Exam Ref 70-532
Developing Microsoft
Azure Solutions

Zoiner Tejada
Michele Leroux Bustamante
Ike Ellis

PUBLISHED BY
Microsoft Press
A Division of Microsoft Corporation
One Microsoft Way
Redmond, Washington 98052-6399

Library of Congress Control Number: 2014951860
ISBN: 978-0-7356-9704-1

Printed and bound in the United States of America.

2   16

Microsoft Press books are available through booksellers and distributors worldwide. If you need support related to this book, email Microsoft Press Book Support at mspinput@microsoft.com. Please tell us what you think of this book at http://www.microsoft.com/learning/booksurvey.

Microsoft and the trademarks listed at http://www.microsoft.com/en-us/legal/intellectualproperty/Trademarks/EN-US.aspx are trademarks of the Microsoft group of companies. All other marks are property of their respective owners.

The example companies, organizations, products, domain names, email addresses, logos, people, places, and events depicted herein are fictitious. No association with any real company, organization, product, domain name, email address, logo, person, place, or event is intended or should be inferred.

This book expresses the author's views and opinions. The information contained in this book is provided without any express, statutory, or implied warranties. Neither the authors, Microsoft Corporation, nor its resellers, or distributors will be held liable for any damages caused or alleged to be caused either directly or indirectly by this book.

Acquisitions Editor: Karen Szall
Developmental Editor: Karen Szall
Editorial Production: Box Twelve Communications
Technical Reviewer: Magnus Märtensson; Technical Review services provided by Content Master, a member of CM Group, Ltd.
Cover: Twist Creative • Seattle

Contents

What do you think of this book? We want to hear from you!

Microsoft is interested in hearing your feedback so we can continually improve our
books and learning resources for you. To participate in a brief online survey, please visit:

www.microsoft.com/learning/booksurvey/

Chapter 5   Manage application and network services   313

What do you think of this book? We want to hear from you!

Microsoft is interested in hearing your feedback so we can continually improve our
books and learning resources for you. To participate in a brief online survey, please visit:

www.microsoft.com/learning/booksurvey/

Introduction

This book covers Microsoft Azure from a high-level perspective, consistent with the Microsoft Certification Exam 70-532: Developing Microsoft Azure Solutions. The target audience for this book includes solution architects, DevOps engineers, and QA engineers already familiar with building, deploying, and monitoring scalable solutions with existing development tools, to some extent including Microsoft Azure. The material covered in this book builds on your existing knowledge and experience designing, developing, implementing, automating, and monitoring Microsoft Azure, extending that knowledge to the current state of platform features, development techniques, and management tools. In this book, you'll find coverage of design and implementation concepts, guidance on applying features, step-by-step instructions, and references to appropriate code listings for specific examples.

The 70-532 and 70-533 exams collectively validate that you have the skills and knowledge necessary to design, deploy, and manage Microsoft Azure solutions. This book focuses on exam 70-532 and prepares you from a development and DevOps perspective. Beyond supporting your exam preparation, where possible, we endeavored to include insights from our own experiences helping customers migrate and manage their solutions on the Microsoft Azure platform.

This book covers every exam objective, but it does not cover every exam question. Only the Microsoft exam team has access to the exam questions themselves and Microsoft regularly adds new questions to the exam, making it impossible to cover specific questions. You should consider this book a supplement to your relevant real-world experience and other study materials. If you encounter a topic in this book that you do not feel completely comfortable with, use the links you'll find in text to find more information and take the time to research and study the topic. Great information is available on MSDN, TechNet, and in blogs and forums.

Microsoft certifications

Microsoft certifications distinguish you by proving your command of a broad set of skills and experience with current Microsoft products and technologies. The exams and corresponding certifications are developed to validate your mastery of critical competencies as you design and develop, or implement and support, solutions with Microsoft products and technologies both on-premises and in the cloud. Certification brings a variety of benefits to the individual and to employers and organizations.

> **MORE INFO** **ALL MICROSOFT CERTIFICATIONS**
>
> For information about Microsoft certifications, including a full list of available certifications, go to *http://www.microsoft.com/learning/en/us/certification/cert-default.aspx*.

Acknowledgments

We'd like to thank the following people:

- To Colin Lyth at Microsoft, thank you for recommending us to author this book; we appreciate the opportunity.

- A well-deserved cheers to Devon Musgrave at Microsoft for helping us kick-start the editorial process, and a big thank you to our editor, Karen Szall at Microsoft, for seeing the whole editing process through and dealing with the insanity of an ever-changing platform under tight deadlines. Thank you also to the entire Microsoft Press team working on this book. It's incredible to see all of the effort you put in and how fast you move things forward!

- To the amazing people behind the features of Microsoft Azure: Many of you have provided first class support and guidance by our side to several of our marquee customers whom we have migrated to Azure. To name a few, we thank you Yochay Kieriati, Brady Gaster, Charles Sterling, Anna Timasheva, Suren Machiraju, and others who have enhanced our understanding of the underlying Microsoft Azure platform through our experiences together. Where appropriate, we share these insights with you, dear reader.

- To Brian Noyes, a founding member of Solliance, and several members of our Solliance Partner Network whom we work with regularly to implement Azure solutions: Our collective knowledge base is continually enhanced working together, and certainly that influences the quality of this book.

- To our technical reviewer, Magnus Martensson, thank you for your very thoughtful and detailed review of each chapter and for helping us by turning those reviews around quickly!

- To our families, thank you for your support and patience through the inevitable pressure that comes with publishing. We love you!

Free ebooks from Microsoft Press

From technical overviews to in-depth information on special topics, the free ebooks from Microsoft Press cover a wide range of topics. These ebooks are available in PDF, EPUB, and Mobi for Kindle formats, ready for you to download at:

http://aka.ms/mspressfree

Check back often to see what is new!

Errata, updates, & book support

We've made every effort to ensure the accuracy of this book and its companion content. You can access updates to this book—in the form of a list of submitted errata and their related corrections—at:

http://aka.ms/ER532/errata

If you discover an error that is not already listed, please submit it to us at the same page.

If you need additional support, email Microsoft Press Book Support at mspinput@microsoft.com.

Please note that product support for Microsoft software and hardware is not offered through the previous addresses. For help with Microsoft software or hardware, go to *http://support.microsoft.com.*

We want to hear from you

At Microsoft Press, your satisfaction is our top priority, and your feedback our most valuable asset. Please tell us what you think of this book at:

http://aka.ms/tellpress

The survey is short, and we read every one of your comments and ideas. Thanks in advance for your input!

Stay in touch

Let's keep the conversation going! We're on Twitter: *http://twitter.com/MicrosoftPress.*

Preparing for the exam

Microsoft certification exams are a great way to build your resume and let the world know about your level of expertise. Certification exams validate your on-the-job experience and product knowledge. While there is no substitution for on-the-job experience, preparation through study and hands-on practice can help you prepare for the exam. We recommend that you round out your exam preparation plan by using a combination of available study materials and courses. For example, you might use this Exam Ref and another study guide for your "at home" preparation and take a Microsoft Official Curriculum course for the classroom experience. Choose the combination that you think works best for you.

Note that this Exam Ref is based on publicly available information about the exam and the author's experience. To safeguard the integrity of the exam, authors do not have access to the live exam.

CHAPTER 1

Design and implement websites

Azure Websites provides a Platform-as-a-Service (PaaS) approach for hosting your web applications, whether they are webpages or web services. The platform approach provides more than just a host for running your application logic; it also includes robust mechanisms for managing all aspects of your web application lifecycle, from configuring continuous and staged deployments to managing runtime configuration, monitoring health and diagnostic data, and, of course, helping with scale and resilience. Related to Azure Websites, WebJobs enables you to perform background processing within the familiar context of Websites. These key features are of prime importance to the modern web application, and this chapter explores how to leverage them.

> **IMPORTANT**
>
> **Have you read page xiv?**
>
> It contains valuable information regarding the skills you need to pass the exam.

Objectives in this chapter:

- Objective 1.1: Deploy websites
- Objective 1.2: Configure websites
- Objective 1.3: Configure diagnostics, monitoring, and analytics
- Objective 1.4: Implement web jobs
- Objective 1.5: Configure websites for scale and resilience
- Objective 1.6: Design and implement applications for scale and resilience

---

MICROSOFT VIRTUAL ACADEMY   **MICROSOFT AZURE FUNDAMENTALS: WEBSITES**

Microsoft Virtual Academy offers free online courses delivered by industry experts, including a course relevant to this exam. Microsoft Azure Fundamentals: Websites provides a helpful video tour of many of the Azure Websites features covered in this chapter. You can access the course at *http://www.microsoftvirtualacademy.com/training-courses/microsoft-azure-fundamentals-websites*.

Objective 1.1: Deploy websites

When you are ready to move beyond local development of your website to make it accessible to the Internet at large, you have quite a few things to consider. For example, how will subsequent deployments affect existing users of your site? How can you minimize the impact of broken deployments? How can you achieve the right level of website density per instance so that you balance cost with performance and still leverage the Azure Websites SLA? To make the right decisions, you need to understand how to deploy websites to deployment slots, how to roll back deployments, and how to manage hosting plans.

> ***MORE INFO*** **PREREQUISITES**
>
> Refer to the book *Microsoft Azure Essentials Fundamentals of Azure* by Michael Collier and Robin Shahan for a review of the various deployment options available. In this book, it is assumed you are familiar with the basic process of deploying from Visual Studio and deploying from a local repository (such as git) or from hosted source control (such as Visual Studio Online, GitHub, BitBucket, or CodePlex).

This objective covers how to:

- Define deployment slots
- Roll back deployments
- Create hosting plans
- Migrate websites between hosting plans
- Create a website within a hosting plan

> ***IMPORTANT*** **NO PACKAGES IN AZURE WEBSITES**
>
> While the Objective Domain includes "implement pre- and post-deployment actions" and "create, configure, and deploy a package" as topics, don't expect any questions about these on the exam. There is currently no information available on this topic in the context of Websites since websites are not managed or deployed with packages.

Defining deployment slots

Deployment slots enable you to perform more robust deployment workflows than deploying your website directly to production. When you create an Azure website, you are automatically provisioned with a production slot that represents your live website. With each deployment slot, you can create up to four additional deployment slots (for a total of five) that you can swap with the production slot (or even with other non-production slots). When you swap, the site content and certain slot configurations are exchanged with no downtime. This is useful in the following scenarios:

- **Staged deployment**   In a staged deployment, you deploy to a non-production slot that is acting as a staging environment. In this environment, you test whether the website is working as expected, and when you are satisfied that it is, you swap the production slot with the staging slot, making the staged content and certain parts of the configuration the new production website.

- **Incremental deployment**   If your website deployment includes incremental steps that you need to take post-deployment, you can deploy to a non-production slot, make those changes, and then swap with the production slot to make the updated website live.

- **Rolling back deployment**   If, after swapping a non-production slot into production, you need to roll back the deployment, you can swap the production slot again with the slot that contains the previous production content and configuration, thereby rolling back the deployment.

> **CAUTION   SLOT RESOURCES ARE SHARED**
>
> All deployment slots for a given website share the same web hosting plan and are created within the same virtual machine (VM) instance that is hosting the production slot. Therefore, take care when performing stress tests on a non-production slot because you will in effect be stressing the production website by virtue of stressing the VM that hosts it. Because the same VM instance is used for all slots, you cannot scale a non-production deployment slot independently of the production slot—you can only adjust the scale settings for the production slot.

The website for which you want to create a second deployment slot must be using the Standard web hosting plan mode (also referred to as tier). In other words, you cannot create a deployment slot with the Free, Shared, and Basic modes.

Creating a new deployment slot (existing portal)

To create a new deployment slot in the management portal, complete the following steps:

1.   Navigate to the dashboard of your website in the management portal accessed via *https://manage.windowsazure.com*.

2.   Under Quick Glance, click Add A New Deployment Slot.

quick glance

⬤ Visit the new portal PREVIEW

⬤ View Applicable Add-ons

ⓘ View connection strings

⬇ Download the publish profile

↻ Reset your deployment credentials

↻ Reset your publish profile credentials

⏎ Delete Git repository

ⓘ Add a new deployment slot PREVIEW

3. In the dialog box that appears, name your deployment slot. This name will be added as a suffix to the name used by the existing slot. Optionally, choose an existing slot as the source from which to copy configuration settings to be applied to the new deployment slot.

```
ADD NEW DEPLOYMENT SLOT                                    ✕

NAME

[                                              ❗ ]

CONFIGURATION SOURCE

✓ Don't clone configuration from an existing slot
  sol-deployslots
  sol-deployslots(stage)
  sol-deployslots(fourth)
  sol-deployslots(third)
  sol-deployslots(fifth)


                                                        ✓
```

4. Click the check mark to create the new deployment slot.

Creating a new deployment slot (Preview portal)

To create a new deployment slot in the Preview portal, complete the following steps:

1. Navigate to the blade of your website in the portal accessed via *https://portal.azure.com*.

2. Scroll to Deployment and click Deployment Slots.

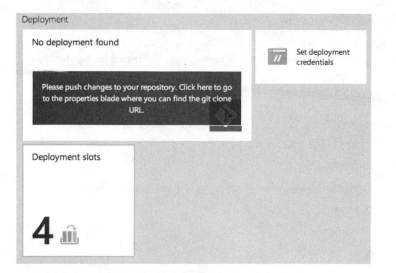

3. In the blade that appears, click Add Slot.

4. Name your deployment slot. This name will be added as a suffix to the name used by the existing slot. Optionally, choose an existing slot as the source from which to copy configuration settings to be applied to the new deployment slot.

Deployment slots let you deploy different versions of your site to different URLs. You can test a certain version and then swap content and configuration between slots.

NAME ⓘ

sol-deployslots-second

CONFIGURATION SOURCE

sol-deployslots

5. Click OK to create the new deployment slot.

Swapping and website configuration

When you swap deployment slots, all of the website content is swapped, but the same is not true of the configuration. The following configuration items will move to the destination slot:

- General settings (for example, .NET framework version, Web Sockets, Always On)
- Connection strings
- Handler mappings
- Application and site diagnostics settings
- Monitoring settings

The following configuration items will not move to the destination slot:

- Publishing endpoints
- Custom domain names
- SSL certificates and bindings
- Scale settings

In effect, this means that settings such as your database connection strings should be configured with the production values prior to the swap. It also means that you do not have to worry about your non-production SSL certificate bindings or domain names accidentally overwriting your production settings. The fact that publishing endpoints do not swap also implies that if you are deploying to websites via source control (for example, Visual Studio Online), your production slot will not suddenly be updated from source control just because you swapped into production a slot that is configured for deployment from source control.

Swapping website slots (existing portal)

To swap website slots in the management portal, complete the following steps:

1. Navigate to the dashboard of your website in the management portal accessed via *https://manage.windowsazure.com*.

2. On the command bar, click Swap.

3. In the Swap Deployments dialog box, from the Destination list, select the destination slot to swap with the current website slot.

4. Click the check mark to begin the swap.

Swapping website slots (Preview portal)

To swap website slots in the Preview portal, complete the following steps:

1. Navigate to the blade of your website in the portal accessed via *https://portal.azure.com*.

2. On the command bar, click Swap.

3. On the Choose Destination Slot blade, click the name of the destination slot with which to swap.

Rolling back deployments

Along with the ability to swap websites between slots comes the ability to roll back a failed or broken deployment. In the context of deployment slots, to roll back a deployment, select the production slot that represents the broken deployment, click Swap, and for the destination, choose the slot that contains the deployment that was previously in the production slot.

Creating hosting plans

A web hosting plan defines the supported feature set and capacity of a group of virtual machine resources that are hosting one or more websites. Each web hosting plan is configured with a pricing tier (for example, Free, Shared, Basic, and Standard), and each tier describes its own set of capabilities and cost. A web hosting plan is unique to the region, resource group, and subscription (see Figure 1-1). In other words, two websites can participate in the same web hosting plan only when they are created in the same subscription, resource group, and region (with the same pricing tier requirements).

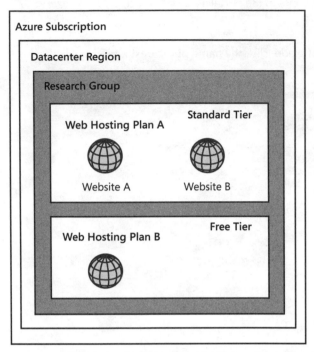

FIGURE 1-1 The relationship between web hosting plans and websites

Web hosting plans are created as a part of website creation and are not created directly.

Creating a new web hosting plan (existing portal)

To create a new web hosting plan in the management portal, complete the following steps:

1. Navigate to the management portal accessed via *https://manage.windowsazure.com*.

2. On the command bar, click New, and then select Compute, Website, Quick Create.

3. Provide a prefix for your website in the URL field.

4. From the Web Hosting Plan list, select Create New Web Hosting Plan.

5. Select a region in which to create the website and the web hosting plan that encompasses it.

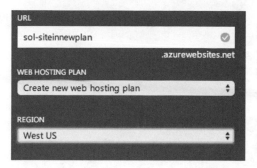

6. Click Create Website.

Creating a new web hosting plan (Preview portal)

To create a new web hosting plan in the Preview portal, complete the following steps:

1. Navigate to the portal accessed via *https://portal.azure.com*.

2. Click New.

3. Click Website.

4. Enter a name for the website.

5. Click the Web Hosting Plan ribbon

6. Under Create New, provide a name for the new web hosting plan, select a pricing tier, and then click OK.

Web hosting plan

Choose a new or existing web hosting plan.
Learn more ☑

⟁ **Create new**

NAME

My New Web Hosting Plan

S1 STANDARD	**B1** BASIC	**S3** STANDARD
44.64	32.74	178.56

1	Core	
1.75	GB RAM	
▭	Storage	50 GB
◉	Custom domains / SSL	5 SNI, 1 IP
↗	Auto scale	Up to 10 instances
☁	Backup	Daily
⚖	Website staging	5 slots
◉	Geo availability	Traffic Manager

7. Return to the Website blade, set the Resource Group, Subscription, and Location options as desired.

8. Click Create to create the new web hosting plan and the new website.

When you create your website, you create a new web hosting plan with your active subscription, in a new or existing resource group, in the selected geographic region.

Migrating websites between hosting plans

You can migrate a website between web hosting plans to change the scale of the website, to leverage the features of a different pricing tier, or to redistribute the website hosting load, all without affecting the other websites belonging to the web hosting plan currently in use. Websites can be migrated between web hosting plans provided they meet two conditions. First, the website and the web hosting plan must reside in the same region. Second, the web hosting plans in question must be a part of the same resource group.

Migrating a website between hosting plans (existing portal)

There is currently no support for migrating a website between web hosting plans using the management portal.

Migrating a website between hosting plans (Preview portal)

To migrate a website between hosting plans in the Preview portal, complete the following steps:

1. Navigate to the blade of your website in the portal accessed via *https://portal.azure.com*.

2. Click the ellipses (...) on the menu bar.

3. Click Web Hosting Plan.

4. On the Web Hosting Plan blade, click an existing web hosting plan to move the website to that hosting plan.

5. Alternately, you can create a new web hosting plan, name it, select the pricing tier, and then click OK to move the website into the newly created web hosting plan.

Creating a website within a hosting plan

If you have already provisioned a web hosting plan and want to create a new website within that existing plan, select the web hosting plan as a part of the website creation process.

Creating a website within an existing web hosting plan (existing portal)

To create a website within a hosting plan in the management portal, complete the following steps:

1. Navigate to the management portal accessed via *https://manage.windowsazure.com*.

2. On the command bar, click New, and then select Compute, Website, Quick Create.

3. Provide a prefix for your website in the URL field.

4. In the Web Hosting Plan list, choose the desired web hosting plan.

5. Click Create Website.

Creating a website within an existing web hosting plan (Preview portal)

To create a website within a hosting plan, complete the following steps:

1. Navigate to the portal accessed via *https://portal.azure.com*.

2. Click New.

3. Click Website.

4. Enter a name for the website.

5. Click the Web Hosting Plan ribbon.

6. Under Use Existing, select one of the existing web hosting plans, and then click OK.

7. Click Create to create the new website within the selected web hosting plan.

Thought experiment
Website deployment

In this thought experiment, apply what you've learned about this objective. You can find answers to these questions in the "Answers" section at the end of this chapter.

You are preparing a new website for deployment and are planning how your deployment process will proceed.

1. You envision a need for multiple related deployments of the website for staging and testing purposes. Explain how deployment slots can help with this.

2. You want to guarantee that this website will have its own VM resources and not compete against other deployed websites. How can you use web hosting plans to do this?

Objective summary

- Websites can be deployed to a primary slot or to as many as four additional slots you can use for staging or testing.
- Web hosting plans describe the capacity characteristics of the infrastructure supporting your websites as well as the pricing tier.
- Multiple websites can be hosted within a single web hosting plan.

Objective review

Answer the following questions to test your knowledge of the information in this objective. You can find the answers to these questions and explanations of why each answer choice is correct or incorrect in the "Answers" section at the end of this chapter.

1. How many deployment slots can a website have (besides the main slot)?
   - **A.** Two
   - **B.** Three
   - **C.** Four
   - **D.** Five

2. For a website to be co-located with other websites in the same web hosting plan, what must they have in common? (Choose all that apply.)
   - **A.** Subscription
   - **B.** Region
   - **C.** Resource group
   - **D.** Pricing tier

3. How can you create a new web hosting plan?
   - **A.** Directly, by clicking New on the command bar
   - **B.** By creating a new website and then choosing an existing web hosting plan
   - **C.** By creating a new website and then creating a new web hosting plan
   - **D.** None of the above

Objective 1.2: Configure websites

Azure Websites provides a comprehensive collection of settings that you can adjust to establish the environment in which your website runs, as well as tools to define and manage the values of settings used by your web application code. A fundamental pattern embraced by the configuration model of Azure Websites is the separation of code from configuration, and particularly the notion that the deployment environment can override configuration. This simplifies management of configuration in your source code. For example, code on your local machine can use a development configuration that targets only development resources, a local development database for instance, but upon deployment to the production website, the production settings can transparently override the development settings so that the code uses the appropriate production configuration, for instance to target an Azure SQL database, all without any explicit effort on your part. Understanding website configuration is critical to succeeding with Azure Websites.

This objective covers how to:

- Define and use app settings, connection strings, handlers, and virtual directories
- Configure certificates and custom domains
- Configure SSL bindings
- Manage websites by using the API, Windows PowerShell, and the Cross-Platform Command-Line Interface (xplat-cli)

IMPORTANT **RUNTIME CONFIGURATIONS**

While the Objective Domain includes "runtime configurations" as a topics, don't expect any questions about this on the exam. There is currently no information available on this topic in the context of Websites.

Defining and using app settings

App settings are represented as name-value pairs made available to your web application when it starts. The mechanism you use to access these values depends on the web platform in which your web application is programmed. If your application is built using .NET, then you access the values of app settings just as you would access the AppSettings values stored in web.config. If your web application is built using another supported web platform, such as Node.js, PHP, Python, or Java, the app settings are presented to your application as environment variables.

Defining an app setting in the management portal (existing portal)

To define an app setting in the management portal, complete the following steps:

1. Navigate to the Configure tab of your website in the management portal accessed via *https://manage.windowsazure.com.*

2. Scroll down to App Settings.

3. In the list, type a name for the setting in the text box with the placeholder text KEY, and type a value for the setting in the text box with the placeholder text VALUE.

app settings		
WEBSITE_NODE_DEFAULT_VERSION	0.10.29	
mysettings	foobar	
KEY	VALUE	

4. Click Save on the command bar to persist and apply the new app setting.

Defining an app setting in the management portal (Preview portal)

To define an app setting in the Preview portal, complete the following steps:

1. Navigate to the blade of your website in the portal accessed via *https://portal.azure.com*.

2. Click the Settings box in the Summary section, and then click Application Settings and scroll down to App Settings.

3. In the list, type a name for the setting in the text box with the placeholder text KEY, and type a value for the setting in the text box with the placeholder text VALUE.

App settings	
WEBSITE_NODE_DEFAULT_VERSION	0.10.29
mysettings	foobar
Key	Value

4. Click Save on the command bar to persist and apply the new app setting.

Using an app setting from .NET

To retrieve an app setting, use the AppSettings property of the ConfigurationManager class and access the setting by name, using it as the key to retrieve the value from the AppSettings collection. Listing 1-1 shows an example of this in C#.

LISTING 1-1 Using a configured app setting from C#

```
using System;
using System.Configuration;
...
string key = "mySetting";
string value = ConfigurationManager.AppSettings[key];
```

Using an app setting from Node.js

AppSettings properties are exposed to JavaScript code running in Node.js by means of environment variables. By convention, these are exposed as environment variables (accessible via process.env) with the same name. They can also be accessed with the APPSETTING_ prefix. Listing 1-2 shows an example of how to retrieve a setting in Node.js using both the non-prefixed and prefixed approaches.

LISTING 1-2 Using a configured app setting from Node.js

```
var value = process.env.MYSETTING;
var value = process.env.APPSETTING_MYSETTING;
```

Defining and using connection strings

Like app settings, connection strings represent name-value pairs, but they are used specifically for settings that define the connection string to a linked resource (typically a database) such as a SQL database, a SQL server, MySQL, or some other custom resource. Connection strings are given special treatment within the portal, beyond that offered to app settings, in that you can specify a type for the connection string to identify it as a SQL server, MySQL, a SQL database, or a custom connection string. Additionally, the values for connection strings are not displayed by default, requiring an additional effort to display the values so that their sensitive data is not displayed or editable until specifically requested by the portal user.

Just as for app settings, the mechanism you use to access connection string values depends on the web platform in which your web application is programmed. If your application is built using .NET, then you access the values of connection strings just as you would access the connectionStrings values stored in web.config. If your web application is built using another supported web platform, such as Node.js, PHP, Python, or Java, the connection strings are presented to your application as environment variables.

Defining a connection string in the management portal (existing portal)

To define a connection string in the management portal, complete the following steps:

1. Navigate to the Configure tab of your website in the management portal accessed via *https://manage.windowsazure.com*.

2. Scroll down to Connection Strings.

3. In the list, type a name for the connection string in the text box with the placeholder text NAME, type a value for the connection string in the text box with the placeholder text VALUE, and select a type for the connection string from the drop-down list, choosing SQL Database, SQL Server, MySQL, or Custom, as appropriate.

4. Click Save on the command bar to persist and apply the new connection string.

Defining a connection string in the management portal (Preview portal)

To define a connection string in the Preview portal, complete the following steps:

5. Navigate to the blade of your website in the portal accessed via *https://portal.azure. com*.

6. Scroll down to Connection Strings.

7. In the list, type a name for the connection string in the text box with the placeholder text NAME, type a value for the connection string in the text box with the placeholder text VALUE, and select a type for the connection string from the drop-down list, choosing SQL Database, SQL Server, MySQL, or Custom, as appropriate.

8. Click Save on the command bar to persist and apply the new connection string.

Using a connection string from .NET

To retrieve a connection string, use the ConnectionStrings property of the ConfigurationManager class, and access the setting by name as the index into ConnectionStrings. Listing 1-3 shows an example of this in C#.

LISTING 1-3 Using a configured connection string from C#

```
using System;
using System.Configuration;
…
string key = "myConnectionString";
string value = ConfigurationManager.ConnectionStrings[key].ConnectionString;
```

Using a connection string from Node.js

Connection strings are exposed to JavaScript code running in Node.js by means of environment variables. By convention, these are exposed as environment variables (accessible via process.env) with the same name prefixed by the type of the connection string indicated in the portal (which is SQLAZURECONNSTR_ for SQL Database, SQLCONNSTR_ for SQL Server, MYSQLCONNSTR_ for MySQL, and CUSTOM_CONNSTR_ for Custom). Listing 1-4 shows an example of how to retrieve a MySQL connection string in Node.js for a connection string with the name MYDB.

LISTING 1-4 Using a configured connection string from Node.js

```
var value = process.env.MYSQLCONNSTR_MYDB;
```

> **NOTE APP SETTINGS AND CONNECTION STRINGS**
>
> App settings and connection strings, while editable in the portal, are strictly read-only when accessed through your web application code. Changes made to these settings at run-time are not persisted and may be lost if your application (or its VM host) restarts. If you need to alter these settings, you can do so manually via the portal or you can use the Azure Management API, Windows PowerShell, or xplat-cli to change them at the website level.

Defining and using request handler mappings

Request handler mappings, or handlers, instruct websites how to handle requests for files with particular file extensions by running a script that processes the request. These handlers are invoked instead of websites performing further processing on the request (for example, if a handler is configured, the request does not get to ASP.NET). Handler mappings are commonly used to respond to a *.php file request using a custom PHP runtime that invokes a php-cgi executable runtime or to respond to requests with a Python application by means of the FastCGI handler for Python.

> **REAL WORLD PHP HANDLER MAPPING**
>
> Azure Websites has built-in support for PHP. You need to configure a handler mapping for PHP only if you want to use a different PHP runtime than that which is included with Azure Websites.

Defining a handler mapping in the management portal (existing portal)

To define a handler mapping in the management portal, complete the following steps:

1. Navigate to the Configure tab of your website in the management portal accessed via *https://manage.windowsazure.com*.

2. Scroll down to Handler Mappings.

3. In the list, in the text box with the placeholder text EXTENSION, type a value for the file extension that should be processed by the handler (for example, *.php).

4. Type the path to the script processor in the text box with the placeholder text SCRIPT PROCESSOR PATH. Note that this value must be an absolute path. For example, if your website's bin directory is located at D:\home\site\wwwroot\bin and you have a custom PHP runtime, you would enter D:\home\site\wwwroot\bin\php\php-cgi.exe for the script processor path.

handler mappings

.php	D:\home\site\wwwroot\bin\php\p	ADDITIONAL ARGUMENTS (OPTI
EXTENSION	SCRIPT PROCESSOR PATH	ADDITIONAL ARGUMENTS (OPTI

5. If the script processor takes input arguments, enter them in the text box with the placeholder text ADDITIONAL ARGUMENTS (OPTIONAL).

6. Click Save on the command bar to persist and apply the new handler.

Defining a handler mapping in the management portal (Preview portal)

To define a handler mapping in the Preview portal, complete the following steps:

1. Navigate to the blade of your website in the portal accessed via *https://portal.azure.com*.

2. Under Summary, click the Settings box, and then click Applications Settings and scroll down to Handler Mappings.

3. In the list, in the text box with the placeholder text EXTENSION, type a value for the file extension that should be processed by the handler (for example, *.php).

4. Type the path to the script processor in the text box with the placeholder text PROCESSOR PATH. Note that this value must be an absolute path. For example, if your website's bin directory is located at D:\home\site\wwwroot\bin and you have a custom PHP runtime, you would enter D:\home\site\wwwroot\bin\php\php-cgi.exe for the script processor path.

Handler mappings

*.php	D:\home\site\wwwroot\bin\php	
Extension	Processor path	Additional arguments

5. If the script processor takes input arguments, enter them in the text box with the placeholder text ADDITIONAL ARGUMENTS.

6. Click Save on the command bar to persist and apply the new handler.

Defining and using virtual directories and virtual applications

You can use virtual directories to logically define a hierarchy of web content that is potentially different from the physical directory structure of the web content as it appears on disk. You can change how the hierarchy is exposed to the browser without altering the file structure, and you can collapse deeply nested directory structures by representing them with a top-level virtual directory. For example, if your website root / maps to site\wwwroot, but your images are located at the physical path site\wwwroot\static\content\current\images, you can simplify the path to the images by creating a virtual directory that maps the physical path to something much shorter, such as /images.

You can also isolate a virtual directory within its own w3wp.exe worker process by making it an application. A common scenario is to expose a subdirectory of wwwroot as the root website while also exposing a peer to that subdirectory as a separate web application. For example, under wwwroot, you might have three separate web applications:

- /website
- /blog
- /store

where /website represents your site's main web application, /blog is a separate web application that runs a blogging platform, and /store is an e-commerce application. You could configure each of these to run as a separate web application within the same website by configuring them as virtual applications.

Defining a virtual directory in the management portal (existing portal)

To define a virtual directory in the management portal, complete the following steps:

1. Navigate to the Configure tab of your website in the management portal accessed via *https://manage.windowsazure.com*.

2. Scroll down to Virtual Applications And Directories.

3. In the list, in the text box with the placeholder text VIRTUAL DIRECTORY, type a value for the virtual directory you want to surface.

4. In the text box with the placeholder text PHYSICAL PATH RELATIVE TO SITE ROOT, type the physical path to the directory that the virtual directory should map to. Note that this value must be a path relative to the site root. For example, if your website has an images directory under a directory named *content* within the root, you would enter a value of site\wwwroot\content\images for this path.

virtual applications and directories				
/	site\wwwroot\website	Application	☑	
/images	site\wwwroot\static\content\images	Application	☐	
/blog	site\wwwroot\blog	Application	☑	
/store	site\wwwroot\store	Application	☑	
VIRTUAL DIRECTORY	PHYSICAL PATH RELATIVE TO SITE RO	Application	☐	

5. To make this virtual directory a virtual application, select the Application check box.

6. Click Save on the command bar to persist and apply the new virtual directory or virtual application changes.

Defining a virtual directory in the management portal (Preview portal)

To define a virtual directory in the Preview portal, complete the following steps:

1. Navigate to the blade of your website in the portal accessed via *https://portal.azure.com*.

2. Under Summary, click the Settings box, and then click Applications Settings and scroll down to Virtual Applications And Directories.

3. In the list, in the text box with the placeholder text VIRTUAL DIRECTORY, type a value for the virtual directory you want to surface.

4. In the text box with the placeholder text PHYSICAL PATH RELATIVE TO SITE, type the physical path to the directory that the virtual directory should map to. Note that this value must be a path relative to the site root. For example, if your website has an images directory under a directory named *content* within the root, you would enter a value of site\wwwroot\content\images for this path.

Virtual applications and directories			
/	site\wwwroot\website	☑	
/images	site\wwwroot\static\images	☐	
/blog	site\wwwroot\blog	☑	
/store	site\wwwroot\store	☑	
Virtual directory	Physical path relative to site	☐	Application

5. To make this virtual directory a virtual application, select the Application check box.

6. Click Save on the command bar to persist and apply the virtual directory or virtual application changes.

Configure custom domains

When you first create your website, it is accessible through the subdomain you specified in the website creation process, where it takes the form *<yoursitename>*.azurewebsites.net. To map to a more user-friendly domain name (such as *www.contoso.com*), you must set up a custom domain name. Additionally, to enable your visitors to securely browse your website using HTTPS, consider using certificates bound to the domain name you have selected.

Mapping custom domain names

Azure Websites supports mapping to a custom domain that you purchase from a third-party registrar either by mapping the custom domain name to the virtual IP address of your website or by mapping it to the *<yoursitename>*.azurewebsites.net address of your website. This mapping is captured in domain name system (DNS) records that are maintained by your domain registrar. Two types of DNS records effectively express this purpose:

- A records, or address records, map your domain name to the IP address of your website.

- CNAME records, or alias records, map a subdomain of your custom domain name to the canonical name of your website, expressed as *<yoursitename>*.azurewebsites.net.

Table 1-1 shows some common scenarios along with the type of record, the typical record name, and an example value based on the requirements of the mapping.

TABLE 1-1 Mapping domain name requirements to DNS record types, names, and values

Requirement	Type of Record	Record Name	Record Value
contoso.com should map to my website's IP address	A	@	138.91.225.40 IP address
contoso.com and *all* subdomains demo.contoso.com and www.contoso.com should map to my website's IP address	A	*	138.91.225.40 IP address
www.contoso.com should map to my website's IP address	A	www	138.91.225.40 IP address
www.contoso.com should map to my website's canonical name in Azure	CNAME	www	contoso.azurewebsites.net Canonical name in Azure

Note that whereas A records enable you to map the root of the domain (like contoso.com) and provide a wildcard mapping for all subdomains below the root (like www.contoso.com and demo.contoso.com), CNAME records enable you to map only subdomains (like the www in www.contoso.com).

These are the high-level steps for creating a custom domain name for your website:

1. Ensure that your website is in the correct web hosting plan mode.

2. If using an A record, collect the IP address of your website from the management portal.

3. If using an A record to map your domain to Azure, add a CNAME record with a subdomain of awverify to prove to Azure that you own the domain name you want to point to your website.

4. Add an A record or CNAME record for your custom domain to map the domain or subdomain to the address of the website.

5. Associate the custom domain name with your website by editing its configuration.

> **NOTE   USING A CUSTOM DOMAIN NAME**
>
> Use of a custom domain name requires your website to be in a web hosting plan mode of Shared, Basic, or Standard. You cannot map a custom name to your website if it is in Free mode.

Configuring a custom domain (existing portal)

To configure a custom domain in the management portal, complete the following steps:

1. Ensure your website is in the correct web hosting plan mode:

   A. Navigate to the Scale tab of your website in the management portal accessed via *https://manage.windowsazure.com*.

   B. Verify that the mode is set to Shared, Basic, or Standard.

2. If using an A record, collect the IP address of your website from the management portal:

   A. Navigate to the Configure tab of your website in the management portal accessed via *https://manage.windowsazure.com*.

   B. Scroll down to Domain Names.

   C. Click Manage Domains.

   D. In the dialog box that appears, note the IP address labeled The IP Address To Use When You Configure A Records.

   THE IP ADDRESS TO USE WHEN YOU CONFIGURE A RECORDS ⓘ
   138.91.225.40

3. If using an A record to map your domain to Azure, add a CNAME record with a subdomain of awverify to prove to Azure that you own the domain name you want to point to your website:

   A. Log in to your domain registrar's DNS management page for your custom domain.

   B. Following the instructions provided by your domain name registrar, add a new CNAME record with the name **awverify** and the value **awverify.<yourwebsitename>.azurewebsites.net**.

4. Add an A record or CNAME record for your custom domain to map the domain or subdomain to the address of the website:

    A. Log in to your domain registrar's DNS management page for your custom domain.

    ■ If using an A record, following the instructions provided by your domain name registrar, add a new A record with the appropriate name (refer to Table 1-1 to choose the name), and for the value, specify the previously collected IP address of your website.

    ■ If using a CNAME record, following the instructions provided by your domain name registrar, add a new CNAME record with the name of the subdomain, and for the value, specify your website's canonical name in Azure (*<youwebsitename>*.azurewebsites.net).

    B. Save your DNS changes. Note that it may take some time for the changes to propagate across DNS. In most cases, your changes will be visible within minutes, but in some cases, it may take up to 48 hours. You can check the status of your DNS changes by doing a DNS lookup using third-party websites like *http://mxtoolbox.com/DNSLookup.aspx*.

5. Associate the custom domain name with your website by editing its configuration:

    A. Navigate to the Configure tab of your website in the management portal accessed via *https://manage.windowsazure.com*.

    B. Scroll down to Domain Names.

    C. Click Manage Domains.

    D. In the Domain Names list, enter the domain name for which you previously added either an A record or CNAME record. When you stop typing, the dialog box will validate the value you entered by checking for the CNAME record you created previously. If the validation fails, you may have to wait a little longer for the DNS settings to propagate, or you may need to check the DNS configuration you made in step 4.

DOMAIN NAMES
posesbykhalil.com
www.posesbykhalil.com
posesbykhalil.azurewebsites.net
DOMAIN NAME

    E. Click the check mark to associate the custom domain name with your website.

Configuring a custom domain (Preview portal)

To configure a custom domain in the Preview portal, complete the following steps:

1. Ensure your website is in the correct web hosting plan mode:

A. Navigate to the blade of your website in the portal accessed via *https://portal.azure.com*.

B. Click the ellipses (...), and then click Change Web Hosting Plan.

C. On the Web Hosting Plan blade, ensure that the selected web hosting plan is not in Free mode (the mode appears directly below the plan name).

2. If using an A record, collect the IP address of your website from the management portal:

A. Navigate to the blade of your website in the portal accessed via *https://portal.azure.com*.

B. Under Summary, click Settings, and then click Custom Domains And SSL.

C. On the SSL Settings blade, note the IP address listed under the heading The IP Address To Use When You Configure A Records.

The IP Address to use when you configure A Records
ⓘ
138.91.225.40

---

3. If using an A record to map your domain to Azure, add a CNAME record with a subdomain of awverify to prove to Azure that you own the domain name you want to point to your website:

A. Log in to your domain registrar's DNS management page for your custom domain.

B. Following the instructions provided by your domain name registrar, add a new CNAME record with the name **awverify** and the value **awverify.<yourwebsitename>.azurewebsites.net**.

4. Add an A record or CNAME record for your custom domain to map the domain or subdomain to the address of the website:

A. Log in to your domain registrar's DNS management page for your custom domain.

- If using an A record, following the instructions provided by your domain name registrar, add a new A record with the appropriate name (refer to Table 1-1 to choose the name), and for the value, specify the previously collected IP address of your website.

- If using a CNAME record, following the instructions provided by your domain name registrar, add a new CNAME record with the name of the subdomain, and for the value, specify your website's canonical name in Azure (*<youwebsitename>.azurewebsites.net*).

B. Save your DNS changes. Note that it may take some time for the changes to propagate across DNS. In most cases, your changes will be visible within minutes, but in some cases, it may take up to 48 hours. You can check the status of your DNS changes by doing a DNS lookup using third-party websites like *http://mxtoolbox.com/DNSLookup.aspx.*

5. Associate the custom domain name with your website by editing its configuration:

   A. Navigate to the blade of your website in the portal accessed via *https://portal. azure.com.*

   B. Under Summary, click Settings, and then click Domains And SSL.

   C. Scroll down to Domain Names.

   D. In the Domain Names list, enter the domain name for which you previously added either an A record or CNAME record. When you tab out of the text box, the dialog box will validate the value you entered by checking for the CNAME record you created previously. If the validation fails, you may have to wait a little longer for the DNS settings to propagate, or you may need to check the DNS configuration you made in step 4.

   > Learn more about managing custom domains
   >
   > posesbykhalil.com
   >
   > www.posesbykhalil.com
   >
   > posesbykhalil.azurewebsites.net
   >
   > Domain names

6. Click Save on the command bar to associate the custom domain name with your website.

> **IMPORTANT IP ADDRESS CHANGES**
>
> The IP address that you get by following the preceding steps will change if you move your website to a Free web hosting plan, if you delete and re-create it, or if you subsequently enable SSL with the IP-based type. This can also happen unintentionally if you reach your spending limit and the website is changed to the Free web hosting plan mode. If the IP address changes and you are using an A record to map your custom domain to your website, you will need to update the value of the A record to use the new IP address.

Configuring certificates

If your website will use HTTPS to secure communication between it and the browser using Transport Layer Security (TLS), more commonly (but less accurately) referred to in the industry as Secure Socket Layer (SSL), you will need to utilize an SSL certificate. There are multiple types of SSL certificates, but the one you choose primarily depends on the number of different custom domains (or subdomains) that the certificate secures. Some certificates apply to only a single fully qualified domain name (sometimes referred to as *basic certs*), some certificates apply to a list of fully qualified domain names (also called *subjectAltName* or *UC certs*), and other certificates apply across an unlimited number of subdomains for a given domain name (usually referred to as *wildcard certs*).

With Azure Websites, you can use an SSL certificate with your website in one of two ways:

- You can use the "built-in" wildcard SSL certificate that is associated with the *.azurewebsites.net domain.

- You can use a certificate you purchase for your custom domain from a third-party certificate authority.

Using the certificate for the *.azurewebsites.net domain

No special configuration is required to use the SSL certificate provided for *.azurewebsites.net since it is provided by Microsoft, is automatically available, and is enabled for any website. To use SSL with your website, clients need only communicate with your website using the HTTPS endpoint, as in https://<yourwebsitename>.azurewebsites.net.

> **SECURITY** **VULNERABILITY OF THE *.AZUREWEBSITES.NET CERTIFICATE**
>
> Wildcard certificates, particularly as utilized by Azure Websites, are viewed as inherently less secure because they are shared by all Azure Websites customers, versus certificates that are specifically created only for your website or website properties. This wildcard certificate creates two possible (though remote) vulnerabilities:
>
> - **Phishing attacks** Because the certificate is associated with *.azurewebsites. net, it is relatively easy for an attacker to create a mock version of your website and trick users into visiting and trusting it because the certificate still appears properly secured and validated in the browser. In this case, the certificate cannot be trusted to help users identify that the website they are accessing is truly yours.
>
> - **Private key compromise** If somehow an attacker compromised Azure Websites and obtained the private key behind the wildcard certificate, he or she could decrypt all SSL traffic flowing across Azure Websites.
>
> Therefore, while you can rely on the *.azurewebsites.net wildcard certificate during development and arguably for certain non-public scenarios, ultimately it's best practice to secure your website using a custom certificate.

Using certificates with your custom domain

Custom domain names and SSL certificates are inextricably linked. In fact, to create a certificate, you need a custom domain name. The following are the high-level steps for obtaining a certificate:

1. Complete the steps for enabling a custom domain for your website.

2. Create a certificate signing request (CSR) on a local machine using one of the tools listed in Table 1-2.

3. Request a certificate from a certificate authority, and submit your CSR as a part of that request.

4. After obtaining the certificate, download the IIS-compatible certificate to the same local machine you used to generate the CSR.

5. Using the tool you used to generate the CSR (running on the same machine), export the certificate as a personal information exchange (*.pfx) file that bundles both the private and public keys.

6. Upload the *.pfx certificate to your website using the portal.

7. Bind your domain name to the uploaded certificate using the portal.

Table 1-2 lists the tools commonly used to request the CSR (step 2) and to export the certificate (step 5) and provides selection guidance.

TABLE 1-2 Tools used to generate the CSR

Tool Name	Supported Platform	When to Use
Certreq.exe and CertMgr.msc	Windows XP/Windows Server 2000 and later	Use if the machine you are generating the certificate on is running Windows.
IIS Manager	Windows with IIS 7 or later installed	Use if you are already familiar with IIS Manager.
OpenSSL	Most platforms including Windows, Linux, and Mac	Use if you are developing on a Mac or otherwise using Linux, or to create a self-signed certificate.
Makecert	Windows with Visual Studio installed	Use if you are developing with Visual Studios on Windows and want to create a self-signed certificate.

Assuming you already have a website properly configured with a custom domain name, you can explore the steps for getting and using a certificate in greater detail. For the purposes of this chapter, the following discussion focuses on using Certreq.exe and Certmgr. msc, but if you want to use one of the other tools for step 2 and step 3, you can find step-by-step instructions at *http://azure.microsoft.com/en-us/documentation/articles/web-sites-configure-ssl-certificate*.

> **IMPORTANT WEB HOSTING PLAN MODE REQUIREMENTS**
>
> SSL certificates for custom domain names require that the website is configured in the Basic or Standard mode (unlike the requirement for custom domain names, which supports the Shared mode in addition to Basic and Standard).

Before you begin, make sure that you understand the requirements for an SSL certificate in Azure:

- The certificate must contain both the public and private keys.
- The certificate needs to be created for key exchange and ultimately must be exportable to a *.pfx file.
- The subject name in the certificate must match the domain used to access the website.
- The certificate needs to use 2,048-bit encryption at minimum.

Complete the following steps to ensure your certificate meets the requirements:

1. Use Certreq.exe to generate the CSR. Certreq.exe relies on an .ini file to provide the certificate request details, as shown in Listing 1-5. You can create this file in the text editor of your choice.

   LISTING 1-5 Sample Certreq.exe request configuration file

   ```
   [NewRequest]
   Subject = "CN=yourwebsitename.com"
   Exportable = TRUE
   KeyLength = 2048
   KeySpec = 1
   KeyUsage = 0xA0
   MachineKeySet = True
   ProviderName = "Microsoft RSA SChannel Cryptographic Provider"
   ProviderType = 12
   RequestType = CMC

   [EnhancedKeyUsageExtension]
   OID=1.3.6.1.5.5.7.3.1
   ```

2. Save this file with any name you choose, although naming it with the subject name can be helpful if you need to regenerate the CSR later. For example, name it *yourwebsitename.ini*.

3. After you create the .ini file, run Certreq.exe. From the Start menu or Start screen, run Cmd.exe, and in the command window, navigate to the directory containing your .ini file and enter the command shown in Listing 1-6.

   LISTING 1-6 Command line to run CertReq with a request configuration file

   ```
   certreq -new yourwebsitename.ini yourwebsitename.csr
   ```

4. Navigate to your certificate authority's website and provide the CSR as a part of requesting the SSL certificate. The exact approach will vary by certificate authority, but you will typically either upload the CSR or be directed to open the CSR in a text editor, copy the contents, and paste them into a field in a form on the webpage.

5. After your certificate authority has completed the required validations (such as verifying that you are the actual owner of the domain referenced in the subject name of the certificate), your certificate should be ready in the form of a *.cer file. Download this file to the same local machine that you used to generate the CSR.

> **IMPORTANT** **CUSTOM CERTIFICATES**
>
> You should not attempt to create a custom certificate for your website using the subject name azurewebsites.net, no matter what the subdomain is. When you make a request to create such a certificate, the certificate authority will contact the owner of the domain to confirm that the requestor of the certificate in fact owns the domain. Since Microsoft owns the azurewebsite.net domain, this request will either not get a response or will be automatically denied—your certificate will not be issued in either case.

Next, install the certificate from the .cer file and export it to a .pfx file. To do this, complete these steps:

1. Navigate to the file in Windows Explorer, right-click it, and select Install Certificate. The Certificate Import Wizard appears—you can leave the default values on each page and click Next until the import is finished.

2. To export the certificate as a .pfx file, from the Start menu, Start screen, or command prompt, run **certmgr.msc**. In the navigation pane, expand the Personal folder, and then click the Certificates folder (see Figure 1-2). In the details pane, click the Issued To column header to sort the listing by the subject name. In the listing, locate the item that matches the subject name you entered, right-click the certificate, select All Tasks, and then select Export.

FIGURE 1-2 Selecting the Personal and Certificates folders in CertMgr

3. On the Export Private Key page of the wizard, select Yes, Export The Private Key, and click Next. On the Export File Format page, select the Personal Information Exchange – PKCS #12 (.PFX) option, and then select the Include All Certificates In The Certification Path If Possible and Export All Extended Properties options. Do not select Delete The Private Key If The Export Is Successful unless you are sure you will not need to perform this export again. Click Next.

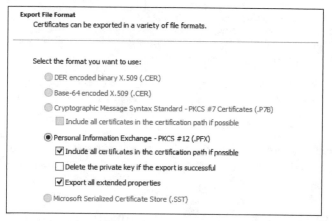

FIGURE 1-3 The Export File Format screen in CertMgr

4. On the Security screen, select the Password check box and enter and confirm a password. (Remember this password; you will need it later when uploading your certificate to Azure.) Click Next.

5. Finally, on the File To Export screen, select a file name path for where to export your .pfx file, and then click Next. A good practice is to export it to the same directory as your .ini file and CSR, and name it according to the subject name, such as yourwebsitename.com.pfx.

After creating the *.pfx file, you can upload your certificate to Azure Websites and then bind it to your custom domain name.

Uploading your certificate to Websites (existing portal)

To upload your certificate to Azure Websites in the management portal, complete the following steps:

1. Navigate to the Configure tab of your website in the management portal accessed via *https://manage.windowsazure.com*.

2. Scroll down to Certificates and click Upload A Certificate.

3. In the dialog box, browse to and click your .pfx file, click Open, and then specify the password you used during the export process.

4. Click the check mark to upload the certificate.

Uploading your certificate to Websites (Preview portal)

To upload your certificate to Azure Websites in the Preview portal, complete the following steps:

1. Navigate to the blade of your website in the portal accessed via *https://portal.azure.com*.

2. Scroll down to Configuration and click Domains And SSL.

3. On the SSL Settings blade, under Certificates, click Upload.

4. In the Upload Certificate blade, browse to and click your .pfx file, click Open, and then specify the password you used during the export process.

5. Click Save on the command bar to upload the certificate.

Configuring SSL bindings

With the certificate uploaded to Azure Websites, the only remaining step is to bind the certificate for use with a custom domain. Binding is what enables Websites to map a request from a client to the appropriate certificate to use for securing communication.

Binding your SSL certificate to a custom domain (existing portal)

To bind your SSL certificate to a custom domain in the management portal, complete the following steps:

1. Navigate to the Configure tab of your website in the management portal accessed via *https://manage.windowsazure.com*.

2. Scroll down to SSL Bindings, and from the drop-down lists, choose the domain name to bind to, the certificate to be bound to it, and how these are associated (either IP SSL or SNI SSL).

3. In the dialog box, browse to your .pfx file, and then specify the password you used during the export process.

4. Click the check mark to upload the certificate.

Binding your SSL certificate to a custom domain (Preview portal)

To bind your SSL certificate to a custom domain in the Preview portal, complete the following steps:

1. Navigate to the blade of your website in the portal accessed via *https://portal.azure.com*.

2. Scroll down to Configuration and click Domains And SSL.

3. In the SSL Settings blade, scroll down to SSL Bindings, and from the drop-down lists, choose the domain name to bind to, the certificate to be bound to it, and how these are associated (either IP SSL or SNI SSL).

4. Click Save on the command bar to apply the binding.

   With the binding saved, you should be able to visit your website using HTTPS.

> **IMPORTANT IP ADDRESS CHANGE**
>
> If you originally configured your custom domain name in DNS to use an A record to point to the IP address of your website and you are using IP-based SSL, you will need to update the IP address used for the A record with the new IP address assigned to your website before you will be able to access it via HTTPS.

EXAM TIP

Server Name Indication (SNI) is an extension of the TLS standard that enables a web server to host multiple different certificates at a single web server host accessed using a single IP address that is shared among all the websites it hosts. Essentially, its function is very practical; it enables a client to indicate the host name of the server it is trying to access during the TLS handshake that sets up the secure connection, and then the web server is able to use this name to select the appropriate certificate from its certificate store to use in securing the communication with the client. This enables greater website density per web server because it allows a single web server host to provide HTTPS across different websites, where each is accessed using a different domain and using its own certificate for securing communication. Contrast this with the IP-based approach, which is limited to one certificate per IP address. To host multiple websites each with different certificates, you would typically need multiple hosts each with a different IP address. In the context of Azure, SNI frees Websites from having to dedicate an IP address (which are a limited resource) to a single website—leading to greater hosting efficiency and, ultimately, cost savings.

The primary obstacle to using SNI is browser support—legacy browsers do not support it and will display certificate warnings. However, the list of modern browsers supporting SNI is not insignificant, and It Includes the most common browsers in use today: Microsoft Internet Explorer 7 (on Vista or higher), Mozilla Firefox 2.0 or later, Google Chrome 6 or later, and Safari 3.0 or later.

Managing websites by using the API, Windows PowerShell, and the Cross-Platform Command Line Interface (xplat-cli)

In addition to configuring and managing Websites via the management portal, programmatic or script-based access is available for much of this functionality and can satisfy many development requirements. The options for this include the following:

- **Service Management REST API** This is a low-level REST API interface that you can call from almost any client that can make REST requests. These are the APIs the management portal utilizes behind the scenes. For a complete reference on the REST API, visit *http://msdn.microsoft.com/en-us/library/azure/ee460799.aspx*.

- **Microsoft Azure Management Libraries for .NET**   Also known as MAML, these assemblies enable programmatic access to manage your websites using .NET code and provide a convenient, Intellisense-aware wrapper around the Service Management REST APIs. The best place to start learning about these is the blog *http://www.jeff. wilcox.name/2014/04/wamlmaml/*.
- **Azure PowerShell management cmdlets**   These enable script-based access for Windows users to create, manage, and monitor websites using Windows PowerShell. For details on using the Azure cmdlets, visit *http://msdn.microsoft.com/en-us/library/ azure/dn495240.aspx*.
- **Cross-Platform Command Line Interface**   Also known as the xplat-cli, this open source SDK provides a command-line interface that enables script-based access for users of Mac OSX and Linux platforms to create, manage, and monitor Websites. For details on using the xplat-cli, visit *https://github.com/Azure/azure-sdk-tools-xplat*.

> ## *Thought experiment*
> ### Domains and SSL
>
> In this thought experiment, apply what you've learned about this objective. You can find answers to these questions in the "Answers" section at the end of this chapter.
>
> Your new website is almost ready for a production launch, and you are tasked with determining the order of steps to take in preparing the deployment with regards to setting up SSL and configuring the custom domain name.
>
> 1. Which should you acquire and set up first: a custom domain name or the SSL certificate?
>
> 2. Given that you have yet to acquire the SSL certificate, how can you test that your website works well over SSL?

Objective summary

- App settings, connection strings, handlers, and virtual directories can all be configured using the management portal.
- Custom domains can be mapped to your website, but doing so requires you to validate ownership of the domain by adding a record to DNS.
- Websites can be configured to use SSL and support utilizing multiple certificates per website instance.
- Beyond using the portal, you can manage websites by using the API, Windows PowerShell, and the xplat-cli.

Objective review

Answer the following questions to test your knowledge of the information in this objective. You can find the answers to these questions and explanations of why each answer choice is correct or incorrect in the "Answers" section at the end of this chapter.

1. Why should you set up your own SSL certificate versus using the certificate for *.azurewebsites.net? (Choose all that apply.)

   A. The *.azurewebsites.net certificate is more susceptible to phishing attacks.

   B. The *.azurewebsites.net certificate is less secure.

   C. You cannot use the *.azurewebsites.net certificate with a custom domain name.

   D. Your data is not encrypted in transit with the *.azurewebsites.net certificate.

2. If you are developing a Node.js web application on Mac for deployment to Azure Websites, which tools might you use to manage your website? (Choose all that apply.)

   A. Windows PowerShell

   B. xplat-cli

   C. Management portal

   D. None of the above

3. Which of the following changes require you to update your DNS settings if you are using an A record to map your custom domain to your website? (Choose all that apply.)

   A. Deleting and re-adding the SSL certificate

   B. Deleting the website and re-deploying

   C. Enabling SSL after configuring the A record

   D. Switching your web hosting plan to Free tier and then back to Standard

Objective 1.3: Configure diagnostics, monitoring, and analytics

Operating a website without suitably configuring and leveraging diagnostics, monitoring, and analytics is like relying exclusively on your users calling to tell you about their experiences, what is working, and what is not. Without diagnostics, monitoring, and analytics, you cannot reactively investigate the cause of a failure, nor can you proactively prevent potential problems before your users experience them. Azure Websites provides multiple forms of logs, features for monitoring availability and automatically sending email alerts when the availability crosses a threshold, features for monitoring your website resource usage, and support for remotely debugging web application code.

Retrieving diagnostics data and viewing streaming logs

A web application hosted by Websites can leverage many different types of logs, each focused on presenting a particular source and format of diagnostic data. The following list describes each of these logs:

■ **Event Log** The equivalent of the logs typically found in the Windows Event Log on a Windows Server machine, this is a single XML file on the local file system of the website. In the context of Websites, the Event Log is particularly useful for capturing unhandled exceptions that may have escaped the application's exception handling logic and surfaced to the web server. Only one XML file is created per website.

■ **Web server logs** Web server logs are textual files that create a text entry for each HTTP request to the website.

■ **Detailed error message logs** These HTML files are generated by the web server and log the error messages for failed requests that result in an HTTP status code of 400 or higher. One error message is captured per HTML file.

■ **Failed request tracing logs** In addition to the error message (captured by detailed error message logs), the stack trace that led to a failed HTTP request is captured in these XML documents that are presented with an XSL style sheet for in-browser consumption. One failed request trace is captured per XML file.

■ **Application diagnostic logs** These text-based trace logs are created by web application code in a manner specific to the platform the application is built in. For ASP.NET applications, these are created by invoking the logging methods in the System.Diagnostics.Trace class. Java, Node.js, Ruby, and Python applications running in Websites can emit similar text-based application diagnostic traces, with the log names, locations, and format specific to each platform.

You can retrieve diagnostic data by using Visual Studio, the Site Control Management (SCM) website, the command line in Windows PowerShell or the xplat-cli, or direct download via FTP to query Table or Blob storage.

Table 1-3 describes where to find each type of log when retrieving diagnostic data stored in the website's local file system. The Log Files folder is physically located at D:\home\LogFiles.

TABLE 1-3 Locations of the various logs on the website's local file system

Log Type	Location
Event Log	\LogFiles\eventlog.xml
Web server logs	\LogFiles\http\RawLogs*.log
Detailed error message logs	\LogFiles\DetailedErrors\ErrorPage######.htm
Failed request tracing logs	\LogFiles\W3SVC**.xml Also includes one *.xsd file that is used to format the XML file for display in supported browsers.
Application diagnostic logs (.NET)	\LogFiles\Application*.txt

Retrieving diagnostic data and log streaming using Visual Studio

Diagnostic data that's configured to log to the file system of websites can be retrieved and viewed using Server Explorer within Visual Studio.

1. Launch Visual Studio.

2. From the View menu, select Server Explorer.

3. Expand the node labeled Azure. If you are prompted to log in, log in with your organizational account or the Microsoft account that is associated with the website you want to manage.

4. Expand Websites.

5. Expand the website you want to manage.

6. Expand the Log Files folder to reveal the subfolders listed in Table 1-3, which contain the various diagnostic log files.

7. Expand any of the subfolders until you get to the desired file listing, and then double-click the file to download and open it within Visual Studio.

8. Alternately, to download the entire Log Files folder, complete the following steps:

    A. In Server Explorer, right-click the website whose log files you want to download.

    B. Select View Settings.

    C. Click the Logs tab.

    D. Under Actions, click the Download Logs link to download a *.zip file that contains all of the logs.

If in addition to or instead of having the application logs stored in the website's local file system you want to retrieve the application logs stored in Azure Storage, complete the following steps:

1. In Server Explorer, right-click the website whose log files you want to download.

2. Select View Settings.

3. Click the Logs tab.

4. Click the View All Application Logs link to open the logs table from Table storage.

EXAM TIP

Your own Failed Request Tracing Logs folder may include multiple folders that start with *W3SVC*. There are always two such folders because one is for your website and one is for the Site Control Manager (also known as Kudu) that runs in parallel to your website.

In addition to being able to download and view your application diagnostic logs, you can view them line by line as they are generated in real time in response to activity on the website. To view the logs in Visual Studio, in Server Explorer, right-click the website you want to monitor and select View Streaming Logs. The Output window appears and updates to indicate it has connected to the log streaming service. When the window is connected, any requests that generate application diagnostic trace output should cause the trace to appear in the output window.

Retrieving diagnostic data using Site Control Manager (Kudu)

Site Control Manager (SCM) (also known as Kudu) is a parallel website that is available with every deployed website, providing various management functions. In particular, it can be used to access and view diagnostic log data using only the browser. To access SCM, you must have administrator rights to the website. (If you can access the website via the portal, then you will be able to access SCM.) To retrieve data using SCM, complete the following steps:

1. Open your browser, and navigate to *https://<yoursitename>.scm.azurewebsites.net*. In the URL, ensure that you are accessing using SSL, that you replace *<yoursitename>* with the name of your website, and that you add *.scm.* between your website's name and *.azurewebsites.net*.

2. If you are not currently logged in with your organizational account or Microsoft account, you will be prompted to log in. Be sure to use the credentials you would use to manage the website in the portal.

3. When you are logged in, click the Debug console menu, and select CMD.

4. In the screen that appears, you can explore the local file system of your website using a tabular view (top part of the screen) and a command line view (bottom part of the screen). In the tabular view, click the LogFiles folder.

5. A screen showing the root of all your log files appears. To view any of the files, click the download button (the left-most icon next to any file). To download a complete subdirectory (such as the entire DetailedErrors folder), click the download button to the far left of any subdirectory.

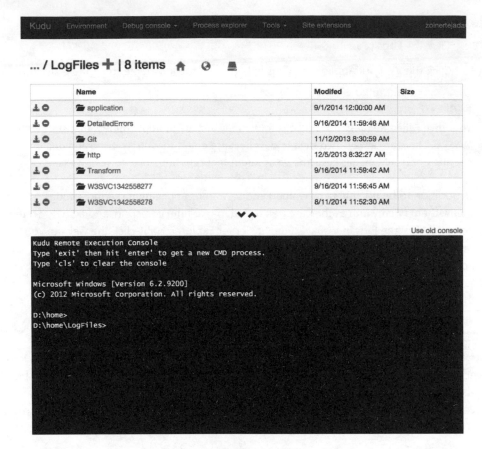

In SCM, you can also stream the logs, just as you can within Visual Studio. To do this, log in to the SCM website for your website, and complete the following steps:

6. From the Tools menu, select Log Stream.

7. When the page loads, you are connected to the log streaming service and can view the log entries as they are created in real time.

Retrieving diagnostic data using Windows PowerShell

Using the Azure PowerShell cmdlets, you can stream diagnostic logs. Ensure the cmdlets are installed and configured to connect to your subscription, and then use the command shown in Listing 1-7 to stream your diagnostic logs.

LISTING 1-7 Using Windows PowerShell to retrieve the streaming logs

```
Get-AzureWebsiteLog -Name contoso -Tail
```

You will be connected to the log-streaming service and able to view the log records as they come in.

Retrieving diagnostic data using the xplat-cli

Using the xplat-cli, you can download diagnostic logs, as well as stream application diagnostic logs. When the xplat-cli is installed, make sure that the default account is set to the subscription containing the website you are interested in, and then you can retrieve diagnostic data.

To download your diagnostic logs, from the command prompt, type the command shown in Listing 1-8.

LISTING 1-8 Downloading diagnostic logs using xplat-cli

```
azure site log download
```

When prompted for the name of the website, enter just the name (not the full URL), and press Enter. When prompted for the website slot, press Enter to accept the default, or type the name of the slot and then press Enter. The diagnostic logs will download to your current directory as a file named Diagnostic.zip.

To connect your command window to the log-streaming service, enter the command shown in Listing 1-9.

LISTING 1-9 Using the xplat-cli to view streaming logs

```
azure site tail
```

When prompted for the name of the website, enter just the name (not the full URL), and press Enter. When prompted for the website slot, press Enter to accept the default, or type the name of the slot and then press Enter.

You will be connected to the log-streaming service and able to view the log records as they come in.

Retrieving diagnostic data from FTP

You can download all of the diagnostic data using an FTP client. To do so, you must first set your deployment credentials for your website (these are different than your organizational or Microsoft account credentials used to access the portal). When those credentials are set, using the FTP client your choice, connect to the FTP host and enter your credentials to log in. From the folder you connect to, drill down to the LogFiles folder where you can download your diagnostic logs.

RETRIEVING DIAGNOSTIC DATA FROM FTP (EXISTING PORTAL)

To retrieve diagnostic data from FTP in the management portal, complete the following steps:

1. Navigate to the dashboard of your website in the management portal accessed via *https://manage.windowsazure.com*.

2. Under Quick Glance, click Reset Your Deployment Credentials.

quick glance

◉ Visit the new portal PREVIEW

◉ View Applicable Add-ons

ⓘ View connection strings

⊕ Download the publish profile

↻ Reset your deployment credentials

↻ Reset your publish profile credentials

↩ Delete Git repository

ⓘ Add a new deployment slot PREVIEW

3. In the dialog box that appears, enter a username and password, and then confirm that password.

4. Click the check mark to save the deployment credentials, which are your FTP credentials.

5. Under Quick Glance, note the Deployment/FTP User. This is your username for FTP. (You must include the website name that precedes the user you entered, so make sure you note it is *<yourwebsitename>\<user>* and not just *<user>*.)

6. Collect the FTP endpoint to connect to. Under Quick Glance, copy either the FTP Host Name or FTPS Host Name value (depending on what your FTP client supports and what you prefer to use).

7. Open your FTP client, and for the address, enter the FTP or FTPS host name. When prompted, enter your credentials. You are now connected via FTP and can download any of the log files from the LogFiles folder.

RETRIEVING DIAGNOSTIC DATA FROM FTP (PREVIEW PORTAL)

To retrieve diagnostic data from FTP in the Preview portal, complete the following steps:

1. Navigate to the blade of your website in the portal accessed via *https://portal.azure.com*.

2. Scroll down to Deployment and click Set Deployment Credentials.

3. On the blade that appears, enter a username and password, and then confirm that password.

4. Click Save on the command bar.

5. Return to the blade of your website, click Settings, and then click Properties.

6. On the blade that appears, take note of the FTP/Deployment User. This is your username for FTP. (You must include the website name that precedes the user you entered, so make sure you note it is *<yourwebsitename>\<user>* and not just *<user>*.)

7. Collect the FTP endpoint to connect to. On the same blade as the user, copy either the FTP Host Name or FTPS Host Name value (depending on what your FTP client supports and what you prefer to use).

8. Open your FTP client, and for the address, enter the FTP or FTPS host name. When prompted, enter your credentials. You are now connected via FTP and can download any of the log files from the LogFiles folder.

Configuring diagnostics

The portal makes the configuration of diagnostic data a straightforward process, but you can also use the Azure PowerShell cmdlets and the xplat-cli to achieve the same results.

Configuring diagnostic data collection (existing portal)

To configure diagnostic data in the management portal, complete the following steps:

1. Navigate to the Configure tab of your website in the management portal accessed via *https://manage.windowsazure.com*.

2. Scroll down to Application Diagnostics. Application diagnostic logs are configured using the controls in this section.

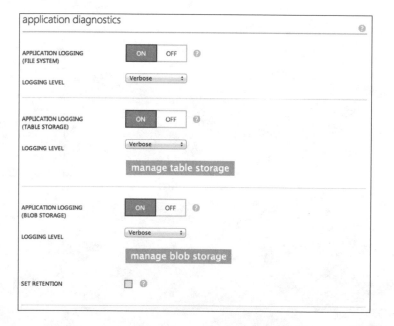

3. To enable collection of application diagnostic logs to the local file system of the website, change the Application Logging (File System) option to On, and select a logging level.

4. To enable collection of application diagnostic logs to Table storage, change the Application Logging (Table Storage) option to On, and select a logging level. Click Manage Table Storage to choose a storage account from within your active subscription, as well as to create a new table or to write the log data to an existing table. Click the check mark to close the dialog box.

5. To enable writing the diagnostic logs to files in Blob storage, change the Application Logging (Blob Storage) option to On, and select a logging level. Optionally, select the Set Retention check box and enter a number of days to keep the log files. Click Manage Blob Storage to choose a storage account from within your active subscription, as well as to create a new blob container or to write the log data to an existing blob container. Click the check mark to close the dialog box.

> **IMPORTANT   AZURE STORAGE AND LOG DATA LIMITATIONS**
>
> Application diagnostic logging to Table or Blob storage is supported only for .NET applications. While the portal may let you enable it for any website, log data will be collected to Azure Storage only from a .NET application.

6. To configure web server logs, detailed error message logs, and failed request tracing logs, on the Configure tab, scroll down to Site Diagnostics.

7. To enable writing the diagnostic logs to the local file system of the website, change the Web Server Logging option to File System and set a quota for the space consumed by these logs to between 25 and 100 MB. Optionally, select the Set Retention check box and enter a number of days to keep the log files.

8. To enable writing the diagnostic logs to Blob storage, change the Web Server Logging option to Storage. Optionally, select the Set Retention check box and enter a number of days to keep the log files. Click Manage Blob Storage to choose a storage account from within your active subscription, as well as to create a new blob container or to write the log data to an existing blob container. Click the check mark to close the dialog box.

9. To enable writing of detailed error message logs to the local file system of the website, change the Detailed Error Messages option to On.

10. To enable writing of failed request logs to the local file system of the website, change the Failed Request Tracing option to On.

11. After completing your application and site diagnostic configuration, be sure to click Save on the command bar to apply the changes to your website.

Configuring diagnostic data collection (Preview portal)

To configure diagnostic data collection in the Preview portal, complete the following steps:

1. Navigate to the blade of your website in the portal accessed via https://portal.azure.com.

2. Under Summary, click Settings, and then click Diagnostic Logs.

3. On the Logs blade, switch the desired logs to the On position.

4. Click Save.

> **NOTE** **EVENT LOG IS ALWAYS ENABLED**
>
> You may have noticed that there is no configuration setting for Event Log. This log is always enabled.

Using remote debugging

Remote debugging enables you to use your local copy of Visual Studio to debug an ASP.NET application running in Websites. When you are remote debugging, you can use Visual Studio to set breakpoints, examine variable values, and step through code. To debug a deployed website, you must ensure that it is a debug build (for example, it has the debug symbols). After you have deployed a debug build, complete the following steps to start a debug session within Visual Studio.

1. Ensure the project you are debugging is built and that you have made no changes to it since you deployed it to Websites.

2. From the View menu, select Server Explorer.

3. Expand the node labeled Azure. If prompted to log in, login with your organizational account or the Microsoft account that is associated with the website you want to manage.

4. Expand Websites.

5. Right-click the website to debug and select Attach Debugger.

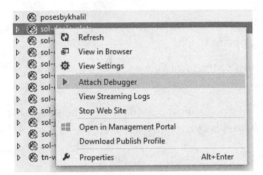

6. If you have never attached the remote debugger before, this process might take up to 30 seconds as it automatically configures the website for debugging.

7. When your web application's home page has loaded in the browser, start debugging as you would if the code were running locally.

> **IMPORTANT** **HOW DEBUGGING AFFECTS YOUR WEBSITE**
>
> When you attach the debugger and pause at a breakpoint, you are stopping the deployed Azure website for all requests, so it is not a good idea to rely on this technique for production debugging because users will think your website is down. Also, if you spend more than a few minutes stopped at any one breakpoint, Azure will treat your Websites worker process as having become unresponsive and try to restart it, so be prepared to move quickly when attached with the remote debugger to a website.

Configuring endpoint monitoring

You can use endpoint monitoring to leverage Azure to provide outside-in monitoring of your website. That is, you leverage a service remote to your website, possibly in multiple regions around the world, to periodically ping your website to assess its health. To enable endpoint monitoring, provide the URL of the endpoint on your website that it should ping, and choose where you want to ping from. The results of these pings appear in the status dashboards for your website and can also be used to create alerts that send out an email when the results fall outside of thresholds you configure.

Configuring endpoint monitoring (existing portal)

To configure endpoint monitoring in the management portal, complete the following steps:

1. Navigate to the Configure tab of your website in the management portal accessed via *https://manage.windowsazure.com*.

2. Scroll down to Monitoring.

3. Provide a short name for the endpoint and the URL you want Azure to ping. Also pick from one to three locations from which to ping.

4. To add another, different URL to ping, fill in the row that was added as soon you started typing in the first row.

5. Click Save on the command bar to apply the changes.

Configuring endpoint monitoring (Preview portal)

To configure endpoint monitoring in the Preview portal, complete the following steps:

1. Navigate to the blade of your website in the portal accessed via *https://portal.azure.com*.

2. Scroll down to Monitoring and click Webtests.

3. On the Create Test blade that appears, specify a name for this test endpoint, the URL, and the test locations.

4. Click Create.

Configuring alerts

You can configure rules for your website to evaluate metrics you specify and, when the values of those metrics exceeds your designated threshold, to send an email to a service administrator, a co-administrator, or to an email address you specify.

Configuring alerts (existing portal)

To configure alerts in the management portal, complete the following steps:

1. Navigate to the Configure tab of your website in the management portal accessed via *https://manage.windowsazure.com*.

2. In the main navigation pane, click Management Services.

3. On the Alert tab that appears, click Add Rule on the command bar.

4. In the Define Alert dialog box, provide a short name for your alert, as well as a description to help you understand the alert in the future.

5. From the Service Type drop-down list, select Web Site, and from the Service Name drop-down list, select the website for which you are configuring an alert. Click the right arrow to move to the next step.

CREATE ALERT RULE

Define Alert

NAME ⊙

Website Slow

DESCRIPTION

Things are not working like they should

SERVICE TYPE

Web Site ⬍

SERVICE NAME

sol-deployslots ⬍

6. In the Define A Condition For Notifications dialog box, choose the metric to define your threshold condition. If you have enabled endpoint monitoring for the selected website, in addition to the standard set of metrics (memory, CPU, data and HTTP status counts, and so on), there are also entries for response time and uptime as measured from each of the configured monitoring locations.

CREATE ALERT RULE

Define a condition for notifications.

METRIC ⓘ

Response Time (Endpoint 1/US : IL-Chicago)   ▲▼

CONDITION   THRESHOLD VALUE   UNIT

greater than   ▲▼   1   Seconds

ALERT EVALUATION WINDOW ⓘ

Average over the last 15 minutes   ▲▼

ACTIONS ⓘ

☑ Send an email to the service administrator and co-administrators.

☐ Specify the email address for another administrator.

7. In the Condition field, choose how to compare the selected metric's value against the threshold value, and enter the threshold value in the Threshold Value text box.

8. Select a window of time over which to compute the rule.

9. Set the desired email actions by selecting the appropriate check boxes.

10. Click the check mark to create the new rule, automatically enabled.

Configuring alerts (Preview portal)

To configure alerts in the Preview portal, complete the following steps:

1. Navigate to the blade of your website in the portal accessed via *https://portal.azure.com*.

2. Scroll down to Operations and click Alert Rules.

3. On the Alert Rules blade, click Add Alert.

4. On the Add An Alert Rule blade, choose the metric to define your threshold condition. If you have enabled endpoint monitoring for the selected website, in addition to the standard set of metrics (memory, CPU, data and HTTP status counts, and so on), there are entries for response time and uptime as measured from each of the configured monitoring locations.

METRIC ⓘ

Http Server Errors ▾

```
100 ..................................................
 80
 60
 40
 20

      06 PM    TUE 16    06 AM    12 PM
```

CONDITION

greater than ▾

THRESHOLD ⓘ

100   ⟳

count

PERIOD ⓘ

Over the last 5 minutes ▾

EMAIL SERVICE AND CO-ADMINISTRATORS
☑

ADDITIONAL ADMINISTRATOR EMAIL

additional administrator email

OK

5. In the Condition field, choose how to compare the selected metric's value against the threshold, and enter the threshold value in the Threshold text box.

6. From the Period drop-down list, select a period of time over which to compute the rule.

7. If desired, select the Email Service And Co-Administrators check box.

8. Additionally, if desired, enter an email address in the Additional Administrator Email text box.

9. Click OK to create the new rule.

Monitoring website resources

You can use the management portal to monitor the status, health, and resource consumption of your website. From the portal, you can examine and chart metrics (for example, memory, CPU, data transfer, requests, and endpoint uptime/response time); examine resource usage and compare it against your web hosting plan quota (for example, CPU time, outbound data transfer, file system usage, and memory usage); review the status of your monitored endpoints and alert rules; and review an audit log of management events.

Monitoring website resources (existing portal)

To monitor website resources in the management portal, complete the following steps:

1. To examine resource usage against your web hosting plan quota, navigate to the dashboard of your website in the management portal accessed via *https://manage.windowsazure.com*.

   Depending on the web hosting plan mode, you will see the quotas that are in effect and how your consumption compares to the cap. For example, a website in the Free web hosting plan mode will show resource consumption for CPU Time, data transfer out, usage of the local file system, and memory usage. However, a website in the Standard mode will show only file system storage. On the dashboard, you can also view the status of your monitored web endpoints.

2. To view detailed metrics for your website, navigate to the Monitor tab. A chart of the collected metrics is displayed above a table of the same metrics. To add additional metrics, click Add Metrics on the command bar, and select the desired metrics or endpoint statistics.

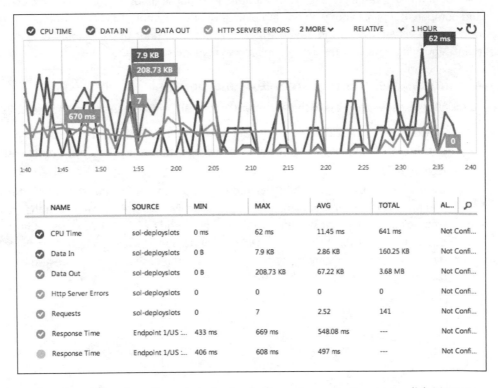

NAME	SOURCE	MIN	MAX	AVG	TOTAL	AL...
CPU Time	sol-deployslots	0 ms	62 ms	11.45 ms	641 ms	Not Confi...
Data In	sol-deployslots	0 B	7.9 KB	2.86 KB	160.25 KB	Not Confi...
Data Out	sol-deployslots	0 B	208.73 KB	67.22 KB	3.68 MB	Not Confi...
Http Server Errors	sol-deployslots	0	0	0	0	Not Confi...
Requests	sol-deployslots	0	7	2.52	141	Not Confi...
Response Time	Endpoint 1/US :...	433 ms	669 ms	548.08 ms	---	Not Confi...
Response Time	Endpoint 1/US :...	406 ms	608 ms	497 ms	---	Not Confi...

3. To view the status of configured alert rules, in the main navigation pane, click Management Services. This screen will provide you with a list of all the alerts you have configured, along with their status.

RULE NAME	ALERT STATUS	SERVICE	SUBSCRIPTION
BusyDay	✔ Not activated	Web Site: fall-...	
ForbiddenRequests sol-tempone	⚠ Limited	Web Site: sol-...	
Http Errors Alert	✔ Not activated	Web Site: fall-...	
ServerErrors sol-tempone	⚠ Limited	Web Site: sol-...	
ServerErrors-test-devintersection	⚠ Limited	Web Site: test...	

4. To view the audit log of management events that have occurred, on the Management Services page, click Operation Logs.

Monitoring website resources (Preview portal)

To monitor website resources in the Preview portal, complete the following steps:

1. To examine resource usage against your web hosting plan quota, navigate to the blade of your website in the portal accessed via *https://portal.azure.com*.

2. Scroll down to Usage and click Quotas.

   Depending on the web hosting plan mode, you will see the quotas that are in effect and how your consumption compares to the cap. For example, a website in the Free web hosting plan mode will show resource consumption for CPU Time, data transfer out, usage of the local file system, and memory usage. However, a website in the Standard mode will show only memory and CPU usage.

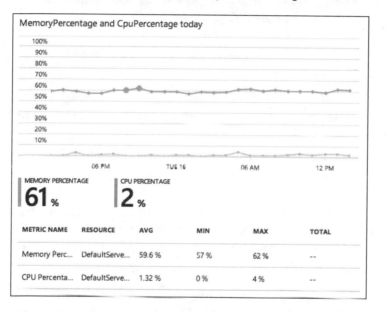

3. On the Website blade of your website, click Webtests to view the status of your monitored web endpoints.

4. To view detailed metrics and alert status for your website, return to the Website blade of your website and scroll down to Monitoring. Click Requests And Errors.

5. To view the audit log of management events that have occurred, return to the Website blade of your website and scroll down to Operations. Click Events In The Past Week.

OPERATION		STATUS	TIME	CALLER
UpdateWebSite	✓	Succeeded	1 h ago	--
UpdateWebSite	▶	Started	1 h ago	--

Objective summary

- Diagnostic data can be stored locally on the website or in Azure Storage and later retrieved by using SCM, downloaded from the website via FTP, viewed via SCM streaming logs, or retrieved from Azure Storage.

- You can use Visual Studio to attach to a website instance with remote debugging, but you should be careful in doing so because hitting breakpoints will stop your website instance from responding to all requests.

- Websites can be configured to use outside-in endpoint monitoring to remotely monitor the availability and responsiveness of your website, and these metrics can also be used as alerts sent out via email when configured thresholds are crossed.

- You can monitor website resources using the management portal.

Objective review

Answer the following questions to test your knowledge of the information in this objective. You can find the answers to these questions and explanations of why each answer choice is correct or incorrect in the "Answers" section at the end of this chapter.

1. Which of the following tools would you *not* use to diagnose a problem on a production site to avoid disturbing visitors while diagnosing?

   A. Log streaming

   B. Remote debugger

   C. Event log

   D. Application log

2. With endpoint monitoring, you can perform all of the following *except* what?

   A. Configure alerts to send automated emails

   B. Auto-scale

   C. Perform outside-in monitoring

   D. Monitor from multiple geographic locations

3. Out of the box, where can website diagnostic logs be stored? (Choose all that apply.)

   A. Website file system

   B. Azure Storage

   C. SQL Database

   D. Email

Objective 1.4: Implement WebJobs

WebJobs enables you to run a .NET console application (as well many types of scripts, in-cluding batch, Windows PowerShell, PHP, Python, and Node.js) within the context of Azure Websites, enabling you to perform background processing. These jobs can be scheduled to run on demand, continuously, or on a predefined schedule with a recurrence. Additionally, operations defined within WebJobs can be triggered to run either when the job runs or when a new file is created in Blob storage or a message is sent to an Azure queue.

> **This objective covers how to:**
> - Write WebJobs using the SDK
> - Package and deploy WebJobs
> - Schedule WebJobs

Writing WebJobs using the SDK

With the WebJobs SDK, the work of connecting the logic of the console application to Azure blobs and queues becomes little more than a matter of decorating your public static meth-ods in your console application with parameter level attributes (the attributes precede the parameter name and type in the method signature). With these attributes, the WebJobs SDK knows to invoke your methods so they run based on the appearance of a blob in Blob storage or a message in a queue and then just as easily output a new blob or message as a result of the invocation. WebJobs SDK handles the triggering of your decorated methods, and binding takes care of passing you a reference to the blob or message as desired. Table 1-4 describes these attributes by example, the syntax of which is demonstrated later.

TABLE 1-4 WebJobs SDK binding attributes in C#

Example Attribute	Meaning
[BlobTrigger("input/{blob-Name}")]	Triggers the method to run when a new blob is detected within the input container. The name of the blob is captured (much like for MVC routes) into blobName and can be reused later by the Blob attribute as well as by adding a parameter to the method named blobName.
[QueueTrigger("queueName")]	Triggers the method to run when a new message appears in the queue indicated.
[Blob("output/{blobName}", FileAccess.Write)]	Provides access to the blob identified by the parameter. Often used with the optional FileAccess.Write parameter to output the results of the method to the indicated blob.
[Queue("queueName")]	Provides access to the queue identified by the queue name, particularly to add a new message to the queue.

The following example shows how to create a new, standalone WebJobs project. WebJobs always run within a website, but they can be created independently of a Websites project.

1. Within Visual Studio, click File, New Project.

2. In the New Project dialog box navigation pane, expand Installed, Templates, Visual C#, and then click Cloud.

3. In the list of templates, select Microsoft Azure WebJob.

4. Name your project, and click OK.

5. Open Program.cs.

6. Modify the class Program so that it is public. If you do not make the class public, WebJobs will not detect and run your operations.

7. Inside Program.cs, add a using statement for Microsoft.Azure.WebJobs as well as System.IO (because the example will process blobs as Stream objects), as shown in Listing 1-10.

LISTING 1-10 Using statements needed for WebJobs

```
using Microsoft.Azure.WebJobs;
using System.IO;
```

8. Within Main(), add the code to initialize and configure the behavior of JobHost, in this case, to invoke host.RunAndBlock() so that the WebJob runs continuously as shown in Listing 1-11.

LISTING 1-11 Initializing a JobHost

```
static void Main()
{
    JobHost host = new JobHost();
    host.RunAndBlock();
}
```

9. Next, add a method to be invoked by WebJobs as shown in Listing 1-12. In this case, it "listens" for files with the .png extension being added in the "input" container of Blob storage and then re-writes the file with a new file name to the "ouput" container, where the new file name is the original .png file name without the extension, prefixed with "processed_" and suffixed with "_final.png."

LISTING 1-12 WebJob operation triggered by a blob appearing

```
public static void RenameFile(
    [BlobTrigger("input/{blobName}.png")] Stream input,
    [Blob("output/processed_{blobName}_final.png", FileAccess.Write)] Stream
output)
{
    input.CopyTo(output);
}
```

10. To run this WebJob locally, you need to apply some local configuration. Open the App.config file and add connection strings for the canonical storage account connection strings expected by WebJobs SDK, AzureWebJobsDashboard, and AzureWebJobsStorage as shown in Listing 1-13. Be sure to replace name and key values with the values from your own storage account.

LISTING 1-13 Storage connection configuration that enables the WebJob to run locally

```
<connectionStrings>
    <add name="AzureWebJobsStorage" connectionString="DefaultEndpointsProtocol=http
s;AccountName=name;AccountKey=key"/>
    <add name="AzureWebJobsDashboard" connectionString="DefaultEndpointsProtocol=ht
tps;AccountName=name;AccountKey=key"/>
</connectionStrings>
```

11. Using Server Explorer, connect to the storage account you will be using, right-click Blobs, and select Create Blob Container.

12. In the dialog box that appears, for the blob container name, enter **input**, and click OK.

13. Upload a few .png files to process the input blob container. One way to do this is to double-click the container in Server Explorer, and in the document window, click the Upload Blob button (which is the third button from the left in the toolbar at the top of the document window), and select the .png files to upload.

14. Finally, press F5 or click the Debug menu, Start Debugging. The console window should appear with an indicator of "Job host started." About 10 to 15 seconds later, you should see diagnostic traces indicating "Executing: 'Program.RenameFile because New blob detected."

15. To confirm the files were copied to the output container, open the container in the tool of your choice (you can use the Server Explorer approach for this also).

Packaging and deploying WebJobs

Using Visual Studio 2013 and the Azure SDK 2.4 or later, you can package a WebJob console application and deploy it without leaving Visual Studio.

While it can be convenient to deploy a WebJob alongside a web project (for example, an ASP.NET Web Application), this makes it difficult to scale the WebJob independently of the website and also introduces the potential for resource contention between the website handling requests and the WebJob performing its processing. Additionally, within a Visual Studio solution, it is possible to associate a WebJob with a web project at a later time if you consolidate the deployment. Therefore, it is pragmatic to start your WebJob development as a standalone console project.

> *MORE INFO*   **WEBJOBS AND WEB PROJECTS SIDE BY SIDE**
>
> If you would like to learn how to deploy a WebJob project alongside a web project, see *http://azure.microsoft.com/en-us/documentation/articles/websites-dotnet-deploy-webjobs/.*

1. Open the project you created previously in the section "Writing WebJobs using the SDK."

2. In Server Explorer, right-click the project and select Publish As Azure WebJob.

3. In the Add Azure WebJob dialog box, set the WebJob run mode to Run Continuously, and then click OK.

Microsoft Azure WebJobs

Project name:

WebJobSample

WebJob name:

WebJobSample

WebJob run mode:

Run Continuously

4. In the Publish Web dialog box, select Microsoft Azure Websites as your publish target.

5. In the dialog box that appears, sign in if you have not done so already, and then click New to create a new website for this WebJob.

6. In the Create A Site On Microsoft Azure dialog box, provide a site name for the new website, and then specify a subscription and region as desired.

7. Click Create.

8. Return to the Publish Web dialog box, and click Publish to deploy your WebJob.

9. Before your WebJob will run, you need to navigate to the website you just created using the portal and add the same two connection strings (AzureWebJobsStorage and AzureWebsJobsDashboard) you previously added to App.config.

10. After you apply the connection strings, upload some .png files to the input folder.

11. Check on the status of the WebJob by using your browser to navigate to the Azure WebJobs Dashboard (which is a special WebJobs area within SCM), located at *https://<yourwebsitename>.scm.azurewebsites.net/azurejobs*.

Scheduling WebJobs

WebJobs can run on-demand (when run from the portal), continuously (and possibly in response to input from a Storage blob, Storage queue, or Service Bus queue), on a scheduled date and time, or at certain recurring intervals within a specified date range. The schedule to use depends on your scenario. Scenarios that run only occasionally may work best as on-demand; scenarios that run in response to input from storage or service queues should run continuously; others may need to be scheduled according to the calendar.

In the previous example, the WebJob was configured to run continuously. If instead you want the WebJob to run on a schedule, you can complete the following steps to reconfigure it in Visual Studio and then re-deploy:

1. With the project open in Visual Studio, open Solution Explorer.

2. Expand the project, and then expand Properties. Right-click the file named Webjob-publish-settings.json, select Delete, and then confirm the selection in when prompted. You will re-create this file later using the Add Azure WebJob dialog box.

3. Return to Solution Explorer, right-click the project and select Publish As Azure WebJob.

4. In the Add Azure WebJob dialog box, select Run On A Schedule in the WebJob Run Mode list.

5. Specify a recurrence, a starting date and time, and, if you selected Recurring Job as recurrence, specify an ending date and time and a recurrence pattern (for example, Recur Every 1 Day).

6. Click OK to re-create the Webjob-publish-settings.json file with the new configuration and open the Publish Web dialog box.

7. Click Publish to deploy the WebJob with the new schedule.

Objective summary

- WebJobs enables you to run background processing tasks that run within the context of Azure Websites.

- When authoring a WebJob in .NET, you can use WebJobs SDK to trigger processing based on the appearance of a blob or queue message.

- Alternately, you can run a WebJob once or configure it to run according to a schedule.

Objective review

Answer the following questions to test your knowledge of the information in this objective. You can find the answers to these questions and explanations of why each answer choice is correct or incorrect in the "Answers" section at the end of this chapter.

1. Which of the following is NOT true about WebJobs?

   A. They can only be triggered by a queue message.

   B. They must be deployed with a web application.

   C. They can only be written in C#.

   D. All of the above.

2. A recurring WebJob can be configured to recur every how often? (Choose all that apply.)

   A. Second

   B. Minute

   C. Hour

   D. Day

   E. Week

   F. Month

3. A WebJob can be triggered as a result of which of the following? (Choose all that apply.)

   A. A new blob added to a container

   B. A new message in a storage queue

   C. An on-demand request

   D. A SQL trigger

Objective 1.5: Configure websites for scale and resilience

Azure Websites provides various mechanisms to scale your websites up and down by adjusting the number of VM instances serving requests and by adjusting the instance size. You can, for example, increase (scale up, or more precisely, scale out) the number of instances to support the load you experience during business hours, but then decrease (scale down, or more precisely, scale in) the number of instances during less busy hours to save costs. Websites enables you to scale the instance count manually, automatically via a schedule, or automatically according to key performance metrics. Within a datacenter, Azure will load balance traffic between all of your website instances using a round-robin approach.

You can also scale up a website by deploying to multiple regions around the world and then utilizing Microsoft Azure Traffic Manager to direct website traffic to the appropriate region based on a round robin strategy or according to performance (approximating the latency perceived by clients of your website). Alternately, you can configure Traffic Manager to use the alternate regions as targets for failover if the primary region becomes unavailable.

In addition to scaling instance counts, you can manually adjust your instance size. For example, you can scale up your website to utilize more powerful VMs that have more RAM memory and more CPU cores to serve applications that are more demanding of memory consumption or CPU utilization, or scale down your VMs if you later discover your requirements are not as great.

> **This objective covers how to:**
> - Configure auto-scale using built-in and custom schedules
> - Configure auto-scale by metric
> - Change the size of an instance
> - Configure Traffic Manager

EXAM TIP

Unlike other Azure compute services, Websites provides a high availability SLA of 99.9 percent using only a single standard instance. You do not need to provision more than one instance to benefit from this SLA.

Configuring auto-scale using built-in and custom schedules

Scheduling is enabled via the Auto-Scale feature and requires that your website is in Standard web hosting plan mode. You can use one of the predefined recurring schedules (for example, day/night or weekdays/weekends) or define your own custom schedules (for example, according to a set of non-overlapping date ranges) to control the instance count of your website.

Configuring auto-scale by schedule (existing portal)

To configure auto-scale by schedule in the management portal, complete the following steps:

1. Navigate to the Scale tab of your website on the management portal accessed via *https://manage.windowsazure.com*.

2. Scroll down to Capacity.

3. Click Set Up Schedule Times.

4. In the dialog box that appears, define the schedule:

   - To enable a day/night recurring schedule, under Recurring Schedules, select Different Scale Settings For Day And Night, and then, under Time, specify what hours are considered daytime. (Azure will infer the remaining hours are nighttime.)

   - To enable a weekdays and weekends recurring schedule, under Recurring Schedules, select Different Scale Settings For Weekdays And Weekends (where weekdays are defined as Monday morning through Friday evening and weekends are Friday evening through Monday morning). Under Time, adjust the time for morning and evenings.

   - To enable usage of specific date ranges, under Specific Dates, fill in the grid. Specify a user-friendly name for the date range, a start date and time, and an end date and time. You can add multiple date ranges as long as they do not overlap.

5. When you finish defining schedules, click the check mark to make these schedules configurable on the Scale tab.

6. Return to the Scale tab and select one of your newly defined schedules from the Edit Scale Settings For Schedule.

7. Use the Instance Count slider to adjust the target number of instances for your website during that schedule.

8. Repeat the previous two steps as necessary for any other schedules you have defined.

9. Click Save to save both the newly defined schedules and your instance count configurations for each schedule.

Configuring auto-scale by schedule (Preview portal)

It is not currently possible to configure auto-scale using a schedule with the Preview portal.

Configuring auto-scale by metric

Auto-scale by metric enables Azure to automatically adjust the number of instances provisioned to your web hosting plan based on one or more configured rules, where each rule has a condition, a metric, and an action to take in response to the threshold being exceeded.

The performance-related metrics currently available include the following:

- **CPU Percentage**   Percent of CPU utilization
- **Memory Percentage**   Percent of RAM memory utilization
- **Disk Queue Length**   Count of pending disk operations
- **Http Queue Length**   Count of pending HTTP operations
- **Data In**   Amount of traffic ingress in kilobytes
- **Data Out**   Amount of traffic egress in kilobytes

Each metric is measured as an aggregate (typically an average) across all of your website instances over a period of time. For example, if you choose CPU Percentage as a metric, your condition will evaluate a threshold against the average CPU utilization percentage for all of your website VMs over a period of time and not the CPU percentage of a single VM.

For each rule, you choose a metric and then define a condition for it. This condition compares against a threshold. Above this threshold, a scale up action (adding instances) occurs, and below this threshold, a scale down action (removing instances) occurs. You also specify the number of instances by which to scale up or down.

You can specify both scale up and scale down actions for the same metric by using different rules. You can also specify multiple rules, using different conditions, metrics, and actions.

The frequency with which these rules are triggered is important to manage—you do not want to constantly add and remove instances because adding instances always takes some amount of time (no matter how little). As a practical approach, it is better to scale up aggressively (to better address your applications' demands) and scale down conservatively (so your application performance is more stable). Scaling frequency and how you choose to stabilize it is within your control. You stabilize scaling by specifying the period of time over which the threshold is computed and setting a cool-down period that follows a scaling operation, during which, scaling will not be triggered again.

This is all best explained by example. Consider a scenario where you start with one instance and you configure the following rule:

- **Metric**   CPU Percentage
- **Threshold**   Greater than 80 percent
- **Over Past**   20 minutes
- **Scale Up By**   1 instance
- **Cool Down**   20 minutes

Over a 20-minute period, your website experiences an average CPU utilization of 85 percent. Auto-scale adds one instance, increasing your total scale to two instances. However, assume that the CPU utilization remains at 85 percent for the next 5 minutes, even with the additional instance helping to reduce the average CPU load. Auto-scale will not trigger again for another 15 minutes because it is within the cool-down period for the scaling rule.

> **NOTE**   **NON-CONTIGUOUS THRESHOLDS**
>
> It is important to note that the scale-up threshold and the scale-down threshold do not have to be contiguous. For example, you can specify that one instance should be added every time the CPU utilization exceeds 80 percent, and only begin to remove one instance when the CPU utilization drops below 50 percent. This is another way to control the frequency of scaling operations.

Configuring auto-scale by metric (existing portal)

The existing portal allows you to define only a single pair of scale-up and scale-down rules based on the CPU percentage metric. You do not have control over the Over Past period, the step (or number of instances added/removed), or the cool-down period used each time a scaling rule is triggered—these default to 20 minutes, one instance, and 20 minutes, respectively. To specify this pair of rules, complete the following steps:

1. Navigate to the Scale tab of your website on the management portal accessed via *https://manage.windowsazure.com*.

2. Scroll down to Capacity.

3. For Scale By Metric, click CPU. This is the only metric supported by the existing portal.

4. Adjust the Target CPU slider to specify the threshold below which scale down actions will be taken. Do this by entering a value in the left-most text box or by dragging the left-most slider handler.

5. Repeat the previous step to define the threshold for the scale up action, using the right-most text box or slider handle to adjust the threshold.

6. Using the Instance Count slider, define the minimum and maximum number of instances that auto-scale can reach at any point in time.

7. Click Save to apply your auto-scale by metric rules.

Configuring auto-scale by metric (Preview portal)

The Preview portal enables you to define multiple scaling rules, using all the metrics previously introduced in this section, and provides granular control over scaling frequency. To configure your rules, complete the following steps:

1. Navigate to the blade of your website in the portal accessed via *https://portal.azure.com*.

2. Scroll down to Usage and click Scale.

3. In the Scale blade that appears, under Choose Scale, click Performance.

4. By default, one pair of rules for CPU percentage is already present. To quickly set scale up and scale down thresholds for the CPU percentage metric, leave the over past period and cool down period at their defaults.

5. Adjust the left and right control knobs on the Target Metrics slider to the desired threshold values.

6. To change the metric used or to add rules using different metrics, click the ">" button to the right of the Target Metrics slider and then do the following:

   A. Choose a metric from the Metric drop-down list.

   B. Specify the condition (greater or less), threshold, over past, scale up/down by, and cool down values.

C. To add another rule, click Add Scale Up Rule or Add Scale Down Rule and then repeat step 6 for the new rule.

D. Click Save on the command bar.

7. On the Scale blade for your web hosting plan, using the Instance Count slider, define the minimum and maximum number of instances that auto-scale can reach at any point in time.

8. To remove any undesired rules, click the X button to the right of its slider.

9. Click Save to apply your auto-scale rules.

> **NOTE   SCOPE OF AUTO-SCALE**
> Auto-scale affects the instance count of your web hosting plan and therefore affects all websites hosted within that plan. It does not apply directly to an individual website.

Changing the size of an instance

You can adjust the number of CPU cores and the amount of RAM memory available to your Websites VMs by adjusting the instance size (in the existing portal) or the by changing your pricing tier (in the Preview portal). In either case, you are adjusting the size of the instances used for your web hosting plan and therefore for all websites that are a part of it.

Changing the size of an instance (existing portal)

The existing portal allows you to change the instance size for your web hosting plan by selecting an instance size from the Scale tab of your website. To do so, your website must be in the Basic or Standard web hosting plan tier.

1. Navigate to the Scale tab of your website on the management portal accessed via *https://manage.windowsazure.com*.

2. Scroll down to Capacity.

3. From Instance Size, choose the desired instance size.

4. Click Save on the command bar.

Changing the size of an instance (Preview portal)

The Preview portal allows you to change the instance size for your web hosting plan by selecting a new pricing tier for it.

1. Navigate to the blade of your website in the portal accessed via *https://portal.azure.com*.

2. Scroll down to Usage and click Pricing Tier.

3. In the new blade, click on a pricing tier, and then click Select.

Configuring Traffic Manager

Traffic Manager combines endpoint monitoring of your website with DNS so that client traffic is always directed toward a viable endpoint. It is important to understand that traffic does not flow through Traffic Manager to your website endpoint, but rather it is guided to your website endpoint as a result of DNS resolution.

To understand this better, assume you have a website at www.contoso.com. You would configure your DNS for contoso.com to have a CNAME record with a key of "www" pointing to contoso.trafficmanager.net. When a client, such as a browser, first tries to browse to www.contoso.com, it does a domain name lookup that ultimately leads it to Traffic Manager. Traffic Manager evaluates its configuration for a viable endpoint (effectively evaluating rules and choosing from a list of endpoints you configured) and then Traffic Manager replies with the domain name of the viable endpoint for your website, such as contoso-west.azurewebsites.net. This domain name is then resolved to the IP address of your website endpoint by DNS. The browser actually sends its request to this IP address. For a period of time, the IP address to which www.contoso.com ultimately resolves is cached by the browser (to avoid the DNS lookup for every request). This period is referred to as the time-to-live, or TTL, for the local DNS cache entry, and it controls how long the client will continue to use a resolved endpoint—basically, until the TTL expires. When it expires, the client may perform another DNS lookup and, at this point, may learn of a new endpoint domain name (and by extension, a new IP address) from Traffic Manager.

> **NOTE CUSTOM DOMAIN NAMES AND TRAFFIC MANAGER**
>
> If you plan to use a custom domain name with Traffic Manager, you must configure the DNS settings for the custom domain to use a CNAME record that maps to the *<yourprefix>*.trafficmanager.net address. You cannot use an A record to map to an IP address exposed by Traffic Manager. This means that you can only use Traffic Manager for subdomains, such as www.contoso.com and not for contoso.com.

The fact that the resolution is time-based has a very important implication—at a given point in time, individual clients may resolve to different endpoints for load balancing or failover, but when resolved, clients may not become aware they need to be communicating with a different endpoint until the TTL expires.

> **NOTE CHOOSING A TTL VALUE**
>
> The default TTL used by Traffic Manager in response to DNS queries is 300 seconds (5 minutes). If you are using Traffic Manager primarily for failover, you might be tempted to set the TTL to a very low value to ensure clients who had been communicating with a now unreachable endpoint can quickly start communicating with a functioning endpoint. The minimum TTL allowed is 30 seconds, and you can use this value, but be aware you are creating additional DNS traffic as well as incurring additional Traffic Manager costs to handle the increased load of DNS queries.

Traffic Manager load balancing methods

Traffic Manager provides three different load balancing methods to guide traffic to a viable website endpoint. Each load balancing method can define its own TTL, list of endpoints, and monitoring configuration. The difference between them is primarily in how Traffic Manager chooses the endpoint from the list of endpoints when responding to a DNS query.

- **Failover**   When a DNS query comes in from a client, Traffic Manager picks the first endpoint from the ordered list of endpoints that it determines is healthy based on periodic monitoring of the endpoints.

- **Round robin**   Traffic Manager treats each active endpoint in its list of endpoints equally and tries to evenly distribute traffic among the endpoints in a round-robin fashion.

- **Performance**   Traffic Manager picks the "closest" endpoint from the configured list of endpoints that should have the lowest latency for the client. To do this, Traffic Manager maintains a lookup table (called the Internet Latency Table) of DNS server IP address ranges, and for each IP range, it periodically collects the round-trip latency from servers in that range to an Azure datacenter region. It locates the entry in the table that contains the IP address of the DNS server where the DNS query originated and then selects the website endpoint whose datacenter had the lowest latency.

You can think of these methods as all having a failover element because if Traffic Manager monitoring detects an endpoint as unhealthy, it is removed from the rotation and traffic is not guided to it.

> **NOTE AVOIDING CASCADING FAILURES**
>
> When using the performance load balancing method, be aware that if all the endpoints in the closest datacenter are not available, then Traffic Manager will switch to a round-robin method, distributing traffic to endpoints located in other datacenters to avoid overwhelming the endpoints in the next closest datacenter and potentially causing a chain of failures.

Configuring Traffic Manager (existing portal)

You configure Traffic Manager by creating profiles. Each profile contains a DNS prefix (of the form *<yourhost>*.trafficmanager.net), the load balancing method and configuration, and a list of endpoints. To configure Traffic Manager in the management portal, complete the following steps.

1. Navigate to the management portal accessed via *https://manage.windowsazure.com*.

2. On the command bar, click New, and then click Network Services, Traffic Manager, Quick Create.

3. Provide a DNS prefix for your Traffic Manager endpoint.

4. Choose a load balancing method (Performance, Round Robin, or Failover).

5. Click Create to create the basic Traffic Manager profile.

6. Click the name of the profile in the list of profiles.

7. Click the Endpoints tab.

8. Click Add Endpoints.

9. In the dialog box that appears, under Service Type, select Web Site.

10. In the Service Endpoints list, select the website endpoints you want to include in this Traffic Manager profile.

11. Click the check mark to complete selecting the endpoints.

12. Click the Configure tab.

13. Under General, in the DNS Time To Live (TTL) text box, enter a value in seconds.

14. Optionally, under Load Balancing Method Settings, change the load balancing method. If you choose the Failover method, modify the order of the endpoints by using the up and down arrows that appear when you hover over a website.

15. Under Monitoring Settings, choose the protocol (http or https) to use for monitoring your website endpoints, and specify the port number.

16. If desired, provide a relative path to monitor.

---

sol-tmdemo1

DASHBOARD   ENDPOINTS   **CONFIGURE**

general

DNS NAME   `sol-tmdemo1.trafficmanager.net`

DNS TIME TO LIVE (TTL)   `300`   seconds

load balancing method settings

LOAD BALANCING METHOD   `Performance ⬍`

monitoring settings

PROTOCOL   `HTTP` HTTPS

PORT   `80`

RELATIVE PATH AND FILE NAME   `/`

---

17. Click Save on the command bar.

Configuring Traffic Manager (Preview portal)

Currently, Traffic Manager cannot be configured using the Preview portal.

Scalability

In this thought experiment, apply what you've learned about this objective. You can find answers to these questions in the "Answers" section at the end of this chapter.

Congratulations! Your website is becoming quite successful, and traffic is growing steadily every day. Before the media frenzy, you are tasked with considering what steps you should take to support the future scalability requirements of your increasing traffic.

1. You are based in the United States. Users in Asia are complaining that the site is sluggish and slow to load. How might you apply Traffic Manager to improve their experience?

2. You have noticed a pattern: there are no traffic bursts on weekends or evenings. How might you configure auto-scale to optimize your number of instances and, therefore, hosting costs?

Objective summary

- Auto-scale adjusts the count of instances supporting your website in response to the crossing of configured metric thresholds or according to a schedule.

- You can change the size of the instances supporting your website by adjusting the size or tier of the web hosting plan. Auto-scale does not affect instance size.

- Azure Traffic Manager provides a DNS-level solution for direction requests to your geographically distributed websites according to one of three load balancing methods: performance, failover, and round robin.

Objective review

Answer the following questions to test your knowledge of the information in this objective. You can find the answers to these questions and explanations of why each answer choice is correct or incorrect in the "Answers" section at the end of this chapter.

1. The failover load balancing method is also a feature of which of the following?

   A. Failover

   B. Round robin

   C. Performance

   D. All of the above

2. Which one of the following does auto-scale control?

   A. Instance size

   B. Instance count

   C. Instance region

   D. Instance memory

3. If you have a website set up with Traffic Manager for failover and the primary endpoint fails, what is the minimum amount of time active users will wait to failover to the next endpoint?

   A. 0 seconds

   B. 30 seconds

   C. 500 seconds

   D. 3,600 seconds

Objective 1.6: Design and implement applications for scale and resilience

If your website will be accessible to any nominal amount of users, you are likely concerned about its ability to scale to current and future loads, as well as its ability to remain available to those users. Availability includes resiliency, which is the application's ability to recover from some form of failure, whether transient (temporary in nature, such that retrying the same operation will likely succeed) or permanent (where the fault will continue until explicitly addressed). Azure Websites provides a great deal of functionality for providing a scalable and resilient platform for hosting web applications, but how you design and implement your website, and the patterns you follow, equally impact how successful you are in achieving your target scale and resilience.

> **This objective covers how to:**
> - Select a pattern
> - Implement transient fault handling for services and respond to throttling
> - Disable Application Request Routing (ARR) affinity

Selecting a pattern

You can choose various patterns to implement a scalable and resilient web application. This section focuses on three frequently applied web application patterns in particular: throttling, retry, and circuit breaker.

> **MORE INFO**   **CLOUD PATTERNS**
>
> For comprehensive coverage of a number of cloud design patterns, see the material supplied by Microsoft Patterns & Practices at *http://msdn.microsoft.com/en-us/library/dn568099.aspx*. There you can read about the patterns online, download the documentation in PDF form (or order a printed copy), and view a poster summarizing all of the patterns.
>
> The following patterns are particularly useful to the availability, resiliency, and scalability of Websites and WebJobs.
>
> **USEFUL FOR WEBSITES AND WEBJOBS**
>
> - Static Content Hosting pattern
> - Cache-Aside pattern
> - Health Endpoint Monitoring pattern
> - Compensating Transaction pattern
> - Command and Query Responsibility Segregation pattern
>
> **USEFUL FOR WEBJOBS**
>
> - Competing Consumers pattern
> - Priority Queue pattern
> - Queue-Based Load Leveling pattern
> - Leader Election pattern
> - Scheduler Agent Supervisor pattern

Throttling pattern

When a website returns a 503 Service Unavailable status to a client, it is typically informing the browser that it is overloaded. This is an example of throttling in action. The throttling pattern quickly responds to increased load by restricting the consumption of resources by an application instance, a tenant, or an entire service so that the system being consumed can continue to function and meet service level agreements. The example in Figure 1-4 shows a scenario where paying customers get priority when the system is under heavy load.

Throttling Inactive

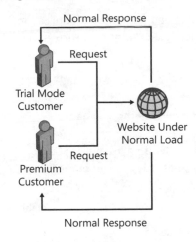

Throttling Active

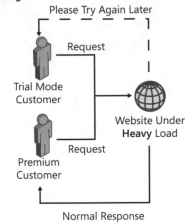

FIGURE 1-4 Throttling activated for a busy website

This pattern allows resource consumption up to some soft limit (that is, below the hard, maximum capacity of the system) that, when reached, causes the system to begin throttling the requests. This could be by outright rejecting requests, degrading functionality (such as switching to a lower bit rate video stream), focusing on high priority requests (such as only processing messages from paid subscribers and not trial users), or deferring the requests for the clients to retry later (as in the HTTP 503 case). Throttling is often paired with auto-scaling; since the time required to scale up is not instantaneous, the throttling can help keep the system operational until the new resources come online and then raise the soft limit after they are available.

If your web application consumes an external service (such as the SQL Database or Storage service), your application code must be aware of how the service may throttle your requests and handle the throttling exceptions properly (perhaps by retrying the operation later). This makes your website more resilient instead of immediately giving up when a throttling exception is encountered.

If your web application is a service itself, implementing the Throttling pattern as a part of your service logic makes your website more scalable in the face of rapid increases in load.

Retry pattern

If your application experiences a short-lived, temporary (or transient) failure connecting to an external service, it should transparently retry the failed operation. The most common example of this type of transient failure is connecting to a database that is overloaded and responding to new connection requests by refusing the connection (see Figure 1-5).

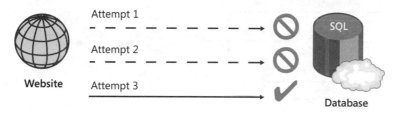

FIGURE 1-5 A website retrying to connect with a database multiple times

For applications depending on this database, you should define a retry policy to retry the connection multiple times, with a back-off strategy that waits an increasing amount of time between retries. With these definitions, only after the desired number of attempts have been made and failed does the retry mechanism raise an exception and abort further retry attempts.

When your web application is a client of an external service, implementing smart retry logic increases the resiliency of your website because it will recover from transient failures that occur in communicating with the external service.

Implementing the Retry pattern for a website that is a service by returning error codes for transient failures that are distinct from error codes for permanent failures improves your website's scalability and resiliency. This occurs because the service logic can guide client requests expecting that the client will retry the operation that resulted in a transient failure in the near future.

Circuit Breaker pattern

An implementation of the Circuit Breaker pattern prevents an application from attempting an operation that is likely to fail, acting much like the circuit breaker for the electrical system in a house (see Figure 1-6). The circuit breaker acts like a proxy for the application when invoking operations that may fail, particularly where the failure is long lasting. If everything is working as expected, the circuit breaker is said to be in the closed state, and any requests from the application are routed through to the operation. If the number of recent failures invoking the operation exceeds a threshold over some defined period of time, the circuit breaker is tripped and changes to the open state. In the open state, all requests from the application fail immediately without an actual attempt to invoke the real operation (for example, without trying to invoke the operation on a remote service). In the open state, a timer controls the "cool-down" period of the proxy. When this cool-down period expires, the circuit breaker switches to a half-open state, and a limited number of trial requests are allowed to flow through to the operation while the rest fail immediately, or the code queries the health of the service hosting the operation. In the half-open state, if the trial requests succeed or the service responds as healthy, then the failure is deemed repaired, and the circuit breaker changes back to the closed state. Conversely, if the trial requests fail, then the circuit breaker returns to the open state, and the timer starts anew.

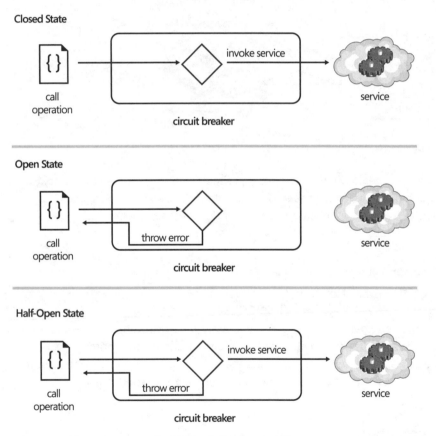

FIGURE 1-6 The various states in the Circuit Breaker pattern

For an application that consumes an external service, implementing the Circuit Breaker pattern in your client code increases your website resiliency because it more efficiently handles faults from the external service that may be long lasting, but eventually self-correct.

If your application is a service provider, encouraging clients to use the Circuit Breaker pattern when invoking your service increases the scalability of your website because your service logic does not have to deal with a flood of repeated requests that all result in the same exception while there is an issue.

Implementing transient fault handling for services and responding to throttling

Within your website application logic, you implement transient fault handling for services by configuring how your client code invokes the operations on the service. From a website, if you are accessing Azure SQL Database or Azure Storage using .NET, you do not have to author the transient fault handling logic yourself—each service provides mechanisms either directly by the client library or the client works in combination with the Transient Fault Handling Application Block. These ready-made clients include all of the logic for identifying transient failures received from the service (including failures resulting from throttling). If you are using a service that does not provide support for transient fault handling, you can use the Transient Fault Handling Application Block, which provides a framework for encapsulating the logic of which exceptions are transient, defines retry policies, and wraps your operation invocation so that the block handles the retry logic.

Adding the Transient Fault Handling Application Block to your project

To add the Transient Fault Handling Application Block to your Visual Studio web application project, you generally must add two NuGet packages: One that represents that base Transient Fault Handling Application Block itself and another "integration" package that contains the exception handling specific to the service you are using.

To add the block to your project in Visual Studio, right-click your project, select Manage NuGet Packages, and then search for "topaz." In the results, click Install for the item with the label Enterprise Library – Transient Fault Handling Application Block. Make sure to accept the license prompt.

With the Manage NuGet Packages dialog box still open and displaying the results of you're your "topaz" search, click Install for the integration package. For example, for SQL Database, you would choose Enterprise Library – Transient Fault Handling Application Block – Windows Azure SQL Database integration. Again, make sure to accept the license prompt. Close the Manage NuGet Packages dialog box. You should have all the references you need added to your project.

Transient fault handling for SQL Database

Your approach to transient fault handling for SQL Database depends on the client you are using against SQL Database. If you are using ADO.NET, the Transient Fault Handling Application Block provides the retry logic for you. To use it, add the Transient Fault Handling Application Block and the Windows Azure SQL Database – Integration package as described previously.

Within your code, add a using statement for Microsoft.Practices.EnterpriseLibrary.-TransientFaultHandling, and then use the block as shown in Listing 1-14. Notice that you must first create the default Retry Manager, after which you can create a ReliableSql-Connection that respects the retry and back-off settings you specify in the RetryPolicy. You can then use that connection to run whatever commands you desire.

LISTING 1-14 Enabling transient fault handling in ADO.NET

```
//Set up the Default Retry Manager
string defaultRetryStrategyName = "fixed";
int retryCount = 10;
var retryInterval = TimeSpan.FromSeconds(3);

var strategy = new FixedInterval(defaultRetryStrategyName, retryCount, retryInterval);
var strategies = new List<RetryStrategy> { strategy };
var manager = new RetryManager(strategies, defaultRetryStrategyName);

RetryManager.SetDefault(manager);

//Perform your queries with retries
var connStr = "Data Source=<serverName>.database.windows.net,1433;
    Initial Catalog=sql-temp-demo2;User ID=some-user;Password=some-password";
var policy = new RetryPolicy<SqlDatabaseTransientErrorDetectionStrategy>(3,
    TimeSpan.FromSeconds(5));

using (var conn = new ReliableSqlConnection(connStr, policy))
{
    conn.Open();
    var cmd = conn.CreateCommand();
    cmd.CommandText = "SELECT COUNT(*) FROM Sample";
    var result = cmd.ExecuteScalar();
}
```

If you are using Entity Framework 6 (EF 6), the retry logic for transient faults is built in to the framework. When your EF 6 model is in your project, you need to create a new class that derives from DbConfiguration and customizes the execution strategy in the constructor. EF 6 will look for classes that derive from DbConfiguration in your project and use them to provide resiliency. To set this, add a new Class file to your project and add using statements for System.Data.Entity and System.Data.Entity.SqlServer. Then replace the class code with the code shown in Listing 1-15.

LISTING 1-15 Configuring Entity Framework 6 to use transient fault handling

```
public class EFConfiguration : DbConfiguration
{
    public EFConfiguration()
    {
        this.SetExecutionStrategy("System.Data.SqlClient",
    () => new SqlAzureExecutionStrategy());
    }
}
```

If desired, you can specify a MaxRetryCount and MaxDelay parameter in the SqlAzureExecutionStrategy constructor to override the default number of retries and wait time between retries, respectively.

When this configuration is in place, you can use your model as you normally do and take advantage of the built-in transient fault handling.

> **MORE INFO** **LIMITATIONS OF EF 6 RETRY EXECUTION STRATEGIES**
>
> You should be aware of some limitations when using EF 6 retry execution strategies. To read about these, see *http://msdn.microsoft.com/en-us/data/dn307226*.

Transient fault handling for Azure Storage

Since the release of Azure Storage Client Library 2.0, support for retries is built in and uses sensible defaults without any special steps. You use the client to access blobs, tables, or queues as you normally would. However, if you would like to tailor the behavior, you can control the back-off strategy, delay, and number of retries. The code in Listing 1-16 shows an example of how you could alter the delay and number of retries. Although the Exponential-Retry policy is the recommended strategy, you could also use LinearRetry or NoRetry if you want to have a linear back off or no retry at all, respectively.

LISTING 1-16 Configuring transient fault handling for Azure Storage

```
string accountName = "<accountName>";
string accountKey = "<accountKey>";
string blobContainerName = "images";

var storageAccount = new CloudStorageAccount(new StorageCredentials(accountName,
    accountKey), true);
CloudBlobClient blobClient = storageAccount.CreateCloudBlobClient();
blobClient.DefaultRequestOptions.RetryPolicy = new ExponentialRetry(TimeSpan.
FromSeconds(2), 10);
CloudBlobContainer blobContainer = blobClient.GetContainerReference(blobContainerName);
bool containerExists = blobContainer.Exists();

if (containerExists)
{
    //...other code that works with container...
}
```

> **MORE INFO** **RETRY POLICIES**
>
> If you would like to learn more about your options for configuring retry polices, see the blog post at *http://gauravmantri.com/2012/12/30/storage-client-library-2-0-implementing-retry-policies/*.

Disabling Application Request Routing (ARR) affinity

Application Request Routing (ARR) is a feature of Websites that effectively enables sticky sessions between the client (such as the browser) and the first instance of the website it connects to by providing the client with a cookie that encodes identification for that website instance. All subsequent requests from the client are guided to that original website instance, irrespective of how many other instances a website may have available, what the load is on that instance, or even if that instance is available.

ARR can be a useful technology if a lot of state is loaded into memory for any given client and moving that state between server instances is prohibitively expensive or not possible at all. However, its use introduces the problem of statefulness in Websites, and by extension, limits the scalability of the system because clients get attached to a particular website instance. It can also become a problem since users tend to keep their browsers open for long periods of time. In this case, the website instance they originally connected to may have failed, but on their next request, ARR will try to guide them to the unavailable website instance instead of one of the other instances that are available.

It is possible to disable ARR for Websites by modifying the web.config to send an Arr-Disable-Session-Affinity custom header as shown in Listing 1-17.

LISTING 1-17 Configuring the Arr-Disable-Session-Affinity header

```
<system.webServer>
    <httpProtocol>
      <customHeaders>
        <add name="Arr-Disable-Session-Affinity" value="True" />
      </customHeaders>
    </httpProtocol>
</system.webServer>
```

Thought experiment
Scalability and resilience

In this thought experiment, apply what you've learned about this objective. You can find answers to these questions in the "Answers" section at the end of this chapter.

You are designing the logic for a REST service you will host in a website and are examining it from a scalability perspective.

1. You are trying to decide between implementing throttling in the service logic versus using auto-scale. Should you choose one over the other?

2. Your service is completely stateless. Should you disable ARR?

Objective summary

- Transient faults are temporary issues that occur when attempting an operation, such that if the operation is retried it is likely to succeed. Transient fault handling is the pattern used to handle these issues for services.

- Throttling is a service-imposed limit that restricts the amount of throughput of requests to a service, which can usually be addressed by trying again at a later point or, for some services, scaling up the service in use.

- Application Request Routing (ARR) affinity ensures that clients establish sticky sessions with a particular website instance so that information about the client can be stored in the website's local memory instead of in a distribute store. While this can simplify a solution architecture, it can also cause scalability bottlenecks because a few instances may become overloaded.

Objective review

Answer the following questions to test your knowledge of the information in this objective. You can find the answers to these questions and explanations of why each answer choice is correct or incorrect in the "Answers" section at the end of this chapter.

1. Which of these is *not* an example of throttling?

    A. Server crash

    B. Responding with server busy

    C. Switching over to lower bit-rate streaming

    D. Handling high-priority requests differently than low-priority requests when under load

2. If a transient fault is expected to take a long time to resolve for a service operation that is frequently invoked, which pattern might you consider implementing for the client?

    A. Throttling

    B. Retry

    C. Transient

    D. Circuit Breaker

3. After deploying a website that has multiple instances, you discover that one instance in particular seems to be handling most of the load. What is one possible culprit?

    A. ARR affinity

    B. Throttling

    C. Transient fault handling

    D. Retries

Answers

This section contains the solutions to the thought experiments and answers to the objective review questions in this chapter.

Objective 1.1: Thought experiment

1. You can use different deployment slots for testing and staging, and you can ultimately swap between staging and production to complete the deployment.

2. You should ensure that the website is the only one within a web hosting plan. Also, be careful about using deployment slots if your goal is isolation; these will share the resources of the web hosting plan.

Objective 1.1: Objective review

3. **Correct answer:** C

   A. **Incorrect:** A website can have up to four deployment slots besides the main slot, not just two.

   B. **Incorrect:** A website can have up to four deployment slots besides the main slot, not just three.

   C. **Correct:** A website can have up to four deployment slots besides the main slot.

   D. **Incorrect:** A website can have a maximum of four deployment slots besides the main slot.

4. **Correct answers:** A, B, C, and D

   A. **Correct:** Websites must share the same subscription.

   B. **Correct:** Websites must share the same region.

   C. **Correct:** Websites must share the same resource group.

   D. **Correct:** Websites must share the same pricing tier.

5. **Correct answer:** C

   A. **Incorrect:** Web hosting plans cannot be created directly.

   B. **Incorrect:** This would not result in a new web hosting plan.

   C. **Correct:** A web hosting plan can only be created as a step in creating a new website or in migrating the website to a new web hosting plan.

   D. **Incorrect:** A web hosting plan can only be created as a step in creating a new website or in migrating the website to a new web hosting plan.

Objective 1.2: Thought experiment

1. You should set up the custom domain name first because it is a prerequisite for requesting the SSL certificate.

2. While testing, you can use SSL via the endpoint at https://<yoursitename>.azurewebsites.net.

Objective 1.2: Objective review

1. **Correct answers:** A, B, and C

   A. **Correct:** Because the certificate does not identify the subdomain, it becomes possible to lure users to a similarly named website pretending to be yours.

   B. **Correct:** Because the private key is used to decrypt all Azure traffic, its compromise would mean compromising your website security—which would not be possible if you had your own certificate.

   C. **Correct:** You can only use the *.azurewebsites.net certificate against that domain.

   D. **Incorrect:** Data is encrypted with the certificate for the *.azurewebsites.net domain.

2. **Correct answers:** B and C

   A. **Incorrect:** Windows PowerShell is supported only on Windows.

   B. **Correct:** The cross-platform command line interface (xplat-cli) would be useful here.

   C. **Correct:** The management portal is accessible using a browser on a Mac.

   D. **Incorrect:** Options B and C are valid.

3. **Correct answers:** A, B, C, and D

   A. **Correct:** This will likely yield a new IP address for the website, so the A record needs to be updated.

   B. **Correct:** This will likely yield a new IP address for the website, so the A record needs to be updated.

   C. **Correct:** This will likely yield a new IP address for the website, so the A record needs to be updated.

   D. **Correct:** This will likely yield a new IP address for the website, so the A record needs to be updated.

Objective 1.3: Thought experiment

1. You should consider using monitoring (through the portal) and configuring alerts.

2. You should enable and review the diagnostic logs. You could also monitor streaming logs to see any traces that happen in real time (but after the issue has occurred). You might also try remote debugging within a test environment.

Objective 1.3: Objective review

1. **Correct answer:** B

    A. **Incorrect:** This will not disturb visitors since log-streaming displays logs that are collected in the background.

    B. **Correct:** When you are stopped in a breakpoint, this will stop the website from responding to all requests, and therefore certainly disturb visitors.

    C. **Incorrect:** This will not disturb visitors. Event logs are collected in the background without interfering with requests.

    D. **Incorrect:** This will not disturb visitors. Application logs are collected in the background without interfering with requests.

2. **Correct answer:** B

    A. **Incorrect:** The sending of automated alert emails can be enabled along with endpoint monitoring.

    B. **Correct:** Auto-scale is not related to endpoint monitoring.

    C. **Incorrect:** Outside-in monitoring can be enabled along with endpoint monitoring.

    D. **Incorrect:** Monitoring from multiple geographic locations can be enabled along with endpoint monitoring.

3. **Correct answers:** A and B

    A. **Correct:** The file system is a storage location for diagnostic logs.

    B. **Correct:** Azure Storage is a storage location for diagnostic logs.

    C. **Incorrect:** This is not a valid location for diagnostic logs out of the box.

    D. **Incorrect:** This is not a valid location for diagnostic logs.

Objective 1.4: Thought experiment

1. You can trigger a WebJob with a blob, a message, or on demand using the portal.

2. You can schedule a WebJob to run on schedule with a daily recurrence starting at a specific time in the evening.

Objective 1.4: Objective review

1. **Correct answer:** D

   A. **Incorrect:** WebJobs can be triggered by both queue messages and blobs.

   B. **Incorrect:** WebJobs can be created as standalone executables or scripts.

   C. **Incorrect:** WebJobs can be written in multiple languages.

   D. **Correct:** All options in A, B, and C are not true.

2. **Correct answers:** B, C, D, E, and F

   A. **Incorrect:** WebJobs do not support a 1-second recurrence.

   B. **Correct:** WebJobs can recur every minute.

   C. **Correct:** WebJobs can recur every hour.

   D. **Correct:** WebJobs can recur every day.

   E. **Correct:** WebJobs can recur every week.

   F. **Correct:** WebJobs can recur every month.

3. **Correct answers:** A, B, and C

   A. **Correct:** WebJobs can be triggered from a blob.

   B. **Correct:** WebJobs can be triggered from a message in a Storage queue.

   C. **Correct:** WebJobs can be triggered on demand.

   D. **Incorrect:** WebJobs cannot be triggered from a SQL trigger.

Objective 1.5: Thought experiment

1. You can deploy your website to datacenters in the Asia region and configure Traffic Manager with the performance load balancing method, listing your United States and Asia endpoints.

2. You could configure auto-scale to scale down on weekends and evenings and scale up during the weekdays.

Objective 1.5: Objective review

1. **Correct answer:** D

   A. **Incorrect:** While correct, failover load balancing can occur with round robin and performance methods.

   B. **Incorrect:** While correct, failover load balancing can occur with failover and performance methods.

   C. **Incorrect:** While correct, failover load balancing can occur with failover and round robin methods.

   D. **Correct:** Failover occurs with all load balancing methods.

2. **Correct answer:** B

   A. **Incorrect:** Instance size is not affected by auto-scale.

   B. **Correct:** Instance count is controlled by auto-scale.

   C. **Incorrect:** The region is not affected by auto-scale.

   D. **Incorrect:** The memory (or instance size) is not affected by auto-scale.

3. **Correct answer:** B

   A. **Incorrect:** The minimum TTL is 30 seconds; a user would experience at least that.

   B. **Correct:** The minimum TTL is 30 seconds; a user would experience at least that.

   C. **Incorrect:** The minimum TTL is 30 seconds; a user would experience at least that.

   D. **Incorrect:** The minimum TTL is 30 seconds; a user would experience at least that.

Objective 1.6: Thought experiment

1. You should consider using both: Throttling to handle spikes in load in the immediate term and auto-scale to correctly provision your website for the load over time.

2. Most likely, yes. ARR is typically needed with stateful services because shipping the state between instances is difficult or impractical.

Objective 1.6: Objective review

1. **Correct answer:** A

   A. **Correct:** This is not an example of throttling.

   B. **Incorrect:** This is an example of throttling.

   C. **Incorrect:** This is an example of throttling.

   D. **Incorrect:** This is an example of throttling.

2. **Correct answer:** D

   A. **Incorrect:** Throttling would not benefit the client.

   B. **Incorrect:** Retry is best for faults that will get resolved within a short period.

   C. **Incorrect:** This is not a pattern.

   D. **Correct:** The Circuit Breaker pattern is best for dealing with faults that might take some time to resolve.

3. **Correct answer:** A

   A. **Correct:** It might be that users are all being directed to one server due to ARR affinity.

   B. **Incorrect:** This is not a likely culprit for this load on a single instance.

   C. **Incorrect:** This is not a likely culprit for this load on a single instance.

   D. **Incorrect:** This is not a likely culprit for this load on a single instance.

CHAPTER 2

Create and manage virtual machines

Virtual machines (VMs) are part of the Microsoft Azure Infrastructure-as-a-Service (IaaS) offering. With VMs, you can deploy Windows Server and Linux-based workloads and have greater control over the infrastructure, your deployment topology, and configuration as compared to Platform-as-a-Service (PaaS) offerings such as Websites and Cloud Services. That means you can more easily migrate existing applications and VMs without modifying code or configuration settings, but still benefit from Azure features such as management through a centralized web-based portal, monitoring, and scaling.

Objectives in this chapter:

- Objective 2.1: Deploy workloads on Azure virtual machines
- Objective 2.2: Create and manage a VM image or virtual hard disk
- Objective 2.3: Perform configuration management
- Objective 2.4: Configure VM networking
- Objective 2.5: Scale VMs
- Objective 2.6: Design and implement VM storage
- Objective 2.7: Monitor VMs

Objective 2.1: Deploy workloads on Azure virtual machines

VMs can run more than just Windows and .NET applications. They provide support for running many forms of applications using various operating systems. This section describes where and how to analyze what is supported and how to deploy three different forms of VMs.

Identifying supported workloads

A workload describes the nature of a solution, whether it is an application that runs on a single machine or it requires a complex topology that prescribes the operating system used, the additional software installed, the performance requirements, and the networking environment. Azure enables you to deploy a wide variety of VM workloads, including "bare bones" VM workloads that run various versions of Windows Server and Linux; database and big-data workloads (such as Microsoft SQL Server, IBM DB2, Couchbase, Cloudera, and Hortonworks Data Platform); complete application infrastructures (for example, those requiring server farms or clusters like SharePoint, Biztalk Server, SQL Server AlwaysOn, and SAP); workloads that provide security and protection (such as antivirus, intrusion detection systems, firewalls, data encryption, and key management); and workloads that support developer productivity (such as the Windows 7 and Windows 8 client operating system, Visual Studio, or the Java Development Kit).

There are two approaches to identifying supported Azure workloads. The first is to determine whether the workload is already explicitly supported and offered through the Marketplace, which provides a large collection of free and for-pay solutions from Microsoft and third parties that deploy to VMs. The Marketplace also offers access to the VM Depot, which provides a large collection of community provided and maintained VMs. The VM configuration and all the required software it contains on the disk (or disks) is called a *VM image*.

The second approach is to compare the requirements of the workload you want to deploy directly to the published capabilities of Azure VMs or, in some cases, to perform proof of concept deployments to measure whether the requirements can be met. The following is a representative, though not exhaustive, list of the requirements you would typically need to take into consideration:

- CPU and RAM memory requirements
- Disk storage capacity requirements, in gigabytes (GB)
- Disk performance requirements, usually in terms of input/output operations per second (IOPS) and data throughput (typically in megabytes per second)
- Operating system compatibility
- Networking requirements
- Availability requirements
- Security and compliance requirements

This section covers what is required to deploy the "bare bones" VM (that is, one that has the operating system and minimal features installed) that can serve as the basis for your more complex workloads and describes the options for deploying a pre-built workload from the Marketplace.

Creating a VM

Fundamentally, there are two approaches to creating a new VM. You can upload a VM that you have built on-premises, or you can instantiate one from the pre-built images available in the Marketplace. This section focuses on the latter and defers coverage of the upload scenario until the next section.

Creating a Windows Server VM (existing portal)

To create a Windows Server VM in the management portal, complete the following steps:

1. Navigate to the management portal accessed via *https://manage.windowsazure.com*.

2. Click New on the command bar, and then click Compute, Virtual Machine, From Gallery.

3. Select a Windows Server image (such as Windows Server 2012 R2 Datacenter) from which to create the VM, and then click the right arrow.

4. Provide a name, tier, instance size, and administrator credentials, and then click the right arrow.

5. On the Virtual Machine Configuration screen, click Create A New Cloud Service, and then provide a DNS name, region, and storage account.

6. Leave the availability set value configured to none. (Availability sets are covered later in the chapter.) Leave the endpoints at their defaults, and click the right arrow.

7. Leave the Install VM Agent check box selected, and leave the remaining extensions cleared.

8. Click the check mark to provision the Windows Server VM.

Creating a Windows Server VM (Preview portal)

To create a Windows Server VM in the Preview portal, complete the following steps:

1. Navigate to the management portal accessed via *https://portal.azure.com*.

2. Click New on the command bar.

3. To navigate to the Marketplace, click the Everything link located near the upper-right corner of the blade that appears.

4. On the Marketplace blade, select Virtual Machines.

5. On the Virtual Machines blade, select Windows Server in the Recommended area.

6. On the Windows Server blade, select the image for the version of Windows Server you want for your VM (such as Windows Server 2012 R2 Datacenter).

7. Click Create.

8. On the Create VM blade, provide a host name, user name, and password for the new VM.

9. Review the Pricing Tier, Optional Configuration, Resource Group, Subscription, and Location settings and change as necessary.

10. Click Create to provision the Windows Server VM.

Creating a Linux VM (existing portal)

To create a bare bones Linux VM in the management portal, complete the following steps:

1. Navigate to the management portal accessed via *https://manage.windowsazure.com*.

2. Click New on the command bar, and then click Compute, Virtual Machine, From Gallery.

3. In the navigation pane, select Ubuntu.

4. Choose an Ubuntu Server image (such as Ubuntu Server 14.04 LTS) from which to create the VM, and then click the right arrow.

5. Provide a name, tier, instance size, and administrator user name.

6. Clear the Upload Compatible SSH Key For Authentication check box.

7. Select the Provide A Password check box, and provide the password for the administrator. Click the right arrow.

8. On the Virtual Machine Configuration screen, select Create A New Cloud Service, and enter a DNS name, region, and storage account.

9. Leave the availability set value configured to none. (Availability sets are covered later in the chapter.)

10. Leave the endpoints at their defaults, and click the right arrow.

11. Leave the listed extensions cleared.

12. Click the check mark to provision the Ubuntu Server Linux VM.

Creating a Linux VM (Preview portal)

To create a bare bones Linux VM in the Preview portal, complete the following steps:

1. Navigate to the management portal accessed via *https://portal.azure.com*.

2. Click New on the command bar.

3. To navigate to the Marketplace, click the Everything link located near the upper-right blade that appears.

4. On the Marketplace blade, select Virtual Machines.

5. On the Virtual Machines blade, select Ubuntu Server in the Recommended area.

6. On the Ubuntu Server blade, select the image for the version of Ubuntu Server you want for your VM (such as Ubuntu Server 2014.04 LTS).

7. Click Create.

8. On the Create VM blade, provide a host name and user name for the new VM.

9. Use an external tool to generate a public SSH key, and then copy and paste it in the SSH Public Key text box. See the More Info readeraid titled, "SSH key generation" for instructions on how to do this.

10. Review the Pricing Tier, Optional Configuration, Resource Group, Subscription, and Location settings and change as necessary.

11. Click Create to provision the Ubuntu Server VM.

> **MORE INFO**   **SSH KEY GENERATION**
>
> To create the SSH public key that you need to provision your Linux VM, run **ssh-keygen** on a Mac OSX or Linux terminal, or, if you are running Windows, use **Puttygen**. A good refer ence for the latter, if you are not familiar with it, is available at *http://azure.microsoft.com/ en-us/documentation/articles/virtual-machines-linux-use-ssh-key/*.

Creating a SQL Server VM (existing portal)

The steps for creating a VM that has SQL Server installed on top of Windows Server are identical to those described earlier for provisioning a Windows Server VM using the existing portal. The only difference surfaces in the third step: instead of selecting a Windows Server image, select a SQL Server image (such as SQL Server RTM 2014 Enterprise).

Creating a SQL Server VM (Preview portal)

The steps for creating a VM that has SQL Server installed on top of Windows Server are identical to those described earlier for provisioning a Windows Server VM using the Preview portal. The only differences surface in the fifth and sixth steps: instead of selecting a Windows Server from the Recommended area, select SQL Server from the Database Servers area, and on the SQL Server blade, select the SQL Server version you want (such as SQL Server RTM 2014 Enterprise).

Objective summary

- There are two approaches to identifying supported workloads in Azure: looking for explicit support by a listing in the Marketplace and performing a manual comparison of the workload requirements against the capacities of VMs.

- New VMs can be created by uploading a VM you have already created on-premises or by instantiating one from a selection of pre-built images that are available in the Marketplace.

- Azure supports the creation of "bare-bones" VMs that provide just Windows or Linux operating system from pre-built images available in the Marketplace.

- The Marketplace provides the ability to provision single VMs with pre-configured applications. The example shown in this chapter provisions SQL Server in a VM.

- The Marketplace provides images that can configure a complex topology consisting of multiple VMs, such as a SQL Server AlwaysOn or a SharePoint farm.

Objective review

Answer the following questions to test your knowledge of the information in this objective. You can find the answers to these questions and explanations of why each answer choice is correct or incorrect in the "Answers" section at the end of this chapter.

1. Which of the following are true regarding the types of workloads that you can deploy from the Marketplace? (Choose all that apply.)

   A. Single instance virtual machines

   B. Linux virtual machines

   C. Clusters of virtual machines

   D. None of the above

2. Which of the following is *not* true about the Marketplace?

    A. All images are community provided.

    B. Some of the images have no additional costs beyond the Azure VM pricing.

    C. Some of the images have additional costs for the software they provide.

    D. There is a mixture of first-party, third-party, and community images.

3. Which of the following is a supported VM workload? (Choose all that apply.)

    A. Running Visual Studio (with an MSDN account)

    B. Running Windows 8

    C. Running Ubuntu

    D. Running the Java Development Kit

Objective 2.2: Create and manage a VM image or virtual hard disk

The previous section covered how to create VMs by using an image from the Marketplace. But what if you already have the VHDs for an on-premises VM that you would like to use as the basis for future VMs in Azure? Alternately, what if you have already created a VM and have its VHD disks in Azure Storage in one region (for example, in the West US region) but want to create the VM in another region (for example, in the Japan West region)? To answer these questions, this section examines the definition of a VM image more closely, compares it to a disk, and examines how images and disks are managed.

> **This objective covers how to:**
> - Create specialized and generalized VM images
> - Upload VHDs to Azure
> - Copy images between storage accounts

Creating specialized and generalized VM images

Before getting into the details, you should understand a few important concepts. The first is the relationship between virtual hard drives (VHDs), VM disks, and VM images. On a high level, VHDs are ultimately the file format a running VM uses to store its data. These VHDs must be packaged into disks so that they can be attached to a VM. When your VM is provisioned, you can create a VM image that captures all the details about the VM, its disks, and VHDs and creates a template that you can use to create new VM instances.

Creating this template generates a question: Should the operating system settings in these VM templates be exact copies of the VM instance, including things like the machine identifiers and the administrator credentials, or can some of these settings be "generalized" or "reusable" so that they can be changed when the VM instance is provisioned from a template?

This notion surfaces important operating system disk terminology: specialized images and generalized images. Think of these concepts as two different scenarios in which you might provision a VM.

In the specialized image scenario, you are interested in creating a golden copy of a VM, or in other words, a snapshot, from which you can create exact duplicates of the VM. You might stop the VM, capture a snapshot of it in an image, re-create that exact VM somewhere else, and then turn on the VM again. Any time you provision an instance of the image, it maintains the identity it had at the time of the snapshot. It is like turning on the original VM from the point in time at which the snapshot was taken, except that any modifications you make as the VM runs do not alter the image from which it was created.

Compare this with the generalized images scenario, where you want to turn the VM you have created into a template from which you can stamp out new cloned instances of the VM, each of them unique with respect to certain settings in the operating system. For example, to scale out a cluster, you add new instances of the template VMs, each of them similarly configured but uniquely identified. In this case, each instance has its own identity and is therefore slightly different. The instances identify themselves as "VM-A," "VM-B," and "VM-C" instead of always being "VM-A." In fact, when you create VMs from images available in the Marketplace, you utilize generalized images.

A VM created from the Marketplace consists of a set of VHDs—an operating system disk and zero or more data disks are attached to the VM. Each of these disk VHDs were created from an image, which is also a VHD. So what is the difference between an image and a disk?

With an understanding of the difference between specialized and generalized images, you can consider the steps necessary to create these two forms of images.

At the highest level, if you are starting with a VM created in Azure (such as one from the Marketplace), you follow these steps:

1. **Create the source VM.** Start with a VM you created from an existing image, such as one from the Marketplace.

2. **Generalize the VM.** To create a generalized image, you must take specific steps to prepare the VM before you create an image from it. You do not perform these steps to create a specialized VM.

3. **Capture the VM image.** With the VM in the desired state, take a snapshot of it by capturing a VM image.

4. **Instantiate instances of the image.** With an image ready, you can launch specialized instances that act like a copy of the original, right down to operating system details like the administrator user name and password. Generalized images start up differently as they configure themselves to take on new identities during their first start up and can be configured to draw their administrator user name and password from an Azure-provided configuration during startup.

Similarly, if you are starting with a VM created on-premises, you follow these steps:

1. **Upload the source VHDs to Azure.** If you created your VM on-premises, for example using Hyper-V, upload its constituent VHD disks to Azure.

2. **Create disks from the VHDs.** To attach a VHD to a VM, it must be created as a disk. It can be an operating system disk if it is to be bootable or a data disk if not.

3. **Create a VM.** Create a new VM by attaching the operating system disk and any data disks.

4. **Generalize the VM.** To create a generalized image, you must take specific steps to prepare the VM before you create an image from it.

5. **Capture the VM image.** With the VM in the desired state, take a snapshot of it by capturing a VM image.

6. **Instantiate instances of the image.** With an image ready, you can launch a specialized instance that acts like a copy of the original. Instances of generalized images start up differently as they configure themselves to take on new identities during their first startup.

The sections that follow focus on a scenario in which you are uploading a VM from on-premises to show the contrast with provisioning VMs from the Marketplace, as covered in the previous objective.

Uploading VHDs to Azure

If you have a VM on-premises that you would like to upload to Azure to serve as the basis for an image, complete the following steps:

1. Ensure that your VM meets the requirements to run on Azure. This means that it must be running an Azure-compatible guest operating system and that the disks are stored in the VHD format (not the expanding VHDX format)

2. Turn off the VM so you can be certain you are capturing a consistent state of the VM.

3. Open the Azure PowerShell cmdlets and make sure that your default Azure Subscription and Storage accounts are configured as the accounts in which to deploy your VM. You can use the following three commands to download your publish settings file to disk using the browser, import it into the Windows PowerShell context, and set the default Subscription and Storage accounts:

```
Get-AzurePublishSettingsFile

Import-AzurePublishSettingsFile "<path to file>\<fileName>.publishsettings"

Set-AzureSubscription "<Subscription Name> -CurrentStorageAccountName
"<StorageAccountName>"
```

4. If you prefer not to deal with the downloading, storing, and securing of the publish settings file, you can use Azure Active Directory to authenticate. Instead of using Get-AzurePublishSettingsFile and Import-AzurePublishSettingsFile, run Add-AzureAccount, log in to your Azure account, and then set the default Subscription and Storage accounts:

```
Add-AzureAccount

Set-AzureSubscription "<Subscription Name> -CurrentStorageAccountName
"<StorageAccountName>"
```

5. Within Blob storage, ensure you have a container that will hold the uploaded VHDs, and then run the following Windows PowerShell cmdlet to upload each VHD to that container:

```
Add-AzureVhd -Destination
http://<StorageAccountName>.blob.core.windows.net/<ContainerName>/<DestinationFile
Name>.vhd -LocalFilePath C:\<PathToSourceImage>\<SourceFileName>.vhd
```

6. Repeat step 5 for every VHD belonging to your VM.

Creating disks

After you have uploaded all of the VHDs that make up your VM, you can directly create a disk from any single VHD. This section covers how to create an operating system disk or data disk from a VHD.

Creating an operating system disk or data disk from a VHD (existing portal)

Using a single VHD file uploaded to Blob storage, you can use the existing portal to create either an operating system disk or a data disk.

1. Navigate to the Disks tab in the Virtual Machines area in the management portal accessed via *https://manage.windowsazure.com*.

2. Click Create on the command bar.

3. In the Create A Disk From A VHD dialog box, provide a name for the new disk.

4. Click the file area under VHD URL, and select the VHD you uploaded to Azure Storage from the list that appears.

5. Indicate that the disk you have selected contains an operating system image and that you intend to use it as a specialized disk by selecting This VHD Contains An Operating System. If you do so, also indicate whether the operating system is Windows or Linux using the Operating System Family drop-down list. Otherwise, leave the check box clear to create the disk as a data disk.

6. Click the check mark to create the disk.

Creating a disk from a VHD (Preview portal)

Currently, you cannot create a disk from a VHD using the Preview portal.

Creating an operating system disk or data disk from a VHD using Windows PowerShell

You can create a disk from a VHD using Windows PowerShell by running the Add-AzureDisk cmdlet. To create a bootable Windows operating system disk from a VHD, use the following syntax:

```
Add-AzureDisk -DiskName "<DiskName>" -MediaLocation
"http://<StorageAccountName>.blob.core.azure.com/<ContainerName>/<FileName>.vhd"
-Label "<Label>" -OS "Windows"
```

Similarly, to create a bootable Linux operating system disk from a VHD, use the following syntax:

```
Add-AzureDisk -DiskName "<DiskName>" -MediaLocation
"http://<StorageAccountName>.blob.core.azure.com/<ContainerName>/<FileName>.vhd"
-Label "<Label>" -OS "Linux"
```

To create a data disk from a VHD, omit the operating system parameter:

```
Add-AzureDisk -DiskName "<DiskName>" -MediaLocation
"http://<StorageAccountName>.blob.core.azure.com/<ContainerName>/<FileName>.vhd"
-Label "<Label>"
```

Creating a VM using existing disks

When you have created a disk from a VHD, you can create new VMs that can start up from the operating system disk you have created or attach any data disks you have created.

Creating a new VM from an operating system disk (existing portal)

To create a new VM from an operating system disk in the management portal, complete the following steps:

1. Navigate to the management portal accessed via *https://manage.windowsazure.com*.

2. Click New on the command bar, and select New, Virtual Machine, From Gallery.

3. In the dialog box that appears, in the navigation pane, click My Disks.

4. In the list that appears, select the operating system disk to use for this VM. Click the right arrow.

5. Provide a name, tier, and instance size, and then click the right arrow.

6. On the Virtual Machine Configuration screen, click Create A New Cloud Service, and enter a DNS name, region, and storage account. Leave the remaining settings at their default values and click the right arrow.

7. Leave the endpoints at their defaults and click the right arrow.

8. Leave the VM Agent selected, and leave the remaining extensions clear.

9. Click the check mark to provision the VM.

Creating a new VM from an operating system disk (Preview portal)

Creating a new VM from an operating system disk is not currently supported in the Preview portal.

Attaching data disks to a VM (existing portal)

To attach data disks to a VM in the management portal, complete the following steps:

1. Navigate to the VM in the management portal accessed via *https://manage.windowsazure.com*, and click the Dashboard tab.

2. Click Attach on the command bar, and select Attach Disk.

3. In the Available Disks drop-down list, select the data disk.

4. Set your host cache preferences (this is discussed later in this chapter).

5. Click the check mark to attach the disk to the VM.

Attaching data disks to a VM (Preview portal)

To attach data disks to a VM in the Preview portal, complete the following steps:

1. Navigate to the blade for your VM in the management portal accessed via *https://portal.azure.com*.

2. Scroll down to the Configure section and click the Disks tile.

3. On the Disks blade, on the command bar, click Attach Existing.

4. On the Attach An Existing Disk blade, click VHD File.

5. On the Choose A Disk blade, select the storage account, the container, and the disk that you want to attach, and then click OK.

6. Return to the Choose A Disk blade, and click OK.

7. Return to the Attach An Existing Disk blade, and click OK to attach the data disk to the VM.

Attaching data disks to a VM using Windows PowerShell

To attach a data disk to a VM using Windows PowerShell, you need to use the Import parameter set of the Add-AzureDataDisk cmdlet as follows:

```
Get-AzureVM "<CloudServiceName>" -Name "<VMName>" |
Add-AzureDataDisk -Import -DiskName "<DiskName>" -LUN <LUN#> |
Update-AzureVM
```

In this example, the <LUN#> parameter is an ordinal with a value from 0 to 15 that identifies logical unit number location for the data disk in the VM.

Generalizing a VM

The steps to generalize a VM vary depending on the operating system you have installed. The following sections show how to generalize Windows and Linux VMs.

Generalizing a Windows VM

To generalize a Windows VM, run Sysprep.

1. Launch Remote Desktop and connect to the VM.

2. From the Run area on the Start menu or Start screen, type **sysprep** and press Enter.

3. In the System Preparation Tool dialog box that appears, for the System Cleanup Action, select Enter System Out-of-Box Experience (OOBE), and select the Generalize check box. Under Shutdown Options, select Shutdown, and click OK. The VM will shut down. It is now ready to be captured as an image.

Generalizing a Linux VM

To generalize a Linux VM, the Azure Virtual Machine Agent (VM Agent) must be installed. With the VM Agent installed, run the following command and shut down the VM.

```
waagent -deprovision
```

> **MORE INFO** **MANUALLY INSTALLING THE AZURE VM AGENT**
>
> If your uploaded Windows or Linux VM does not have the VM Agent installed, you can download it to your VM instance and install it manually. For detailed instructions on how to install the VM Agent, visit *http://msdn.microsoft.com/en-us/library/dn832621.aspx*.

Creating or capturing a VM image

There are two ways to create a VM image: you can create it directly from a single VHD, or you can capture an existing VM.

Creating an image from a single VHD (existing portal)

If your VM consists of only a single VHD, the operating system disk, you can directly create an image using the existing portal.

1. Navigate to the Images tab in the Virtual Machines area in the management portal accessed via *https://manage.windowsazure.com*.

2. Click Create on the command bar.

3. In the Create An Image From A VHD dialog box, provide a name and description for the new image.

4. Click VHD URL to select the VHD you want from Blob storage.

5. In the Operating System Family drop-down list, select the operating system that is installed on the VHD.

6. To create a reusable image from a VHD, select the I Have Run Sysprep On The Virtual Machine check box (for a Windows VHD) or the I Have Run waagent -deprovision On The Virtual Machine check box (for a Linux VHD).

7. Click the check mark to create the image.

Creating an image from a single VHD (Preview portal)

Currently, it is not possible to create an image from a VHD using the Preview portal.

Capturing a VM as a VM image (existing portal)

If you have built a VM in Azure, you can capture the VM and create a VM image for future reuse. Note that for a generalized image, you must generalize and shut down your VM before you perform the capture operation. If you attempt to capture a running VM, you effectively take a snapshot of that VM to create a specialized image, but you risk not capturing any changes that are currently in the running VM's memory because this state is not captured.

1. Navigate to the Instances tab in the Virtual Machines area in the management portal accessed via *https://manage.windowsazure.com*.

2. In the list of VMs, select the VM to capture to an image.

3. Click Capture on the command bar.

4. In the Capture The Virtual Machine dialog box, provide a name and description.

5. If you selected a VM that was stopped, select the I Have Run Sysprep On The Virtual Machine check box (for a Windows VM) or the I Have Run The Windows Azure Linux Agent On The Virtual Machine check box (for a Linux VHD).

6. Click the check mark to create the VM image.

Capturing a VM as a VM image (Preview portal)

Capturing a VM as a VM image is not currently supported in the Preview portal.

Capturing a VM as a VM image using Windows PowerShell

- You can capture a stopped VM as a VM image using the Windows PowerShell Save-AzureImage cmdlet.

```
Save-AzureVMImage -ServiceName "<CloudServiceName>" -Name "<VMName>" -OSState
"<GeneralizedOrSpecialized>" -NewImageName "<ImageName>" -NewImageLabel "<ImageLabel>"
```

With the Save-AzureImage cmdlet, you indicate that the VM has been generalized by providing an OSState parameter with a value of Generalized. Otherwise, you provide a value of Specialized. Note that when the cmdlet finishes, the target VM is deleted.

Instantiating a VM instance from a VM image

- With a VM image at the ready, you can create instances of the VM using either the management portal or Windows PowerShell.

Creating a VM instance from a VM image (existing portal)

To create a VM instance from a VM image in the management portal, complete the following steps:

1. Navigate to the management portal accessed via *https://manage.windowsazure.com*.

2. Click New on the command bar, and select New, Virtual Machine, From Gallery.

3. In the Create A Virtual Machine dialog box that appears, in the navigation pane, click My Images.

4. In the list that appears, select the image you want to use for this VM. Click the right arrow.

5. Provide a name, tier, instance size, and administrator credentials. Click the right arrow.

6. On the Virtual Machine Configuration screen, select Create A New Cloud Service, and provide a DNS name, region, and storage account. Leave the remaining settings at their default values and click the right arrow.

7. Leave the endpoints at their defaults and click the right arrow.

8. Leave the VM agent selected, and leave the remaining extensions clear.

9. Click the check mark to provision the VM.

Creating a VM instance from a VM image (Preview portal)

Creating a VM instance from a VM image is not currently supported in the Preview portal.

Creating a VM instance from a VM image using Windows PowerShell

You can provision a VM instance from a VM image using the Windows PowerShell New-AzureQuickVM cmdlet:

```
New-AzureQuickVM -Windows -Location "<LocationName>" -ServiceName "<CloudServiceName>"
-Name "<VMName>" -InstanceSize "<InstanceSize>" -ImageName "<ImageName>"
-AdminUsername "<Username>" -Password "<Password>" -WaitForBoot
```

If you are provisioning a Linux VM, supply the -Linux switch in place of the -Windows switch and provide the -LinuxUser and –Password:

```
New-AzureQuickVM –Linux –Location "<LocationName>" –ServiceName "<CloudServiceName>"
–Name "<VMName>" –InstanceSize "<InstanceSize>" –ImageName "<ImageName>"
–LinuxUser "<Username>" –Password "<Password>" -WaitForBoot
```

Copying images between storage accounts

To create instances of your VM image in a region different than the one where the storage account containing the VM image exists, copy the VM image to Storage Accounts in the target region. To accomplish this effectively, consider using the AZCopy utility. You can download this utility from *http://azure.microsoft.com/en-us/documentation/articles/storage-use-azcopy/*.

With the utility downloaded and installed, open a command prompt window and run the following command:

```
AzCopy /Source:
https://<SourceStorageAccountName>.blob.core.windows.net/<SourceContainerName>
/Destination:https://<DestinationStorageAccountName>.blob.core.windows.
net/<DestinationContainerName> /Sourcekey:<SourceStorageKey> /Destkey:<DestinationStora
geKey>
/Pattern:<ImageFileName>
```

> **MORE INFO**   **AZCOPY**
>
> AZCopy has a feature-rich command line. For more details, see *http://azure.microsoft.com/en-us/documentation/articles/storage-use-azcopy/*.

> ### *Thought experiment*
> #### Lift and shift
>
> In this thought experiment, apply what you've learned about this objective. You can find answers to these questions in the "Answers" section at the end of this chapter.
>
> You have an application configured to run in Hyper-V on-premises, which runs atop Windows Server 2012 R2. The VM consists of a single VHD disk that contains the operating system and all application files. You never run multiple instances of the VM at the same time on the same network, and you want Azure to run this VM periodically.
>
> 1. How would you transfer the VM from on-premises to Azure?
> 2. Would you create a specialized disk or a generalized disk?

Objective summary

- You can provision VMs from two different kinds of images: specialized images and generalized images.
- A specialized image is the equivalent of a snapshot or golden copy of a VM from which you create instances that have the same identity.
- A generalized VM is the equivalent of a template created from a VM, where each instance you create receives a unique identity.
- You upload a VM to Azure by uploading its constituent VHD disks, creating disks from those VHDs, and then attaching the disks to a VM. You can then capture a VM image from the VM instance. The VM image is what you use to subsequently create new VM instances.
- VM images are copied between Storage accounts using the AZCopy utility.

Objective review

Answer the following questions to test your knowledge of the information in this objective. You can find the answers to these questions and explanations of why each answer choice is correct or incorrect in the "Answers" section at the end of this chapter.

1. Which of the following is *not* a tool used for generalizing a VM? (Choose all that apply.)

   A. Sysprep

   B. waagent

   C. reset

   D. generalize

2. Which of the following diagnostics are valid options for creating a disk?

   A. Create an operating system disk from a single VHD

   B. Create an operating system disk from multiple VHDs

   C. Create a data disk from a single VHD

   D. Create a data disk from multiple VHDs

3. Which of the following are valid options for creating a VM image? (Choose all that apply.)

   A. Capture a VM image from a running VM instance

   B. Capture a VM image from a stopped (de-allocated) VM instance

   C. Create a VM image from a single VHD

   D. Capture a VM image from a VM instance running Linux

Objective 2.3: Perform configuration management

A number of configuration management tools are available for provisioning, configuring, and managing your VMs. In this section, you learn how to use Windows PowerShell Desired State Configuration (DSC) and the Custom Script Extension to perform configuration management tasks, including automating the process of provisioning VMs, deploying applications to those VMs, and automating configuration of those applications based on the environment, such as development, test, or production. In addition, this section explores how to take advantage of unique features offered by Puppet and Chef extensions for similar configuration management activities.

> **This objective covers how to:**
> - Automate configuration management with the Custom Script Extension and PowerShell Desired State Configuration (DSC)
> - Enable Puppet and Chef extensions
> - Enable remote debugging

VM Agent and VM extensions

Before describing the details of using PowerShell DSC and the Custom Script Extension, this section provides some background on the relationship between these tools and the relevance of the Azure Virtual Machine Agent (VM Agent) and Azure virtual machine extensions (VM extensions).

When you create a new VM in the existing portal or Preview portal, the VM Agent is installed by default. The VM Agent is a lightweight process used for bootstrapping additional tools on the VM by way of installing, configuring, and managing VM extensions. VM extensions can be added through the management portal, but they are also commonly installed with Windows PowerShell cmdlets or through the Azure Cross Platform Command Line Interface (Azure CLI, or xplat-cli).

> **NOTE VM AGENT INSTALLATION**
>
> When you create a new VM through the management portal (existing portal or Preview portal), or with Windows PowerShell, the VM Agent is installed by default on the VM. If you create a VM from the gallery, you can optionally clear the option for installing the VM Agent and later install it with Windows PowerShell if necessary.

With the VM Agent installed, you can add VM extensions. Popular VM extensions include the following:

- DSC (to enable PowerShell DSC commands)
- Custom Script Extension (for Windows or Linux)
- Visual Studio Release Manager (DSC-based extension)
- Octopus Deploy (DSC-based extension)
- Docker extension
- Puppet Enterprise agent
- Chef client (for Windows or Linux)

You can add some VM extensions as you create the VM through either portal; you can manage others (such as PowerShell DSC) only through the Preview portal. You enable the remainder using Windows PowerShell scripts.

Configuring VMs with Custom Script Extension

Custom Script Extension makes it possible to automatically download files from Azure Storage and run Windows PowerShell scripts to copy files and otherwise configure the VM. This can be done when the VM is being created or when it is already running. You can do this from the Preview portal or from a Windows PowerShell command line interface.

Configuring a new VM with Custom Script Extension (existing portal)

Create a Windows Server VM following the steps presented in the earlier section, "Creating a Windows Server VM (existing portal)." In the final step, in the Virtual Machine Configuration dialog box where the check mark appears, complete the following steps:

1. Ensure the VM Agent check box is selected.

2. Select the Custom Script check box.

3. Under Custom Script Configuration, browse for the Windows PowerShell script on the local drive or in your storage account.

4. Provide any arguments to the script if applicable.

5. Click the check mark to create the VM.

Configuring a new VM with Custom Script Extension (Preview portal)

Create a Windows Server VM following the steps presented in the earlier section, "Creating a Windows Server VM (Preview portal)." After creating the VM, complete the following steps to set up the Custom Script Extension:

6. Navigate to the blade for your VM in the management portal accessed via *https://portal.azure.com*.

7. Scroll down to the Configure section, and click the Extensions box.

8. On the Extensions blade, click Add on the command bar.

9. On the New Resource Disk blade, click Custom Script.

10. On the Custom Script blade, click Create.

11. On the Add Extension blade, click the area for Script File and select the .ps1 file containing the script you want to run when the VM starts. Optionally, provide arguments.

12. Click Create.

> **MORE INFO   CUSTOM SCRIPT EXTENSION AND WINDOWS POWERSHELL**
>
> You can also configure Custom Script Extension using the Set-AzureVMCustomScriptExtension Windows PowerShell cmdlet. For details on this, see *http://msdn.microsoft.com/en-us/library/azure/dn722462.aspx*.

Using PowerShell DSC

PowerShell Desired State Configuration (DSC) is a management platform introduced with Windows PowerShell 4.0, available as a Windows feature on Windows Server 2012 R2. PowerShell DSC is implemented using Windows PowerShell. You can use it to configure a set of servers (or nodes) declaratively, providing a description of the desired state for each node in the system topology. You can describe which application resources to add, remove, or update based on the current state of a server node. The easy, declarative syntax simplifies configuration management tasks.

With PowerShell DSC, you can instruct a VM to self-provision to a desired state on first deployment and then have it automatically update if there is "configuration drift." Configuration drift happens when the desired state of the node no longer matches what is described by DSC.

DSC resources

Resources are core building blocks for DSC. A script can describe the target state of one or more resources, such as a Windows feature, the registry, the file system, and other services. For example, a DSC script can describe the following intentions:

- Manage server roles and Windows features
- Manage registry keys
- Copy files and folders
- Deploy software
- Run Windows PowerShell scripts

> **MORE INFO** **DSC BUILT-IN RESOURCES**
>
> For a more extensive list of DSC resources, see *http://technet.microsoft.com/en-us/library/dn249921.aspx*.

Configuration keyword

DSC extends Windows PowerShell 4.0 with a new Configuration keyword used to express the desired state of one or more target nodes. For example, the following configuration indicates that a server should have IIS enabled during provisioning:

```
Configuration EnableIIS
{
    Node WebServer
    {
        WindowsFeature IIS {
                Ensure = "Present",
                Name = "Web-Server"
        }
    }
}
```

The Configuration keyword can wrap one or more Node elements, each describing the desired configuration state of one or more resources on the node. In the preceding example, the server node is named WebServer and the DSC ensures that the IIS Windows feature is enabled.

EXAM TIP

After the DSC runs, a Managed Object Format (MOF) file is created, which is a standard endorsed by the Distributed Management Task Force (DTMF). See *http://www.dmtf.org/education/mof.*

Custom resources

Many resources are predefined and exposed to DSC; however, you may also require extended capabilities that warrant creating a custom resource for DSC configuration. You can implement custom resources by creating a Windows PowerShell module. The module includes a MOF schema, a script module, and a module manifest.

> **MORE INFO** **CUSTOM DSC RESOURCES**
>
> For more information on building custom DSC resources, see *http://technet.microsoft.com/en-us/library/dn249927.aspx*.

> **MORE INFO** **DSC RESOURCE KIT**
>
> The Windows PowerShell team released a number of DSC resources to simplify working with Active Directory, SQL Server, and IIS. See *https://gallery.technet.microsoft.com/DSC-Resource-Kit-All-c449312d*.

Local Configuration Manager

Local Configuration Manager runs on all target nodes and enables the following scenarios for DSC:

- Pushing configurations to bootstrap a target node
- Pulling configuration from a specified location to bootstrap or update a target node
- Applying the configuration defined in the MOF file to the target node, either during the bootstrapping stage or to repair configuration drift

Local Configuration Manager runs dscboot.ps1 to evoke the configuration specified by your DSC configuration file. You can optionally configure Local Configuration Manager to apply new configurations only, to report differences resulting from configuration drift, or to automatically correct configuration drift.

> **MORE INFO** **LOCAL CONFIGURATION MANAGER**
>
> For additional details on the configuration settings available for Local Configuration Manager, see *http://technet.microsoft.com/en-us/library/dn249922.aspx*.

Configuring VMs with DSC

To configure a VM using DSC, first create a Windows PowerShell script that describes the desired configuration state. As discussed earlier, this involves selecting resources to configure and providing the appropriate settings. When you have a configuration script, you can use one of a number of methods to initialize a VM to run the script on startup.

Creating a configuration script

Use any text editor to create a Windows PowerShell file. Include a collection of resources to configure, for one or more nodes, in the file. If you are copying files as part of the node configuration, they should be available in the specified source path, and a target path should also be specified. For example, the following script ensures IIS is enabled and copies a single file to the default website:

```
configuration DeployWebPage
{
    node ("localhost")
    {
        WindowsFeature IIS
        {
            Ensure = "Present"
            Name = "Web-Server"
        }

        File WebPage
        {
            Ensure          = "Present"
            DestinationPath = "C:\inetpub\wwwroot\index.html"
            Force           = $true
            Type            = "File"
            Contents        = '<html><body><h1>Hello Web Page!</h1></body></html>'

        }
    }
}
```

Preparing the DSC configuration package

After creating your configuration script and allocating any resources it requires, produce a compressed zip file containing the configuration and the resources using Windows PowerShell as follows:

```
Publish-AzureVMDSCConfiguration DeployWebPage.ps1 -ConfigurationArchivePath
DeployWebPage.ps1.zip
```

> **NOTE** **ADDING RESOURCES TO THE ZIP FILE**
>
> When you build your configuration zip using Publish-AzureVMDSCConfiguration, it will not automatically include the resources you specify, for example additional Windows PowerShell module dependencies or any files or folders that you intend to deploy. You must add those manually to the zip file before configuring the VM with the DSC script.

Configuring an existing VM (existing portal)

Configuring an existing VM is not currently supported in the existing portal.

Configuring an existing VM (Preview portal)

To configure an existing VM in the Preview portal, complete the following steps:

1. Navigate to the blade for your VM in the management portal accessed via *https://portal.azure.com*.

2. Scroll down to the Configure section and click the Extensions box.

3. On the Extensions blade, click Add on the command bar.

4. On the New Resource Disk blade, click PowerShell Desired State Configuration.

5. On the PowerShell Desired State Configuration blade, click Create.

6. On the Add Extension blade, click the area for Configuration Modules or Script and select the .ps1 file containing the DSC script you want to run when the VM starts. Then, for Module-Qualified Name Of Configuration, type the name of the .ps1 file followed by the configuration type name for example, DeployWebPage.ps1\DeployWebPage.

7. Click Create on the Add Extension blade.

Using the Puppet and Chef configuration management tools

Puppet and Chef are two well-known configuration management tools. They each provide a way to turn infrastructure into code to automate build process, deployment, and management of IT infrastructure. There are synergies between these tools and the DSC in terms of the ability to script many aspects of configuration management. Puppet and Chef build upon this theme to provide IT operations with a set of management tools for the global view of an entire system topology. With both Puppet and Chef, you can leverage your Windows PowerShell and DSC scripts as part of this holistic experience.

The sections that follow provide an overview of the steps to set up these extensions as part of your VM topology to support configuration management.

Enabling Puppet extensions

This section describes how to set up a Linux VM pre-configured as a puppet master node and a managed Windows Server node with the Puppet agent installed.

MORE INFO   **PUPPET SETUP ON AZURE**

The following references provide additional information related to learning Puppet and for setting up Puppet on Azure. The first reference links to the Puppet Labs site. The second reference links to, "Getting Started Guide: Deploying Puppet Enterprise in Microsoft Azure."

- *http://puppetlabs.com/*
- *http://info.puppetlabs.com/pe-azure-gsg.html*

Creating a Linux VM with the puppet master (existing portal)

Complete the following steps to set up a Linux VM with the puppet master installed using the existing portal:

1. Navigate to the management portal accessed via *https://manage.windowsazure.com*.

2. Click New on the command bar, and then click Compute, Virtual Machine, From Gallery.

3. In the navigation pane, select Puppet Labs.

4. Select the Puppet Enterprise 3.2.3 image (the only one available). Click the right arrow.

5. Provide a name, tier, instance size, and administrator user name. Be sure to use an instance size minimum of A2 to support the puppet master extension.

6. Clear the Upload Compatible SSH Key For Authentication option.

7. Select Provide A Password, and type the password for the administrator. Click the right arrow.

8. On the Virtual Machine Configuration screen, select Create A New Cloud Service, and provide a DNS name, region, and storage account.

9. Leave the availability set value configured to none.

10. Add an endpoint for HTTPS assigning port 443 for both the public and private port.

11. Add an endpoint for MCollective assigning port 61613 for both the public and private port.

12. Add an endpoint for Puppet assigning port 8140 for both the public and private port.

13. Click the right arrow, and then click the check mark to provision the Linux VM with a pre-configured puppet master.

Creating a Linux VM with the puppet master (Preview portal)

Complete the following steps to set up a Linux VM with the puppet master installed using the Preview portal:

1. Navigate to the management portal accessed via *https://portal.azure.com*.

2. Click New on the command bar.

3. Navigate to the Marketplace by clicking the Everything link located near the upper-right blade that appears.

4. On the Marketplace blade, select Virtual Machines.

5. On the Virtual Machines blade, scroll to the Linux-based section and select Puppet Enterprise 3.2.3 by Puppet Labs.

6. On the Puppet Enterprise blade, click Create.

7. On the Create VM blade, provide a host name and a user name for the new VM.

8. Using an external tool, generate a public SSH key, and then copy and paste it into the SSH Public Key text box. See the More Info titled, "SSH key generation" earlier in this chapter for instructions on how to do this.

9. Review the Pricing Tier, Optional Configuration, Resource Group, Subscription, and Location settings, and change as necessary.

10. Click Create to provision the Puppet Enterprise VM.

> *NOTE* **SETTING UP A PUPPET MASTER**
>
> You can select the Puppet Enterprise pre-configured VM to set up a puppet master node, or you can create a new Linux VM and enable the puppet master agent manually. Using the pre-configured VM is preferred for setup simplicity.

Accessing the Puppet Enterprise console

After the VM is provisioned, browse to the Puppet Enterprise console as follows:

1. Open a browser and navigate to your VM using HTTPS. For example, use *https://<VMName>.cloudapp.net*.

2. Ignore the certificate error that appears (this server has a self-signed certificate).

3. On the login page, enter your credentials to log in to the Enterprise Puppet console.

At this point, you need your administrative credentials to log in to the console. These credentials are created when the VM is generated. They are not the same as the VM credentials you supplied while creating the VM in the portal. To get the credentials, connect to the Linux VM using SSH (for example, use PuTTY from Windows or Terminal from iOS platforms).

For more information on how to gather the credentials, follow the instructions in the reference guide. For example, type the following SSH command, follow the prompts to ignore certificate errors, and then provide your password supplied in the portal. Note that

<VMUSERNAME> should be replaced by the user name you supplied when creating the VM in the portal:

```
ssh <VMUSERNAME>@<VMNAME>.cloudapp.net
```

After connecting using SSH, type the following command to retrieve the administrator user name:

```
sudo grep 'auth_user_email' /etc/puppetlabs/installer/answers.install
```

The response should be something like following:

```
<q_puppet_enterprise_auth_user_email=admin@<VMNAME>.cloudapp.net
```

where *admin@<VMNAME>.cloudapp.net* is the user name.

To retrieve the password, type the following similar command:

```
sudo grep 'auth_password' /etc/puppetlabs/installer/database_info.install
```

The response should be something like the following:

```
q_puppet_enterpriseconsole_auth_password=<PASSWORD>
```

Use this user name and password to log in to the Puppet Enterprise console, where you can manage any nodes subsequently registered to this puppet master instance.

Creating a Windows Server VM with the Puppet agent (existing portal)

Complete the following steps to create a Windows Server VM with the Puppet agent in the management portal:

1. Navigate to the portal accessed via *https://manage.windowsazure.com*.

2. Click New on the command bar, and then click Compute, Virtual Machine, From Gallery.

3. In the navigation pane, select Windows Server.

4. Select Windows Server 2012 R2 Datacenter, and click the right arrow.

5. Provide a name, tier, instance size, and administrator user name. Be sure to select an instance size minimum of A2 to support the Puppet agent extension.

6. Provide a user name and password for the administrator. Click the right arrow.

7. On the Virtual Machine Configuration screen, select Create A New Cloud Service, and provide a DNS name, region, and storage account.

8. Leave the availability set value configured to none.

9. Leave the default endpoints for PowerShell and Remote Desktop. Click the right arrow.

10. Ensure that Install The VM Agent is selected.

11. Select Puppet Enterprise Agent.

12. Under Puppet Enterprise Agent Configuration, supply the fully qualified address to the puppet master server node.

13. Click the check mark to provision the Linux VM with the Puppet Enterprise agent configured.

Creating a Windows Server VM with the Puppet agent (Preview portal)

Before completing these steps, create a Windows Server VM following the same steps recommended in the "Creating a Windows Server VM (Preview portal)" section earlier in this chapter. Next, complete the following steps to set up the Puppet Enterprise agent extension:

1. Navigate to the blade for your VM in the management portal accessed via *https://portal.azure.com*.

2. Scroll down to the Configure section and click the Extensions box.

3. On the Extensions blade, click Add on the command bar.

4. On the New Resource Disk blade, click the Puppet Enterprise Agent ribbon.

5. On the Puppet Enterprise Agent blade, click Create.

6. On the Add Extension blade, supply the fully qualified address to the puppet master server node.

7. Click Create.

Accepting agent node registration

When you create a Puppet agent node, it registers with the puppet master node at the supplied fully qualified address and sends a certificate request. Log in to the Puppet Enterprise console to accept the request so that you can add the agent node to your managed group of servers.

EXAM TIP

If you supply the wrong fully qualified address to the puppet master node during this configuration process, the agent will not automatically register with the puppet master node. If this happens, to fix the address, you must manually edit the Puppet agent configuration on the machine and manually send a registration request from a remote desktop session.

See the guide, "Getting Started Guide: Deploying Puppet Enterprise in Microsoft Azure" at *http://info.puppetlabs.com/pe-azure-gsg.html* for additional details on these steps.

Configuring puppet scripts

When your agent nodes are registered with the puppet master, you can create your modules to configure those nodes by accessing the puppet master VM using SSH and editing the /etc/puppetlabs/puppet/manifests/site.pp file to configure any existing or custom modules that should be used to initialize each agent node.

> **MORE INFO** **INTRODUCTION TO PUPPET**
>
> If you are new to Puppet, you can start learning more about it with the documentation at *https://docs.puppetlabs.com/guides/introduction.html.*

To configure Azure resources and DSC scripts, you can leverage existing modules created by the Puppet Forge community. MS Open Tech released a Microsoft Azure module for Puppet, and there is a community-driven PowerShell DSC module as well.

> **MORE INFO** **PUPPET FORGE RESOURCES**
>
> You can search for modules at Puppet Forge. The following links lead to the Microsoft Azure and DSC modules:
>
> - *https://forge.puppetlabs.com/msopentech/windowsazure*
> - *https://forge.puppetlabs.com/msutter/dsc*

Enabling Chef extensions

This section describes how to set up a Linux VM pre-configured as a Chef server node and a managed Windows Server node with the Chef client installed.

> **MORE INFO** **CHEF SETUP ON AZURE**
>
> The following references provide additional information related to learning Chef and for setting up Chef on Azure:
>
> - *http://learn.getchef.com/*
> - *https://www.getchef.com/partners/microsoft/*

Creating a Linux VM with a Chef server

Currently, there is no pre-configured VM for a Chef server on Azure. You can use one of the following options to set up a Chef server:

- Use the multi-tenant solution for the Chef server hosted by OpsDev
- Create a Linux VM and manually set up the Chef server following instructions supplied by OpsDev

MORE INFO CHEF SERVER SETUP

The following reference can guide you through setting up the OpsDev hosted or self-hosted Chef server: *https://www.getchef.com/chef/choose-your-version*.

Creating a Chef workstation

You must set up an administrative workstation to manage your configuration management workflow with Chef. This can be a local or hosted workstation. To do this, choose a Windows Server VM as your workstation and follow the instructions to set up the Chef Development Kit found at *http://docs.getchef.com/install_dk.html*.

Creating a Windows Server VM with a Chef client (existing portal)

To create a Windows Server VM with a Chef client in the management portal, complete the following steps:

1. Navigate to the management portal accessed via *https://manage.windowsazure.com*.

2. Click New on the command bar, and then click Compute, Virtual Machine, From Gallery.

3. In the navigation pane, select Windows Server.

4. Select a Windows Server R2 datacenter from which to create the VM, and then click the right arrow.

5. Provide a name, tier, instance size, and administrator user name. Be sure to select an instance size minimum of A2 to support the Chef client extension.

6. Provide a user name and password for the administrator. Click the right arrow.

7. On the Virtual Machine Configuration screen, select Create A New Cloud Service, and provide a DNS name, region, and storage account.

8. Leave the availability set value configured to none.

9. Leave the default endpoints for Windows PowerShell and Remote Desktop. Click the right arrow.

10. Ensure that Install The VM Agent is selected.

11. Select the Chef check box.

12. Under Chef Configuration, supply your client.rb and validation.pem files to configure the Chef client node.

13. Click the check mark to provision the VM.

Creating a Windows Server VM with a Chef client (Preview portal)

Before completing these steps, first create a Windows Server VM following the same steps presented in the "Creating a Windows Server VM (Preview portal)" section earlier in this chapter. Next, complete the following steps to set up the Chef client extension:

1. Navigate to the blade for your VM in the management portal accessed via *https://portal.azure.com*.

2. Scroll down to the Configure section, and click the Extensions box.

3. On the Extensions blade, click Add on the command bar.

4. On the New Resource Disk blade, click the Chef Client ribbon.

5. On the Chef Client blade, click Create.

6. On the Add Extension blade, supply your client.rb and validation.pem files to configure the Chef client node.

7. Click Create.

> ### Thought experiment
> #### Choosing a configuration management tool
>
> In this thought experiment, apply what you've learned about this objective. You can find answers to these questions in the "Answers" section at the end of this chapter.
>
> You are currently setting up your development, test, and production environments manually through a combination of Visual Studio deployment steps and portal commands to create and manage resources and swapping activities. You want a tool to help with automation, with a vision toward the future scale and management requirements of your system.
>
> 1. Can you start with Windows PowerShell scripts, or should you start by using PowerShell DSC?
>
> 2. Do you need a management tool such as Puppet or Chef?

Enabling remote debugging

You can use remote debugging to debug applications running on your VMs. Server Explorer in Visual Studio shows your VMs in a list, and from there you can enable remote debugging and attach to a process following these steps:

1. In Visual Studio, open Server Explorer.

2. Expand the Azure node, and expand the Virtual Machines node.

3. Right-click the VM you want to debug and select Enable Debugging. Click Yes in the dialog box to confirm.

   This installs a remote debugging extension to the VM so that you can debug remotely. After this is installed, you can continue.

4. Right-click the virtual machine again and select Attach Debugger. This presents a list of processes in the Attach To Process dialog box.

5. Select the processes you want to debug on the VM and click Attach. To debug a web application, select w3wp.exe, for example.

MORE INFO   DEBUGGING PROCESSES IN VISUAL STUDIO

For additional information about debugging processes in Visual Studio, see this reference: *http://msdn.microsoft.com/en-us/library/jj919165.aspx.*

Objective summary

- The VM Agent is a very lightweight process. When installed on a VM, it makes it possible to bootstrap additional VM extensions such as DSC, Chef, and Puppet extensions.

- The Custom Script Extension makes it possible to download files from Azure Storage, run Windows PowerShell scripts, and automate copying files and configuring a VM.

- DSC helps you avoid configuration drift by specifying the desired state for VM provisioning and subsequent updates.

- Puppet and Chef are configuration management tools that, like DCS, provide a way to describe the desired state of a VM on provisioning and for updates. They also respectively have rich tooling for visualizing aspects of your VMs in your system deployment, manage updates to collections of VMs, and more.

Objective review

Answer the following questions to test your knowledge of the information in this objective. You can find the answers to these questions and explanations of why each answer choice is correct or incorrect in the "Answers" section at the end of this chapter.

1. Which of the following statements are true? (Choose all that apply.)

   A. The VM Agent is always installed with a new Windows VM image.

   B. The Custom Script Extension can be enabled while creating a VM in either management portal.

   C. PowerShell DSC is always installed on a new Windows VM image.

   D. Chef client can be enabled for both Windows and Linux-based VM images.

   E. Puppet Enterprise agent can be enabled for both Windows and Linux-based VM images.

2. What are examples of built-in resources that you can configure using PowerShell DSC? (Choose all that apply.)

   A. Windows features

   B. Network topology

   C. Files and directories

   D. File archives (zip files)

   E. Registry settings

   F. Windows PowerShell scripts

   G. Users

3. Which of the following are accurate statements? (Choose all that apply.)

   A. Custom Script Extension and PowerShell DSC are one and the same.

   B. DSC provides the same features and functionality as Puppet and Chef.

   C. Windows PowerShell scripts can be leveraged by Custom Script Extension, DSC, Puppet, and Chef configuration management tools.

   D. DSC cannot automatically update VMs without pushing an instruction via Windows PowerShell.

Objective 2.4: Configure VM networking

In this objective, you explore additional ways to configure communication with your Azure VMs, beyond configuring endpoints and communicating via the virtual IP address and port.

> **This objective covers how to:**
> - Configure DNS at the cloud service level
> - Configure endpoints with instance-level public IP addresses
> - Configure endpoints with reserved IP addresses
> - Configure access control lists (ACL)
> - Load balance endpoints and configure health probes
> - Configure Direct Server Return and keep-alive
> - Configure firewall rules

Configuring DNS at the cloud service level

In Objective 2.1, the steps for creating a new VM using the existing management portal include providing a DNS name for the cloud service. When provisioned, this DNS name can be used to access the VM. This DNS name resolves to the public virtual IP address of the cloud service, and after the cloud service has been created, the DNS name cannot be changed. Alternately, the VM can be accessed directly by the public virtual IP address.

Configuring endpoints with instance-level public IP addresses

Public endpoints created for a VM use port forwarding to expose a single port on the publicly available virtual IP (VIP) assigned to the cloud service to which the VM belongs and map that public IP and port to a private IP and port available on a single VM instance. If instead you want to make a VM instance available across a range of ports, or if you don't want to specify specific ports, you can configure an instance-level public IP address (PIP) for that VM instance to use in addition to the VIP plus port endpoint you have configured for it. With this configuration, you can communicate directly with your VM instance using this public IP address (and any port) instead of (or in addition to) using the VIP address and a specific port.

PIP has two typical advantages. First, by removing the need to define ports, you can enable scenarios, such as passive FTP, that rely on choosing ports dynamically. Second, you can rely on the PIP to uniquely identify your VM on outgoing requests to external services that have access control or firewall rules that allow or deny based on IP address.

To assign a PIP to your VM, first ensure that your VM is deployed to a regional virtual network (VNET) since a PIP cannot be assigned to VMs that do not belong to a VNET. Second, configure that VM instance with a PIP.

Creating a regional VNET (existing portal)

To create a regional VNET using the management portal, complete the following steps:

1. Navigate to the VM in the management portal accessed via *https://manage. windowsazure.com.*

2. Click New on the command bar, and then click Virtual Network, Quick Create.

3. Specify a name for the new virtual network, an address space (the group of IP addresses that are available for use by VMs), the maximum VM count, and a location (the region in which to create the regional VNET).

4. Click Create A Virtual Network to create the regional VNET.

Creating a regional VNET (Preview portal)

Currently, virtual networks cannot be created using the Preview portal.

> **NOTE   PROVISIONING THE VM IN THE VNET**
>
> After you have created a regional VNET, be sure to select that VNET when you provision your VM since you cannot easily move a VM into a VNET after creating it.

Configuring the public IP address (existing portal)

Public IP addresses cannot be configured using the existing portal.

Configuring the public IP address (Preview portal)

To configure the PIP for a VM using the Preview portal, complete the following steps.

1. Navigate to the blade for your VM in the management portal accessed via *https://portal.azure.com.*

2. Scroll down to the Configure section and click the IP Addresses tile.

3. In the IP Addresses blade, under the Instance IP Address blade, click Instance IP Address to turn on the option.

4. Click Save on the command bar to apply the change.

In the Preview portal, you can view the address by navigating to the blade for the VM, scrolling down to the Configure section, and viewing the value under Instance in the IP Addresses tile. This value is not shown in the existing portal.

Configuring endpoints with reserved IP addresses

Public virtual IP addresses (VIP) used to access your VM via an endpoint are assigned to the cloud service to which that VM belongs, not to the VM itself. This IP address remains unchanged until all of the VMs in that cloud service are stopped and de-allocated or deleted; when either of these happen, the IP address is released. This means that the next time you provision a VM, the cloud service is likely to have a new and different VIP. If you want to ensure that the IP address remains fixed and reflected as being owned by your Azure subscription, even if the cloud service it is associated with is deleted, then you need to configure a reserved IP address.

To use a reserved IP address with a VM, you must request it as a part of creating both a new cloud service and new VM. There is currently no support for assigning a reserved IP address to an existing cloud service and VM.

Creating a VM with a reserved IP address (existing portal)

It is not possible to provision a VM with a reserved IP address using the existing portal.

Creating a VM with a reserved IP address (Preview portal)

To provision a VM with a reserved IP address using the Preview portal, complete the following steps:

1. Navigate to the management portal accessed via *https://portal.azure.com*.

2. Click New.

3. Select a VM image (such as Windows Server 2012 R2 Datacenter).

4. On the Create VM blade, provide a host name for the VM, along with an administrator user name and password.

5. Set your pricing tier as desired.

6. Click the Optional Configuration ribbon, and then click the Network ribbon.

7. On the Network blade, click the Virtual Network ribbon, and on the Virtual Network blade do one of the following:

   A. To create a new virtual network, click the Virtual Network ribbon, provide a name, address space, and DNS servers as desired, and then click OK.

   B. Click one of the existing virtual networks listed on the blade.

8. Return to the Network blade and click the IP Addresses ribbon.

9. On the IP Address blade, click the Virtual IP Address Assignment toggle to reserve the assignment.

10. Click the Reserved IP Address ribbon.

11. On the Reserved IP Address blade, click the Create A Reserved IP Address ribbon.

12. On the Create A Reserved IP Address blade that appears, provide a name for the reserved IP address, and click OK.

13. Return to the IP Address blade and click OK. Click OK again on the Network blade, and then click OK once more on the Optional Config blade.

14. On the Create VM blade, click Create to provision the new cloud service, new VM, and new reserved IP address.

Configuring access control lists

A network access control list (ACL) allows you to restrict access to your VMs to specific ranges of IP addresses by defining a list of permit or deny rules. They perform packet filtering on the host node running your VM, controlling what external traffic is allowed to reach it via the endpoint. They are defined on a VM endpoint or load balanced set and apply only to external traffic (for example, traffic that flows through the VIP and load balancer). They are not applied to internal traffic and cannot be applied to a VNET or to a subnet within a VNET.

Within an ACL, you can combine permit and deny rules for specific IP address ranges. When you have no ACL defined on an endpoint, all traffic is allowed. When you define one or more Permit rules, only traffic from IP ranges explicitly specified are allowed, and the rest are denied. If you define one or more Deny rules, all traffic from all IP ranges is allowed except those ranges specifically identified. When you combine Permit and Deny rules, you can tightly restrict access.

ACL rule evaluation proceeds in priority order, where rules with the lowest order value have highest priority and are evaluated before rules with higher order values that have a lower priority. The first rule to match the traffic in the list, if there is a match, is applied and stops further rule evaluation.

Configuring ACL (existing portal)

To configure ACL in the management portal, complete the following steps:

1. Navigate to the Endpoints tab of your VM in the management portal accessed via *https://manage.windowsazure.com*.

2. In the endpoints table, click an endpoint in the list of standalone or load balanced endpoints to select it.

3. Click Manage ACL on the command bar.

4. In the Manage Endpoint ACL dialog box that appears, add ACL entries by specifying the description of the ACL, action (allow or deny), and the remote subnet of the IP address range to which this ACL should apply.

5. Add additional ACL entries as desired, and use the up or down arrows that appear to the right of the ACL entry to adjust the order of the rule.

6. Click the check mark to apply the changes to the VM.

Configuring ACL (Preview portal)

To configure ACL using the Preview portal, complete the following steps:

1. Navigate to the blade of your VM in the management portal accessed via *https://portal.azure.com.*

2. Scroll down to the Configure section.

3. If the endpoint you want to secure is a standalone endpoint, complete the following steps:

   A. Click the Endpoints tile to display the Endpoints blade.

   B. On the Endpoints blade, click an endpoint from the list of standalone endpoints to display the blade for that endpoint.

4. If the endpoint you want to secure is part of a load balanced set, complete the following steps:

   A. Click the Load Balanced Sets tile to display the Load Balanced Sets blade.

   B. Click a load balanced set in the list of public endpoints to display the blade for that load balanced set.

5. In the access control list table, add ACL entries by specifying the order (lowest value gets highest priority), name of the ACL, action (allow or deny), and the remote subnet of the IP address range to which this ACL should apply.

6. Add additional ACL entries as desired. You can adjust the priority of the rules by changing the value of the order field.

7. Click Save to apply the changes to the VM.

> **EXAM TIP**
>
> You can use ACL to restrict access to a single host instead of the many hosts that would be described by an IP address range. To do so, when specifying the remote subnet, use the /32 subnet mask, for example 70.0.0.1/32.

Load balancing endpoints and configuring health probes

If you have multiple VMs listening for requests on the same port and want to distribute external (or Internet) traffic between them, you can use the Azure Load Balancing service (see Figure 2-1). If you do not need to expose your VMs to the public Internet, but still want to distribute traffic internal to a cloud service or occurring within a VNET between the VMs, you can leverage the Azure Internal Load Balancing (ILB) service. In either case, the load balancer handles the task of mapping traffic to available servers in a fairly random fashion. The load balancer uses a hashing function to achieve a relatively even distribution of load between the VMs while also ensuring the subsequent requests use the same protocol, from the same source IP/source port to the same destination IP/destination port hash to the same value, and therefore map to the same VM and continue to be sent to the same VM as long as it remains available. The load balancer polls the VM periodically to validate this availability.

No Load Balancing

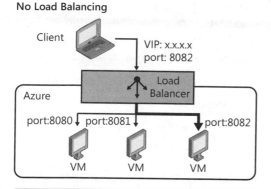

Load Balancing

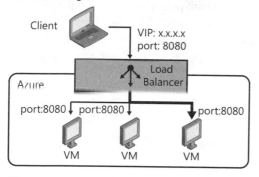

Internal Load Balancing

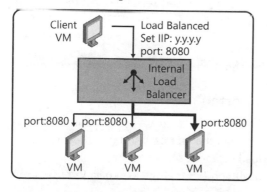

FIGURE 2-1 Comparing load balancing options available with the Azure load balancer. Without load balancing, requests flow directly to the VM whose VIP and port have been requested. With load balancing, the load balancer chooses a VM to send the request to from among the endpoints present in the load balanced set.

Configuring load balancing (existing portal)

It is not currently possible to configure internal load balanced endpoints using the existing portal, but you can configure load balancing for public endpoints. To enable a VM endpoint to participate in load balancing, first create a load balanced set as a part of creating your first load balanced endpoint, and then for each VM that should participate, create a new endpoint and add it to the load balanced set. As a part of configuring the load balanced set, configure the HTTP or TCP health probes that the load balancer uses to determine the availability of a VM.

1. Navigate to the Endpoints tab of your VM in the management portal accessed via *https://manage.windowsazure.com*.

2. Click Add on the command bar.

3. Select Add A Stand-Alone Endpoint, and click the right arrow.

4. Provide a name for the new endpoint, the protocol (TCP or UDP), the public port, and the private port, and be sure to select Create A Load Balanced Set. Click the right arrow.

5. Name the load balanced set and configure the health probe by specifying the protocol used for probes, the health probe path (if you selected HTTP for the health probe protocol), the health probe port, the probe interval (seconds between load balancer health probes), and the number of retries (before the load balancer decides an endpoint is unavailable).

6. Click the check mark to create both the new public endpoint and the load balanced set.

7. To add additional endpoints from other VMs to the load balanced set, for each VM complete the following steps:

   A. Navigate to the Endpoints tab for the next VM.

   B. Select Add An Endpoint To An Existing Load-Balanced Set, and select the name of the load balanced set you previously created.

   C. Click the right arrow.

   D. Provide a name for the new endpoint, and then click the check mark.

Configuring load balancing (Preview portal)

To enable a VM endpoint to participate in load balancing, first create a load balanced set as a part of creating your first load balanced endpoint, and then for each VM that should participate, create a new endpoint and add it to the load balanced set. As a part of configuring the load balanced set, configure the HTTP or TCP health probes that the load balancer uses to determine the availability of a VM.

1. Navigate to the blade of your VM in the management portal accessed via *https://portal.azure.com*.

2. Scroll down to the Configure area.

3. Click the Load Balanced Sets tile.

4. In the Load Balanced Sets blade, click Join on the command bar.

5. To create a new load balanced set for a new public endpoint, in the Join A Load Balanced Set blade, complete the following steps:

6. Set the Load Balanced Set Type toggle to Public.

7. Click the Configure Required Settings ribbon, and select Create A Load Balanced Set.

8. On the Create A Load Balanced Set blade, provide a name for the set, the protocol (TCP or UDP), the public port, the health probe protocol, the health probe path (if you selected HTTP for the health probe protocol), the health probe port, the interval (between load balancer health probes), and the number of retries (before the load balancer decides an endpoint is unavailable).

9. Click OK to create the load balanced set.

10. To create a new load balanced set for a new internal endpoint, on the Join A Load Balanced Set blade, complete the following steps:

    A. Set the Load Balanced Set Type toggle to Internal.

    B. Click the Configure Required Settings ribbon, and select Create A Load Balanced Set.

    C. On the Create A Load Balanced Set blade, provide a name for the set, the protocol (TCP or UDP), the public port, the health probe protocol, the health probe path (if you selected HTTP for the health probe protocol), the health probe port, the interval (between load balancer health probes), and the number of retries (before the load balancer decides an endpoint is unavailable).

    D. Click OK to create the load balanced set.

11. To create a new endpoint and add it to an existing load balanced set, click the Configure Required Settings ribbon, and then click an existing load balanced set to select it.

12. Return to the Join A Load Balanced Set blade, provide an endpoint name and private port for the new endpoint for use by the selected VM, and click OK to join the VM to the load balanced set.

> **NOTE LOAD BALANCED ENDPOINTS AVAILABILITY**
>
> Load balanced endpoints (public or internal) is functionality available only to VMs in the Standard tier and not to VMs in the Basic tier.

Configuring Direct Server Return and keep-alive

During the previous processes of creating and configuring endpoints, you may have noticed the option for enabling Direct Server Return (DSR). When responding to a request from a client, the typical flow is for the request to enter through the load balancer, which then forwards the request to a VM. That VM processes the request and responds to the load balancer, which then forwards the request to the client. DSR changes the last two steps of this process and enables the VM to return the response directly to the client instead of sending it through the load balancer. DSR is most commonly needed to support SQL Server AlwaysOn Availability Groups.

While DSR addresses responses from the VM, keep-alives are intended to keep the TCP connection with the VM open even in the absence of application communication. Keep-alives accomplish this by periodically sending a keep-alive packet from the client application to the server-side application, which instructs both the server-side application and any load balancers along the way not to close the idle connection. TCP keep-alives in the context of Azure VMs were intended to ensure that the Azure load balancer did not close the connection prematurely (at one time, the load balancer had a 4-minute idle timeout). This has since changed, however, and you can now configure the idle timeout for endpoints and load balanced endpoint sets as high as 30 minutes, which is more than sufficient for most applications.

> **MORE INFO**   **KEEP-ALIVES**
>
> If you want some more background reading on keep-alives, the following links provide good information on how to enable it in .NET for a TCP connection and for Windows using the registry.
>
> - .NET   *http://msdn.microsoft.com/en-us/library/system.net.servicepoint.settcpkeepalive.aspx*
> - Windows   *http://blogs.technet.com/b/nettracer/archive/2010/06/03/things-that-you-may-want-to-know-about-tcp-keepalives.aspx*

Configuring Direct Server Return (existing portal)

Direct Server Return can be enabled only during the creation of an endpoint, and it requires that the public and private ports have the same value.

1. Navigate to the Endpoints tab of your VM in the management portal accessed via *https://manage.windowsazure.com*.

2. Click Add on the command bar.

3. Select Add A Stand-Alone Endpoint, and click the right arrow.

4. Provide a name for the new endpoint, the protocol (TCP or UDP), the public port, and the private port (ensuring these are the same), and be sure to select Enable Direct Server Return.

5. Click the check mark to create the endpoint with DSR enabled.

Configuring Direct Server Return (Preview portal)

Currently, Direct Server Return cannot be configured using the Preview portal.

Configuring idle timeout for an endpoint

The idle timeout for a public Azure endpoint can only be configured at the time of creating the endpoint, and can be done with the following Windows PowerShell script:

```
Get-AzureVM -ServiceName "<CloudServiceName>" -Name "<VMName> " |
Add-AzureEndpoint -Name "<EndpointName>" -Protocol "tcp" -PublicPort <PublicPort>
-LocalPort <PrivatePort> -IdleTimeoutInMinutes <NumMinutes> |
Update-AzureVM
```

Configuring idle timeout for a load balanced endpoint set

The idle timeout for a load balanced endpoint set can only be configured after creation, using the following Windows PowerShell script:

```
Set-AzureLoadBalancedEndpoint -ServiceName "<CloudServiceName>" -LBSetName "<SetName>"
-Protocol tcp -LocalPort <PrivatePort> -ProbeProtocol tcp -ProbePort <ProbePort>
-IdleTimeoutInMinutes <NumMinutes>
```

Leveraging name resolution within a cloud service

Azure provides an internal DNS that allows a VM hosted within a cloud service to resolve the IP address of another VM also hosted within that cloud service using the target VM's host name. The host name, and therefore the fully qualified domain name, is set when you provision the VM. If you want to change the VM host name, you must log in to the VM and rename the host using the native operating system's mechanisms. For example, in Windows, you would remote desktop into the VM and, using Server Manager, open the computer name properties, change the computer name, and restart. After the restart, the VM would have a new host name (which you could verify using the management portal).

Configuring firewall rules

Firewalls and firewall rules may be configured on each of the VMs to provide an additional layer of protection for inbound and outbound requests. The actual firewall configuration steps will vary based on the guest operating system and firewall software in use.

In addition to the firewall provided by the guest operating system, VMs can now be created within the portal with security extensions from Trend Micro or Symantec, which provide additional firewall functionality (as well as antivirus and malware and intrusion detection functions). To access these extensions in the existing portal, click New, Virtual Machine, and From Gallery, and then select a Windows Server image. These extensions are listed as check boxes you can select on the last page of the Create a Virtual Machine dialog box.

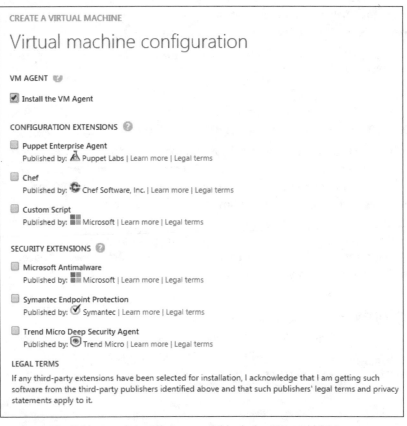

FIGURE 2-2 Available security extensions available during VM provisioning

Objective summary

- By default, VMs can be accessed using either the cloud service DNS name and a port or the VIP address and port.

- Instance-level public IP addresses enable access to a VM using an IP address that will forward requests to the VM, irrespective of the port used.

- The IP address assigned to the cloud service containing a VM can change. To prevent unwanted changes, configure reserved IP addresses.

- Traffic to a VM can be stopped before it reaches the VM endpoint if it does not match permit rules of an access control lists (ACL).

- Both internal and external traffic to VMs can be load balanced, and performed according to the health of the VMs.

- Direct Server Return (which enables a VM to reply to a request directly to the client instead of through the load balancer) and keep-alive (which controls how long an idle connection is maintained open) are two TCP settings that certain server applications may require to function properly.

- Firewall rules and security extensions enable VMs to provide an additional layer of security beyond ACLs.

Objective review

Answer the following questions to test your knowledge of the information in this objective. You can find the answers to these questions and explanations of why each answer choice is correct or incorrect in the "Answers" section at the end of this chapter.

1. Which of the following is *not* true regarding instance-level public IP (PIP) address endpoints? (Choose all that apply.)

   A. Requests using PIPs do not flow through the load balancer.

   B. If you enable PIPs, you can no longer communicate via the VIP and port configured for a VM.

   C. PIPs free you from having to expose a VM endpoint on specific ports.

   D. A PIP can be assigned only to VMs that are a part of a regional virtual network.

2. In which of the following conditions will a reserved IP address be released?

   A. VM associated with it is stopped and de-allocated.

   B. The cloud service using it is deleted.

   C. All VMs using it are deleted.

   D. None of the above

3. How does the Azure load balancer distribute load?

   A. In a round-robin fashion

   B. Randomly

   C. Based on resource utilization

   D. Based on network response times

Objective 2.5: Scale VMs

Similar to Azure Websites, Azure Virtual Machines provides the capability to scale in terms of both instance size and instance count and supports auto-scale on the instance count. However, unlike Websites which can automatically provision new instances as a part of scale out, Virtual Machines must be pre-provisioned in order for auto-scale to turn instances on or off during a scaling operation.

> **This objective covers how to:**
> - Scale up and scale down VM sizes
> - Configure availability sets
> - Configure auto-scale

Scaling up and scaling down VM sizes

Using the management portal or Windows PowerShell, you can scale VM sizes up or down to alter the capacity of the VM, which collectively adjusts:

- The number of VHD disks that can be attached and the total IOPS capacity
- The size of the local temp disk
- The number of CPU cores
- The amount of RAM memory available
- The network performance

Note that there are two pricing tiers for Virtual Machines: Basic and Standard. The Standard tier offers load balancing, auto-scale, and a larger set of VM sizes (high memory, SSD-based D-series) as compared to the Basic tier, which lacks these.

Scaling up and scaling down VM size (existing portal)

You can scale a VM up or down while it is shutdown or even if it is running.

1. Navigate to the Configure tab of your VM in the management portal accessed via *https://manage.windowsazure.com*.

2. From the Instance Size drop-down list, select an instance size. Select a large instance size to scale up or a smaller one to scale down.

3. Click Save on the command bar to apply the change.

Scaling up and scaling down VM size (Preview portal)

To scale a VM up or down in the Preview portal, complete these steps:

1. Navigate to the blade of your VM in the management portal accessed via *https://portal.azure.com*.

2. Scroll down to the Usage area and click the Pricing Tier tile.

3. On the Choose Your Pricing Tier blade, select the new size and tier you would like for the VM.

4. Click Select to apply the new size and tier.

Scaling up and scaling down VM size using Windows PowerShell

The instance size can also be adjusted using the following Windows PowerShell script:

```
Get-AzureVM -ServiceName "<CloudServiceName>" -Name "<VMName>" |
Set-AzureVMSize -InstanceSize "<InstanceSize>" |
Update-AzureVM
```

In the previous script, you specify the name of the cloud service containing your VM, the name of the VM you want to scale, and the label of the size (for example, "A2") to which you want to scale it.

> **NOTE** **INSTANCE SIZES**
>
> At the time of this writing, the following are the valid values for the instance size parameter of Set-AzureVMSize:
>
> ExtraSmall, Small, Medium, Large, ExtraLarge, A5, A6, A7, A8, A9, Basic_A0, Basic_A1, Basic_A2, Basic_A3, Basic_A4, Standard_D1, Standard_D2, Standard_D3, Standard_D4, Standard_D11, Standard_D12, Standard_D13, Standard_D14
>
> For an up-to-the-minute list, see *http://msdn.microsoft.com/library/azure/dn197896.aspx*. 1

Configuring availability sets

Availability sets enable you to improve the availability of VMs deployed to your cloud service by identifying to Azure a group of VMs that should never be brought down simultaneously during updates and that should be physically separated (that is, connected to a separate power source and network switch) so that the failure of a host does not cause all of the VMs in that group to fail. In other words, an availability set does what it says—it describes a set of VMs that Azure will respect to ensure that the service provided by the VMs remains available because at no point in time should all VMs in the set be offline.

By defining an availability set, you constrain how Azure locates your VM in update and fault domains.

Update domains

An update domain constrains how Azure performs updates to the underlying host machine that is running your VM. VMs located in separate update domains will never experience an update (or a restart of the host machine) at the same time. Azure provides a fixed set of five update domains in which it places your VMs in a round-robin process. When you add VMs to an availability set, Azure places the first five VMs in separate update domains, then continues to distribute additional VMs across update domains in a round-robin fashion, assigning the sixth VM to the first update domain, the seventh VM to the second update domain, and so on until all VMs have been assigned to one of the five update domains. The constraint on update domains is that Azure will never bring down more than one update domain at a time, effectively ensuring that when Azure updates the host machines, never more than 50 percent of your VMs will be affected (assuming you have two VMs) or, if you are filling all update domains, 20 percent (assuming you have five or more VMs).

Fault domains

Whereas update domains apply to the roll out of host machine updates, fault domains consider isolation in terms of power and network. When two VMs are placed in separate fault domains, they will never be located such that they share the power source or network switch, which basically means that they will not be on the same host machine or even on the same server rack as one another. When you add VMs to an availability set, they are distributed between two fault domains in round-robin fashion.

In short, the strategic placement of your VMs across update and fault domains is controlled simply by their membership in an availability set.

Availability sets and application tiers

For multi-tier applications (such as those having separate front-end, middle, and back-end tiers), it is a best practice to place all the VMs belonging to a single tier in a single availability set and to have separate availability sets for each application tier. This helps ensure that at no point are all instances for a particular tier in the solution down and, therefore, that the complete solution across all tiers is available.

Configuring availability sets

There are multiples ways to define an availability set and to configure the VMs that belong to it. When you are creating a new VM, you can create a new availability set and add the VM to it or you can specify an existing availability set and add the new VM to it. The same options exist if you have an existing VM. The primary requirement of an availability set is that all member VMs must belong to the same cloud service.

Configuring an availability set (existing portal)

To configure an availability set in the existing portal, complete these steps:

1. Navigate to the management portal accessed via *https://manage.windowsazure.com*.

2. To create a new VM and associate it with an availability group, complete the following steps:

    A. Click New on the command bar, and then click Compute, Virtual Machine, From Gallery.

    B. Select the image from which to create the VM, and click the right arrow.

    C. Provide a name, tier, instance size, and administrator credentials, and click the right arrow.

    D. On the Virtual Machine Configuration screen, select a cloud service, and provide a DNS name, region/VNET, and storage account.

    E. To create a new availability set, from the Availability Set drop-down list, select Create An Availability Set, and then provide a name for it in the text box. To use an existing availability set, select it from the drop-down list.

  F. Specify any endpoints desired, and then click the right arrow.

  G. Select any VM agents, and click the check mark to provision the new VM in the availability set.

 3. To add an existing VM to an availability set, complete the following steps:

  A. Navigate to the Configure tab for your VM.

  B. To create a new availability set, from the Availability Set drop-down list, select Create An Availability Set, and then provide a name for it in the text box. To use an existing availability set, select it from the drop-down list.

  C. Click Save on the command bar to add the VM to the availability set.

Configuring an availability set (Preview portal)

To configure an availability set in the Preview portal, complete these steps:

 1. Navigate to management portal accessed via *https://portal.azure.com*.

 2. To create a new VM and associate it with an availability group, complete the following steps:

  A. Click New on the command bar, and select one of the images, or navigate to the Marketplace to select the image you want to use.

  B. On the Create VM blade, provide a host name, user name, and password for the new VM.

  C. Select a pricing tier.

  D. Click Optional Configuration to display that blade.

  E. Review or change the operating system settings.

  F. On the Optional Config blade, click Availability Set.

  G. On the Availability Set blade, to use an existing availability set, click its name in the list. To create a new availability set, click New on the command bar. In the blade that appears, provide a name for the new availability set in the text box, and click OK.

  H. Complete the VM configuration by adjusting the Network, Storage Account and Diagnostics settings as desired.

  I. Click OK, and then click Create to provision the VM in the availability set.

 3. To add an existing VM to an availability set, complete the following steps:

  A. Navigate to the blade of your VM in the management portal.

  B. Scroll down to the Configuration area, and click the Availability Set tile.

  C. On the Availability Set blade, to use an existing availability set, click its name in the list. To create a new availability set, click New on the command bar. In the blade that appears, provide a name for the new availability set in the text box, and click OK.

Configuring an availability set using Windows PowerShell

Currently, an availability set can be created using Windows PowerShell only during the process of creating a new VM:

```
New-AzureVMConfig -Name <VMName> -InstanceSize <InstanceSize> -ImageName <ImageName>
-AvailabilitySetName <AvailabilitySetName> |
Add-AzureProvisioningConfig -Windows -Password <Password> -AdminUsername <UserName> |
New-AzureVM -ServiceName <CloudServiceName>
```

After the preceding command, use the following cmdlet to provision and start the VM:

```
Start-AzureVM -ServiceName <CloudServiceName> -Name <VMName>
```

After you create it, the availability set for a given VM can be changed using the following Windows PowerShell script:

```
Get-AzureVM -ServiceName "<CloudServiceName>" -Name "<VMName>" |
Set-AzureAvailabilitySet -AvailabilitySetName "<AvailabilitySetName>" |
Update-AzureVM
```

Configuring auto-scale

Auto-scale automatically adjusts the number of VM instances running within an availability set based on load or according to a schedule. It does this by turning on additional VM instances in the availability set during a scale-up event, and stopping (de-allocating) them during a scale-down event. For this to happen, these machines must have already been provisioned, but they can be in the stopped (de-allocated) state as they wait for auto-scale to turn them on. Auto-scale is configured at the level of the availability set within the cloud service, much like it is configured at the level of the web hosting plan for Websites or at the role level for web and worker roles. Auto-scale can be configured to make scaling decisions based on a schedule (predefined or custom schedules are supported) or with respect to the queue depth of an Azure Storage queue or Service Bus queue.

Using auto-scale is predicated upon a few requirements. To begin, all VMs involved must be in the Standard tier (the Basic tier does not provide auto-scale support). All the VMs you want to turn on or off with auto-scale must belong to the same availability set, and because you cannot create a single availability set that includes VMs spanning multiple cloud services, these VMs must also exist within the same cloud service. Also, all VMs in the availability set must be of the same instance size or you will be prevented from configuring auto-scale.

Configuring VM auto-scale (existing portal)

To configure VM auto-scale in the existing portal, complete the following steps:

1. Navigate to the management portal accessed via *https://manage.windowsazure.com*.

2. Navigate to the cloud service containing your VM, and click the Scale tab.

3. To configure auto-scale to operate according to a schedule, click Set Up Schedule Times, and, in the dialog box that appears, do the following to define the schedules:

- Enable usage of the day/night recurring schedule by selecting Different Scale Settings For Day And Night, and then using the Day Starts, Day Ends, and Time Zone drop-down lists to specify what hours are considered daytime (Azure will infer the remaining hours are night time).

- Enable usage of the weekdays and weekends recurring schedule by electing Different Scale Settings For Weekdays And Weekends, where weekdays are defined as Monday morning through Friday evening and weekends are Friday evening through Monday morning. You can adjust the time that is used for morning and for evening by using the Day Starts, Day Ends, and Time Zone drop-down lists.

- Enable usage of specific data ranges by filling in the grid below Specific Dates. You can specify a user-friendly name for the date range, a start date and time, and an end date and time. You can add multiple date ranges as long as they do not overlap.

4. When you are finished defining schedules, click the check mark to make these schedules configurable on the Scale tab. Return to the Scale tab and complete the following steps:

   A. Select the newly defined schedule you want to configure from the Edit Scale Settings For Schedule drop-down list.

   B. Using the Instance Count slider, adjust the number of instances to the target number for your website during that schedule.

   C. Repeat the previous two steps as necessary for any other schedules you have defined.

   D. Click Save to save both the newly defined schedules and your instance count configurations for each schedule.

5. To scale by CPU, complete the following steps:

   A. In the Scale by Metric toggle, click CPU.

   B. Using the Target CPU slider, specify the lower threshold below which scale-down actions will be taken. Do this by entering a value in the left-most text box or by dragging the left-most slider handle.

   C. Repeat the previous step to define the threshold for the scale-up action, using the right-most text box or slider handle to adjust the threshold.

   D. Using the Instance Count slider, define the minimum and maximum number of instances that auto-scale can reach at any point in time.

E. Using the Scale Up By slider, select the number of instances to add at one time and the cool-off period to wait after scaling up from the Scale Up Wait Time drop-down list.

F. Similarly, configure the number of instances to scale down by using the Scale Down By and Scale Down Wait Time settings.

G. Click Save to apply your auto-scale by metric rules.

6. To scale by queue depth, complete the following steps:

7. On the Scale By Metric toggle, click Queue.

8. Using the Instance Count slider, define the minimum and maximum number of instances that auto-scale can reach at any point in time.

9. Select the storage account and queue name (for an Azure queue) or service bus namespace and queue name (for a Service Bus queue) to monitor queue depth.

10. In the Target Per Machine text box, specify the target number of messages that Azure will scale to support per VM.

11. Using the Scale Up By slider, select the number of instances to add at one time and the cool-off period to wait after scaling up from the Scale Up Wait Time drop-down list.

12. Similarly, configure the number of instances to scale down by using the Scale Down By and Scale Down Wait Time settings.

13. Click Save to apply your auto-scale by metric rules.

Also note that you can combine schedule and metric-based scaling. When you define a schedule and select that schedule from the Edit Scale Settings for Schedule drop-down list, you can configure scaling by CPU or by queue conditions within the time frame represented by that schedule.

Configuring VM auto-scale (Preview portal)

Auto-scale cannot currently be configured using the Preview portal.

Configuring VM auto-scale using Windows PowerShell

Auto-scale cannot currently be configured using Windows PowerShell.

Objective summary

- Azure VM sizes control the capacity of the resources available to a VM instance. The size can be scaled up and scaled down using the management portal or Windows PowerShell.

- Availability sets list VMs that should never be updated (or fail) together, such that within the set, a VM is always available. You should typically create an availability set for each logical tier of your application.

- Auto-scale for VMs relies on availability sets to contain the list of pre-provisioned VMs that auto-scale can start up to scale up or shut down to scale down.

Objective review

Answer the following questions to test your knowledge of the information in this objective. You can find the answers to these questions and explanations of why each answer choice is correct or incorrect in the "Answers" section at the end of this chapter.

1. Which of the following are true regarding the capacity and performance-related features that are affected by changing an instance size? (Choose all that apply.)

    A. The number of attachable disks

    B. The size of attachable disks

    C. The number of CPU cores

    D. The amount of RAM

2. Which of these is *not* true regarding availability sets?

   A. All VMs within an availability set must have the same instance size.

   B. The VMs within an availability set can be within different cloud services.

   C. It is a best practice to place VMs from a single application tier in the same availability set.

   D. You can assign a VM to an availability set after it has been created.

3. On what resource do you configure auto-scale?

   A. Cloud service

   B. Virtual machine

   C. Availability set

   D. Update domain

Objective 2.6: Design and implement VM storage

There is more to managing your VM storage than attaching data disks. In this objective, you explore multiple considerations that are critical to your VM storage strategy.

> **This objective covers how to:**
> - Plan for storage capacity
> - Configure storage pools
> - Configure disk caching
> - Configure geo-replication
> - Configure shared storage using Azure File storage

Planning for storage capacity

VMs leverage a local disk provided by the host machine for the temp drive (D) and Azure Storage for the operating system and data disks, wherein each data disk is a VHD stored as a blob in Blob storage. The temp drive, however, uses a local disk provided by the host machine. The physical disk underlying this temp drive may be shared among all the VMs running on the host and, therefore, may be subject to a noisy neighbor that competes with your VM instance for read/write IOPS and bandwidth.

For the operating system and data disks, use of Azure storage blobs means that the storage capacity of your VM in terms of both performance (for example, IOPS and read/write throughput MB/s) and size (such as in GBs) is governed by the capacity of a single blob in Blob storage. For VMs, the critical scalability targets for a single blob include the following:

- Maximum of 500 IOPS for Standard tier instances, 300 IOPS for Basic tier instances
- Maximum throughput of 60 MB/s
- Maximum size of 1 terabyte

> **MORE INFO   IOPS**
>
> An IOPS is a unit of measure counting the number of input/output operations per second and serves as a useful measure for the number of read, write, or read/write operations that can be completed in a period of time for data sets of a certain size (usually 8 KB). To learn more, you can read about IOPS at *http://en.wikipedia.org/wiki/IOPS*.

Given the scalability targets, how can you configure a VM that has an IOPS capacity greater than 500 IOPS or 60 MB/s throughput, or provides more than 1 terabyte of storage? The answer is to use multiple blobs, which means using multiple disks striped into a single volume (in Windows Server 2012 and later VMs, the approach is to use Storage Spaces and create a storage pool across all of the disks). For Azure VMs, the general rule governing the number of disks you can attach is twice the number of CPU cores. For example, an A4-sized VM instance has 8 cores and can mount 16 disks. Currently, there are only a few exceptions to this rule: The A9 and D-series instances, which map on one times the number of cores (so an A9 has 16 cores and can mount 16 disks). Also, the maximum number of disks that can currently be mounted to a VM is 16. This means that the theoretical maximum storage capacity you can provision for a Standard tier VM having 16 disks mounted in a storage pool is 8,000 IOPS, throughput that can exceed 60 MB/s (depending on the data access pattern), and 16 terabytes of storage.

> **MORE INFO   HOW MANY DISKS CAN YOU MOUNT?**
>
> As the list of VM sizes grows and changes over time, you should review the following web page that details the number of disks you can mount by VM size and tier: *http://msdn. microsoft.com/library/azure/dn197896.aspx*.

Configuring storage pools

Storage Spaces enables you to group together a set of disks and then create a volume from the available aggregate capacity. Assuming you have created your VM and attached all of the empty disks you want to it, the following steps explain how to create a storage pool from those disks, then create a storage space in that pool, and from that storage space, mount a volume you can access with a drive letter.

1. Launch Remote Desktop and connect to the VM on which you want to configure the storage space.

2. If Server Manager does not appear by default, run it from the Start screen.

3. Click the File And Storage Services tile near the middle of the window.

4. In the navigation pane, click Storage Pools.

5. In the Storage Pools area, click the Tasks drop-down list and select New Storage Pool.

6. In the New Storage Pool Wizard, click Next on the first page.

7. Provide a name for the new storage pool, and click Next.

8. Select all the disks you want to include in your storage pool, and click Next.

9. Click Create, and then click Close to create the storage pool.

After you create a storage pool, create a new virtual disk that uses it by completing the following steps:

1. In Server Manager, in the Storage Pools dialog box, right-click your newly created storage pool and select New Virtual Disk.

2. Click Next on the first page of the wizard.

3. Select your storage pool, and click Next.

4. Provide a name for the new virtual disk, and click Next.

5. Select the simple storage layout (because your VHDs are already triple replicated by Azure Storage, you do not need additional redundancy), and click Next.

6. For the provisioning type, leave the selection as Fixed. Click Next.

7. For the size of the volume, select Maximum so that the new virtual disk uses the complete capacity of the storage pool. Click Next.

8. On the Summary page, click Create.

9. Click Close when the process completes.

When the New Virtual Disk Wizard closes, the New Volume Wizard appears. Follow these steps to create a volume:

1. Click Next to skip past the first page of the wizard.

2. On the Server And Disk Selection page, select the disk you just created. Click Next.

3. Leave the volume size set to the maximum value and click Next.

4. Leave Assign A Drive Letter selected and select a drive letter to use for your new drive. Click Next.

5. Provide a name for the new volume, and click Next.

6. Click Create.

7. When the process completes, click Close.

8. Open Windows Explorer to see your new drive listed.

Applications running within your VM can use the new drive and benefit from the increased IOPS and total storage capacity that results from having multiple blobs backing your multiple VHDs grouping in a storage pool.

> **MORE INFO**   **D-SERIES AND SSD DRIVES**
>
> At the time of this writing, the D-series of VMs was just announced, which provide your VM an SSD drive mounted at D:\. Be careful. This disk should still be used only for temporary storage of page files, buffers, and other forms of non-persistent data that can benefit from the high IOPS and higher read/write throughput.
>
> For more information, read *http://azure.microsoft.com/blog/2014/10/06/d-series-performance-expectations/.*

Configuring disk caching

Each disk you attach to a VM has a host cache preference setting for managing a local cache used for read or read/write operations that can improve performance (and even reduce storage transaction costs) in certain situations by averting a read or write to Azure Storage. This local cache does not live within your VM instance; it is external to the VM and resides on the machine hosting your VM. The local cache uses a combination of memory and disk on the host (outside of your control). There are three cache options:

- **None**   No caching is performed.
- **Read Only**   Assuming an empty cache or the desired data is not found in the local cache, reads read from Azure Storage and are then cached in local cache. Writes go directly to Azure Storage.
- **Read/Write**   Assuming an empty cache or the desired data is not found in the local cache, reads read from Azure Storage and are then cached in local cache. Writes go to the local cache and at some later point (determined by algorithms of the local cache) to Azure Storage.

When you create a new VM, the default is set to Read/Write for operating system disks and None for data disks. Operating system disks are limited to read only or read/write, data disks can disable caching using the None option. The reasoning for this is that Azure Storage can provide a higher rate of random I/Os than the local disk used for caching. For predominantly random I/O workloads, therefore, it is best to set the cache to None and let Azure Storage handle the load directly. Because most applications will have predominantly random I/O workloads, the host cache preference is set to None by default for the data disks that would be supporting the applications.

However, for sequential I/O workloads, the local cache will provide some performance improvement and also minimize transaction costs (because the request to storage is averted). Operating system startup sequences are great examples of highly sequential I/O workloads and why the host cache preference is enabled for the operating system disks.

You can configure the host cache preference when you create and attach an empty disk to a VM or change it after the fact.

Configuring disk caching (existing portal)

To configure disk caching in the management portal, complete the following steps:

1. Navigate to the VM in the management portal accessed via *https://manage.windowsazure.com*, and click the Dashboard tab.

2. Click Attach on the command bar, and select Attach Empty Disk.

3. In the Attach An Empty Disk To The Virtual Machine dialog box, provide a file name for the new disk and a size.

4. Use the Host Cache Preference toggle to configure the cache setting.

5. Click the Read Only or Read/Write toggle button to create the disk with the host cache preference, and then click the check mark to apply it.

6. To change the host cache preference at a later time, click Virtual Machines in the navigation bar to view the list of VMs in your subscription.

7. Click the Disks tab.

8. Click the disk whose cache setting you want to edit.

9. Click Edit Cache on the command bar.

10. In the Edit Host Cache Preference dialog box that appears, use the Host Cache Preference toggle to set the value you want, and click the check mark to apply it.

Configuring disk caching (Preview portal)

To configure disk caching using the Preview portal, complete the following steps:

1. Navigate to the blade for your VM in the management portal accessed via *https://portal.azure.com*.

2. Scroll down to the Configuration section, and click the Disks tile.

3. On the Disks blade, click Attach New on the command bar.

4. In the Choose A Container blade that appears, select a storage account and container for your new disk, and then click OK.

5. Return to the Attach A New Disk blade, provide a file name and size for the new disk. Use the Host Caching toggle to configure the cache setting.

6. Click OK to create the disk with the host caching setting.

7. To change the host caching setting at a later time, return to the blade for your VM in the portal and click the Disks tile under the Configuration section.

8. On the Disks blade, click the disk whose setting you want to alter.

9. In the blade that appears, use the New Host Caching toggle to set the value you want, and click Save on the command bar to apply it.

Configuring geo-replication

With Azure Storage, you can leverage geo-replication for blobs to maintain replicated copies of your VHD blobs in multiple regions around the world in addition to three copies that are maintained within the datacenter. However, note that geo-replication is not synchronized across blob files and, therefore, VHD disks, which means writes for a file that is spread across multiple disks, as happens when you use storage pools, could be replicated out of order. As a result, if you mount the replicated copies to a VM, the disks will almost certainly be corrupt. To avoid this problem, configure the disks to use locally redundant replication which does not add any additional availability and reduces costs (since geo-replicated storage is more expensive).

Configuring shared storage using Azure File storage

If you have ever used a local network on-premises to access files on a remote machine through a Universal Naming Convention (UNC) path like \\server\share, or if you have mapped a drive letter to a network share, you will find Azure File storage familiar.

Azure File storage enables your VMs to access files using a share located within the same region as your VMs. It does not matter if your VMs' data disks are located in a different storage account or even if your share uses a storage account that is within a different Azure subscription than your VMs. As long as your shares are created within the same region as your VMs, those VMs will have access.

Azure File storage provides support for most of the Server Message Block (SMB) 2.1 protocol, which means it supports the common scenarios you might encounter accessing files across the network:

- Supporting applications that rely on file shares for access to data
- Providing access to shared application settings
- Centralizing storage of logs, metrics, and crash dumps
- Storing common tools and utilities needed for development, administration, or setup

Azure File storage is built upon the same underlying infrastructure as Azure Storage, inheriting the same availability, durability, and scalability characteristics.

Azure File storage requires an Azure Storage account. Access is controlled with the storage account name and key; therefore, as long as your VMs are in the same region, they can access the share using your storage credentials. Note that currently this means you cannot mount shares across regions (even if you set up VNET-to-VNET connectivity) or access shares from your on-premises resources (if you are using a point-to-site or site-to-site VPN with a VNET). Also, while Azure Storage provides support for read-only secondary access to your blobs, this does not enable you to access your shares from the secondary region.

Within each Azure Storage account, you can define one or more shares. Each share is an SMB 2.1 file share. All directories and files must be created within this share, and it can contain an unlimited number of files and directories (limited in depth by the length of the path name and a maximum depth of 250 subdirectories). Note that you cannot create a share below another share. Within the share or any directory below it, each file can be up to 1 terabyte (the maximum size of a single file in Blob storage), and the maximum capacity of a share is 5 terabytes. In terms of performance, a share has a maximum of 1,000 IOPS (when measured using 8-KB operations) and a throughput of 60 MB/s, so it can offer double the maximum IOPS as compared to a single file in Blob storage (which has a cap of 500 IOPS).

A unique feature of Azure File storage is that you can manage shares (create or delete shares, list shares, get share ETag and LastModified properties, get or set user-defined share metadata key and value pairs), and share content (list directories and files, create directories and files, get a file, delete a file, get file properties, get or set user-defined metadata, and get or set ranges of bytes within a file) using REST APIs available through endpoints named *https://<accountName>.file.core.windows.net/<shareName>* and through the SMB protocol. In contrast to Azure Storage, Azure File storage only allows you to use a REST API to manage the files. This can prove beneficial to certain application scenarios. For example, it can be helpful if you have a web application (perhaps running in an Azure website) receiving uploads from the browser. Your web application can upload the files through the REST API to the share, but your back-end applications running on a VM can process those files by accessing them using a network share. In situations like this, the REST API will respect any file locks placed on files by clients using the SMB protocol.

> **MORE INFO** **FILE LOCK INTERACTION BETWEEN SMB AND REST**
>
> If you are curious about how file locking is managed between SMB and REST endpoints for clients interacting with the same file at the same time, the following is a good resource for more information: *http://msdn.microsoft.com/en-us/library/azure/dn194265.aspx*.

Creating a file share

Because it is layered on Azure Storage, Azure File storage functionality may not be available within older Azure Storage accounts you may have already provisioned. You may have to create a new Azure Storage account to be able to use Azure File storage. With a compatible Storage account in place, currently the only way to provision a share is to use the Windows PowerShell cmdlets for Azure Storage v0.8.5 or later. The following cmdlet first creates an Azure Storage context, which encapsulates your Storage account name and key, and then uses that context to create the share with the name of your choosing:

```
$ctx = New-AzureStorageContext <Storage-AccountName> <Storage-AccountKey>

New-AzureStorageShare <ShareName> -Context $ctx
```

With a share in place, you can access it from any VM that is in the same region as your share.

Mounting the share

To access the share within a VM, you mount it to your VM. You can mount a share to a VM so that it will remain available indefinitely to the VM, regardless of restarts. The following steps show you how to accomplish this, assuming you are using a Windows Server guest operating system within your VM.

1. Launch Remote Desktop to connect to the VM where you want to mount the share.

2. Open a Windows PowerShell prompt or the command prompt within the VM.

3. So they are available across restarts, add your Azure Storage account credentials to the Windows Credentials Manager using the following command:

   ```
   cmdkey /add:<Storage-AccountName>.file.core.windows.net /user:<Storage-
   AccountName> /pass:<Storage-AccountKey>
   ```

4. Mount the file share using the stored credentials by using the following command (which you can issue from the Windows PowerShell prompt or a command prompt). Note that you can use any available drive letter (drive Z is typically used).

   ```
   net use z: \\<Storage-AccountName>.file.core.windows.net\<ShareName>
   ```

5. The previous command mounts the share to drive Z, but if the VM is restarted, this share may disappear if net use was not configured for persistent connections (it is enabled for persistent connection by default, but that can be changed). To ensure a persistent share that will survive a restart, use the following command that adds the persistent switch with a value of *yes*.

```
net use z: \\<Storage-AccountName>.file.core.windows.net\<ShareName>
/Persistent: YES
```

6. To verify that your network share was added (or continues to exist) at any time, run the following command:

```
net use
```

After you mount the share, you can work with its contents as you would work with the contents of any other network drive. Drive Z will show a 5-terabyte drive mounted in Windows Explorer.

Accessing files within the share

With a share mounted within a VM, you may next consider how to get your files and folders into that share. There are multiple approaches to this, and you should choose the approach that makes the most sense in your scenario.

- **Remote Desktop (RDP)**   If you are running a Windows guest operating system, you can remote desktop into a VM that has access to the share. As a part of configuring your RDP session, you can mount the drives from your local machine so that they are visible using Windows Explorer in the remote session. Then you can copy and paste files between the drives using Windows Explorer in the remote desktop session. Alternately, you can copy files using Windows Explorer on your local machine and then paste them into the share within Windows Explorer running in the RDP session.

- **AZCopy**   Using AZCopy, you can recursively upload directories and files to a share from your local machine to the remote share, as well as download from the share to your local machine. For examples of how to do this, see *http://blogs.msdn.com/b/windowsazurestorage/archive/2014/05/12/introducing-microsoft-azure-file-service.aspx*.

- **Azure PowerShell**   You can use the Azure PowerShell cmdlets to upload or download a single file at a time. You use Set-AzureStorageFileContent (*http://msdn.microsoft.com/library/ad030d10-8c7c-481a-a58d-f10404bec338*) and Get-AzureStorageFileContent (*http://msdn.microsoft.com/en-us/library/dn806384.aspx*) to upload and download, respectively.

- **Storage Client Library**   If you are writing an application in .NET, you can use the Azure Storage Client Library, which provides a convenience layer atop the REST APIs. You will find all the classes you need below the Microsoft.WindowsAzure.Storage. File namespace, primarily using the CloudFileDirectory and CloudFile classes to access directories and file content within the share. For an example of using these classes, see *http://azure.microsoft.com/en-us/documentation/articles/storage-dotnet-how-to-use-files/#create-console-app.*

- **REST APIs**   If you prefer to communicate directly using any client that can perform REST style requests, you can use REST API. The reference documentation for REST APIs is available at *http://msdn.microsoft.com/en-us/library/azure/dn167006.aspx/.*

While you do have several options, note that currently you cannot access files within a share using the existing tools commonly used for browsing Azure Storage blobs.

Thought experiment
Performance targets

In this thought experiment, apply what you've learned about this objective. You can find answers to these questions in the "Answers" section at the end of this chapter.

Assume you have profiled your Windows Server hosted application running on-premises and discovered it needs close to 8,000 IOPS during peak loads.

1. What size of VM would you choose, and how many disks would you need to attach?

2. How would you configure the disks within Windows Server?

Objective summary

- Storage capacity for VMs is dictated by the scalability limits (IOPS, throughput, and maximum file size) of Azure Storage as well as per-VM limits that adjust with the VM size (the number of VHD disks that can be attached).

- Disk caching provides a cache on the machine hosting your VM that can avert the need to read from or write to Blob storage. The options are None, Read Only, and Read/Write.

- Geo-replication should not be used for Azure Storage accounts that store VHDs because the added redundancy does not provide additional protection against corrupting the data and may in fact result in data loss if you attempt to restore from a geo-replication.

- Azure File storage enables you to use network shares to provide distributed access to files from your VMs.

Objective review

Answer the following questions to test your knowledge of the information in this objective. You can find the answers to these questions and explanations of why each answer choice is correct or incorrect in the "Answers" section at the end of this chapter.

1. Which of the following is *not* an option for managing and interacting with Azure File storage? (Choose all that apply.)

    A. AZCopy

    B. Windows PowerShell

    C. Storage Client Library

    D. REST APIs

    E. SMB 3.0

2. Which of the following scenarios is *not* a valid option for host caching?

    A. An operating system disk with a host caching setting of None

    B. An operating system disk with a host caching setting of Read Only

    C. A data disk with a host caching setting of None

    D. A data disk with a host caching setting Ready Only

3. If you are using storage pools, which of the following is a valid replication option for the Azure Storage account that stores the VHD blobs? (Choose all that apply.)

    A. Locally redundant

    B. Geo-redundant

    C. Read-access geo-redundant

    D. Zone redundant

Objective 2.7: Monitor VMs

Monitoring an Azure VM involves collecting and analyzing metrics as well as collecting log data from system log files and from applications running within the VM. You can configure an email alert to an administrator that's triggered when certain criteria involving these metrics is met. With monitoring, you gain insight into the status of your VMs, their resource utilization, their operational health, and diagnostic details that can help you troubleshoot problems.

Configuring monitoring and diagnostics

When you provision a VM, by default you install the Azure Virtual Machine Agent, which installs and manages extensions running within your VM. Both Windows and Linux VMs collect the following metrics at the host level. In other words, no extension needs to be installed to collect them out of the box:

- Disk read, disk write (in terms of KB/s or MB/s)
- CPU percentage
- Network in, network out (in terms of KB/s or MB/s)

On Windows guest operating system VMs, the agent also installs the IaaSDiagnostics extension for collecting monitoring and diagnostic data. You can enable diagnostics, and when you do, the IaaSDiagnostics extension is installed and used to collect additional metrics. The data collection can be configured to include data from the following groups of performance counter data:

- Basic metrics
- Network and web metrics
- .NET metrics

The diagnostics can also be configured to include data collected from the various logs:

- Windows event logs: system, security, and application logs
- Diagnostic infrastructure logs
- IIS logs

These additional diagnostics are collected to tables within an Azure Storage account that you designate. Metric data is written to the WADPerformanceCountersTable, with aggregates of these performance counter metrics aggregated to the minute or to the hour written to tables that start with the name WADMetricsPT1M for by minute and WADMetricsPT1H for by hour. All event log entries for the three event logs are written to the WADWindowsEventLogsTable, where the log is indicated by the Channels column, which has the values System, Security, or Application. Diagnostic infrastructure logs are written to the WADDiagnosticInfrastructure-LogsTable, and application logs are stored in WADLogsTable. The IIS logs are different in that they are written as blobs to Blob storage under the wad-iis-log-files container.

Configuring monitoring and diagnostics (existing portal)

Monitoring and diagnostics cannot be configured using the existing portal.

Configuring monitoring and diagnostics (Preview portal)

To configure monitoring and diagnostics using the Preview portal, complete the following steps:

1. Navigate to the management portal accessed via *https://portal.azure.com*.

2. To enable and configure monitoring and diagnostics while provisioning a new VM, complete the following steps:

3. Click New on the command bar, and select one of the images, or navigate to the Marketplace to select the image you want to use.

4. On the Create VM blade, provide a host name, user name, and password for the new VM.

5. Select a pricing tier.

6. Click Optional Configuration to display that blade.

7. On the Optional Config blade, click Diagnostics.

8. On the Diagnostics blade, use the Status toggle to turn on the option.

9. Select an Azure Storage account in which to store the metrics and diagnostic logs.

10. Note that if you want to select which groups of metrics and logs you want to enable, you will have to do this after the VM is created.

11. Click OK.

12. Complete the VM configuration by adjusting the network, storage account, and diagnostics as desired.

13. Click OK, and then click Create to provision the VM with monitoring and diagnostics enabled.

14. To enable and configure monitoring and diagnostics for an existing VM, complete the following steps:

15. Navigate to the blade for your VM.

16. Scroll down to the Monitoring section and click any of the graphs (CPU, Disk read and write, Network in and out).

17. In the blade that appears, click Diagnostics on the command bar.

18. On the Diagnostics blade, use the Status toggle to turn on the option.

19. Select an Azure Storage account in which to store the metrics and diagnostic logs.

20. Select the check box next to the metric and log groups you want to enable.

21. Click OK to apply the change to the VM. Note that it may take a few minutes for data to appear within your Azure Storage account.

> **IMPORTANT** **DIAGNOSTICS ON LINUX VMS**
>
> Currently, monitoring and diagnostics data beyond disk read, disk write, CPU percentage, and network in and network out cannot be enabled or viewed for Linux VMs.

Configuring endpoint monitoring

In addition to monitoring data collected within a VM by an extension, you can also enable outside-in monitoring of HTTP or HTTPS web endpoints provided by your VM, where Azure itself makes GET requests against these endpoints periodically (and from configurable locations around the world) and exposes additional metrics that report on the latency and availability experienced.

Configuring endpoint monitoring (existing portal)

To configure endpoint monitoring in the management portal, complete the following steps:

1. Navigate to the Configure tab of your VM on the management portal accessed via *https://manage.windowsazure.com*.

2. Scroll down to the Monitoring section.

3. Provide a short name for the endpoint and the URL you want Azure to ping. Also pick one to three locations from which to ping.

4. To add another, different URL to ping, fill in the row that was added as soon you started filling in the first row with a name.

5. Click Save on the command bar to apply the changes.

Configuring endpoint monitoring (Preview portal)

You cannot configure web endpoint monitoring using the Preview portal.

Configuring alerts

After your VM is configured to collect metrics or monitor endpoints, you can configure alerts that send an email when a particular threshold is crossed.

Configuring alerts (existing portal)

To configure alerts in the management portal, complete the following steps:

1. Navigate to the management portal accessed via *https://manage.windowsazure.com*.

2. In the main navigation pane, click Management Services.

3. The Alert tab should open automatically. Click Add Rule on the command bar.

4. In the Define Alert dialog box, provide a short name for your alert as well as a description to help you recognize the alert in the future.

5. For the service type, select Virtual Machine, and for the service name, select the cloud service containing the VM for which you want to configure an alert. Click the right arrow at the bottom to move to the next step.

6. In the Define A Condition For Notifications dialog box, select the metric to define your threshold condition. If you have enabled endpoint monitoring for the selected VM, in addition to the standard set of metrics (memory, CPU, data and HTTP status counts, and so on), there are entries for response time and uptime as measured from each of the configured monitoring locations.

7. In the Condition text box, indicate how to compare the selected metric's value against the threshold value you type in the Threshold text box.

8. Specify a window of time over which to compute the rule.

9. Select the desired email actions by selecting the appropriate check boxes.

10. Click the check mark to create the new rule, which is automatically enabled.

Configuring alerts (Preview portal)

To configure alerts using the Preview portal, complete the following steps:

1. Navigate to the blade for your VM using the management portal accessed via *https://portal.azure.com*.

2. Scroll down to the Operations area.

3. Click the Alert Rules tile.

4. On the Alert Rules blade, click Add Alert.

5. On the Add An Alert Rule blade, select the metric to define your threshold condition.

6. In the Condition drop-down list, select an option that indicates how to compare the selected metric's value against the threshold value you type in the Threshold text box.

7. Specify a period of time over which to compute the rule by selecting an option from the Period drop-down list.

8. Select the Email The Service Administrators And Co-Administrators check box.

9. Add an additional administrator to the email notification by entering an email address in the Additional Administrator Email text box.

10. Click OK to create the new rule.

Monitoring metrics

You can assess the status and health of your VM by viewing its metrics in the portal, by querying table storage for diagnostic logs, or by downloading IIS logs from Blob storage.

Monitoring metrics (existing portal)

You can use the existing portal to monitor a set of metrics on a single graph and a single table by completing the following steps:

1. Navigate to the Dashboard tab of your VM in the management portal accessed via *https://manage.windowsazure.com*.

2. To view detailed metrics for your VM, navigate to the Monitor tab. A chart of the collected metrics is displayed at the top, and a tabular form of the same metrics is displayed at the bottom. To add additional metrics, click Add Metrics on the command bar, and select the desired metrics or endpoint statistics.

3. To view the status of alert rules you have set up, in the navigation pane, click Management Services. A list of all the alerts you have configured appears along with their status.

Monitoring metrics (Preview portal)

Using the Preview portal, you can change the metrics charted on your VM's blade or you can drill into any of the charts and change the metrics displayed in detail by completing the following steps:

1. Navigate to the blade for your VM using the management portal accessed via *https://portal.azure.com*.

2. Scroll down to the Monitoring section.

3. To change the summary metrics displayed within the tile, complete the following steps:

    A. Right-click any of the graphs (by default these are CPU, Disk read and write, Network in and out). In the context menu that appears, click Edit Chart.

    B. On the Edit Chart blade, select a time frame from which to compute the aggregate metrics (past hour, today, past week, custom). If you select custom, specify the date range using the two date-time pickers.

C. Choose up to two metrics to chart.

D. Click Save to update the chart.

4. To analyze metrics in greater detail, complete the following steps:

A. Click any of the graphs (by default these are CPU, Disk read and write, Network in and out).

B. On the Metric blade that appears, observe that you have a large chart you can point to to get metric details at a point in time, a tabular representation of the charted metrics, and a summary of any configured alerts.

C. To change the metric displayed on this chart, right-click the chart and select Edit Chart.

D. On the Edit Chart blade, select a time frame from which to compute the aggregate metrics (past hour, today, past week, custom). If you select custom, specify the date range using the two date-time pickers.

E. Select up to two metrics to chart.

F. Click Save to update the metrics selection and return to the Metrics blade.

Viewing event logs, diagnostic infrastructure logs, and application logs

You can view Windows event logs, the diagnostic infrastructure logs, and application logs by querying their respective tables (WADWindowsEventLogsTable, WADDiagnosticInfrastructureLogsTable, WADLogsTable) in Table storage using the tool of your choice. The following steps demonstrate how to do this using Visual Studio.

1. Launch Visual Studio.

2. On the View menu, click Server Explorer.

3. Expand the node labeled Azure. If prompted to do so, log in with your organizational account or the Microsoft account that is associated with the website you want to manage.

4. Expand Storage.

5. Expand the storage account containing the logs.

6. Expand Tables.

7. Right-click the table you want to query and select View Table to display its contents.

Viewing IIS logs

IIS logs can be retrieved from Blob storage using the tool of your choice. The following steps show how to do this using Visual Studio.

1. Launch Visual Studio.

2. On the View menu, click Server Explorer.

3. Expand the node labeled Azure. If prompted to do so, log in with your organizational account or the Microsoft account that is associated with the website you want to manage.

4. Expand Storage.

5. Expand Blobs.

6. Right-click wad-iis-logs and select View Blob Container to display its contents. Each log is listed; double-click a log to download and open it.

> ### Thought experiment
> #### Monitoring capacity
>
> In this thought experiment, apply what you've learned about this objective. You can find answers to these questions in the "Answers" section at the end of this chapter.
>
> You believe that the VM on which you are hosting your application is under-provisioned in terms of RAM memory.
>
> 1. How might you monitor for a low memory condition?
>
> 2. If you want to be notified when a low memory condition occurs, how would you enable that?

Objective summary

- A VM can be configured to collect diagnostics data (that is, logs) as well as performance counter metrics (CPU percentage, memory utilization, and so on).

- Endpoint monitoring can be configured on a VM to provide outside-in monitoring of HTTP or HTTPS endpoints provided by your VM.

- You can monitor various metrics using the management portal, and you can configure alerts on these metrics to send out emails when a metric threshold is exceeded.

- Diagnostic logs can be retrieved from Azure Storage (Table or Blob storage, depending on the specific type of log).

Objective review

Answer the following questions to test your knowledge of the information in this objective. You can find the answers to these questions and explanations of why each answer choice is correct or incorrect in the "Answers" section at the end of this chapter.

1. Which of the following is *not* an option for the time period over which metrics used for alerts are evaluated? (Choose all that apply.)

    A. The last value measured

    B. The last 5 minutes

    C. The last hour

    D. The last 24 hours

2. Which of the following diagnostics is *not* available for querying from Table storage?

    A. Diagnostic infrastructure logs

    B. Windows System event logs

    C. Performance counters

    D. IIS logs

3. If you do not enable diagnostics, which of the following diagnostics will you have? (Choose all that apply.)

    A. Disk read and write

    B. CPU percentage

    C. Network in and network out

    D. Disk read guest operating system and disk write guest operating system

Answers

This section contains the solutions to the thought experiments and answers to the objective review questions in this chapter.

Objective 2.1: Thought experiment

1. You could start by searching for documentation about Azure supporting SQL Server AlwaysOn availability groups, but one thing you might check first is the Marketplace in the Preview portal. The Marketplace includes an entry for SQL Server 2014 AlwaysOn that automatically provisions the cluster and configures SQL Server.

2. Using the template from the Marketplace would be less labor intensive than setting up the cluster manually.

Objective 2.1: Objective review

1. **Correct answers:** A, B, and C

   A. **Correct:** The Marketplace supplies a number of choices for single instance VMs including those with only an operating system installed (for example, Windows, Linux), those with pre-installed server software (for example, SQL Server, SharePoint) and those with pre-installed applications based on PHP, Node.js, and other platforms.

   B. **Correct:** The Marketplace supplies a number of pre-configured Ubuntu Linux VM images.

   C. **Correct:** The Marketplace supplies options for creating multi-VM clusters for SharePoint, SQL Server Always On, BizTalk, and SAP. In addition, there are third-party multi-VM templates for products, such as DataStax Cassandra clusters.

   D. **Incorrect:** All of the above are supported workloads.

2. **Correct answer:** A

   A. **Correct:** The Marketplace supports a mixture of free and paid VMs, as well as Microsoft and third-party, and community images.

   B. **Incorrect:** Many images obtained through the Marketplace include the license for the software on the image as part of the cost of the VM. If you upload your own VM with software installed, you must obtain those licenses separately.

   C. **Incorrect:** Some images include software that will require a separate purchase from the third-party vendor (for example, ClearDB MySQL).

   D. **Incorrect:** The Marketplace has a mixture of images provided by Microsoft, by third-party vendors, and by the Open Source community.

3. **Correct answers:** A, B, C, and D

   A. **Correct:** There is a VM image with Visual Studio pre-installed.

   B. **Correct:** There are several VM images with Windows 8 pre-installed.

   C. **Correct:** There are several Ubunto VM images, including the latest versions with Long Term Support (LTS).

   D. **Correct:** There is a VM image with the JDK pre-installed.

Objective 2.2: Thought experiment

1. You could transfer the VM by uploading the VHD to Blob storage using the Add-AzureVhd Windows PowerShell cmdlet.

2. Given that you are not interested in stamping out distinct versions of the image, you could use a specialized image.

Objective 2.2: Objective review

1. **Correct answers:** C and D

   A. **Incorrect:** This is a tool for generalizing Windows VMs.

   B. **Incorrect:** This is a tool for generalizing Linux VMs.

   C. **Correct:** This is *not* a tool for generalizing VMs.

   D. **Correct:** This is *not* a tool for generalizing VMs.

2. **Correct answers:** A and C

   A. **Correct:** An operating system disk can only be created from a single VHD.

   B. **Incorrect:** A data disk *cannot* be created from a single VHD.

   C. **Correct:** A data disk can only be created from a single VHD.

   D. **Incorrect:** A data disk *cannot* be created from a single VHD.

3. **Correct answers:** A, B, C, and D

   A. **Correct:** You can capture a VM image while the VM instance is running.

   B. **Correct:** You can capture a VM image when a VM is stopped.

   C. **Correct:** You can capture a VM image from a single VHD.

   D. **Correct:** You can capture a VM image from an existing VM image that is running Linux.

Objective 2.3: Thought experiment

1. PowerShell DSC enhances your configuration management experience by providing a mechanism for packaging Windows PowerShell instructions in a way that they can bootstrap a VM during creation or post creation to apply updates. If you begin by automating configuration management with Windows PowerShell scripts, you can later incorporate those into an automated experience with DSC.

2. Puppet and Chef are ideal for larger deployments where the number of servers to manage adds complexity and leads to challenges managing multiple environments. These tools are equally useful for smaller topologies, although not required as a starting point. Progressively, you can start with Windows PowerShell and graduate to either DSC or one of these tools. You may also start with DSC scripting and then later incorporate those scripts in your configuration management story using Puppet or Chef.

Objective 2.3: Objective review

1. **Correct answers:** B, D, and E

    A. **Incorrect:** VM Agent is selected by default when you create a VM; however, it can be cleared so that the agent is not installed to the new image.

    B. **Correct:** In both portals, if the VM Agent is enabled, you can also optionally enable the Custom Script Extension.

    C. **Incorrect:** PowerShell DSC is not installed by default, but if the VM Agent is enabled, you can select PowerShell DSC from the Preview portal only.

    D. **Correct:** Chef Client is available for both Windows and Linux operating systems and can be enabled through either portal only if the VM Agent is enabled.

    E. **Correct:** Puppet Enterprise Agent is available for both Windows and Linux operating systems and can be enabled through either portal only if the VM Agent is enabled.

2. **Correct answers:** A, C, D, E, F, and G

    A. **Correct:** Use the Windows Feature resource.

    B. **Incorrect:** Network configuration is not a directly exposed resource.

    C. **Correct:** Use the File resource.

    D. **Correct:** Use the Archive resource.

    E. **Correct:** Use the Registry resource.

    F. **Correct:** Use the Script resource.

    G. **Correct:** Use the User resource.

3. **Correct answer:** C

    A. **Incorrect:** Custom Script Extension is able to run a script and copy resources when a VM starts or is created, but it cannot ensure the VM state matches a defined configuration.

    B. **Incorrect:** DSC overlaps with Puppet and Chef in that it can be used to configure new and existing VMs and can update those VMs to a desired target state. DSC does not provide a management console to manage how scripts are assigned to nodes, to monitor nodes, or to do other global view configuration management tasks.

    C. **Correct:** DSC is based on Windows PowerShell. Windows PowerShell and DSC scripts can be used by Puppet and Chef configurations.

    D. **Incorrect:** DSC can be configured to push updates to server nodes and to have the local configuration manager pull updates periodically to update the state of a node.

Objective 2.4: Thought experiment

1. You would want to configure the VM endpoints with a reserved IP address so that the outbound IP address used by the requests from the application VMs does not change accidentally, thereby differing from what is configured in the whitelist and breaking connectivity with the database.

2. You could obtain the IP address to use by examining the value of the virtual IP (VIP) address in either the existing portal or the Preview portal.

Objective 2.4: Objective review

1. **Correct answers:** A and B

    A. **Correct:** All requests flow through the load balancer.

    B. **Correct:** You can use both the PIP and VIP plus port.

    C. **Incorrect:** PIPs enable you to communicate across all ports.

    D. **Incorrect:** A VM must belong to a regional VNET in order to be assigned a PIP.

2. **Correct answer:** D

    A. **Incorrect:** A VM can safely be stopped without losing the reserved IP address.

    B. **Incorrect:** If a cloud service is deleted, the reserved IP address is preserved.

    C. **Incorrect:** VMs using a reserved IP can be safely deleted without losing the reserved IP address.

    D. **Correct:** A reserved IP is only released explicitly, and its lifetime is associated with a subscription, not a particular VM or cloud service.

3. **Correct answer:** B

    A. **Incorrect:** The load balancer does not distribute load with a round-robin approach.

    B. **Correct:** Load is distributed using a hashing approach, which distributes load fairly randomly.

    C. **Incorrect:** The load balancer does not distribute load based on resource utilization.

    D. **Incorrect:** The load balancer does not distribute load based on network response times.

Objective 2.5: Thought experiment

1. Because the solution architecture has two tiers, you should ensure that you create two availability sets, one for the web tier and one for the services tier. You could use one cloud service for both the availability sets or provision two cloud services (one per tier) since the scenario does not specify any other restrictions. For a single availability set, you would need to pre-provision enough VMs to cover your anticipated peak load and assign the VMs to the appropriate availability set based on the tier the VM will support. In addition, all VMs in the web tier availability set would need to have the same instance size, as would all VMs in the services tier.

2. On each availability set, you could configure auto-scale with a schedule to scale down (turn off VMs) on weekends and scale up (turn on VMs) during the weekdays.

Objective 2.5: Objective review

1. **Correct answers:** A, C, and D

    A. **Correct:** As you increase VM instance size, you increase the number of disks you can attach to the VM.

    B. **Incorrect:** The maximum size of an attached disk is controlled by Azure Storage page blob size constraints (1 terabyte) and not by the VM size.

    C. **Correct:** As you increase VM instance size, you increase the number of cores available to the VM.

    D. **Correct:** As you increase VM instance size, you increase the amount of RAM available to the VM.

2. **Correct answer:** B

    A. **Incorrect:** All VMs within an availability set must have the same instance size.

    B. **Correct:** VMs in the same availability set must exist in the same cloud service.

    C. **Incorrect:** It is a best practice to place VMs from a single application tier in the same availability set.

    D. **Incorrect:** You can assign a VM to an availability set after it has been created.

3. **Correct answer:** C

    A. **Incorrect:** Auto-scale is not configurable on a cloud service, but rather on an availability set within a cloud service.

    B. **Incorrect:** VMs must belong to an availability set to benefit from auto-scale.

    C. **Correct:** Auto-scale can only be configured on an availability set.

    D. **Incorrect:** An update domain is unrelated to auto-scale. VMs in an availability set may traverse several update domains for fault tolerance.

Objective 2.6: Thought experiment

1. You would need a VM that enables you to mount 16 disks. Since each disk can provide a max of 500 IOPS, the total would provide the desired max of 8,000 IOPS. Options for this include A4, A7, A8, and A9.

2. Since the application runs on Windows Server, you should use Windows Server 2012 R2 and configure these 16 disks in a storage pool.

Objective 2.6: Objective review

1. **Correct answer:** E

    A. **Incorrect:** This is a valid way to manage and interact with Azure File storage.

    B. **Incorrect:** This is a valid way to manage and interact with Azure File storage.

    C. **Incorrect:** This is a valid way to manage and interact with Azure File storage.

    D. **Incorrect:** This is a valid way to manage and interact with Azure File storage.

    E. **Correct:** Azure File storage is compatible with SMB 2.1, not SMB 3.0.

2. **Correct answer:** A

    A. **Correct:** The host caching setting of None is not valid for operating system disks.

    B. **Incorrect:** The Host Caching setting of Read Only is valid for operating system disks.

    C. **Incorrect:** The Host Caching setting of None is valid for data disks.

    D. **Incorrect:** The Host Caching setting of Read Only is valid for data disks.

3. **Correct answer:** A

   A. **Correct:** The only valid option is locally redundant replication.

   B. **Incorrect:** Geo-redundant replication yields corrupted disks if you try to restore from a replicated file.

   C. **Incorrect:** Read-access geo-redundant replication yields corrupted disks if you try to restore from a replicated file.

   D. **Incorrect:** Zone redundant replication can only be used with block blobs. VHDs are created using page blobs, so this is not a valid option.

Objective 2.7: Thought experiment

1. Using the portal, you should enable diagnostics and chart the memory percentage metric. If you find that the memory percentage is consistently above 90 percent, you should consider increasing your VM size.

2. You can configure an alert on the memory percentage metric with a threshold of 90 percent to email you when the VM encounters this condition for a period of time.

Objective 2.7: Objective review

1. **Correct answer:** A

   A. **Correct:** Alerts use metrics computed over an aggregate time period, with the minimum period being 5 minutes and the maximum 24 hours.

   B. **Incorrect:** Metrics can be evaluated on a 5-minute interval.

   C. **Incorrect:** Metrics can be evaluated on an hourly interval.

   D. **Incorrect:** Metrics can be evaluated on a 24-hour interval.

2. **Correct answer:** D

   A. **Incorrect:** Diagnostics logs are available from Table storage.

   B. **Incorrect:** Windows System event logs are available from Table storage.

   C. **Incorrect:** Performance Counter metrics are available from Table storage.

   D. **Correct:** IIS logs can be retrieved only from Blob storage, not Table storage.

3. **Correct answers:** A, B, and C

   A. **Correct:** By default, Disk Read and Write diagnostics are collected.

   B. **Correct:** By default, CPU percentage diagnostics are collected.

   C. **Correct:** By default, Network In and Network Out diagnostics are collected.

   D. **Incorrect:** Without diagnostics enabled, you have access only to the five metrics that are exposed by the VM host (Read/Write, CPU percentage, Network In/Out) and not the guest operating system.

CHAPTER 3

Design and implement cloud services

The Cloud Services feature is part of the Microsoft Azure Platform-as-a-Service (PaaS) offering. Cloud Services offers the ability to deploy websites and asynchronous work to Azure servers with simpler deployment options and without the need to manage complex networking and operating system updates. A cloud service is a mechanism for packaging, deploying, and configuring one or more websites (web roles) or asynchronous workers (worker roles).

A cloud service project allows you to group these roles into a single deployment package and to indicate with configuration how websites and workers should be distributed in terms of physical servers and topology. You build a website as you normally would and associate it to a cloud service project as a web role. You build a worker role in a similar fashion to Windows NT services but using Cloud Services tools for managing the lifecycle of the service. You then provide configuration settings to determine the choice of operating system family and version, networking topology, server allocation and instance count, and more. When deployed, Azure takes the package configuration and files to deploy each project to virtual machines (VMs) according to the required configuration and topology.

In this chapter you will learn how to develop, configure, deploy, and debug Cloud Services.

Objectives in this chapter:

- Objective 3.1: Design and develop a cloud service
- Objective 3.2: Configure cloud services and roles
- Objective 3.3: Deploy a cloud service
- Objective 3.4: Monitor and debug a cloud service

Objective 3.1: Design and develop a cloud service

To develop a cloud service, install the Azure SDK. With the Azure SDK installed, you can develop a web or worker role and configure startup tasks within that role to perform additional configuration when an instance starts up. All of these tasks are covered in this section.

> **This objective covers how to:**
> - Install SDKs and emulators
> - Develop a web or worker role
> - Design and implement resiliency
> - Develop startup tasks

Installing SDKs and emulators

To design and develop cloud services, you need to install the Azure SDK. This section walks you through the process.

Assuming you already have Visual Studio installed, you first need to install Azure SDK. This SDK installs many different items, including emulators, tools, and APIs for several different Azure services. One approach to installing the Azure SDK is to create a new cloud project.

1. Open Visual Studio.

2. On the New Project screen, under Templates, click Visual C#.

3. Under Visual C#, click Cloud. On the right, click Get Microsoft Azure SDK For .NET, as shown in Figure 3-1. You can leave everything else the same. Click OK.

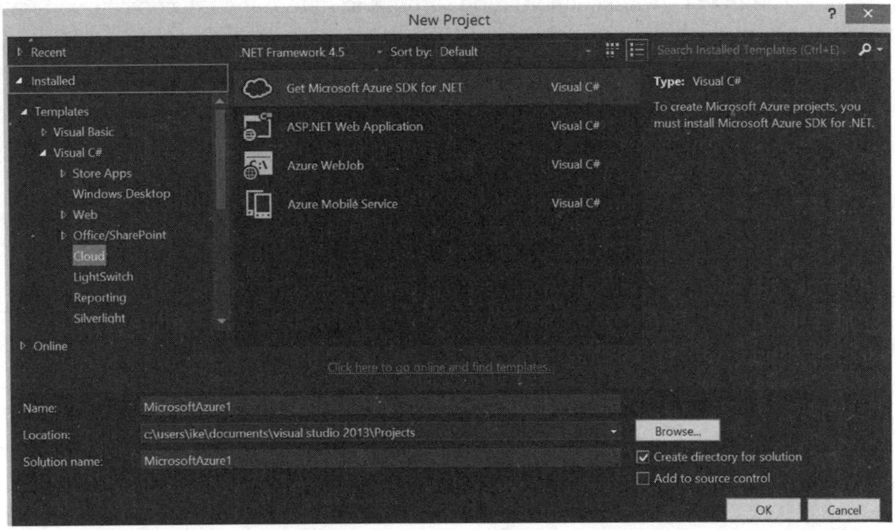

FIGURE 3-1 The Visual Studio New Project dialog box

4. In the download dialog box that appears, click Download Microsoft Azure SDK.

5. In the dialog box that appears, click Run.

6. If a security warning appears, click Run again.

7. On the Web Platform Installer 5.0 welcome screen (see Figure 3-2), click Install.

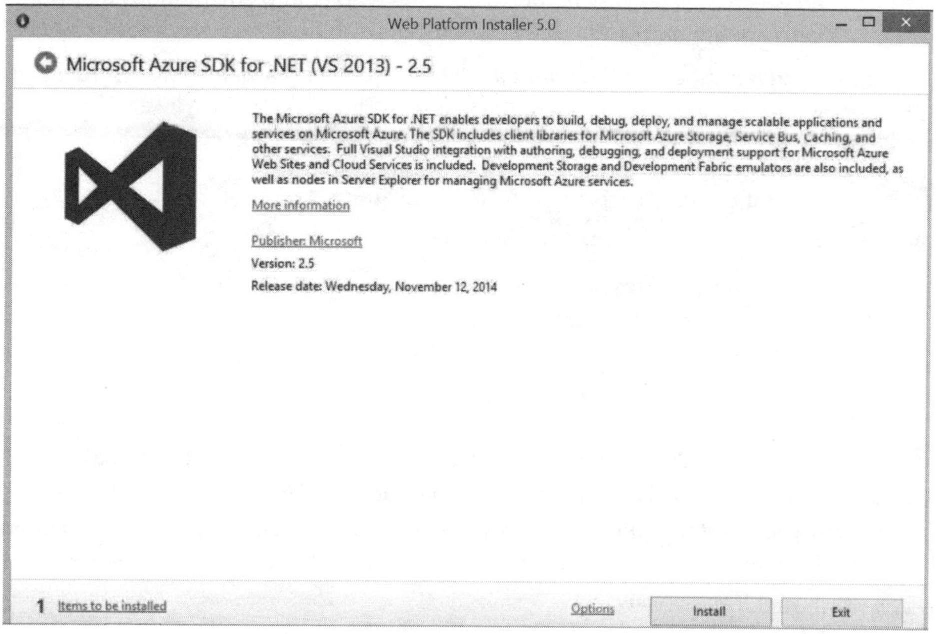

FIGURE 3-2 The Web Platform Installer 5.0 welcome screen

8. Accept the licensing agreement. The Azure ADK will take a minute to download and install.

> **NOTE STAYING UP TO DATE**
>
> It is important to stay up to date on the latest SDK. This allows you to avoid backward com-patibility issues with your code base as the SDK evolves. As if this writing, you can get the latest SDK at *http://azure.microsoft.com/en-us/downloads/archive-net-downloads/*. Click the SDK that targets the Visual Studio version you're using.

When the install completes, the SDK installs two emulators, the Azure Compute Emula-tor and the Azure Storage Emulator. These emulators are useful for debugging applications, which is covered in "Objective 3.4: Monitor and debug a cloud service."

Developing a web or worker role

When you create a cloud service project, you can add one or more cloud service roles (roles) to the project to be included in the deployment package. The type of role defines the compo-sition of the deployment environment for the role. Cloud Services supports two kinds of roles:

- **Web roles**   Used for web server applications hosted in IIS, such as an ASP.NET MVC application or a Web API application

- **Worker roles**   Used for running a compute workload. It can be used to launch an executable process or for background worker implementations that work in a similar manner to a Windows service.

This section describes the templates available for creating a web or worker role and the process for creating each from within Visual Studio.

process for creating each from within Visual Studio.

MORE INFO   **CLOUD SERVICES TERMINOLOGY**

The following link provides some terminology important to Cloud Services: *http://azure. microsoft.com/en-us/documentation/articles/cloud-services-what-is/.*

EXAM TIP

PaaS cloud services discussed in this chapter are conceptually different from IaaS cloud services discussed in Chapter 2, "Create and manage virtual machines." With PaaS cloud services, you are entrusting Azure to manage the operating system updates, patching, and deployment lifecycle of your applications. IaaS cloud services are a mechanism for grouping assets in your VM topology.

Choosing a cloud service template

When you create a new cloud service project from within Visual Studio, you choose the cloud service template and then select a role template as follows:

1.   In Visual Studio, click File, and then click New Project.

2.   In the New Project dialog box, click Installed, Templates, Visual C#, and then Cloud, and select the Azure Cloud Service template.

3.   The New Microsoft Azure Cloud Service dialog box includes a list of role templates available, organized by language (Visual Basic, C#, or F#). Select one or more of the available templates and click the right arrow to add them to the cloud service project you are creating.

4.   Optionally, rename each role to match the desired project name.

5.   After you select the desired roles for the cloud service, click OK.

The cloud service template should be the startup project in the solution. It references the roles associated with the cloud service and holds the configuration settings for each role, including their operating system version, application configuration, topology for VM allocation, and any startup tasks required on VM provisioning.

When creating the cloud service project, you can optionally create web or worker roles by selecting from one of several role templates, including the following:

- **ASP.NET Web Role**   Used to create a new MVC, Web API, Single Page application, Web Forms application, or empty ASP.NET application
- **WCF Service Web Role**   Used to create an ASP.NET website that hosts a WCF Service over HTTP protocol with default configurations
- **Worker Role**   Used to create an empty background worker process where you provide the functionality in Run()
- **Worker Role with Service Bus Queue**   Used to create a background worker process that reads from a Service Bus queue using default configurations

Any of these role templates can be used as a starting point for producing a website or background worker deployed as part of a cloud service package. By default, adding multiple roles will result in multiple VMs. Each role then operates in isolation with its own configuration settings. It is possible to configure multiple roles to deploy to a single VM.

> ***MORE INFO***   **THE ROLEENTRYPOINT CLASS**
>
> Cloud service web and worker roles are projects that include a class that inherits the RoleEntryPoint base type from the Microsoft.WindowsAzure.ServiceRuntime namespace. When each role is allocated to a VM, its entry point is invoked to initialize the environment. There are three key methods to override when you implement RoleEntryPoint: OnStart(), Run(), and OnStop(). For more information about this type, see *http://msdn.microsoft.com/ en-us/library/microsoft.windowsazure.serviceruntime.roleentrypoint.aspx.*

Creating a new web role

To create a new cloud service project with a web role, complete the following steps:

1. In Visual Studio, click File, and then click New Project.

2. In the New Project dialog box, click Installed, Templates, Visual C#, and then Cloud, and then select the Azure Cloud Service template.

3. In the New Microsoft Azure Cloud Service dialog box, select ASP.NET Web Role, and click the right arrow. Edit the name of the web role to match the name you would give the ASP.NET project. Click OK.

4. Accept the defaults for the new ASP.NET Project and click OK. This creates a new MVC website based on the default template.

5. To run the project, click Debug and then click Start Debugging (or press F5).

The web role is running in the Azure Compute Emulator, but since this is a web role, a browser window also opens with the ASP.NET application loaded. Note that the ASP.NET project includes a class called WebRole that extends RoleEntryPoint, as follows:

```
public class WebRole : RoleEntryPoint
{
  public override bool OnStart()
  {
return base.OnStart();
  }
}
```

You can proceed to develop the ASP.NET project as you normally would with a few considerations in mind:

- Consider putting some key configuration settings in the role configuration settings instead of in the web.config application settings. This makes it possible to surface those settings to the management portal for modification.

- If your application has any dependencies that require installation on the destination VM or control over IIS-related settings, use a startup task to provide an unattended deployment for this configuration. Startup tasks are discussed in the following section.

Creating a new worker role

To create a new cloud service project with a worker role, complete the following steps:

1. In Visual Studio, click File and then click New Project.

2. In the New Project dialog box, click Installed, Templates, Visual C#, and then Cloud, and select the Azure Cloud Service template.

3. In the New Microsoft Azure Cloud Service dialog box, click Worker Role and click the right arrow. Edit the name of the worker role to match the name you would give the background worker project. Click OK.

4. To run the project, click Debug and then click Start Debugging (or press F5).

5. The background worker runs in the Azure Compute Emulator. To view the emulator, from the task bar, select the arrow to show hidden icons and right-click the Microsoft Azure icon. From the context menu, select Show Compute Emulator UI (see Figure 3-3).

6. In the Azure Compute Emulator window, expand your cloud service project to reveal the worker role node (see Figure 3-4). Click this node to view the output from the default worker role implementation.

> **MORE INFO   RUNNING THE AZURE COMPUTE EMULATOR FROM THE COMMAND LINE**
>
> The Azure Compute Emulator automatically starts when you run a cloud service from within Visual Studio. You can also start the emulator from the command line as described at *http://msdn.microsoft.com/en-us/library/azure/gg433001.aspx*.

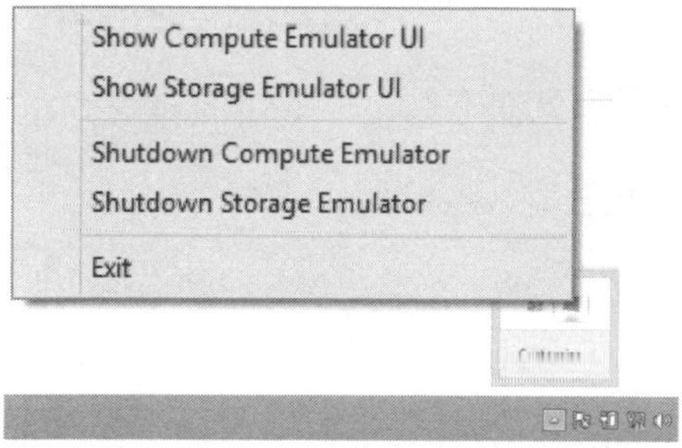

FIGURE 3-3 Showing the Azure Compute Emulator menu from the Microsoft Azure icon

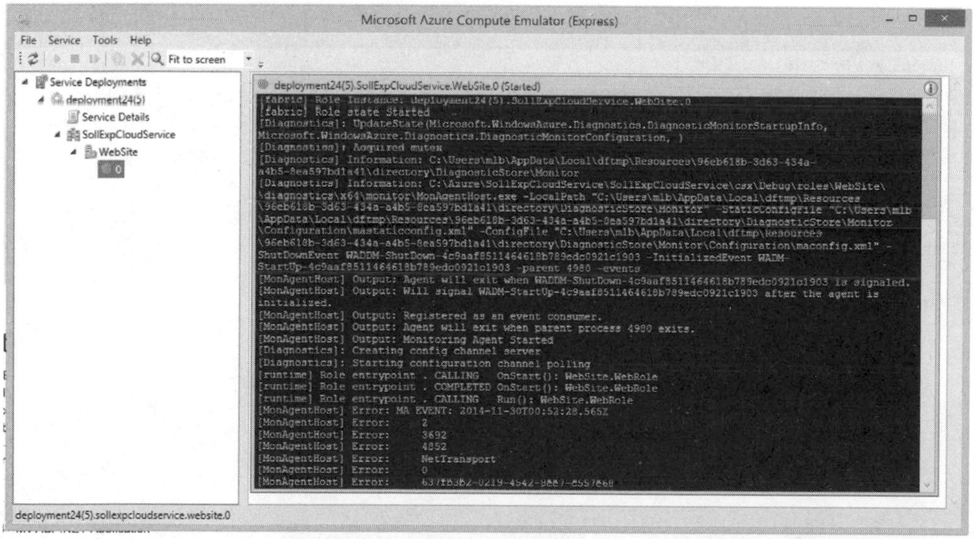

FIGURE 3-4 The Azure Compute Emulator illustrating the output from the default worker role running

For a worker role, the RoleEntryPoint is the heart of its functionality; therefore, providing an implementation for OnStart(), Run(), and OnEnd(), among other interactions with RoleEnvironment events, is implied. The default implementation for a basic worker role is as follows:

```
public class WorkerRole : RoleEntryPoint
{
    private readonly CancellationTokenSource cancellationTokenSource = new
CancellationTokenSource();
    private readonly ManualResetEvent runCompleteEvent = new ManualResetEvent(false);

    public override void Run()
    {
        Trace.TraceInformation("Worker is running");

        try
        {
            this.RunAsync(this.cancellationTokenSource.Token).Wait();
        }
        finally
        {
            this.runCompleteEvent.Set();
        }
    }

    public override bool OnStart()
    {
        ServicePointManager.DefaultConnectionLimit = 12;

        bool result = base.OnStart();

        Trace.TraceInformation("Worker has been started");

        return result;
    }

    public override void OnStop()
    {
        Trace.TraceInformation("Worker is stopping");

        this.cancellationTokenSource.Cancel();
        this.runCompleteEvent.WaitOne();

        base.OnStop();

        Trace.TraceInformation("Worker has stopped");
    }

    private async Task RunAsync(CancellationToken cancellationToken)
    {
        // TODO: Replace the following with your own logic.
        while (!cancellationToken.IsCancellationRequested)
        {
            Trace.TraceInformation("Working");
            await Task.Delay(1000);
        }
    }
}
```

In a typical implementation, you customize the following from this default template:

- **OnStart()** Initialize the environment here. You may hook some RoleEnvironment events, for example.

- **OnStop()** Clean up anything you created before the role shuts down.

- **RunAsync()** Provide your implementation here. For example, you may read from a storage queue, process messages, handle errors, and provide back-off polling when the queue is empty. See Chapter 5, "Manage application and network services," for more information on storage queue processing.

> **MORE INFO** **THE ROLEENVIRONMENT OBJECT**
>
> For more information about the RoleEnvironment object, events you can handle, and information you can gather about the cloud service, see *http://msdn.microsoft.com/en-gb/library/microsoft.windowsazure.serviceruntime.roleenvironment.aspx*.

Adding an existing project as a web role

If you have previously created a web application project such as an ASP.NET MVC or Web API project, you may want to associate that with a cloud service in order to deploy it as part of a package.

Create a new cloud service project without selecting a role template, or open an existing cloud service, and do the following:

1. In Solution Explorer, navigate to the cloud service project.

2. Right-click the Roles node, select Add, and then select Web Role Project In Solution. If this option is unavailable, a web project may not be available to select from within the solution.

3. In the Associate With Role Project dialog box, select the web project from the list. Click OK. A new role node is created under Roles.

> **MORE INFO** **ADDING A ROLE TO A CLOUD SERVICE**
>
> You can also add an existing worker role to a cloud service project using similar steps. The Add and Worker Role Project In Solution menus will be enabled if a valid worker role project exists in the solution.

Reviewing cloud service project elements

The remainder of this chapter covers a few key features of a cloud service project. To provide you with a holistic view, this section reviews the key elements in the solution.

After creating a cloud service project with a web or worker role, navigate to Solution Explorer from within Visual Studio and review the following items:

- At the root of the project is ServiceDefinition.csdef. This file, called the service definition, holds the definition for the cloud service, including a list of any startup tasks you add and a definition for each web and worker role.

- Also at the root of the project are two default service configuration files. One is used when you run ServiceConfiguration.Local.cscfg locally. The other, ServiceConfiguration.Cloud.cscfg, is included when you publish to the cloud. These files are called the service configuration. Configuration settings are edited as you edit the role configuration in the role settings dialog box. You can also create additional or alternate configuration settings, for example for development, test, or production cloud deployments.

- Expand the cloud service project and note the Roles node. When expanded, this will show one or more web or worker role nodes according to what you have added to the cloud service project.

- Double-click any role node to open the role settings dialog box, where you can configure settings used for running locally or in the cloud published version.

Design and implement resiliency

As with websites (discussed in Chapter 1, "Design and implement websites"), you should design your cloud services to support the potential for increases in server load. While Azure provides you with an inherently scalable and available platform for hosting cloud service web roles and worker roles, their design and implementation plays an important role in the overall scalability, availability, and resiliency of the application.

This section covers how to apply those concepts to cloud services.

> **MORE INFO**   **RESILIENT CLOUD ARCHITECTURES**
>
> The following reference provides additional insights, some specific to Azure, regarding designing resilient architectures for the cloud: *http://msdn.microsoft.com/library/azure/jj853352.aspx*.

Selecting a pattern

Factors that influence resiliency of web roles and worker roles are similar to those discussed in "Objective 1.6: Design and implement applications for scale and resilience" in Chapter 1.

For both web roles and worker roles, the following patterns are useful to your availability, resiliency, and scalability strategy for cloud services:

- Static Content Hosting pattern
- Cache-Aside pattern
- Health Endpoint Monitoring pattern

- Compensating Transaction pattern
- Command and Query Responsibility Segregation pattern

Worker roles can be used for background work in a similar fashion to WebJobs. For these implementations, the same patterns that are useful to WebJobs are also useful to the worker role:

- Competing Consumers pattern
- Priority Queue pattern
- Queue-Based Load Leveling pattern
- Leader Election pattern
- Scheduler Agent Supervisor pattern

Implementing transient fault handling

As with website implementations, cloud services should implement transient fault handling to improve resiliency. Specifically, application logic that accesses remote application services requires a form of retry logic to recover from transient connectivity issues. As discussed in Chapter 1, "Objective 1.6: Design and implement applications for scale and resilience," you can leverage the Transient Fault Handling Application Block to assist with this type of implementation for Azure Storage and Azure SQL Database.

Developing startup tasks

Startup tasks are used to perform operations such as running scripts prior to starting a role. The script can be a simple batch file that launches a process, adjusts registry settings, runs an MSI, or invokes Windows PowerShell scripts to configure any number of machine settings. Since startup tasks are invoked prior to role startup, they are typically used to prepare the VM in advance of running your application code.

This section describes developing and running startup tasks for a web or worker role.

Starting a role and startup tasks

The process of starting a role follows this order:

1. A role enters "starting" state and does not receive traffic.
2. Startup tasks run according to their type. Simple tasks run in order. Background and foreground tasks start asynchronously.
3. Role host process starts. For a web role, IIS is initialized.
4. The RoleEntryPoint type OnStart() is called.
5. The role enters "ready" state and traffic is sent to the role endpoints.
6. The RoleEntryPoint type Run() method is called.

If any of the tasks do not complete with exit code 0, the role is not started.

> **MORE INFO**   **LOGGING FROM STARTUP TASKS**
>
> Visibility into your startup task process is important if there are issues that require trouble-shooting. Log activity from your startup tasks to help with this. For more information on this and other helpful tips, see *http://msdn.microsoft.com/en-us/library/azure/jj129545. aspx*.

Creating a batch file to run as a startup task

Each startup task typically references a batch file that contains the instructions to run. Within the batch file you can do things such as:

- Install registry settings with a .reg file
- Call a Windows PowerShell script
- Install software using msiexec.exe
- Launch a process

The following instructions step through creating a simple batch file that edits registry settings and launches a Windows PowerShell script:

1. Using NotePad.exe, create a new file called licensesettings.reg.

2. Add the following text to the file and save it:

```
Windows Registry Editor Version 5.00
[HKEY_LOCAL_MACHINE\SOFTWARE\LicensedApplication]
"Expires"="99999999"
"LicenseType"="Business"
"Key"="12345"
```

3. Using NotePad.exe, create a new file called startup.cmd.

4. Add the following text to the file and save it:

```
@echo off
regedit.exe /s licensesettings.reg
exit /b 0
```

5. Copy both files to the root of your web or worker role project. Set the files to Copy Always so that they will be copied to the \bin folder when the solution is compiled.

You can now reference this file from the startup task configuration discussed in the next section.

> **MORE INFO**   **EXAMPLES OF STARTUP TASK IMPLEMENTATIONS**
>
> See the following reference for an example of how to create batch files that run Windows PowerShell scripts and initialize IIS settings: *http://msdn.microsoft.com/en-us/library/ azure/hh180155.aspx*.

Adding a startup task to a cloud service definition

After you write your startup task implementation, you configure the task for your cloud service as follows:

1. Open the ServiceDefinition.csdef file in Solution Explorer.

2. Add a Startup element to the WebRole or WorkerRole element. Inside the Startup element, add a Task element.

3. Add a commandLine attribute with the name of a batch file to run, such as startup. cmd. This batch file contains the actual task instructions.

4. Add an executionContext attribute with the value "limited" or "elevated." If you add "limited," the task will run without administrator privileges. If you use "elevated," the task will run with administrator privileges and be able to modify the registry, change IIS configurations, and interact with other protected resources.

5. Add a taskType attribute with the value "simple," "foreground," or "background." If you use "simple," the task will run synchronously, in the order it appears alongside other "simple" tasks. If you use "foreground," the task will run asynchronously in a foreground thread, and the role will not start until the thread completes. If you use "background," the task will run as a background thread, in parallel with other background tasks.

The following is the result of the configuration.

```xml
<?xml version="1.0" encoding="utf-8"?>
<ServiceDefinition name="CloudServiceWorker" xmlns="http://schemas.microsoft.com/
ServiceHosting/2008/10/ServiceDefinition" schemaVersion="2014-06.2.4">
 <WorkerRole name="Worker" vmsize="Small">
  <Startup>
   <Task commandLine="startup.cmd" executionContext="elevated" taskType="background"/>
  </Startup>
 </WorkerRole>
</ServiceDefinition>
```

> **MORE INFO**   **STARTUP TASKS AND ROLE RECYCLING**
>
> Startup tasks must be designed to run more than once for the role VM. When roles restart, the startup tasks run again. For information on how to design startup tasks for graceful restarts, see *http://msdn.microsoft.com/en-us/library/azure/jj129544.aspx*.

> **NOTE**   **ROLEENVIRONMENT AND STARTUP**
>
> Information about the role is not guaranteed to be available when the startup task is running. If you must interact with the RoleEnvironment and related information, use the OnStart() override for the RoleEntryPoint.

> **Thought experiment**
>
> ### Complex installation requirements
>
> In this thought experiment, apply what you've learned about this objective. You can find answers to these questions in the "Answers" section at the end of this chapter.
>
> Assume you are migrating an existing ASP.NET MVC application to a cloud service. The application requires the .NET Framework 3.5 Windows feature, some custom registry settings for related application DLL dependencies, and the installation of software with an MSI. To avoid regression testing during migration, the application cannot be upgraded to the latest version of .NET Framework.
>
> 1. How would you convert this ASP.NET application to a cloud service?
>
> 2. Would you use a web role or a worker role?
>
> 3. How would you ensure that the role is set up with all of these requirements?

Objective summary

- The Azure SDK includes the required emulators and Visual Studio templates required to develop cloud services. It is important to stay up to date on this SDK to keep up with changing features.

- Web roles are typically used for applications that run on IIS such as ASP.NET. Worker roles can be used to launch a process such as an alternate web hosting environment or database application, or for background work.

- Cloud services should implement cloud resiliency patterns, and they should implement transient fault handling for calls to remote application services.

- Startup tasks are useful to cloud services, enabling the pre-configuration of the VM for the web role or worker role. For example, you can enable Windows features, control registry settings, and install software.

Objective review

Answer the following questions to test your knowledge of the information in this objective. You can find the answers to these questions and explanations of why each answer choice is correct or incorrect in the "Answers" section at the end of this chapter.

1. Which of the following emulators is installed with the Azure SDK? (Choose all that apply.)

   A. Service bus emulator

   B. Virtual machine emulator

   C. Compute emulator

   D. Storage emulator

2. Which of the following is true about the Cloud Services feature? (Choose all that apply.)

    A. Before you create a cloud service project, you have to know which web and worker roles you will include in the cloud service solution.

    B. The only way to create a worker role that listens to a Service Bus queue is to select the role template while creating the cloud service project.

    C. You must provide an implementation for the RoleEntryPoint when creating a worker role.

    D. Web.config settings do not work with web roles. You have to use cloud service configuration settings.

3. Which of these is true about startup tasks? (Choose all that apply.)

    A. Simple tasks run before the role starts processing requests.

    B. Foreground tasks run before the role starts accepting requests.

    C. Background tasks run before the role starts accepting requests.

    D. A startup task can interact with the RoleEnvironment object.

Objective 3.2: Configure cloud services and roles

Even though the PaaS aspects of Cloud Services shield you from having to manage lower level server details, Cloud Services and Roles are feature rich and highly configurable. This section examines the configuration of key items from networking, storage, scaling, and caching.

> **This objective covers how to:**
> - Configure instance size and count
> - Configure auto-scale
> - Configure cloud service networking
> - Configure HTTPS and upload an SSL certificate
> - Configure local storage
> - Configure multiple websites in a web role
> - Configure custom domains
> - Configure caching

Configuring instance size and count

Similar to websites and VMs, you can scale cloud service roles both in terms of instance size and instance count, and you can use auto-scale for the instance count.

Scaling role instance sizes

Role instance sizes can be scaled up or down to alter the capacity of the VM supporting the instance. For each role instance, scaling collectively adjusts:

- The size of the local temp disk
- The number of CPU cores available
- The amount of RAM memory available
- The network performance

Unlike websites and VMs, whose instance size can be adjusted through the management portal, scaling the instance size of a role instance requires that you change the cloud service definition and re-deploy the package, as described in the following steps.

1. Open your cloud service project in Visual Studio.

2. In Solution Explorer, locate and double-click the role to display the properties page.

3. On the Configuration tab, from the VM Size drop-down list, select the desired VM size for instances in the role.

4. Save your solution.

5. Publish your solution.

When the deployment completes, instances of the affected role should be running on the new instance size.

Scaling role instance count

The role instance count can be scaled using the existing management portal or by adjusting the count in the cloud service configuration and re-deploying.

ADJUSTING ROLE INSTANCE COUNT (EXISTING PORTAL)

To adjust the role instance count using the management portal, complete the following steps:

1. Navigate to the management portal accessed via *https://manage.windowsazure.com*.

2. Navigate to the cloud service containing the role you want to scale and click the Scale tab.

3. Scroll down to the role you want to scale, and use the Instance Count slider to adjust the value for the desired number of instances.

4. Click Save on the command bar.

ADJUSTING ROLE INSTANCE COUNT (PREVIEW PORTAL)

Adjusting role instance count is not currently possible using the Preview portal.

ADJUSTING ROLE INSTANCE COUNT IN VISUAL STUDIO

To adjust the role instance count in Visual Studio, complete the following steps:

1. Open your cloud service project in Visual Studio.

2. In Solution Explorer, locate and double-click the role to display the properties view.

3. On the Configuration tab, in the Instance Count text box, supply the number of instances.

4. Save your solution.

5. Publish your solution.

When the deployment completes, the number of instances requested will be deployed behind the load balancer. This will also be reflected in the Instance Count slider mentioned previously.

Configuring auto-scale

Auto-scale for Cloud Services automatically adjusts the number of instances running within a role based on load or according to a schedule. It does this by provisioning additional instances in the role during a scale-up event, and de-provisioning them during a scale-down event. Auto-scale is configured at the level of the role within a cloud service, much like it is configured at the level of the web hosting plan for websites or at the availability set level for VMs. Auto-scale can be configured to make scaling decisions based on a schedule (predefined or custom schedules are supported) or with respect to the queue depth of an Azure Storage queue or Service Bus queue.

Configuring role auto-scale (existing portal)

To configure role auto-scale using the management portal, complete the following steps:

1. Navigate to the management portal accessed via *https://manage.windowsazure.com*.

2. Navigate to the cloud service containing the role you want to scale and click the Scale tab (as shown in Figure 3-5).

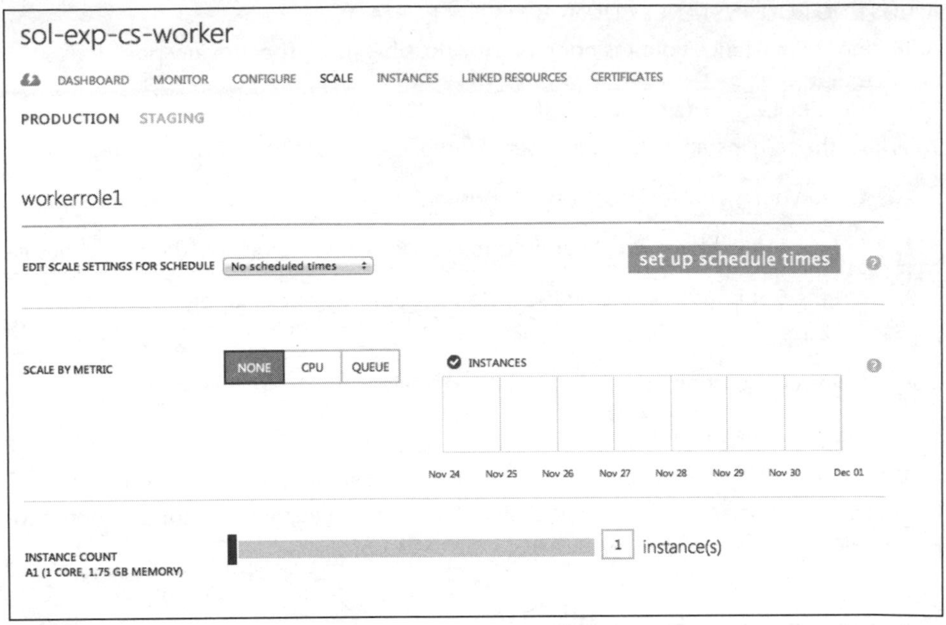

FIGURE 3-5 The scale tab for a cloud service in the management portal

3. To configure auto-scale to operate according to a schedule, complete the following steps, click Set Up Schedule Times, and, in the dialog box that appears, do one or more of the following to define the schedule:

   A. To enable the day/night recurring schedule, select Different Scale Settings For Day And Night, and then use the Day Starts, Day Ends, and Time Zone drop-down lists to specify what hours are considered day time. (Azure will infer the remaining hours are night time.)

   B. To enable the weekdays and weekends recurring schedule, select Different Scale Settings For Weekdays And Weekends, where weekdays are defined as Monday morning through Friday evening and weekends are Friday evening through Monday morning. You can adjust the time that is used for morning and for evening by using the Day Starts, Day Ends, and Time Zone drop-down lists.

   C. Enable specific data ranges by filling in the grid below Specific Dates. Specify a user-friendly name for the date range, a start date and time, and an end date and time. You can add multiple date ranges as long as they do not overlap.

4. When you are finished defining schedules, click the check mark to make these schedules configurable on the Scale tab. Return to the Scale tab and complete the following steps:

   A. From the Edit Scale Settings For Schedule drop-down list, select the schedule you want to configure.

B. Use the Instance Count slider to adjust the number instances to the target number your role should have during that schedule.

C. Repeat the previous two steps as necessary for any other schedules you have defined.

D. Click Save to save both the newly defined schedules and your instance count configurations for each schedule.

5. To scale by CPU, complete the following steps:

A. Click the Scale By Metric toggle key to select CPU.

B. Using the Target CPU slider, specify the lower threshold below which scale-down actions should be taken. You can do this by entering a value in the left-most text box or by dragging the left-most slider handler.

C. Repeat the previous step to define the threshold for the scale-up action, using the right-most text box or slider handle to adjust the threshold.

D. Using the Instance Range slider, define the minimum and maximum number of instances that auto-scale can reach at any point in time.

E. Use the Scale Up By slider to specify the number of instances to add at one time, and select a cool-off period to wait after scaling up from the Scale Up Wait Time drop-down list.

F. Similarly, configure the number of instances to scale down by using the Scale Down By and Scale Down Wait Time controls.

G. Click Save to apply your auto-scale by metric rules.

6. To scale by queue depth, complete the following steps:

A. Click the Scale By Metric toggle to select Queue.

B. Using the Instance Range slider, define the minimum and maximum number of instances that auto-scale can reach at any point in time.

C. Select the Storage Account and Queue Name (for an Azure Queue) or Service Bus Namespace and Queue Name (for a Service Bus Queue) to monitor queue depth.

D. In Target Per Machine, specify the target number of messages that Azure will scale to support per VM.

E. Using the Scale Up By slider, specify the number of instances to add at one time, and select a cool-off period to wait after scaling up from the Scale Up Wait Time drop-down list.

F. Similarly, configure the number of instances to scale down by using the Scale Down By and Scale Down Wait Time controls.

G. Click Save to apply your auto-scale by metric rules.

7. Also note that you can combine schedule-based and metric-based scaling. When you define a schedule and then select it from the Edit Scale Settings For Schedule dropdown list, you can configure scaling by CPU or by queue conditions within the timeframe represented by that schedule.

Configuring role auto-scale (Preview portal)

Auto-scale cannot currently be configured using the Preview portal.

Configuring role auto-scale using Windows PowerShell

Auto-scale cannot currently be configured using Windows PowerShell.

Configuring cloud service networking

Cloud service roles offer many mechanisms for controlling communication between Internet traffic and the role instances and between role instances.

Understanding cloud service endpoint types

Cloud service roles can be configured to expose one of three types of endpoints:

- **Input endpoint**   Controls the transport protocol (http, https, tcp, or udp) and port used by traffic coming from the Internet to instances of the role. When accessed this way, the Azure load balancer determines which role instance will receive a particular request. The IP address used to communicate with this endpoint is the virtual IP (VIP) of the cloud service, and the role instance to which the traffic goes will see the traffic on the configured localPort number or on the one assigned automatically by the Azure fabric controller if a localPort is not provided.
- **InstanceInput endpoint**   Defines a specific protocol (tcp or udp) and port that when used by Internet traffic goes via port forwarding directly to a specific role instance. The IP address used to communicate with this endpoint is the VIP of the cloud service.
- **Internal endpoint**   Configures a protocol (http, tcp, udp, or any of the aforementioned) and a dynamically allocated public port range that can be used for communication between roles and role instances within a cloud service. The IP address used to communicate with this endpoint is the internal IP address assigned to each role instance, and the role instance to which the traffic goes will see the traffic on the configured private port.

Configuring HTTPS endpoints

HTTPS endpoints enable you to secure traffic between the public Internet and your role instances via transport layer security (TLS) by using a certificate (often mislabeled as a standard SSL certificate) that you either generate yourself (in the dev/test scenario) or that you purchase from a certificate authority (in the production scenario). The process has four main tasks. First, you need to acquire a certificate. Second, you need to convert the certificate into the PFX format by exporting it from the keystore. Third, you need to upload the certificate to the certificate store used by your cloud service. Fourth, you need to configure an endpoint in your role that uses the HTTPS protocol and is configured to use the certificate to secure the traffic. The following sections cover each of these tasks.

ACQUIRING A CERTIFICATE

You can acquire a certificate from a certificate authority, such as GoDaddy, Thawte, or Verisign. The process for creating a certificate request and submitting it the certificate authority varies by vendor, and you should follow vendor instructions. However, also creating a self-signed certificate while you develop your solution offers an opportunity to become familiar with how HTTPS endpoints are configured. The steps that follow show how to create a self-signed certificate using the makecert tool that is installed with the Windows SDK (and with Visual Studio).

1. Open the command prompt and be sure to run it as an administrator.

2. Navigate to the Windows SDK you have installed on your machine. If you have Visual Studio, you will have one of the following folders with the corresponding SDK version installed. Look for makecert.exe in the corresponding SDK folder shown here:

    A. C:\Program Files (x86)\Microsoft SDKs\Windows\v7.1A\Bin (win7 SDK)

    B. C:\Program Files (x86)\Windows Kits\8.0\bin\x64 (win8 SDK)

    C. C:\Program Files (x86)\Windows Kits\8.1\bin\x64 (win8.1 SDK)

3. At the command prompt, run the following command:

```
makecert -sky exchange -r -n "CN=<SubjectName>" -pe -a sha1 -len 2048 -sr
LocalMachine -ss My "<PathTo>\<SubjectName>.cer"
```

In the above command, substitute <SubjectName> with a string representing the name you will use for the certificate. (In production certificates, this is your domain name, but for self-signed certificates, this value has little meaning beyond a label.) For the final parameter, provide a path for the makecert utility to write the certificate to disk. Be sure to retain the .cer extension.

This command will both create the *.cer file at the location you specified and add it to your Local Machine\Personal keystore. This latter step makes selecting the certificate within Visual Studio more convenient.

CONVERTING THE CERTIFICATE TO PFX

Before you can upload the certificate to Azure, you need to export it in the PFX format that Azure expects.

1. From the Start menu, run **mmc** to open an empty Microsoft Management Console.

2. From the File menu, select Add/Remove Snap-In.

3. The Add Or Remove Snap-ins dialog box opens as shown in Figure 3-6. Under Available Snap-ins, click Certificates, and then click Add to open the certificates snap-in wizard.

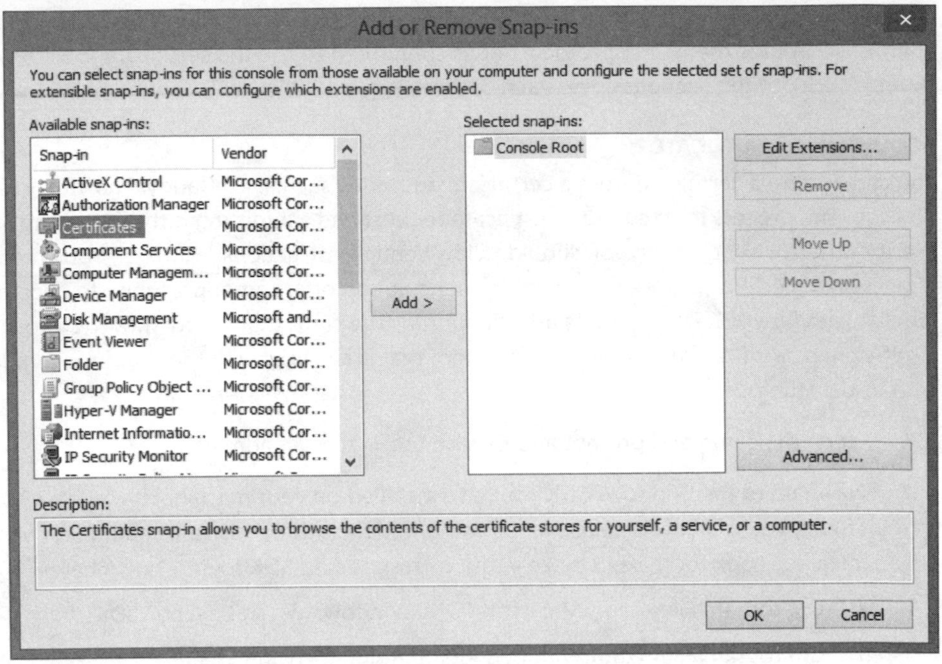

FIGURE 3-6 The Add or Remove Snap-Ins dialog box

4. On the first page of the wizard, click Computer Account, and then click Next.

5. On the next page, leave the options unchanged and click Finish.

6. In the Add Or Remove Snap-ins dialog box, click OK.

7. In the Microsoft Management Console, expand the Certificates node in the navigation pane. The certificates are listed as shown in Figure 3-7.

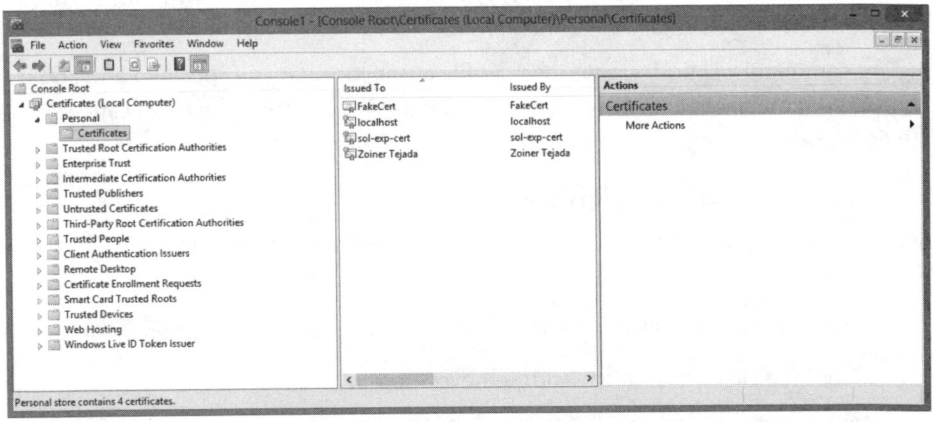

FIGURE 3-7 Certificates listed under the Personal folder

8. Expand Personal, and then click Certificates.

9. Right-click the certificate you just created and select All Tasks, Export.

10. Click Next on the first wizard page.

11. On the Export Private Key page, select Yes, Export The Private Key, and then click Next.

12. On the Export File Format page, click Next.

13. On the Security page, select the Password check box and enter a password to secure access to the certificate. You will use this password when you upload the certificate to Azure. Click Next.

14. On the File To Export page, browse to the path where you would like to save the PFX certificate. Click Next.

15. Click Finish on the summary page to create your certificate in the PFX format.

UPLOADING THE CERTIFICATE

To upload the PFX certificate, complete the following steps.

1. Navigate to the existing portal accessed via *https://manage.windowsazure.com*.

2. If you have not already created a cloud service that will support your deployment, click New on the command bar, and select Compute, Cloud Service, and then Quick Create.

3. When your cloud service is created, navigate to it and click the Certificates tab.

4. On the command bar, click Upload.

5. In the dialog box that appears (as seen in Figure 3-8), browse to select the PFX file you just created, and enter the password you used to secure it. Click the check mark to upload the certificate.

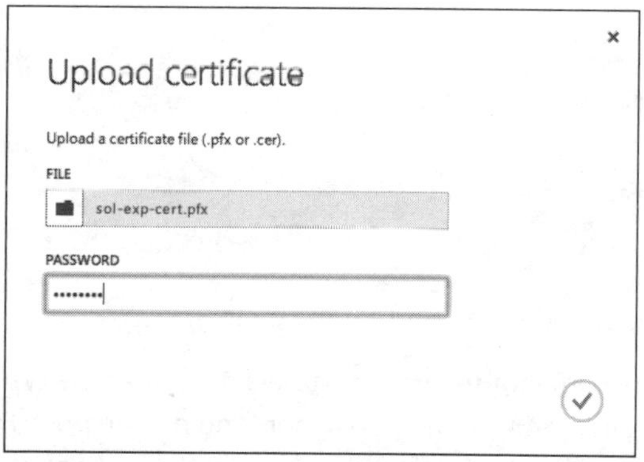

FIGURE 3-8 The Upload Certificate dialog box

CONFIGURING THE ROLE

The final tasks are to associate the certificate with the role and configure an HTTPS endpoint that uses that certificate.

1. Open your cloud service in Visual Studio.

2. In Solution Explorer, double-click the role to open the properties view.

3. Click the Certificates tab.

4. Click Add Certificate. A row is added to the grid on the page.

5. In the row that appears, provide a name for the certificate and leave the Store Location and Store Name options as Local Machine and My, respectively.

6. In the Thumbprint box, click the ellipses to open a dialog box that lists the certificates present in the Local Machine\Personal keystore (as shown in Figure 3-9).

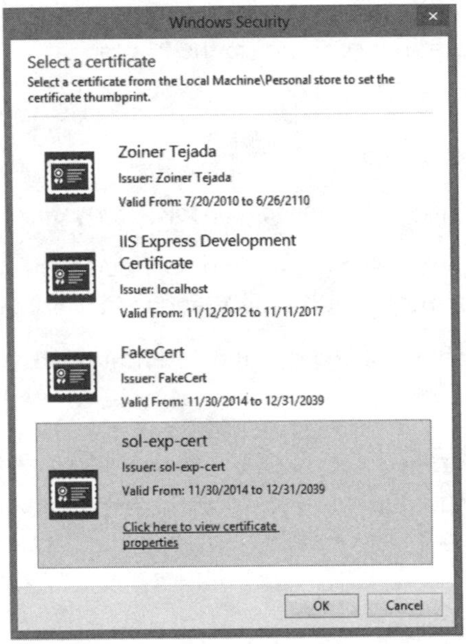

FIGURE 3-9 The Select A Certificate dialog box

7. Select the certificate that you created, and click OK.

8. Click the Endpoints tab.

9. Click Add Endpoint. A row will be added to the grid on the page.

10. In the row that appears, provide a name for the endpoint, select Input as the type, enter **HTTPS** for the protocol, and enter **443** for the public port and private port. Finally, from the SSL Certificate Name drop-down list, select the name of the certificate you just added.

11. Save your solution.

12. Deploy your cloud service. When the deployment completes, you should be able to access your role using the HTTPS endpoint.

Configuring network traffic rules

Network traffic rules are configured to control or restrict how internal communication between roles within a cloud service happens, effectively dictating which roles are allowed to communicate with the internal endpoints of another role within a cloud service.

Network traffic rules are best explained by example. Assume you have a cloud service with two worker roles, and you want WorkerRole2 to be accessible only from WorkerRole1, but you want WorkerRole1 to be accessible to WorkerRole2 plus any future roles you might add to the cloud service. Assuming you have defined an HTTP internal endpoint on each role, you can configure the service definition (the *.csdef) as follows:

```xml
<?xml version="1.0" encoding="utf-8"?>
<ServiceDefinition …>
 <WorkerRole name="WorkerRole1" vmsize="Small">
  <Imports>…</Imports>
  <Endpoints>
   <InternalEndpoint name="httpInternal" protocol="http" port="8080"/>
  </Endpoints>
 </WorkerRole>
 <WorkerRole name="WorkerRole2" vmsize="Small">
  <Imports>…</Imports>
  <Endpoints>
   <InternalEndpoint name="httpInternal" protocol="http" port="8080"/>
  </Endpoints>
 </WorkerRole>
 <NetworkTrafficRules>
  <OnlyAllowTrafficTo>
   <Destinations>
    <RoleEndpoint roleName="WorkerRole2" endpointName="httpInternal" />
   </Destinations>
   <WhenSource matches="AnyRule">
    <FromRole roleName="WorkerRole1" />
   </WhenSource>
  </OnlyAllowTrafficTo>
  <OnlyAllowTrafficTo>
   <Destinations>
    <RoleEndpoint roleName="WorkerRole1" endpointName="httpInternal" />
   </Destinations>
   <AllowAllTraffic/>
  </OnlyAllowTrafficTo>
 </NetworkTrafficRules>
</ServiceDefinition>
```

In the previous example, each WorkerRole element exposes an internal HTTP endpoint named *httpInternal*. The service definition file was modified to add a NetworkTrafficRules element that contains two OnlyAllowTrafficTo child elements. Each OnlyAllowTrafficTo element describes the source role endpoint and destination role endpoint for which communication should be allowed; any other combinations will be denied. The first OnlyAllowTrafficTo element specifies that traffic from WorkerRole1 (as identified within the WhenSource and child FromRole elements) is addressing the httpInternal endpoint on WorkerRole2 (as is identified by the Destination and child RoleEndpoint elements), it should be allowed. The second OnlyAllowTrafficTo element specifies the httpInternal endpoint of WorkerRole1 as the target, but, by using the AllowAllTraffic element, enables any role within the cloud service to communicate with that endpoint.

> **MORE INFO** **NETWORKTRAFFICRULES SCHEMA**
>
> For a complete explanation of the NetworkTrafficRules schema, see *http://msdn.microsoft.com/en-us/library/azure/gg557551.aspx*.

Configuring access control lists

If you need to restrict access to an endpoint within a cloud service, but the source requiring access is not another role in the same cloud service (for example, if it's a VM), you can use an access control list (ACL). Access control lists act on cloud service endpoints the same way they act on VM endpoints (see "Objective 2.4: Configure VM networking" in Chapter 2); you can use them to specify rules for ranges of IP addresses (that is, subnets) to permit or deny access. However, ACLs are configured differently for cloud service endpoints. While you can use the management portal to specify ACLs for VMs, you configure ACLs for cloud services by editing the service configuration file (*.cscfg) and then deploying.

To configure ACLs for your cloud service, open your cloud service project in Visual Studio, and then open the *.cscfg file for the cloud service project (be sure to pick the *.Cloud.cscfg or whichever file you use for deploying to Azure). The configuration of ACLs is best demonstrated by example. Below the closing </Role> tag, enter the following network configuration, which defines a set of access control rules and then applies that set of rules to a particular endpoint:

```
<?xml version="1.0" encoding="utf-8"?>
<ServiceConfiguration …>
 <Role name="WorkerRole1">
  <Instances count="…" />
  <ConfigurationSettings>
   <Setting name="…" value="…"/>
  </ConfigurationSettings>
 </Role>
 <NetworkConfiguration>
  <AccessControls>
   <AccessControl name="corpOnly">
    <Rule action="permit" description="allows corpnet" order="100"
```

```
remoteSubnet="70.181.131.0/28" />
    <Rule action="deny" description="deny rest" order="200" remoteSubnet="0.0.0.0/0"/>
  </AccessControl>
 </AccessControls>
 <EndpointAcls>
  <EndpointAcl role="WorkerRole1" endPoint="httpInput" accessControl="corpOnly"/>
 </EndpointAcls>
 </NetworkConfiguration>
</ServiceConfiguration>
```

> **MORE INFO**   **NETWORKCONFIGURATION SCHEMA**
>
> For the complete schema documentation of the NetworkConfiguration element,
> see *http://msdn.microsoft.com/en-us/library/azure/jj156091.aspx*.

In the previous example, an access control named "corpOnly" is created with two rules. The first rule, with the description "allows corpnet", uses an action of "permit" since it is intended to allow access to machines coming from a fictional corporate range of IP addresses specified in the remoteSubnet attribute. Its order is set to 100 so that it is evaluated first.

The second rule has an action of "deny" and a higher value for the order attribute so that it is evaluated after the allow rule. It effectively acts as the catch all rule because the remoteSubnet is set to "0.0.0.0/0". Then, within the EndpointAcls element, a single EndpointAcl is added that ties together the role and endpoint (in this case WorkerRole1 and the endpoint named httpInput) with the ACL named corpOnly.

With this basic structure in place, you can adjust the configuration to suit your particular environment and access control requirements and then publish the cloud service.

> **IMPORTANT**   **ACL UPDATES AND DEPLOYMENTS**
>
> Currently, you must perform a complete re-deployment if you enable ACLs on a service
> that already exists. An update deployment will fail with an error.

Configuring virtual networks

You can join cloud services to an existing virtual network; however, to do so you must edit the service configuration file and re-deploy. The following abbreviated example shows how to configure a cloud service to have its role instances created within a specific subnet of an existing virtual network:

```
<?xml version="1.0" encoding="utf-8"?>
<ServiceConfiguration …>
 <Role name="WorkerRole1">
  <Instances count="1" />
  <ConfigurationSettings>
   <Setting name="…" value="…"/>
  </ConfigurationSettings>
 </Role>
```

```
<NetworkConfiguration>
 <VirtualNetworkSite name="sol-exp-vm-vnet"/>
 <AddressAssignments>
  <InstanceAddress roleName="WorkerRole1">
   <Subnets>
    <Subnet name="Subnet-1"/>
   </Subnets>
  </InstanceAddress>
 </AddressAssignments>
 </NetworkConfiguration>
</ServiceConfiguration>
```

To join a role to a particular subnet in a virtual network requires two major steps, both performed by adding configuration within the NetworkConfiguration element. First, you must associate the cloud service with a virtual network. This is accomplished by adding a VirtualNetworkSite element and specifying the name of the virtual network as the value for the name attribute. Second, you need to add an AddressAssignments element that contains one InstanceAddress element for each role in the cloud service. The InstanceAddress element is associated with the role by the value specified for the roleName attribute (whose value must be the name of the role). Within the InstanceAddress element, specify a <Subnets> element that will contain a <Subnet> entry whose name attribute indicates the name of the subnet in the virtual network in which instances of the role shall be placed. The previous example is in effect configuring instances of the role WorkerRole1 to be placed in the subnet "Subnet-1" of the virtual network "sol-exp-vm-vnet".

Configuring reserved IPs and public IPs

Cloud services can be assigned a reserved IP that keeps the VIP address from changing, and role instances can be assigned public IPs that enable direct access to each instance without specifying a port. Refer to "Objective 2.4: Configure VM networking" in Chapter 2 for why to use public IPs and how they work with VMs; they serve the same purpose and provide the same function to a cloud service. However, in contrast to the way you configure reserved and public IPs in VMs, for a cloud service role you configure the reserved and public IPs by editing the service configuration file.

CONFIGURING A RESERVED IP

Before you can configure a reserved IP on a cloud service, you need to create a reserved IP in your Azure subscription. Unlike for VMs, the management portals currently do not offer a standalone method for creating the reserved IP resource. To create this resource, use the following Windows PowerShell cmdlet:

```
New-AzureReservedIP -Location "<RegionName>" -ReservedIPName <ReservedIPName>
```

Replace <RegionName> with the region to which the IP will be associated (for example, "West US") and <ReservedIPName> with the name you will use to reference the resource in your cloud service configuration.

With a reserved IP allocated, add configuration within the NetworkConfiguration element of the service configuration. The following code shows an example of associating a reserved IP named "sol-exp-res-ip" with the cloud service:

```xml
<?xml version="1.0" encoding="utf-8"?>
<ServiceConfiguration …>
 <Role name="WorkerRole1">
  <Instances count="1" />
  <ConfigurationSettings>
   <Setting name="…" value="…"/>
  </ConfigurationSettings>
 </Role>
 <NetworkConfiguration>
  <AddressAssignments>
   <ReservedIPs>
    <ReservedIP name="sol-exp-res-ip"/>
   </ReservedIPs>
  </AddressAssignments>
 </NetworkConfiguration>
</ServiceConfiguration>
```

In the previous example, a ReservedIPs element containing a single ReservedIP element is added to the NetworkConfiguration element. This NetworkConfiguration element has only one attribute, the name of the reserved IP resource. With this configuration in place, this cloud service can be deployed with a reserved IP address assigned, in addition to the IP address automatically assigned to its VIP.

CONFIGURING A PUBLIC IP

You enable a public IP for a role instance by enabling it for all instances in that role. Each instance receives a unique public IP. The public IP is also configured within the service configuration, as shown in the following example:

```xml
<?xml version="1.0" encoding="utf-8"?>
<ServiceConfiguration …>
 <Role name="WorkerRole1">
  <Instances count="3" />
  <ConfigurationSettings>
   <Setting name="…" value="…"/>
  </ConfigurationSettings>
 </Role>
 <NetworkConfiguration>
  <AddressAssignments>
   <InstanceAddress roleName="WorkerRole1">
    <PublicIPs>
     <PublicIP name="MyPublicIP"/>
    </PublicIPs>
   </InstanceAddress>
  </AddressAssignments>
 </NetworkConfiguration>
</ServiceConfiguration>
```

In this example, an AddressAssignments element is added to the NetworkConfiguration element. This AddressAssignments element references WorkerRole1 in its InstanceAddress element by referencing WorkerRole1 in the roleName attribute. The AddressAssignments element also includes a PublicIPs element defining a single PublicIP by the name MyPublicIP. These AddressAssignments settings are applied to all instances of the role WorkerRole1.

Unlike a reserved IP, this PublicIP resource is not created in advance. This configuration will result in Azure assigning a distinct public IP for each instance of WorkerRole1. In other words, this configuration yields three public IPs, one pointing to each of the three role instances.

Configuring local storage

Local storage provides temporary disk space for your cloud service application. For example, you can use local storage as a temporary location for file uploads, as storage for files that you have to generate, or as a place for a Microsoft Installer (MSI) to run when your application starts.

Local storage can persist between restarts of the VM that hosts your role. The data will be lost if your role is migrated to a different VM host. If you require durability, you should use Azure Blob storage, which is covered in Chapter 4, "Design and implement a storage strategy."

To configure local storage, complete the following steps:

1. In your Azure cloud services project, open the Roles folder.

2. Right-click the role you would like to configure with local storage.

3. Click Properties.

4. Click the Local Storage tab in the Properties window (shown in Figure 3-10).

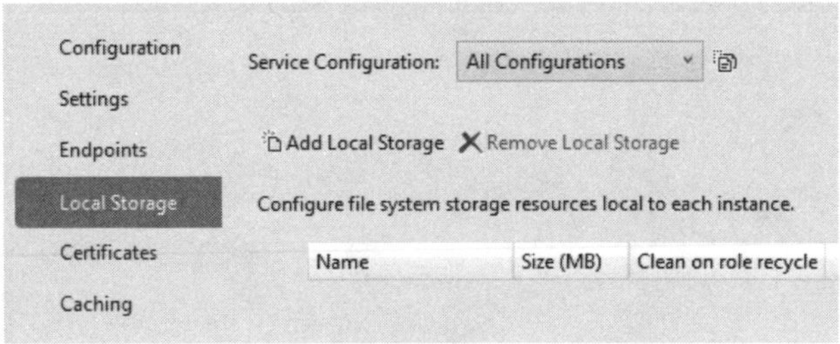

FIGURE 3-10 The Local Storage tab in Visual Studio

5. Click Add Local Storage.

6. Specify the name of the local storage. The default is LocalStorage1 as shown in Figure 3-11.

7. You can specify any size (in MB) between 1 MB and the maximum size allotted for the VM size of the role you have configured. For instance, an ExtraSmall can have 19 GB of local storage, whereas an A6 can have 999 GB of local storage.

Configure file system storage resources local to each instance.

	Name	Size (MB)	Clean on role recycle
▶	LocalStorage1	1024	☐

FIGURE 3-11 Configuring LocalStorage1 in Visual Studio

> **MORE INFO   STORAGE CAPACITY**
>
> **For a detailed listing of the storage capacity available to a cloud service role by the VM size, see *http://msdn.microsoft.com/en-us/library/azure/dn197896.aspx*.**

It is important to be aware of disk space management. If you reach your maximum size of local storage, when you attempt to write again, you will get an out of disk space error message. Note that on the Local Storage configuration tab, you can configure a disk space that is higher than that allotted to your chosen role VM size. No error will be generated until the disk actually fills past the capacity allotted. Always have a method for deleting old files and clearing out space so that writing can continue.

The Clean On Role Recycle option controls persistence between reboots. If this option is cleared, your data will be preserved when the role recycles. If this option is selected, it will be cleared.

Within your role's RoleEntryPoint code, to find the path being used for local storage, call RoleEnvironment.GetLocalResource, for example with this command:

```
LocalResource localResource = RoleEnvironment.GetLocalResource("LocalStorage1");
```

A hard path will be returned, similar to the following:

```
"C:\Users\sol\AppData\Local\dftmp\Resources\d374ab4b-ddd5-41fd-99b6-9f76f44c6779\
directory\LocalStorage1\"
```

When the path is returned, you can use all of the regular .NET file I/O classes, like DirectoryInfo and FileInfo to interact with local storage. To do so, call the RootPath property of the LocalResource object, for example with this code:

```
LocalResource localResource = RoleEnvironment.GetLocalResource("LocalStorage1");
string text = "Azure Rocks! ";
System.IO.File.WriteAllText(localResource.RootPath + "\\myFile.txt", text);
```

Configuring multiple websites in a web role

A single web role is not limited to hosting only a single website. By differentiating between websites using either host headers, a single web role can be configured, by editing the cloud service definition, to host multiple websites.

For these steps, you should begin with a cloud service project that has a web role. The following steps walk through adding another website project and then configuring the web role to serve both the existing website and the newly added website.

1. Open the cloud service project containing your web role in Visual Studio.

2. In Solution Explorer, right-click the solution and select Add, and then click New Project.

3. In the New Project dialog box navigation pane, click the Visual C#\Web or Visual Basic\ Web node.

4. In the listing that appears, click ASP.NET Web Application. Provide a name for the project, and then click OK.

5. In the New ASP.NET Project dialog box, configure the ASP.NET project as desired and clear the Host In Cloud check box under the Microsoft Azure heading. Click OK.

6. In Solution Explorer, navigate to the cloud service deployment project and open the service definition file (*.csdef).

7. Before the closing </Sites> tag, add a new Site element as follows:

   A. The Site element should have a name attribute that uniquely identifies the site. Add a physicalDirectory attribute to the new Site element that provides the relative path to the new web application project. This path is relative to the location of the .csdef file and typically has the form "...\NewWebAppName."

   B. Within the Site element, add a Bindings element with a single Binding element. The Binding element should have the same name and endpointName attribute values as those used by the original website.

   C. To each of the two Binding elements add a hostHeader attribute that will differentiate requests intended for the original website versus the website just added. For example, you might have a public website and an admin website where the public website's Binding element includes hostHeader="www.contoso.com" and the admin website's Binding element includes hostHeader="admin.contoso.com".

```xml
<?xml version="1.0" encoding="utf-8"?>
<ServiceDefinition name="AzureCloudServiceMultiWebsites" xmlns="http://
schemas.microsoft.com/ServiceHosting/2008/10/ServiceDefinition"
schemaVersion="2014-06.2.4">
 <WebRole name="WebRole1" vmsize="Small">
  <Sites>
   <Site name="Web">
    <Bindings>
     <Binding name="Endpoint1" endpointName="Endpoint1" hostHeader="public.
contoso.com" />
    </Bindings>
   </Site>
   <Site name="Web2" physicalDirectory="..\WebApp2">
    <Bindings>
     <Binding name="Endpoint1" endpointName="Endpoint1" hostHeader="admin.contoso.
com"/>
    </Bindings>
```

```
        </Site>
       </Sites>
       <Endpoints>
        <InputEndpoint name="Endpoint1" protocol="http" port="80" />
       </Endpoints>
      </WebRole>
     </ServiceDefinition>
```

When the preceding configuration is deployed, you can access the public site via *http://public.contoso.com* and the admin site *via http://admin.contoso.com*.

To test this configuration locally in the emulator, open your hosts file (located at c:\windows\system32\etc\hosts) in Notepad and add entries to the loopback address (127.0.01) for each host header name value. For the previous example configuration, your hosts file should include the following:

```
127.0.0.1        public.contoso.com
127.0.0.1        admin.contoso.com
```

Run your cloud service project in Visual Studio (with or without debugging). When the browser loads, replace the local host name with one of the previous host header names, but keep the port the same. For example, the browser might load pointing to *http://localhost:27727*. To access the public site, browse to *http://public.contoso.com:27727*. Similarly, to access the admin site, browse to *http://admin.contoso.com:27727*.

An alternative to differentiating the websites via host headers is to use different ports (and therefore different InputEndpoints) for each website. To accomplish this, modify the previous service definition by removing the hostHeader attributes on each Binding element, and for the second website's Binding element, adjust the value of the endpointName so that it references a new InputEndpoint element in the Endpoints section that uses a distinct port from the first endpoint, as shown in the following example:

```
<?xml version="1.0" encoding="utf-8"?>
<ServiceDefinition name="AzureCloudServiceMultiWebsites" xmlns="http://schemas.
microsoft.com/ServiceHosting/2008/10/ServiceDefinition" schemaVersion="2014-06.2.4">
  <WebRole name="WebRole1" vmsize="Small">
   <Sites>
    <Site name="Web">
     <Bindings>
      <Binding name="Endpoint1" endpointName="Endpoint1" />
     </Bindings>
    </Site>
    <Site name="Web2" physicalDirectory="..\..\..\WebApp2">
     <Bindings>
      <Binding name="Endpoint2" endpointName="Endpoint2" />
     </Bindings>
    </Site>
   </Sites>
   <Endpoints>
    <InputEndpoint name="Endpoint1" protocol="http" port="27727" />
    <InputEndpoint name="Endpoint2" protocol="http" port="27728" />
   </Endpoints>
  </WebRole>
</ServiceDefinition>
```

Configuring custom domains

When you deploy a cloud service, any roles for which you have configured an input endpoint will be accessible using the DNS name of the form <cloudServiceName>.cloudapp.net where <cloudServiceName> is the prefix you supplied when creating the cloud service. To have a custom domain (such as www.contoso.com instead of contoso.cloudapp.net) resolve to the IP address of your cloud service, you have to configure DNS. There are two ways to configure DNS:

- **A record**   You can configure a DNS entry that maps contoso.com, www.contoso.com, or *.contoso.com (for example, every subdomain under contoso.com) directly to the VIP address of your cloud service. This type of mapping is expressed by an A record in DNS.

- **CNAME record**   You can configure a DNS entry that maps a subdomain (like the *www* in www.contoso.com) to the DNS name of your cloud service (for example, contoso.cloudapp.net). This type of mapping is expressed by a CNAME in DNS.

These records are configuration entries that you provide to the DNS registrar that is managing your custom domain name. The key difference between the two is that an A record maps a domain to an IP address and a CNAME creates an alias that maps a domain name to another domain name.

Before you begin configuring an A or CNAME record, you should be familiar with where to get the key configuration values you will need to supply to your DNS provider. These values are the IP address of the cloud service and the DNS name of the cloud service. Both of these can be acquired by logging into the existing Azure management portal and navigating to the Dashboard tab for the production slot of your cloud service. In the Quick Glance section on the right, locate the Site URL entry (which provides the DNS name of your cloud service) and the Virtual IP Address entry (which provides the IP address of your cloud service). Which of these two values you use depends ultimately on whether you configure an A record or a CNAME record.

In the following example, assume that the cloud service DNS name is contoso.cloudapp.net and the VIP is currently 191.236.72.93 and that you want to map a custom domain of contoso.com to this.

Configuring an A record

You create an A record in DNS when you want to map a domain name to a static IP address. You can use the VIP of your cloud service for this purpose, whereby you enter an A record of the form in your DNS registrar, following this form:

HOST NAME/SUBDOMAIN	IP ADDRESS
@	191.236.72.93

In most DNS registrars, the at symbol (@) maps to the root of the domain, which in this case means that contoso.com will resolve to 191.236.72.93. With that, you have configured the root or "naked" domain of contoso.com to map to the VIP of your cloud service. Alternately, you can use an asterisk (*) as the host name to map all subdomains to the IP address, or you could provide a single specific host name, such as *www*, to map that host name to the IP address.

When using an A record, you have to be cautious that the IP address value you map to does not change, because if it does, your custom domain will not resolve to your cloud service. If you ever delete the deployment in the production slot of your cloud service and then later re-deploy, your VIP will have changed. If this happens, you will need to update the IP address you have configured in DNS with the new VIP value.

> **NOTE** **PRESERVING YOUR IP ADDRESS**
>
> It is a best practice to deploy to the staging slot first and then perform a VIP swap operation that moves your new deployment into production to ensure you don't lose the VIP associated with production. (VIP swap is covered in "Objective 3.3: Deploy a cloud service" later in this chapter.)
>
> Another way to preserve the IP address of the cloud service is to assign a reserved IP to your cloud service and then use that IP address in the A record.
>
> Yet another alternative is to *not* use an A record at all, and to instead map your custom domain using a CNAME, which is discussed in the following section.

Configuring a CNAME record

Create a CNAME record when you want to map a subdomain of your custom domain to the DNS name of your cloud service. Continuing with the example from the previous section, assume you want to map www.contoso.com to your cloud service. In your DNS registrar, enter a CNAME record of the following form:

HOST/SUBDOMAIN/ALIAS	POINTS TO/TARGET DNS
www	contoso.cloudapp.net

Configuring caching

Besides hosting websites and logic for background processing, a role can also be used to provide a cache cluster using In-Role Cache for Azure Cache. This distributed, in-memory cache can be used to store frequently accessed data so that access to it is fast and offloads the data retrieval work from other resources like your SQL database. In-Role Cache is configured to run within a single role within a cloud service deployment that you manage and deploy, where the instances of your cache role make up the cache cluster. The cache can only be accessed from managed code running within role instances within the same cloud service deployment that contains the cache role. In other words, if you a have a cloud service with a web role, a worker role, and a cacherole, only instances from those three roles can access the cache, in particular, VMs and websites cannot access the cache provided by In-Role Cache.

> *NOTE* **MEMCACHE PROTOCOL SUPPORT**
>
> While the managed cache API can be used only by managed clients, the In-Role Cache also provides support for the memcache protocol, which, when enabled, provides cache access to other non-.NET languages, such as PHP, using the memcache client libraries for that language. For details on how to enable memacache support, see *http://msdn.microsoft.com/en-us/library/azure/hh914167.aspx*.

The In-Role Cache can be configured in the following two different topologies:

- **Co-located cache**   Each role instance contributes a certain percentage of its memory to the cache and joins in as part of the larger cache cluster. In the co-located cache scenario, the cache support is provided in addition to whatever the primary function of the role is (for example, for a web role it might be hosting the website, and for a worker role it might be performing the background processing).

- **Dedicated cache**   Worker roles that are only used for caching and nothing else can form a dedicated cache. Naturally, these have the ability to contribute more of the memory of each role instance toward the cache cluster.

In either topology, you are paying for the time the VM infrastructure supporting your role instances are running and not for any additional cache service (as you might for the Storage Service). As a result, the In-Role Cache feature in Azure does not have an SLA (although you still get a 99.95 percent SLA for multiple role instances supporting the In-Role Cache cluster when they are spread across different fault and upgrade domains).

In-Role Cache stores objects in serialized form within the in-memory cache that is distributed over multiple role instances. By default, this serialization relies on the NetDataContractSerializer (which means any object stored in the cache must be instances of classes marked Serializable), but you can opt to use the BinaryFormatter or implement a custom serializer instead.

Configuring caching on a role

The steps for configuring a co-located versus a dedicated cache are very similar; the following steps call out the difference.

1. Open or create a cloud service project in Visual Studio. You can start from scratch or you can configure an existing role to participate in the cache cluster. When creating a new cloud service, you can add the preconfigured cache worker role directly or you can use a web or worker role.

2. In Server Explorer, right-click the role in which you wish to enable In-Role Cache and select Properties.

3. On the properties page that appears, click the Caching tab as shown in Figure 3-12.

4. To enable In-Role Cache on that role, select the Enable Caching check box.

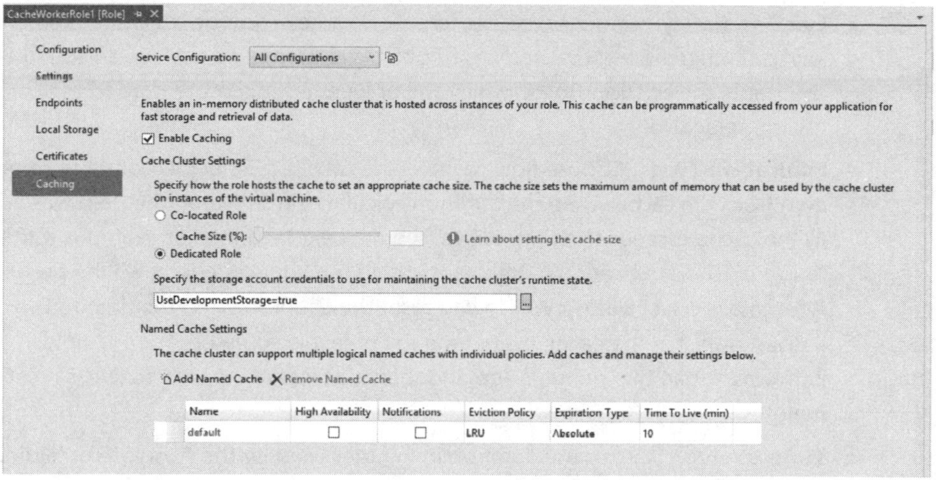

FIGURE 3-12 The caching tab in Visual Studio

When you enable caching, you will have options for a co-located role or a dedicated role, depending on the type of role you selected to configure in step 2. If you are inspecting the properties on a web role, only the Co-located Role option is available because, by definition, this web role will also be hosting a website in addition to its cache duties. If you are inspecting a worker role, both the Co-located Role and the Dedicated Role options are enabled since a dedicated cache role is really just a worker role whose RoleEntryPoint code does not run any application-specific logic.

5. Select the topology you want for your in-role cache:

   A. For a co-located topology, select Co-Located Role and then use the Cache Size slider to indicate the maximum percentage of memory from each instance in the role to contribute toward the cache cluster.

   B. For a Dedicated topology, select Dedicated Role.

6. Select the storage account that the cache cluster will use to persist its runtime state. (Note that this is not used to persist any data in the cache, which is purely maintained within instance memory.)

7. Optionally, configure the policies on the default cache:

   ■ **High Availability**   Select the High Availability check box to ensure that any single piece of cache data is represented by two copies, each on a separate instance within the cluster.

- **Notifications** Select the Notifications check box to enable cache clients to poll the cluster for notifications about data that has changed. These notifications then surface as callbacks that are handled by your cache clients.

- **Eviction Policy** Choose whether to enforce an eviction policy when memory runs low (such that the least recently used objects are removed first) by selecting LRU. To disable the eviction policy, which will prevent adding more data to the cache if it fills up, select None.

- **Expiration Type** Choose how cache data is expired. Select Absolute to remove an item from the cache when the duration calculated from when the item was added to the cache exceeds the time to live (see the next setting). For example, if the time to live is 10 minutes and the item was added ten minutes ago, it will be purged. Alternately, select Sliding Window to reset the countdown to the time to live on a given object in the cache every time the object is accessed. For example, if an item was added two minutes ago and then is accessed, its time to live is reset to 10 minutes.

- **Time to Live** Specify the duration in minutes used by the Absolute or Sliding Window expiration types.

8. Add any additional named caches with other policies as desired. A named cache is a logical grouping of cache data that enables you to have another cache on which different policies are configured.

   A. Add a new named cache by clicking Add Named Cache.

   B. In the grid, provide a name for the new named cache in the new row, under the Name column.

   C. Configure the policies as desired (as in step 7).

9. Set the instance size for the role, which will effectively dictate the amount of memory each role can contribute. Click the Configuration tab, and from the VM Size drop-down list, select an option.

10. Set the number of instances in the role. The number of instances multiplied by the memory provided by each instance yields the total capacity of the cache cluster. On the Configuration tab, type the number of instances you want in the Instance Count text box.

11. Save the solution.

Implementing a cache client

With the previous task complete, you now have a role configured to provide the in-role cache. The next task is to write code within your web or worker role that uses the caching API to read from and write to the cache. First, you will need to set up the Visual Studio project that represents your role with the assembly references required for caching. Second, you will need to place some configuration in web.config (for a web role) or app.config (for a worker role) to configure the cache client. Third, you need to write some code within your client role to use the cache API to read and write from the cache.

ADDING THE CACHING NUGET PACKAGE

To add the caching NuGet package, complete the following steps:

1. Open the solution that contains your cache role in Visual Studio.

2. In Solution Explorer, right-click the Visual Studio project that represents your role and select Manage NuGet Package.

3. In the navigation pane, ensure Online is selected. In the search box at the top right, type **Windows Azure Cache**. The results will appear as shown in Figure 3-13.

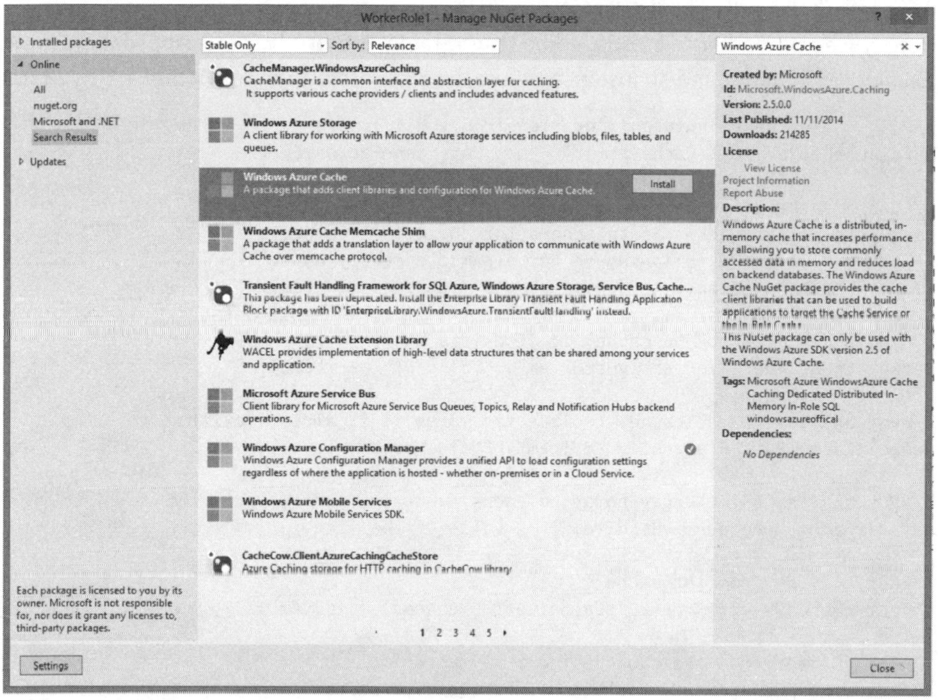

FIGURE 3-13 Search results for NuGet

4. In the search results, click Windows Azure Cache, and then click Install.

5. Review and accept the license when prompted.

6. When the process completes, the assemblies are added and some boilerplate configuration is added to your app.config (for a worker role) or web.config (for a web role).

CONFIGURING THE CACHE CLIENT

The next step is to open the app.config or web.config (as appropriate, depending on the role you are using as a client). Within that configuration is a new <dataCacheClient> section. For the most basic configuration, set the identifier attribute within the <autoDiscover> element to the value of the name of the role within the cloud service that is configured as the in-role cache. For example, if the role on which you enabled caching is named CacheWorkerRole1, then modify this section of the configuration as follows:

```
<dataCacheClients>
 <dataCacheClient name="default">
  <autoDiscover isEnabled="true" identifier="CacheWorkerRole1" />
 </dataCacheClient>
</dataCacheClients>
```

ACCESSING THE CACHE PROGRAMMATICALLY

In your web or worker role code, add a Using statement for Microsoft.ApplicationServer. Caching by instantiating an instance of a cache client from the DataCacheFactory as follows:

```
//Pull the cache client configuration from the *.config
DataCacheFactory dataCacheFactory = new DataCacheFactory();

// Get a cache client to the default cache
DataCache defaultCache = dataCacheFactory.GetDefaultCache();
// or you could the following to get a named cache by name:
// DataCache namedCache = dataCacheFactory.GetCache("default");

// Add a new item to the cache, if it exists an error is thrown
defaultCache.Add("FrequentlyUsedItem", "Value of the item");

// Put an item in the cache, replace the value if it already exists
defaultCache.Put("FrequentlyUsedItem", "Value of the item");

// Put an item using array notation, adds a new item or replaces the value if it exists
defaultCache["FrequentlyUsedItem"] = "Value of the item";

// Get an item from the cache
object cachedObject = defaultCache.Get("FrequentlyUsedItem");

// Get an item from the cache using array notation.
object cachedObject2 = defaultCache["FrequentlyUsedItem"];
```

> **NOTE ROLEENTRYPOINT CODE WITHIN A WEB ROLE**
>
> If you are attempting to use the cache within a web role's RoleEntryPoint logic (for example in WebRole.cs) as opposed to within ASP.NET code behind files, then you must programmatically configure the cache instead of relying on the web.config to provide the settings. See the following link for examples on how to do so: *http://msdn.microsoft.com/en-us/library/azure/jj852128.aspx*.

The previous code creates an instance of the DataCacheFactory so that the cache clients created it from it use the settings you provided in the configuration file. With a reference to an instance of the DataCacheFactory, you create a cache client by calling either GetDefaultCache() to get the default cache or GetCache(string) to request a specific named cache. With a cache client instance ready, you can use the Add, Put, or Item methods (the array accessor style) to add data to the cache. You can retrieve data from the cache using the Get or Item methods (array accessor method).

IMPORTANT **OPTIMAL USE OF DATACACHEFACTORY**

You should be sure to consider the following when working with DataCacheFactory:

- Always dispose of the DataCacheFactory to free underlying resources when you are finished with using the factory reference. Forgetting to dispose of the factory will introduce leaks and could eventually lead to unexpected problems in the application.

- Do not create and dispose of the DataCacheFactory instance for each interaction with the cache. You should hold on to the factory reference and re-use the connection to reduce overhead with creating the cache connection.

- Each factory has a setting for the number of connections to the cache (max-ConnectionsToServer). The default value is 1, but you can adjust this based on the requirements of your application to improve performance.

MORE INFO **OTHER IN-ROLE CACHE FEATURES**

In-Role Cache has many features beyond the core feature of managing data within the cache cluster. These include support for each cache client to manage its own local cache of the data in the cache, the ability to programmatically receive notifications about cache events (for example, items added or removed), the ability to create a searchable group of cache entries using regions and tags, and support for using the in-role cache cluster as the backing for ASP.NET Session and Output Cache via the ASP.NET Session and Output Cache Providers. To read more on these features, see *http://msdn.microsoft.com/en-us/library/azure/hh697523.aspx*.

Objective summary

- Role VM size and instance count is configured as part of the cloud service configuration initially deployed to Azure. You can also adjust the number of instances from the management portal.

- To expose an HTTPS endpoint for a cloud service role, you must upload the certificate to Azure and reference it in the configuration for the endpoint prior to deployment.

- Using the NetworkConfiguration schema, you can configure ACLs to control access by other roles in the deployment package or by remote VMs using IP address restrictions.

- You can combine multiple roles into a single VM by manually adjusting the cloud service configuration. This capability is not exposed through the role properties pages.

Objective review

Answer the following questions to test your knowledge of the information in this objective. You can find the answers to these questions and explanations of why each answer choice is correct or incorrect in the "Answers" section at the end of this chapter.

1. Which of the following is *not* true regarding scaling the instance count of a cloud service? (Choose all that apply.)

   A. You can only scale in even multiples.

   B. You must pre-provision all role instances before scaling up.

   C. You can scale the instance count using auto-scale.

   D. You can scale the instance count using the existing portal.

2. Which of the following is NOT true about cloud service networking?

    A. You can use network traffic rules to restrict inter-role communication.

    B. You can configure ACL to restrict access to a specified subnet.

    C. You cannot join a cloud service to a virtual network.

    D. A public IP does not require a port to reach a role instance.

3. Which of the following are valid configuration options for In-Role Cache? (Choose all that apply.)

    A. Dedicated cache

    B. Persistent cache

    C. Co-located cache

    D. Named cache

Objective 3.3: Deploy a cloud service

There are several ways to publish a cloud service:

- You can publish from Visual Studio.
- You can package from Visual Studio, or the command line, and deploy through the portal or using Windows PowerShell
- You can publish from Visual Studio Online.

There are other topics related to deployment beyond just publishing the cloud service to Azure. This objective reviews how you can upgrade an existing deployment, safely promote a deployment from staging to production, and other topics related to deployment of a cloud service.

> **This objective covers how to:**
>
> - Package a deployment
> - Upgrade a deployment
> - VIP swap a deployment
> - Implement continuous delivery from Visual Studio Online
> - Implement runtime configuration changes using the management portal
> - Configure regions and affinity groups

Packaging a deployment

A cloud service application package includes all of the application and service model files needed to deploy and run an application in an Azure cloud service. When you deploy to Azure using a package, you deploy two files: the application package file and the service configuration file.

Packaging a deployment using Visual Studio

You can package a deployment and create both the package (*.cspkg) and the service configuration (*.cscfg) files by using Visual Studio.

1. Open the cloud service project you want to package in Visual Studio.

2. In Solution Explorer, right-click the cloud service deployment project and select Package.

3. In the Package Azure Application dialog box, specify the service configuration you want to use by selecting the appropriate value from the respective drop-down lists. To enable Remote Desktop, select the Enable Remote Desktop check box and configure the RDP settings in the dialog box that appears. To enable remote debugging, select the Enable Remote Debugger For All Roles check box.

4. Click Package.

5. When Visual Studio finishes creating the package, a new Windows Explorer window appears showing the .cspkg and .cscfg files that were created. You can deploy these using the management portal, such as when upgrading a deployment.

> *NOTE* **PACKAGING FROM THE COMMAND LINE**
>
> You can also use the CSPack command-line tool to create a package from the command line. See the following documentation for details: *http://msdn.microsoft.com/en-us/library/azure/gg432988.aspx*.

Upgrading a deployment

When you re-deploy a cloud service, you have options as to how Azure should roll out changes to the role instances, including the following three options:

- **Incremental**   In this scenario, Azure rolls out the upgrade while attempting to minimize the impact on the overall service. It does this by upgrading instances one upgrade domain at time. For instances in the upgrade domain, this includes stopping the instance, applying the updates, and restarting the instance. Only after all instances in the upgrade domain are back online does Azure move to the instances in the next upgrade domain. While this method ensures availability of the service, it takes significantly more time.

- **Simultaneous** In this scenario, Azure stops all instances at once, applies the update, and brings the instances back online. While this approach takes the shortest time to complete, it makes the service unavailable during the upgrade.

- **Full Deployment** In this scenario, Azure does not attempt to upgrade the instances. It completely removes all the existing instances and performs a fresh deployment with the latest package.

When considering the incremental update option, the most influential setting is the upgradeDomainCount, which sets the number of upgrade domains into which your role instances are distributed. By default, this is set to 5 (such that your instances will be distributed across five upgrade domains), but you can increase that value up to 20. To accomplish this, open the service definition file for your cloud service and add the upgradeDomainCount attribute to the root ServiceDefinition element as follows:

```
<ServiceDefinition name="AzureCloudService2" xmlns="http://schemas.microsoft.
com/ServiceHosting/2008/10/ServiceDefinition" schemaVersion="2014-06.2.4"
upgradeDomainCount="20">
```

When deciding whether to perform an upgrade deployment (either incremental or simultaneous) or a full deployment, note that any of the following changes require a full deployment (or the VIP swap approach, discussed later); you will not be able to perform an upgrade for these changes:

- Change to the name of a role
- Change to the upgrade domain count
- Reduction in the size of local storage resources

MORE INFO **SUPPORTED CHANGES FOR AN UPGRADE**

For a list of all of the changes that you can make to a deployment and still perform an upgrade, see *http://msdn.microsoft.com/en-us/library/azure/hh472157.aspx*.

Deploying an upgrade

You can deploy an upgrade from Visual Studio or by using the management portal. The following sections describe both approaches.

DEPLOYING AN UPGRADE FROM VISUAL STUDIO

To deploy an upgrade from Visual Studio, complete the following steps:

1. In Visual Studio, publish your cloud service. This launches the Publish Azure Application wizard.

2. If you are not already signed in to your subscription, you will be prompted to sign in before the wizard is presented. Sign in to select your subscription.

3. On the Sign In page of the wizard, select your subscription and click Next.

4. On the Settings page of the wizard, on the Common Settings tab, click the Cloud Service drop-down list, and select the target cloud service to upgrade.

5. Click the Advanced Settings tab, and then click the Settings link to the right of the Deployment Upgrade check box.

6. In the dialog box that appears, select either Incremental or Simultaneous as the rollout method for your upgrade. If you select the If Deployment Can't Be Updated, Do A Full Deployment check box, the deployment will automatically perform a full deployment if a change in your cloud service requires it. Click OK.

7. The Deployment Upgrade check box should be selected. If you never want to perform any upgrade and instead always perform a full deployment, clear this check box.

8. Complete configuration of your cloud service as desired, and then click Publish to deploy the cloud service upgrade.

DEPLOYING AN UPGRADE USING THE MANAGEMENT PORTAL (EXISTING PORTAL)

To deploy an upgrade using the management portal, complete the following steps:

1. In Visual Studio, package your cloud service: right-click your cloud service project in Solution Explorer and select Package.

2. When your package is ready, navigate to the existing portal accessed via *https://manage.windowsazure.com*, and then navigate to the dashboard of the cloud service you intend to upgrade.

3. On the command bar, click Update.

4. In the Update Your Deployment dialog box (see Figure 3-14), click From Local to browse for the package you just created, and then click From Local below Configuration to browse for the configuration file (it should be located in the same folder as your .cspkg file). Note that as an alternative, you can upload your package and configuration to blob storage and click From Storage to pull the two files from blob storage instead of your local machine.

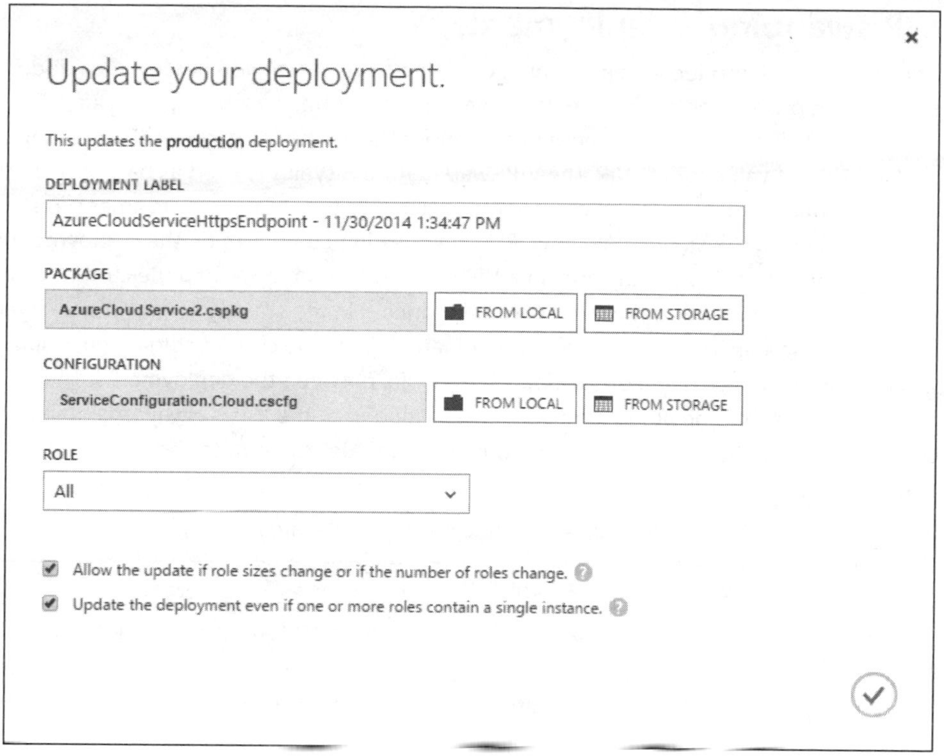

FIGURE 3-14 The Update Your Deployment screen

5. Optionally, select which role to update from the Role drop-down list, or leave the selection as All to upgrade all roles.

6. If your package includes a change to the role instance size or adds or removes roles, select the Allow The Update If Role Sizes Change Or The Number Of Roles Change check box. If you do so, note that this may cause your role instances to be re-deployed to a different host within Azure, and therefore any content written to local storage may be lost.

7. If your cloud service contains single instance roles, select the Update The Deployment Even If One Or More Roles Contain A Single Instance check box. If you do so, understand that any role with a single instance will become unavailable during the upgrade.

8. Click the check mark to upload the package and configuration and to begin the upgrade.

DEPLOYING AN UPGRADE USING THE MANAGEMENT PORTAL (PREVIEW PORTAL)
Deploying an upgrade is not currently supported in the Preview portal.

VIP swapping a deployment

Azure provides a production and staging environment in which you deploy your cloud service. The production environment receives the <dns-prefix>.cloudapp.net URL and a VIP, while the staging environment receives a different URL in the form <Guid-ID>.cloudapp.net and a different value for the VIP. The VIP swap feature is typically used as part of deployment workflow where the newest deployment is published to the staging environment. Testing is performed using the staging VIP and URL. When testing completes on the deployment in the staging environment, you can conduct a VIP swap operation to re-map the current production VIP and URL to the deployment currently running in the staging environment. The current production environment receives the VIP and URL of the current staging environment, effectively swapping both the assigned VIP and URL between the deployments. The benefit of the VIP swap is that the production IP address assigned to the VIP is always maintained, which ensures configuration, such as custom domains, continues to point to the correct VIP of the production cloud service.

For example, consider the following table of the initial state of a deployment:

Deployment	VIP	URL
Staged deployment	104.209.40.255	http://881b1274a08340049735f8dc43b09926.cloudapp.net/
Production deployment	104.309.40.200	http://myservice.cloudapp.net

After a VIP swap, the Azure adjusts which environment is treated as production and staging. As shown here, the deployment slot production now points at staging, and vice versa:

Deployment	VIP	URL
Production deployment	104.209.40.255	http://881b1274a08340049735f8dc43b09926.cloudapp.net/
Staged deployment	104.309.40.200	http://myservice.cloudapp.net

Put another way, what was originally deployed to the staging slot is now available via the production VIP and URL.

VIP swapping a deployment (existing portal)

To VIP swap a deployment in the management portal, complete the following steps:

1. Navigate to the management portal accessed via *https://manage.windowsazure.com*, and then navigate to the dashboard of the cloud service you intend to swap.

2. On the command bar, click Swap.

3. Click Yes to proceed with the swap.

4. The VIPs should swap quickly. If you are finished with the deployment currently occupying the staging slot, you can safely delete it.

VIP swapping a deployment (Preview portal)

VIP swapping a deployment is not currently supported in the Preview portal.

Implementing continuous delivery from Visual Studio Online

Visual Studio Online can be configured to automatically build and deploy a cloud service upon check-in from Visual Studio. By default, the cloud service is deployed to the staging environment, but you can alter this by editing the build configuration. Complete the following steps to set up continuous delivery:

1. As a prerequisite, ensure you have created a team project in Visual Studio Online, to which you will check in your cloud service code. If you are not familiar with this process, see *http://www.visualstudio.com/get-started/connect-to-vs*.

2. Open the cloud service project you want to package in Visual Studio.

3. In Solution Explorer, right-click the solution and select Add Solution To Source Control.

4. In the Choose Source Control dialog box that appears, select Team Foundation Version Control.

5. In the Connect To Team Foundation Server dialog box, select your Visual Studio Online server from the drop-down list, and select the check box next to the team project you will use as the repository for the cloud service. Click Connect.

6. In the Add Solution <Name> To Source Control dialog box, customize where in the team project to locate your solution, and click OK.

7. In Solution Explorer, right-click your solution and select Check In.

8. In the Pending Changes area of Team Explorer (shown in Figure 3-15), enter a comment message, and click Check In.

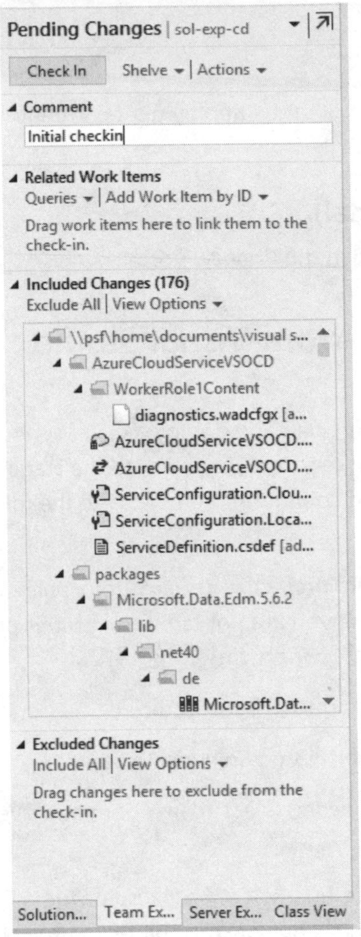

FIGURE 3-15 The Pending Changes pane of Team Explorer

9. Ensure you have deployed your cloud service (or at least create an empty one) using the existing management portal at *https://manage.windowsazure.com*.

10. Click the Cloud tab (to the left of the Dashboard tab) for your cloud service.

11. Click the Setup Publishing With Visual Studio Online link.

12. When prompted to authorize the connection to Visual Studio Online, enter the name of your Visual Studio Online account, and click the Authorize Now link as shown in Figure 3-16.

13. In the OAuth Connection Request dialog box, click Accept.

14. On the next page, from the Project drop-down list, select the team project to deploy, and then click the check mark.

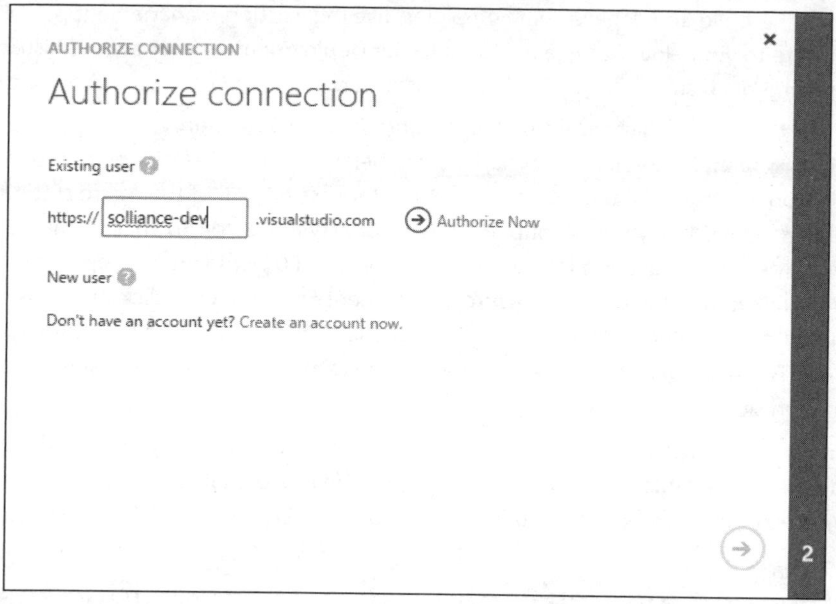

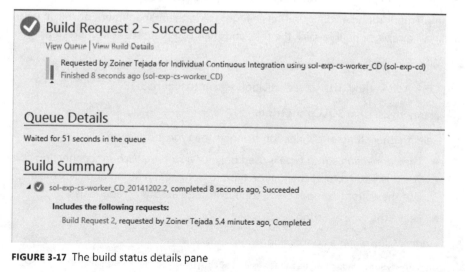

AUTHORIZE CONNECTION

Authorize connection

Existing user ?

https:// | solliance-dev | .visualstudio.com   → Authorize Now

New user ?

Don't have an account yet? Create an account now.

→   2

FIGURE 3-16 Entering a Visual Studio online account

15. Return to Visual Studio, make a change to your cloud service, and then check it in.

16. In Team Explorer, click Home (the house icon).

17. Click Builds.

18. Under My Builds, double-click the build entry to monitor the detailed progress of your active build. A page similar to the one shown in Figure 3-17 appears.

✓ **Build Request 2 – Succeeded**

View Queue | View Build Details

Requested by Zoiner Tejada for Individual Continuous Integration using sol-exp-cs-worker_CD (sol-exp-cd)
Finished 8 seconds ago (sol-exp-cs-worker_CD)

Queue Details

Waited for 51 seconds in the queue

Build Summary

▲ ✓ sol-exp-cs-worker_CD_20141202.2, completed 8 seconds ago, Succeeded

Includes the following requests:
Build Request 2, requested by Zoiner Tejada 5.4 minutes ago, Completed

FIGURE 3-17 The build status details pane

19. When the build and deployment completes, use the existing management portal to navigate to your cloud service and then to the Deployments tab where the history of deployments resulting from check-ins is displayed.

To change the slot to which your build automatically deploys, within Visual Studio, on the Builds screen in Team Explorer, right-click the entry below All Build Definitions, and select Edit Build Definition. On the page that appears, click the Process tab. All of the Azure settings are located under the 6. Deployment grouping in the property inspector. To change the deployment environment to production instead of staging, expand 6.Deployment\Deployment, and click in the value area of the Windows Azure Deployment Environment. Click the ellipses (...) button that appears. In the dialog box, select Production from the Environment drop-down list. Click OK. The next time you check in a change, the cloud service will be pushed directly to the production slot.

Similarly, if you do not want to perform a rolling upgrade upon deployment (and instead want to delete and redeploy all instances at once), on the Process tab under 6. Deployment\ Deployment, set the Allow Upgrade option to False and the Do Not Delete option to False.

Implementing runtime configuration changes using the management portal

A cloud services role might need custom configuration settings stored in an easily accessible place. Those settings can be stored in the configuration settings of the worker or web role. After they are created in the role, they can be changed in the management portal. This allows production environment settings to be managed by other resources and not by the developer. It also allows those configuration settings to vary depending on the deployed environment. For example, in a test environment, the database connection needs to hit the test database, while in production it needs to hit the production database.

To implement runtime configuration changes using the management portal, in your Azure cloud service project, double-click the role, and then complete the following steps:

1. Click Settings.

2. Click Add Setting. The screen will look similar to Figure 3-18.

3. Name the setting **SQLConnString**.

4. Select either string or connection string as the type, as follows:
   - The connection string type is used only for a storage account connection string. If you'd like to explore, change the type to Connection String and click the ellipses. Use the editor that appears to submit storage account credentials
   - Leave the type as String.

5. Under Value, enter a connection string, as follows:

   ```
   Server=myServerAddress;Database=myDataBase;User Id=myUsername;
   Password=myPassword;
   ```

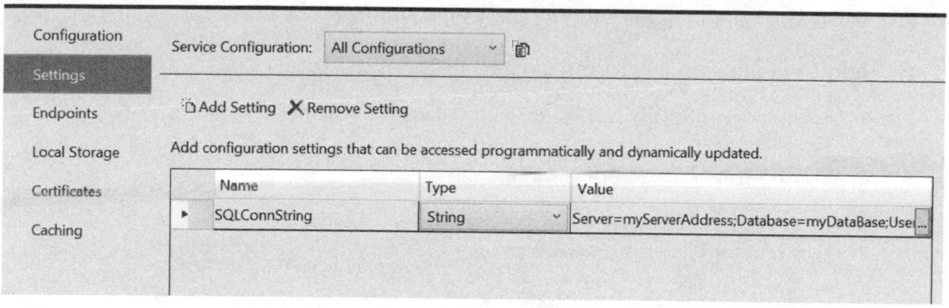

FIGURE 3-18 The Settings tab

6. Add another setting called Environment with the following settings:

   - **Type** String
   - **Value** Development

   The screen will look similar to Figure 3-19.

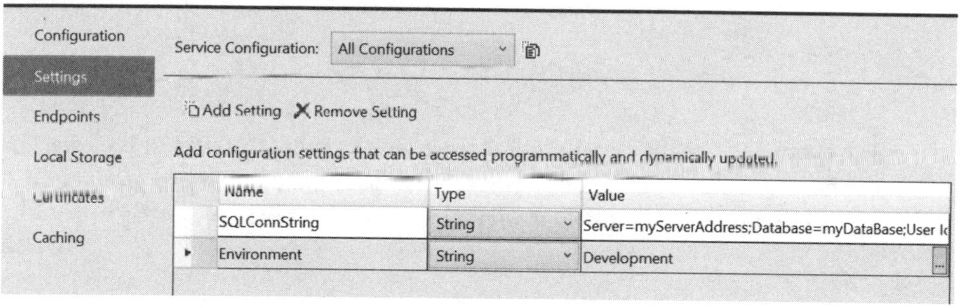

FIGURE 3-19 The Settings tab with two values

Before reviewing how to change these settings in the management portal, you need to understand how settings changes are handled in the role. A setting change in the management portal fires a changing event, followed by a changed event. These events are in the RoleEnvironment class. The following steps focus on the changing event.

> **MORE INFO** **OTHER ROLEENVIRONMENT EVENTS**
>
> For more information other events that the RoleEnvironment supports, see *http://msdn.microsoft.com/en-us/library/microsoft.windowsazure.serviceruntime.roleenvironment_events.aspx.*

1. Open the WorkerRole.cs file.

2. Set a reference to the Microsoft.WindowsAzure.ServiceRuntime.dll. (By default, it's already set.)

3. Verify the Using statement is at the top of the file.

4. Add the following line to the OnStart event of the role:

```
RoleEnvironment.Changing += RoleEnvironmentChanging;
```

5. Create the following event handler:

```
private void RoleEnvironmentChanging(object sender,
RoleEnvironmentChangingEventArgs e)
    {
        foreach (RoleEnvironmentChange rec in e.Changes)
        {
            RoleEnvironmentConfigurationSettingChange recsc = rec as
RoleEnvironmentConfigurationSettingChange;
            if (recsc.ConfigurationSettingName.ToUpper() == "SQLCONNSTRING")
            {
                if (recsc.ToString().ToUpper().Contains("PRODUCTION")
                  && RoleEnvironment.GetConfigurationSettingValue("Environment").
ToUpper() == "DEVELOPMENT")
                {
                    e.Cancel = true;
                }
            }
        }
    }
```

The event handler checks whether this is a development instance of the role. If it is, the handler determines whether you are changing the database to production. Setting e.cancel = true forces the role to recycle before it changes the setting.

6. Deploy your worker role.

7. Login to the management portal.

8. Click Cloud Services.

9. Click your worker role.

10. Click Configure.

11. Under the WorkerRole1 (or whatever you named your version of the role) settings, you should see something similar to Figure 3-20.

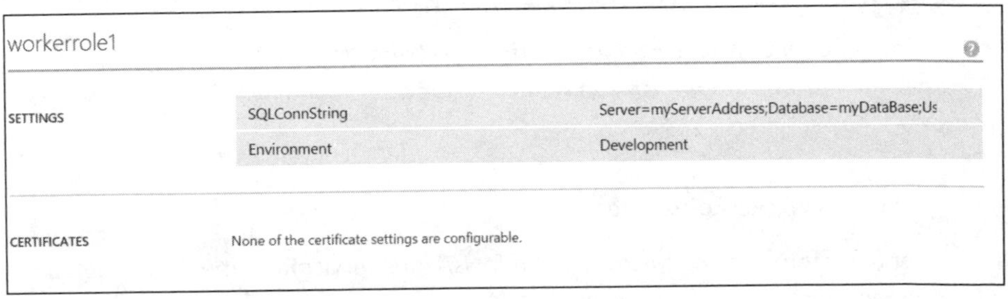

workerrole1		
SETTINGS	SQLConnString	Server=myServerAddress;Database=myDataBase;Us
	Environment	Development
CERTIFICATES	None of the certificate settings are configurable.	

FIGURE 3-20 The Settings tab of the worker role

12. Change the SQLConnString setting and modify the screen so the word PRODUCTION appears someplace in it.

13. Click Save.

The service updates and cycles. The portal notifies you when this is completed.

Configuring regions and affinity groups

A region defines the physical, geographic location of your cloud service. When creating a cloud service, you specify a region, typically based on where the users of that service are geographically located, the geo-political implications of hosting within that region (especially where compliance is concerned), and the proximity of the new cloud service to other services upon which it depends (for example, your worker role should be in the same region as the storage account it uses for the best performance and to minimize data egress costs).

While regions locate and group services by their geographic location, affinity groups describe a scale unit (effectively, a set of co-located server resources) within the Azure datacenter, in which all related resources and services are placed. This logical grouping provided by affinity groups was originally intended to enable you to request that Azure physically locate related services next to each other to minimize the impact of network latency.

As of 2012, however, the Azure datacenter network has undergone a radical restructuring that eliminates the high latencies experienced between services, and with them the need to specify affinity groups. In addition, affinity groups limit you to selecting resources that are part of the scale unit at the time it is created. Using affinity groups therefore restricts your ability to select from new resources that are introduced into the datacenter after you create your affinity group. For example, if you create an affinity group, and then Azure introduces some new, larger VM sizes, you cannot select those VM sizes when provisioning cloud services in the affinity group because they are not a part of the resources included in the scale unit in which your affinity group was defined. By choosing to define only a region, instead of a region and an affinity group, you can always select any of the resources available in the entire region, not just within the subset represented by the scale unit.

You can still use affinity groups and select from a list of existing affinity groups when creating a new service. However, you must create the affinity group first and then create your cloud service.

If you do not have any affinity groups from which to select, you can create a new one using the New-AzureAffinityGroup cmdlet, as follows:

```
New-AzureAffinityGroup -Location <RegionName> -Name <AffinityGroupName>
```

Replace <RegionName> with the Azure datacenter region (such as "West US") in which this affinity group will be provisioned and replace <AffinityGroupName> with the name to use to refer to this new affinity group.

Alternately, you can use the existing management portal to create a new affinity group by completing the following steps:

1. Navigate to the management portal accessed via *https://manage.windowsazure.com*.

2. Click the Settings tab.

3. Within the settings, click the Affinity Groups tab.

4. On the command bar, click Add.

5. Specify a name for the new affinity group, add an optional description, select the region in which to create it, and then click the check mark to create the new affinity group.

To create a cloud service, choose the region or the affinity group in which to provision your cloud service. It is only possible to configure the region or affinity group during the provisioning of the cloud service; you cannot change the region or affinity group after the fact without re-deploying to a new cloud service.

Configuring regions and affinity groups using Windows PowerShell

You can use the New-AzureService cmdlet to create a new cloud service within a region or an affinity group. To create it within an affinity group, created the affinity group, and then run the following:

```
New-AzureService -AffinityGroup <AffinityGroupName> -ServiceName <CloudServiceName>
```

Change <AffinityGroupName> to the name of the existing affinity group and change <CloudServiceName> to the name of the new cloud service.

To create the new cloud service within a region, run the following cmdlet:

```
New-AzureService -Location <RegionName> -ServiceName <CloudServiceName>
```

Change <RegionName> to the name of the datacenter region and change <CloudService-Name> to the name of the new cloud service.

Configuring regions and affinity groups (existing portal)

To configure regions and affinity groups in the management portal, complete the following steps:

1. Navigate to the management portal accessed via *https://manage.windowsazure.com*.

2. On the command bar, click New.

3. Click Compute, Cloud Service, and then Quick Create.

4. Provide a prefix for your cloud service DNS name.

5. In the Region Or Affinity Group drop-down list, select the region or the affinity group in which to create your cloud service.

If there are no affinity group options, you have not created any affinity groups in this subscription. (Use Windows PowerShell or the existing management portal to create one.)

6. Click Create Cloud Service.

Configuring regions and affinity groups (Preview portal)

You cannot currently configure regions and affinity groups in the Preview portal.

Configuring regions and affinity groups in Visual Studio

To configure regions and affinity groups in Visual Studio, complete the following steps:

1. In Visual Studio, publish your cloud service.

2. Sign in to select your subscription.

3. On the Sign In tab, select your Subscription and click Next.

4. Click the Cloud Service drop-down list and select <Create New...>.

5. Provide a name for the new cloud service.

6. In the Region Or Affinity Group drop-down list, select the region or the affinity group in which to create your cloud service.

   If there are no affinity group options, it means you have not created any affinity groups in this subscription. (Use Windows PowerShell or the existing management portal to create one.)

7. Click Create.

8. Complete configuration of your cloud service as desired and then click Publish to deploy the cloud service within the selected region or affinity group.

> ## Thought experiment
> ### Deployments
>
> In this thought experiment, apply what you've learned about this objective. You can find answers to these questions in the "Answers" section at the end of this chapter.
>
> Your cloud service has been successfully deployed to Azure, and now you are thinking about how you will handle future deployments.
>
> 1. What options do you have for deploying upgrades?
>
> 2. What deployment processes might you consider?

Objective summary

- When you deploy a cloud service, you publish a package with the files to deploy for each role and a configuration describing deployment requirements. This package can be created from Visual Studio or from the command line using CSPack.

- You have three options for deploying upgrades to cloud services: Deploy them incrementally to reduce impact to running services, simultaneously to speed the deployment by stopping all instances, or as a full deployment that does not perform an upgrade but replaces the entire deployment.

- VIP swap makes it possible to deploy an update to your cloud service to a staging slot prior to pushing that change to the production slot your users access. When you swap, Azure updates the VIP for production to point at the newly deployed staging slot.

Objective review

Answer the following questions to test your knowledge of the information in this objective. You can find the answers to these questions and explanations of why each answer choice is correct or incorrect in the "Answers" section at the end of this chapter.

1. Which of the following is *not* included within a cloud service application package? (Choose all that apply.)

    A. Compiled application code

    B. Cloud service configuration (*.cscfg)

    C. Dependent assemblies

    D. Cloud service definition (*.csdef)

2. Which of the following situations prevent you from performing an upgrade deployment? (Choose all that apply.)

    A. Increase in the VM instance size

    B. Change in the name of a role

    C. Adjustment in the upgrade domain count

    D. Reduction in the size of local storage resources

3. Which of the following is true regarding VIP swap? (Choose all that apply.)

    A. You can swap an environment from staging to production and back to production.

    B. A VIP swap moves a deployment between hosts.

    C. A VIP swap re-maps only the VIP.

    D. A VIP swap is a time-consuming operation.

Objective 3.4: Monitor and debug a cloud service

Cloud Services provides diagnostics in the form of multiple sources of logs and performance counter metrics to monitor and troubleshoot runtime operation. Additionally, you can debug a cloud service both locally and remotely using Visual Studio. In some cases, you may need to access a machine to troubleshoot a problem, and Cloud Services allows you to use Remote Desktop to do just that.

> **This objective covers how to:**
> - Configure diagnostics
> - Profile resource consumption
> - Enable remote debugging
> - Enable and use Remote Desktop
> - Debug using IntelliTrace
> - Debug using the emulator

Configuring diagnostics

You utilize diagnostics to collect insights into the operational behavior of your cloud service. You configure the collection of diagnostic data first by enabling the Azure Diagnostics module in your service definition, and then configuring the diagnostic data you want to collect. As a result, the Azure Diagnostics monitor will start automatically when the role instance starts. By default, a subset (Azure logs, IIS logs, Azure Diagnostics infrastructure logs) of the available data sources are collected on the local role instance. They are copied to Azure Storage only if you have configured a storage account in the diagnostics configuration. Once your cloud service is deployed with Diagnostics enabled, you can change the Diagnostics monitor configuration.

TABLE 3-1 Diagnostics data sources available to a cloud service

Log Type	RoLE	Location
Azure application logs	Web/Worker	Table storage—WADLogsTable
Diagnostics infrastructure logs	Web/Worker	Table storage—WADDiagnosticInfrastructureLogsTable
Crash dumps	Web/Worker	Blob storage—Container you specify
Event logs	Web/Worker	Table storage—WADWindowsEventLogsTable
Custom error logs	Web/Worker	Blob storage—Container you specify
Performance counters	Web/Worker	Table storage—WADPerformanceCountersTable

Log Type	RoLE	Location
Web Server logs	Web only	Blob storage—Container you specify
Failed request tracing logs	Web only	Blob storage—Container you specify

> **MORE INFO** **DIAGNOSTIC DATA SOURCES**
>
> For a more detailed description of each of the diagnostic data sources, see *http://msdn.microsoft.com/en-us/library/dn205075.aspx*.

As of the Azure SDK 2.5, the only supported mechanism for configuring diagnostics is by using the XML configuration file diagnostics.wadcfgx. This file is automatically created within a cloud service project. To access it, follow these steps:

1. Open Solution Explorer.

2. To configure diagnostics by directly editing the diagnostics.wadcfgx, complete these steps:

    A. For a worker role or web role, in Solution Explorer, expand the cloud service project, expand the Roles folder, and then expand the particular role whose diagnostics you want to configure.

    B. Double-click diagnostics.wadcfgx to open it within Visual Studio where you can edit the contents of the XML file directly.

    C. Make edits and save the file.

3. Alternately, to configure diagnostics using the property dialog boxes in Visual Studio, complete the following steps:

    A. In Solution Explorer, right-click the web or worker role to be configured and select Properties.

    B. On the properties page that appears, leave the Configuration tab selected. In the Diagnostics section, select the Enable Diagnostics check box, and click Configure.

    C. Use the remaining tabs to configure each of the diagnostic log sources.

    D. On the General tab, click Configure to the right of Storage Account Credentials to specify the Azure storage account to which diagnostic data will be copied.

    E. Click OK to apply the changes.

    F. Press Save to persist the changes you made to diagnostics.wadcfgx.

When you have enabled and configured diagnostics, deploy your cloud service. After deployment, you can re-configure diagnostics within Visual Studio by following these steps:

1. Open Solution Explorer and expand the navigation pane until the role you want to configure is visible.

2. Right-click the role and select Update Diagnostics.

3. In the Diagnostics Configuration dialog box, click OK to apply the changes. The settings are applied directly to the running role instead of within your local project.

Viewing Diagnostics data

You can view some diagnostic data your role collects using purpose-built features in Visual Studio or by querying the Azure storage table or blob using Visual Studio tools for navigating storage. The following steps show how to view diagnostic data using the features in Visual Studio:

1. In Server Explorer, right-click the role whose diagnostics you want to examine.

2. Select View Diagnostics Data.

3. In the Diagnostics summary screen that appears, review the summary of all the diagnostics you have configured and the links for details.

4. nostics you have configured and the links for details.

Profiling resource consumption

To measure the performance characteristics to understand which functions are taking the most time, which features are most computationally expensive or memory intensive, or concurrency issues of your cloud service you can use the Visual Studio profiler as it runs remotely in Azure.

Profiling a cloud service in Azure

There are four different performance collection methods you can use to profile your cloud service within Azure, including the following:

- **CPU sampling** In a low impact way, this method periodically collects application statistics that are helpful for analysis of CPU utilization.

- **Instrumentation**   This method adds additional instrumentation to the deployed code so that each function entry, exit, and call is recorded along with timing data and is useful for understanding where a program spends most of its time.

- **.NET memory allocation**   This method periodically collects .NET Framework memory allocation data, providing information such as the quantity and size of allocated objects.

- **Concurrency**   This method collects data for each event that blocks your code from running and is useful in analyzing multi-threaded and multi-process applications.

In addition to these four, with Visual Studio Ultimate you can also collect tier interaction data to gather processing counts and times of the functions that make synchronous calls to a database using ADO.NET.

> **MORE INFO**   **PROFILING METHODS**
>
> For a more detailed exploration of the profiling methods, read *http://msdn.microsoft.com/ en-us/library/dd264994.aspx.*

To enable profiling for a cloud service in Azure, complete the following steps:

1. In Visual Studio, publish your cloud service.

2. Configure your deployment as desired. On the Settings screen, click the Advanced Settings tab.

3. On the Advanced Settings tab, select the Enable Profiling check box.

4. In the Profile Settings dialog box that appears, select the profiling method you want to use. If you have Visual Studio Ultimate and have selected an option other than CPU Sampling, you can select the Enable Tier Interaction Profiling check box.

5. Click OK.

6. Complete configuration of your cloud service, and then click Publish to deploy the cloud service with profiling enabled.

To retrieve the profile report, follow these steps in Visual Studio:

1. On the View menu, click Server Explorer.

2. Expand the Azure node. If prompted to login, log in with your organizational account or the Microsoft account that is associated with the cloud service you intend to debug.

3. Expand Cloud Services, and then expand the cloud service you want to debug.

4. Expand the role whose instance you want to profile, and then right-click an instance and select View Profiling Report.

5. The report downloads and displays in a new document tab within Visual Studio.

Enabling remote debugging

You can use remote debugging to debug one or more instances of a cloud service role using your local copy of Visual Studio. With Visual Studio you can set breakpoints, examine variable values, and step through code. To debug, you must ensure that the deployed cloud service is a debug build (for example, it has the debug symbols) and that the package you have deployed has the remote debugger enabled.

To enable remote debugging, publish your cloud service. On the Settings page of the publish wizard, from the Build Configuration drop-down list, select a debug build. Click the Advanced tab and select the Enable Remote Debugger For All Roles check box. Complete your deployment configuration as desired, and then click Publish.

With the remote debugger enabled, start a debug session in Visual Studio by completing the following steps:

1. Ensure the project you are debugging is built and that you have made no changes to it since you deployed it.

2. On the View menu, click Server Explorer.

3. Expand the Azure node. If prompted to login, log in with your organizational account or the Microsoft account that is associated with the cloud service you intend to debug.

4. Expand Cloud Services, and then expand the cloud service you want to debug.

5. To debug all instances within a role (for example, so you can inspect a breakpoint regardless of the instance on which the code is running), right-click a role and select Attach Debugger. To attach the debugger to a specific role instance, expand the role in the navigation pane, and then right-click an instance and select Attach Debugger.

6. In the Attach To Process dialog box, select a process running within your role to attach to (for example, for a worker role attach to WaWorkerHost.exe), and click OK.

7. When the debugger finishes attaching, debug your code as usual.

> **IMPORTANT** **HOW DEBUGGING AFFECTS YOUR CLOUD SERVICE**
>
> When you attach the debugger and pause at a breakpoint, you are stopping the deployed instance for all requests, so it is not a good idea to rely on this technique for production debugging or users will think your cloud service is down. Also, if you spend more than a few minutes stopped at any one breakpoint, Azure treats the process that is stopped as unavailable and does not send traffic to that instance. Furthermore, if you are stopped too long, the remote debugger service (msvsmon.exe) detaches from the process.

Enabling and using Remote Desktop Protocol

You can enable and use the Remote Desktop Protocol (RDP) to get remote access to a particular instance of a web role or worker role to perform additional configuration of or troubleshooting within the instance. You can enable RDP when you first publish your cloud service using Visual Studio, or you can enable it after deployment using Windows PowerShell or the management portal. When enabled, you can use the management portal to download the RDP file for an instance, open it, enter your credentials, and connect to the instance.

Enabling RDP in the management portal (existing portal)

To enable RDP in the existing management portal, complete the following steps:

1. Navigate to the Configure tab for your cloud service in the management portal accessed via *https://manage.windowsazure.com*.

2. On the command bar, click Remote.

3. Within the Configure Remote Desktop dialog box, from the drop-down list, select a particular role, or leave the selection at (All) to enable RDP for all roles within the cloud service.

4. Select the Enable Remote Desktop check box.

5. Provide a username and password, and confirm the password.

6. Select an existing certificate or leave the default Create A New Certificate option to allow Azure to provision a new one.

7. Click the Expires On field to display a date picker, and select and set an expiration after which RDP access is diabled.

8. Click the check mark to enable RDP.

Enabling RDP in the management portal (Preview portal)

Enabling RDP is currently not supported in the Preview portal.

Enabling RDP using Windows PowerShell

You can enable RDP on a role instance using Windows PowerShell. Run Get-Credential and Windows PowerShell will ask for the username and password to use for RDP access:

```
$cred = Get-Credential
```

Run the following command to enable RDP for all roles within the cloud service:

```
Set-AzureServiceRemoteDesktopExtension -ServiceName <CloudServiceName> -Credential $cred
```

Enabling RDP using Visual Studio

You can enable RDP when publishing your cloud service using Visual Studio by completing the following steps:

1. In Project Explorer, right-click your cloud deployment project and select Publish.

2. On the Sign-In tab, sign in to your Azure account, and select your subscription.

3. Click Next.

4. Select the cloud service to which you want to deploy (or create a new one), and then select the environment (Production or Staging), build configuration, and service configuration.

5. Select the Enable Remote Desktop For All Roles check box.

6. In the dialog box that appears, provide the credentials to use for remote desktop access (enter a username and password and confirm the password). Also, specify an expiration date after which access via RDP is disabled.

7. Click OK.

8. Configure the remaining settings, and then click Publish to deploy your cloud service with RDP enabled.

Using RDP

Using RDP involves downloading the RDP file to a role instance, opening it, and entering your login credentials.

USING THE RDP FILE FROM THE MANAGEMENT PORTAL (EXISTING PORTAL)

To use the RDP file in the management portal, complete the following steps:

1. Navigate to the Instances tab for your cloud service in the management portal accessed via *https://manage.windowsazure.com*.

2. Click an instance in the table to select it.

3. On the command bar, click Connect to download the RDP file for the instance.

4. Open the file.

5. In the Remote Desktop Connection dialog box, click Connect.

6. In the Windows Security dialog box that appears, enter the username and password with which you configured RDP, and click OK.

7. In the Remote Desktop Connection Security dialog box, click Yes to complete the process and connect to the role instance via RDP.

USING THE RDP FILE FROM THE MANAGEMENT PORTAL (PREVIEW PORTAL)
Currently you cannot use the RDP file from the Preview portal.

> *NOTE* **DEPLOYING ROLES WITHOUT RDP**
>
> You can deploy roles without RDP configured and enable it post-deployment. This was not always the case. The Azure guest operating system agent enables this re-configuration using the management portal instead of having to deploy a new package with RDP enabled.

Debugging using IntelliTrace

You use IntelliTrace as an alternative to remote debugging a cloud service that is running within Azure. Unlike remote debugging, which can make your service unresponsive while you are stopped in a breakpoint, IntelliTrace gives you an experience similar to debugging without the potential to interrupt the service operation, which can interfere with your ability to reproduce a problem. With IntelliTrace, you work from a replay of captured events that includes environment data and supports replaying steps through the code.

To debug using IntelliTrace, enable IntelliTrace and publish from Visual Studio with IntelliTrace enabled:

1. In Visual Studio, publish your cloud service.

2. Configure your deployment. On the Settings page, click the Advanced Settings tab.

3. On the Advanced Settings tab, select the Enable IntelliTrace check box, and then click the Settings link.

4. In the IntelliTrace Settings dialog box that appears, indicate what you want to collect by configuring the options on the tabs as follows:

   A. On the General tab, configure the verbosity of logging. Note that collecting both IntelliTrace events and call information impacts your cloud service performance.

   B. On the Module tab, configure the .NET modules from which data is collected. On this tab, you can opt to collect data from all modules, excluding a list of module name patterns or including a list of module name patterns you specify.

   C. On the Processes tab, configure the processes from which data is collected. On this tab, you can opt to collect data from all processes, excluding a list of process name patterns or including a list of process name patterns you specify.

D. On the IntelliTrace Events tab. configure which IntelliTrace events are collected and select the category of event (to collect all events within a category) or expand a category and select an event (to collect a particular event).

E. On the Advanced tab, select a size in MBs from the list tocontrol the amount of event data to collect and therefore the size of the IntelliTrace file you need to download from Azure.

5. Click OK.

6. Complete configuration of your cloud service as desired and then click Publish to deploy the cloud service with IntelliTrace enabled.

> **NOTE INTELLITRACE REQUIREMENTS**
>
> **IntelliTrace requires you to use Visual Studio Ultimate against a cloud service that is running an application built with .NET 4 or .NET 4.5.**

After deploying your cloud service, you can view the IntelliTrace logs for a role instance using Visual Studio by completing the following steps:

1. On the View menu, click Server Explorer.

2. Expand the Azure node. If prompted to login, log in with your organizational account or the Microsoft account that is associated with the cloud service you intend to debug.

3. Expand Cloud Services, and then expand the cloud service you want to debug.

4. Expand the role whose instance you want to profile, and then right-click an instance and select View IntelliTrace Logs.

5. Visual Studio downloads a snapshot of the IntelliTrace logs, and then displays the IntelliTrace summary. Double-click an exception or a thread to start a debugging session with that exception or thread as the point of reference.

> **MORE INFO INTELLITRACE DEBUGGING**
>
> For more details on the types of debugging you can perform using IntelliTrace, see
> *http://msdn.microsoft.com/en-us/library/dd264963.aspx.*

Debugging using the emulator

The Microsoft Azure SDK includes the Azure Compute Emulator that enables you to run a cloud service locally, attach to it with the debugger, and examine the cloud service configuration, roles, and instances. Since Azure SDK 2.3, the default compute emulator is called the Emulator Express because it is lighter-weight, it has a few additional restrictions (specifically, it requires IIS Express and is limited to one instance per role), and it does not require administrative privileges on the system to run. The older emulator (which does require admin rights, but supports multiple instances per role) is referred to as the Full Compute Emulator.

To debug your cloud service project using the Emulator Express complete the following steps:

1. In Visual Studio, right-click your cloud services project and select Properties.

2. On the Web tab of the properties page, ensure the Local Development Server is set to use IIS Express and that the Emulator option is set to use Emulator Express.

3. Click Save to save your changes.

4. Press F5 to run your solution. Emulator Express starts automatically. To access the Emulator Express dialog box, right-click the Azure icon in the system tray and select Show Compute Emulator UI.

Debug your cloud service as you would any other .NET application. The Microsoft Azure SDK also includes the Storage Emulator that provides a local environment emulating blobs, tables, and queues that you use for development purposes. Used together or apart, these emulators collectively enable you to debug a cloud service locally, without first provisioning any resources in Azure.

You can start the Storage Emulator using the following steps:

1. If the Compute Emulator is already running, right-click the Azure icon in the system tray and select Start Storage Emulator.

2. To start the Storage Emulator independently of the Compute Emulator, on the Start menu, search for Azure Storage Emulator.

To use the Storage Emulator from within your applications, you need to set the storage connection strings within your application configuration appropriately. The format of the connection strings for blobs, queues, and tables is as follows (note that you must access these endpoints using HTTP; HTTPS is not supported):

- Blob service: http://127.0.0.1:10000/<account-name>/<resource-path>
- Queue service: http://127.0.0.1:10001/<account-name>/<resource-path>
- Table service: http://127.0.0.1:10002/<account-name>/<resource-path>

In the connection strings above, *account-name* represents the name of your storage account (which you might use when deployed to Azure) and the *resource-path* is the service-specific path to your resource. To set the value appropriately within Visual Studio, in Server Explorer, right-click your role and select Properties. Click the Settings tab. In the settings list, select or add a setting, and set its type to Connection String. Click the ellipses that appears in the Value field to display the Create Storage Connection String dialog box. Select the Microsoft Azure Storage Emulator option, click OK, and then save your solution. Any code that uses that setting will attempt to communicate with the local Storage Emulator.

Thought experiment
Proactive and reactive diagnostics

In this thought experiment, apply what you've learned about this objective. You can find answers to these questions in the "Answers" section at the end of this chapter.

Your cloud service worker role has gone live, and you are planning strategies for monitoring and diagnostics.

1. What features would you use for a proactive, early warning of problems with the worker role?

2. What features could you use to diagnose an issue retroactively so that you can perform root-cause analysis and fix the problem?

Objective summary

- You can no longer configure cloud service diagnostics programmatically. Instead, you provide the configuration for diagnostics in the diagnostics configuration file included in the project. When it is deployed to Azure, you can modify the configuration through Visual Studio or by publishing a full deployment with changes.

- When you enable profiling for your cloud service, you can monitor statistics about CPU usage, function entry and exit with timings, memory allocation, and information about concurrency issues in multi-threaded applications.

- You can troubleshoot issues by running cloud services locally in the emulator, by using remote debugging and IntelliTrace, or by using RDP to access the VM directly.

Objective review

Answer the following questions to test your knowledge of the information in this objective. You can find the answers to these questions and explanations of why each answer choice is correct or incorrect in the "Answers" section at the end of this chapter.

1. Which of the following is *not* true regarding debugging cloud services? (Choose all that apply.)

   A. You can attach the debugger to a role instance running within Azure.

   B. You can attach the debugger to a cloud service running within Azure.

   C. You cannot debug cloud services role instances locally.

   D. You can debug a cloud service role instance using IntelliTrace.

2. Which of the following is the correct way to configure diagnostics?

   A. Configure diagnostics via code.

   B. Configure diagnostics by using the app.config.

   C. Configure diagnostics by editing the diagnostics.wadcfgx.

   D. None of the above.

3. How many instances of a role does the Emulator Express support?

   A. One

   B. Two

   C. Ten

   D. Twenty-five

Answers

This section contains the solutions to the thought experiments and answers to the objective review questions in this chapter.

Objective 3.1: Thought experiment

1. You can add an empty cloud service project to your existing solution that includes the ASP.NET application, and then add the ASP.NET application project as a web role to the cloud service project.

2. For an ASP.NET application, you use a web role since that will provide IIS pre-configured and ready to host the application on deployment.

3. You could create a startup task that runs as a "simple" task with "elevated" processing to ensure that it runs before the role begins accepting requests. Create a registry file (.reg) that sets up the required custom registry settings. Create a Windows PowerShell script (.ps1) that ensures the .NET Framework 3.5 Windows feature is enabled. Create a batch file that runs the registry file, the Windows PowerShell script, and then the MSI using msiexec.exe.

Objective 3.1: Objective review

1. **Correct answers:** C and D

   A. **Incorrect:** The service bus does not have an emulator.

   B. **Incorrect:** Virtual machines do not have an emulator.

   C. **Correct:** The Compute Emulator is installed by the Azure SDK.

   D. **Correct:** The Storage Emulator is installed by the Azure SDK.

2. **Correct answer:** C

   A. **Incorrect:** When you create a new cloud service project, you can choose to add web or worker roles from the provided role templates, or you can create an empty cloud service (no roles) and later add the desired roles to the project using either new role templates or by adding existing projects as roles.

   B. **Incorrect:** Any role template is merely a starting point for creating a role implementation. The Service Bus Queue template includes code to follow a queue but still requires customization and configuration for your specific requirements. Likewise, you could manually write the same code for a worker role you implement from scratch.

C.   **Correct:** By default, the RoleEntryPoint does nothing. To create a worker role with any functionality you have to provide custom code in the Run() override. Optionally, you also override OnStart() and OnStop() to provide functionality that runs before the role receives requests and cleans up before the role shuts down or recycles.

D.   **Incorrect:** Your existing web.config settings work as expected with your web roles while running both locally and in the cloud. The reason for using the role configuration settings is to surface those settings to the management portal for editing without having to redeploy.

3.   **Correct answer:** A

A.   **Correct:** All simple tasks run in sequence prior to the role being put into ready state to start receiving requests.

B.   **Incorrect:** Foreground tasks run asynchronously in parallel to simple and background tasks. The role may be put into ready state after simple tasks are completed but before the foreground or background task has completed. Further, the role cannot be recycled while a foreground task is still running.

C.   **Incorrect:** Background tasks run asynchronously in parallel to simple and foreground tasks. The role may be put into ready state after simple tasks are completed but before the foreground or background task has completed. Unlike foreground tasks, the role CAN be recycled while a background task is still running.

D.   **Incorrect:** Startup tasks cannot rely on any information related to the role environment, nor can they interact with the RoleEnvironment object. To work with RoleEnvironment, use the OnStart() override in the RoleEntryPoint class.

Objective 3.2: Thought experiment

1.   You should consider assigning a reserved IP address to the cloud service hosting your web role and use the IP address of the reserved IP in your DNS settings to ensure that the domain always maps to the IP address of the cloud service. An alternative to this is using a CNAME record (where the host "awesome" maps to appname.cloudapp.net). With a CNAME, a reserved IP is not required.

2.   You could use either a CNAME or an A record (that maps awesome.contoso.com to the IP address of the reserved IP).

Objective 3.2: Objective review

1.   **Correct answers:** C and D

A.   **Incorrect:** You can scale up or down in any increment you specify.

B.   **Incorrect:** This is true for VMs, but not possible or required with cloud services.

C.   **Correct:** Auto-scale only controls the instance count.

D.   **Correct:** You can scale the instance count using the existing portal or by deploying an update from Visual Studio.

2. **Correct answer:** C

    A. **Incorrect:** Inter-role communication can be secured using network traffic rules.

    B. **Incorrect:** ACLs are used to restrict access to a range of IPs (for example, a subnet).

    C. **Correct:** A cloud service can be joined to a virtual network.

    D. **Incorrect:** By using a public IP, you do not have to specify a port to reach an instance of a role.

3. **Correct answers:** A, C, and D

    A. **Correct:** In-role supports configuring a dedicated cache.

    B. **Incorrect:** In-role does not support a persistent cache; all caching is purely in memory.

    C. **Correct:** In-role supports configuring a co-located cache.

    D. **Correct:** In-role supports the creation of named caches.

Objective 3.3: Thought experiment

1. You can deploy upgrades by publishing from Visual Studio or by creating a package in Visual Studio and then deploying the upgrade using the existing portal. You can also use Visual Studio Online to publish upgrades.

2. You should consider using staged deployments and swap your new deployments into the production slot. You should also determine if continuous delivery at check-in from Visual Studio is appropriate for your scenario. In addition, you should consider situations where you may choose between incremental, simultaneous, or full deployment.

Objective 3.3: Objective review

1. **Correct answer:** B

    A. **Incorrect:** Compiled application code is included within a package.

    B. **Correct:** Cloud service configuration is external to the package and is not included in it.

    C. **Incorrect:** Dependent assemblies are included within a package.

    D. **Incorrect:** The cloud service definition is included within a package.

2. **Correct answers:** B, C, and D

    A. **Incorrect:** The instance size can be changed and deployed as an upgrade.

    B. **Correct:** Role name changes require a full deployment.

    C. **Correct:** Changes to the upgrade domain count require a full deployment.

    D. **Correct:** Reducing the size of local resources requires a full deployment (increasing the size, however, is allowed as an upgrade).

3. **Correct answer:** A

    A. **Correct:** A VIP swap can be used to repeatedly swap between slots.

    B. **Incorrect:** A VIP swap operation does not move role VM instances.

    C. **Incorrect:** A VIP swap remaps both the VIP and the URL.

    D. **Incorrect:** A VIP swap is a very fast operation.

Objective 3.4: Thought experiment

1. You should be looking at using monitoring (through the portal) and configuring alerts based on endpoint monitoring and host metrics.

2. You should enable and review the diagnostic logs. You might also try remote debugging or downloading IntelliTrace logs within a test environment.

Objective 3.4: Objective review

1. **Correct answers:** B and C

    A. **Incorrect:** You can attach the debugger to a role instance running in Azure.

    B. **Correct:** It is not possible to attach the debugger to a cloud service; a role instance must be the target to attach to.

    C. **Correct:** It is possible to debug role instances locally by using the Compute Emulator.

    D. **Incorrect:** You can debug a role instance using IntelliTrace.

2. **Correct answer:** C

    A. **Incorrect:** As of Azure SDK 2.5, configuration by code is no longer supported.

    B. **Incorrect:** Diagnostics are configured using the diagnostics.wadcfgx, not app. config.

    C. **Correct:** The only supported way to edit configuration is by editing the diagnostics.wadcfgx file. As of Azure SDK 2.5, configuration by code is no longer supported.

    D. **Incorrect:** Answer C is a correct way to configure diagnostics.

3. **Correct answer:** A

    A. **Correct:** The Emulator Express is limited to one instance per role when debugging a cloud service locally.

    B. **Incorrect:** The Emulator Express is limited to one instance per role.

    C. **Incorrect:** The Emulator Express is limited to one instance per role.

    D. **Incorrect:** The Emulator Express is limited to one instance per role.

CHAPTER 4

Design and implement a storage strategy

Azure Storage and Azure SQL Database both play an important role in the Microsoft Azure Platform-as-a-Service (PaaS) strategy for storage. Azure Storage enables storage and retrieval of large amounts of unstructured data. You can store content files such as documents and media in the Blob service, use the Table service for NoSQL data, use the Queue service for reliable messages, and use the File service for Server Message Block (SMB) file share scenarios. Azure SQL Database provides classic relational database features as part of an elastic scale service.

In this chapter, you will learn how to implement each of the Azure Storage services, how to monitor them, and how to manage access. You'll also learn how to work with Azure SQL Database.

MORE INFO **INTRODUCTION TO STORAGE**

This chapter assumes you have a basic understanding of Azure Storage features. For an introduction to the topic, see *http://azure.microsoft.com/en-us/documentation/articles/ storage-introduction/*.

EXAM TIP

There are many ways to interact with and develop against Azure Storage including the management portal, using Windows PowerShell, using client libraries such as those for the .NET Framework, and using the Storage Services REST API. In fact, the REST API is what supports all other options.

Objectives in this chapter:

- Objective 4.1: Implement Azure Storage blobs and Azure files
- Objective 4.2: Implement Azure Storage tables
- Objective 4.3: Implement Azure Storage queues
- Objective 4.4: Manage access
- Objective 4.5: Monitor storage
- Objective 4.6: Implement SQL databases

Objective 4.1: Implement Azure Storage blobs and Azure files

Azure blob storage is the place to store unstructured data of many varieties. You can store images, video files, word documents, lab results, and any other binary file you can think of. In addition, Azure uses blob storage extensively. For instance, when you mount extra logical drives in an Azure virtual machine (VM), the drive image is actually stored in by the Blob service associated with an Azure blob storage account. In a blob storage account, you can have many containers. Containers are similar to folders in that you can use them to logically group your files. You can also set security on the entire container. Each blob storage account can store up to 500 terabytes of data.

All blobs can be accessed through a URL format. It looks like this:

http://<storage account name>.blob.core.windows.net/<container name>/<blob name>

The Azure File service provides an alternative to blob storage for shared storage, accessible via SMB 2.1 protocol.

This objective covers how to:

- Read data
- Change data
- Set metadata on a container
- Store data using block and page blobs
- Stream data using blobs
- Access blobs securely
- Implement async blob copy
- Configure Content Delivery Network (CDN)
- Design blob hierarchies
- Configure custom domains
- Scale blob storage
- Work with file storage

Creating a container

This section explains how to create a container and upload a file to blob storage for later reading.

Creating a container (existing portal)

To create a container in the management portal, complete the following steps:

1. Navigate to the Containers tab for your storage account in the management portal accessed via *https://manage.windowsazure.com*.

2. Click Add on the command bar. If you do not yet have a container, you can click Create A Container, as shown in Figure 4-1.

FIGURE 4-1 The option to create a container for a storage account that has no containers

3. Give the container a name, and select Public Blob for the access rule, as shown in Figure 4-2.

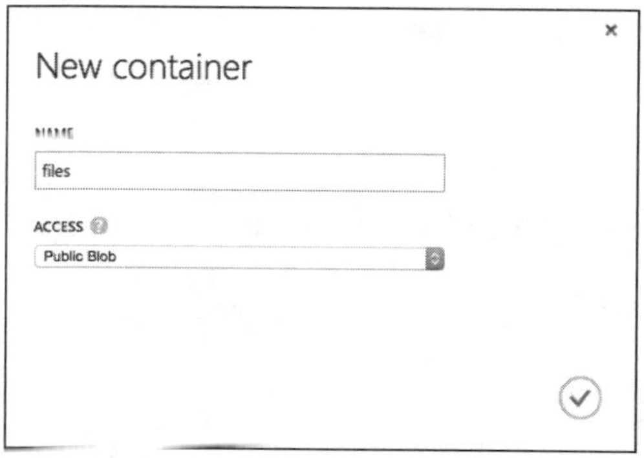

FIGURE 4-2 New container dialog box

4. The URL for the container can be found in the container list, shown in Figure 4-3. You can add additional containers by clicking Add at the bottom of the page on the Containers tab.

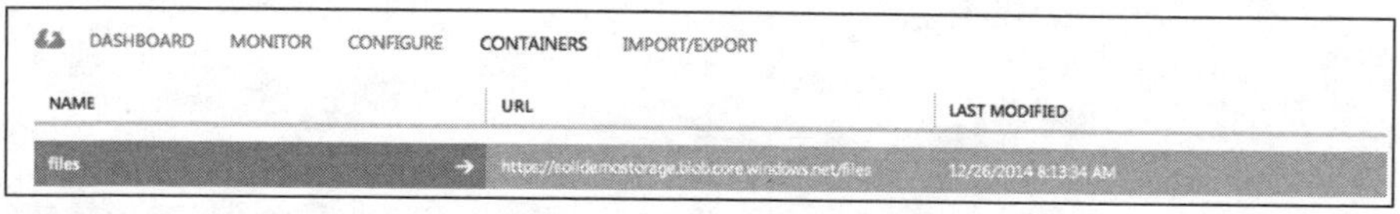

FIGURE 4-3 Containers tab with a list of containers and their URLs

NOTE **CONTAINER ACCESS PERMISSIONS**

You can choose between the following access permissions on the container:

- **Private** All access to the container and its blobs require authentication.
- **Public Container** All access to the container and its blobs are anonymous.
- **Public Blob** You cannot list blobs in the container without authentication, but you can navigate to the blob URL, if you have it, and read it anonymously.

This setting can be changed at any time through the management portal, by using Windows PowerShell, or by configuring it programmatically.

Creating a container (Preview portal)

To create a container in the Preview portal, complete the following steps:

1. Navigate to the management portal accessed via *https://portal.azure.com*.
2. Click Browse on the command bar.
3. Select Storage from the Filter By drop-down list.
4. Select your storage account from the list on the Storage blade.
5. Click the Containers box.
6. On the Containers blade, click Add on the command bar.
7. Enter a name for the container, and select Blob for the access type, as shown in Figure 4-4.

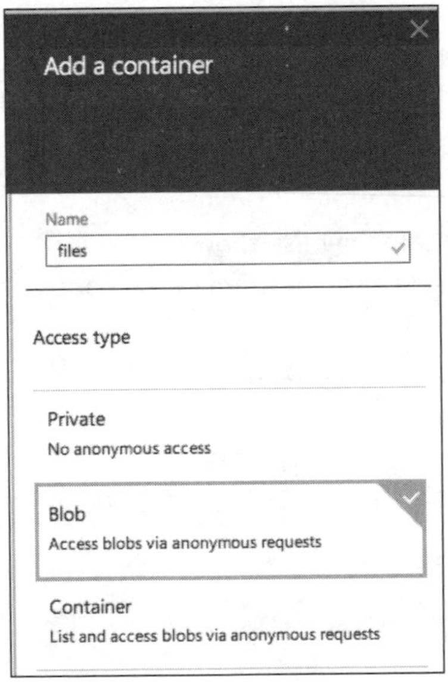

FIGURE 4-4 The Add A Container blade

8. The URL for the container can be found in the container list, as shown in Figure 4-5.

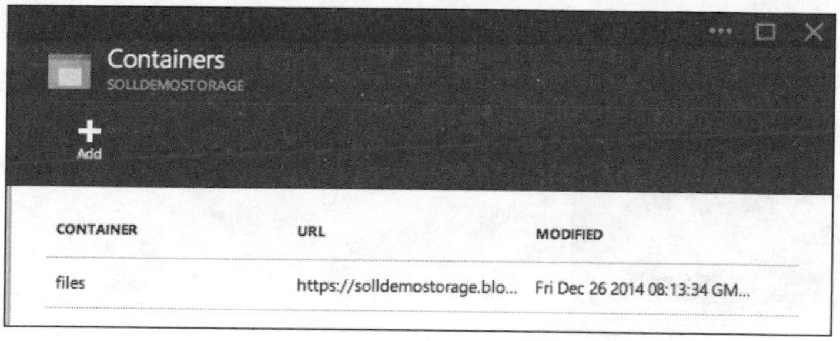

FIGURE 4-5 Containers blade with a list of containers and URLs

Finding your account access key

To access your storage account, you need the account name that was used to build the URL to the account and the primary access key. This section covers how to find the access keys for storage accounts.

Finding your account access key (existing portal)

To find your account access key using the management portal, complete the following steps:

1. Click the Dashboard tab for your storage account.

2. Click Manage Keys to find the primary and secondary key for managing your account, as shown in Figure 4-6. Always use the primary key for management activities (to be discussed later in this chapter).

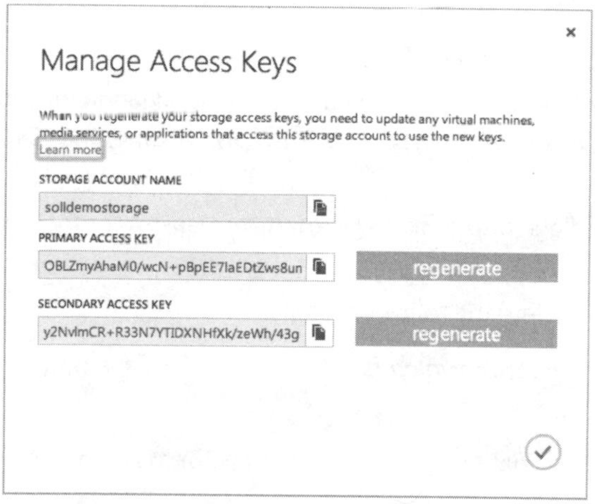

FIGURE 4-6 Manage Access Keys dialog box for a storage account

Finding your account access key (Preview portal)

To find your account access key using the Preview portal, complete the following steps:

1. Navigate to your storage account blade.

2. Click the Keys box on the storage account blade (see Figure 4-7).

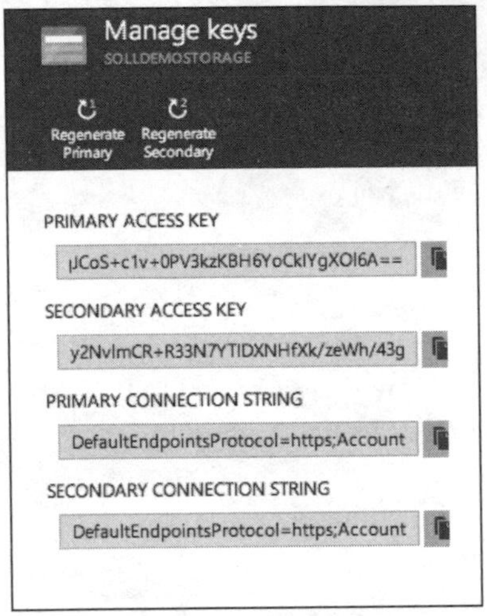

FIGURE 4-7 Manage Keys blade

Uploading a blob

You can upload files to blob storage using many approaches, including the following:

- Using the AzCopy tool provided by Microsoft (*http://aka.ms/downloadazcopy*)
- Directly using the Storage API and writing HTTP requests
- Using the Storage Client Library, which wraps the Storage API into a language and platform-specific library (*http://msdn.microsoft.com/en-us/library/azure/dn806401.aspx*)
- Using Windows PowerShell cmdlets (*http://msdn.microsoft.com/en-us/library/azure/dn806401.aspx*)

To upload a blob using AzCopy, complete the following steps:

1. Download AZCopy from *http://aka.ms/downloadazcopy*. Run the .msi file downloaded from this link.

2. Open a command prompt and navigate to C:\Program Files (x86)\Microsoft SDKs\ Azure\AzCopy.

3. Create a text file in a folder that is easy to get to. Insert some random text in it.

4. In the command window, type a command that looks like this: *AzCopy /Source:c:\test / Dest:https://myaccount.blob.core.windows.net/mycontainer2 /DestKey:key /Pattern:*.txt*.

5. Press Enter to issue the command to transfer the file.

Reading data

You can anonymously read blob storage content directly using a browser if public access to blobs is enabled. The URL to your blob content takes this format:

https://<your account name>.blob.core.windows.net/<your container name>/<your path and filename>

Reading blobs via a browser

Many storage browsing tools provide a way to view the contents of your blob containers. You can also navigate to the container using the existing management portal or the Preview portal to view the list of blobs. When you browse to the blob URL, the file is downloaded and displayed in the browser according to its content type.

Reading blobs using Visual Studio

You can also use Server Manager in Visual Studio 2013 to view the contents of your blob containers and upload or download files.

1. Navigate to the blob storage account that you want to use.

2. Double-click the blob storage account to open a window showing a list of blobs and providing functionality to upload or download blobs.

Changing data

You can modify the contents of a blob or delete a blob using the Storage API directly, but it is more common to do this programmatically as part of an application, for example using the Storage Client Library.

EXAM TIP

Any updates made to a blob are atomic. While an update is in progress, requests to the blob URL will always return the previously committed version of the blob until the update is complete.

The following steps illustrate how to update a blob programmatically. Note that this example uses a block blob. The distinction between block and page blobs is discussed in "Storing data using block and page blobs" later in this chapter.

1. Create a C# console application.

2. In your app.config file, create a storage configuration string and entry, replacing AccountName and AccountKey with your storage account values:

```
<configuration>
  <appSettings>
    <add key="StorageConnectionString" value="DefaultEndpointsProtocol=https;AccountName=<your account name>;AccountKey=<your account key>" />
  </appSettings>
</configuration>
```

3. Use NuGet to obtain the Microsoft.WindowsAzure.Storage.dll. An easy way to do this is by using this command in the NuGet console:

```
Install-package windowsazure.storage –version 3.0.3
```

4. Create a new console application, and add the following using statements to the top of your Program.cs file:

```
using Microsoft.WindowsAzure.Storage;
using Microsoft.WindowsAzure.Storage.Auth;
using Microsoft.WindowsAzure;
using Microsoft.WindowsAzure.Storage.Blob;
using System.Configuration
```

5. Add a reference to System.Configuration. Add the following code in the main entry point:

```
var storageAccount = CloudStorageAccount.Parse( ConfigurationManager.AppSettings["StorageConnectionString"]);
```

6. Use CloudBlobClient to gain access to the containers and blobs in your Azure storage account. After it is created, you can set permissions to make it publicly available:

```
CloudBlobClient blobClient = storageAccount.CreateCloudBlobClient();
```

7. Use a CreateIfNotExists method to ensure a container is there before you interact with it:

```
CloudBlobContainer container = blobClient.GetContainerReference("files");
container.CreateIfNotExists();

container.SetPermissions(new BlobContainerPermissions {PublicAccess =
BlobContainerPublicAccessType.Blob });
```

8. To upload a file, use the FileStream object to access the stream, and then use the UploadFromFileStream method on the CloudBlockBlob class to upload the file to Azure blob storage:

```
CloudBlockBlob blockBlob = container.GetBlockBlobReference("myblob");
using (var fileStream = System.IO.File.OpenRead(@"path\myfile"))
{
  blockBlob.UploadFromStream(fileStream);
}
```

9. To list all of the blobs, use the following code:

```
foreach (IListBlobItem item in container.ListBlobs(null, false))
{
  if (item.GetType() == typeof(CloudBlockBlob))
  {
    CloudBlockBlob blob = (CloudBlockBlob)item;
    Console.WriteLine("Block blob of length {0}: {1}", blob.Properties.Length,
blob.Uri);

  }
  else if (item.GetType() == typeof(CloudPageBlob))
  {
    CloudPageBlob pageBlob = (CloudPageBlob)item;
    Console.WriteLine("Page blob of length {0}: {1}", pageBlob.Properties.Length,
pageBlob.Uri);
  }
  else if (item.GetType() == typeof(CloudBlobDirectory))
  {
    CloudBlobDirectory directory = (CloudBlobDirectory)item;
    Console.WriteLine("Directory: {0}", directory.Uri);
  }
}
```

10. To download blobs, use the CloudBlobContainer class:

```
CloudBlockBlob blockBlob = container.GetBlockBlobReference("photo1.jpg");
using (var fileStream = System.IO.File.OpenWrite(@"path\myfile"))
{
  blockBlob.DownloadToStream(fileStream);
}
```

11. To delete a blob, get a reference to the blob and call Delete():

```
CloudBlockBlob blockBlob = container.GetBlockBlobReference("myblob.txt");
blockBlob.Delete();
```

Setting metadata on a container

Blobs and containers have metadata attached to them. There are two forms of metadata:

- System properties metadata
- User-defined metadata

System properties can influence how the blob behaves, while user-defined metadata is your own set of name/value pairs that your applications can use. A container has only read-only system properties, while blobs have both read-only and read-write properties.

Setting user-defined metadata

To set user-defined metadata for a container, get the container reference using GetContainerReference(), and then use the Metadata member to set values. After setting all the desired values, call SetMetadata() to persist the values, as in the following example:

```
CloudBlobContainer container = blobClient.GetContainerReference("files");
files.Metadata["counter"] = "100";
files.SetMetadata();
```

> **MORE INFO**   **BLOB METADATA**
>
> Blob metadata includes both read-only and read-write properties that are valid HTTP headers and follow restrictions governing HTTP headers. The total size of the metadata is limited to 8 KB for the combination of name and value pairs. For more information on interacting with individual blob metadata, see *http://msdn.microsoft.com/en-us/library/azure/hh225342.aspx.*

Reading user-defined metadata

To read user-defined metadata for a container, get the container reference using GetContainerReference(), and then use the Metadata member to retrieve a dictionary of values and access them by key, as in the following example:

```
CloudBlobContainer container = blobClient.GetContainerReference("files");
Console.WriteLine("counter value: " + files.Metadata["counter"];
```

EXAM TIP

If the metadata key doesn't exist, an exception is thrown.

Reading system properties

To read a container's system properties, first get a reference to the container using GetContainerReference(), and then use the Properties member to retrieve values. The following code illustrates accessing container system properties:

```
CloudBlobContainer container = blobClient.GetContainerReference("files");
Console.WriteLine("LastModifiedUTC: " + container.Properties.LastModified);
Console.WriteLine("ETag: " + container.Properties.ETag);
```

> **MORE INFO**   **CONTAINER METADATA AND THE STORAGE API**
>
> You can request container metadata using the Storage API. For more information on this and the list of system properties returned, see *http://msdn.microsoft.com/en-us/library/azure/dd179370.aspx.*

Storing data using block and page blobs

The Azure Blob service has two different ways of storing your data: block blobs and page blobs. Block blobs are great for streaming data sequentially, like video and other files. Page blobs are great for non-sequential reads and writes, like the VHD on a hard disk mentioned in earlier chapters.

Block blobs are blobs that are divided into blocks. Each block can be up to 4 MB. When uploading large files into a block blob, you can upload one block at a time in any order you want. You can set the final order of the block blob at the end of the upload process. For large files, you can also upload blocks in parallel. Each block will have an MD5 hash used to verify transfer. You can retransmit a particular block if there's an issue. You can also associate blocks with a blob after upload, meaning that you can upload blocks and then assemble the block blob after the fact. Any blocks you upload that aren't committed to a blob will be deleted after a week. Block blobs can be up to 200 GB.

Page bobs are blobs comprised of 512-byte pages. Unlike block blobs, page blob writes are done in place and are immediately committed to the file. The maximum size of a page blob is 1 terabyte. Page blobs closely mimic how hard drives behave, and in fact, Azure VMs use them for that purpose. Most of the time, you will use block blobs.

Streaming data using blobs

You can stream blobs by downloading to a stream using the DownloadToStream() API method. The advantage of this is that it avoids loading the entire blob into memory, for example before saving it to a file or returning it to a web request.

Accessing blobs securely

Secure access to blob storage implies a secure connection for data transfer and controlled access through authentication and authorization.

Azure Storage supports both HTTP and secure HTTPS requests. For data transfer security, you should always use HTTPS connections. To authorize access to content, you can authenticate in three different ways to your storage account and content:

- **Shared Key**   Constructed from a set of fields related to the request. Computed with a SHA-256 algorithm and encoded in Base64.

- **Shared Key Lite**   Similar to Shared Key, but compatible with previous versions of Azure Storage. This provides backwards compatibility with code that was written against versions prior to 19 September 2009. This allows for migration to newer versions with minimal changes.

- **Shared Access Signature**   Grants restricted access rights to containers and blobs. You can provide a shared access signature to users you don't trust with your storage account key. You can give them a shared access signature that will grant them specific permissions to the resource for a specified amount of time. This is discussed in a later section.

To interact with blob storage content authenticated with the account key, you can use the Storage Client Library as illustrated in earlier sections. When you create an instance of the CloudStorageAccount using the account name and key, each call to interact with blob storage will be secured, as shown in the following code:

```
string accountName = "ACCOUNTNAME";
string accountKey = "ACCOUNTKEY";
CloudStorageAccount storageAccount = new CloudStorageAccount(new
StorageCredentials(accountName, accountKey), true);
```

Implementing an async blob copy

The Blob service provides a feature for asynchronously copying blobs from a source blob to a destination blob. You can run many of these requests in parallel since the operation is asynchronous. The following scenarios are supported:

- Copying a source blob to a destination with a different name or URI
- Overwriting a blob with the same blob, which means copying from the same source URI and writing to the same destination URI (this overwrites the blob, replaces metadata, and removes uncommitted blocks)
- Copy a snapshot to a base blob, for example to promote the snapshot to restore an earlier version
- Copy a snapshot to a new location creating a new, writable blob (not a snapshot)

The copy operation is always the entire length of the blob; you can't copy a range.

> **MORE INFO** **COPY BLOB**
>
> For additional details on the underlying process for copying blobs, see *http://msdn. microsoft.com/en-us/library/azure/dd894037.aspx.*

The following code illustrates a simple example for creating a blob and then copying it asynchronously to another destination blob:

```
CloudBlobContainer files = blobClient.GetContainerReference("files");
files.CreateIfNotExists(BlobContainerPublicAccessType.Off);
ICloudBlob sourceBlob = files.GetBlockBlobReference("filetocopy.txt");
sourceBlob.Properties.ContentType = "text/plain";
string sourceFileContents = "my text blob to copy";
byte[] sourceBytes = new byte[sourceFileContents.Length * sizeof(char)];
System.Buffer.BlockCopy(sourceFileContents.ToCharArray(), 0, sourceBytes, 0,
sourceBytes.Length);
sourceBlob.UploadFromByteArray(sourceBytes, 0, sourceBytes.Length);

ICloudBlob blobCopy = files.GetBlockBlobReference("destinationcopy.txt");
AsyncCallback cb = new AsyncCallback(x => Console.WriteLine("copy completed with {0}",
x.IsCompleted));
blobCopy.BeginStartCopyFromBlob(sourceBlob.Uri, cb, null);
```

Ideally, you pass state to the BeginStartCopyFromBlob() method so that you can track multiple parallel operations.

Configuring the Content Delivery Network

The Azure Content Delivery Network (CDN) distributes content across geographic regions to edge nodes across the globe. The CDN caches publicly available objects so they are available over high-bandwidth connections, close to the users, thus allowing the users to download them at much lower latency. You may be familiar with using CDNs to download popular Javascript frameworks like JQuery, Angular, and others.

By default, blobs have a seven-day time-to-live (TTL) at the CDN edge node. After that time elapses, the blob is refreshed from the storage account to the edge node. Blobs that are shared via CDN must support anonymous access.

Configuring the CDN (existing portal)

To enable the CDN for a storage account in the management portal, complete the following steps:

1. In the management portal, click New on the navigation bar.
2. Select App Services, CDN, Quick Create.
3. Select the storage account that you want to add CDN support for, and click Create.
4. Navigate to the CDN properties by selecting it from your list of CDN endpoints.
5. To enable HTTPS support, click Enable HTTPS at the bottom of the page.
6. To enable query string support, click Enable Query String Support at the bottom of the page.
7. To map a custom domain to the CDN endpoint, click Manage Domains at the bottom of the page, and follow the instructions.

To access blobs via CDN, use the CDN address as follows:

```
http://<your CDN subdomain>.vo.msecnd.net/<your container name>/<your blob path>
```

If you are using HTTPS and a custom domain, address your blobs as follows:

```
https://<your domain>/<your container name>/<your blob path>
```

Configuring the CDN (Preview portal)

You currently cannot configure the CDN using the Preview portal.

Designing blob hierarchies

Blob storage has a hierarchy that involves the following aspects:

- The storage account name, which is part of the base URI
- The container within which you store blobs, which is also used for partitioning
- The blob name, which can include path elements separated by a backslash (/) to create a sense of folder structure

Using a blob naming convention that resembles a directory structure provides you with additional ways to filter your blob data directly from the name. For example, to group images by their locale to support a localization effort, complete the following steps:

1. Create a container called **images**.
2. Add English bitmaps using the convention en/bmp/*, where * is the file name.
3. Add English JPEG files using the convention en/jpg/*, where * is the file name.
4. Add Spanish bitmaps using the convention sp/bmp/*, where * is the file name.
5. Add Spanish JPEG files using the convention sp/jpg/*, where * is the file name.

To retrieve all images in the container, use ListBlob() in this way:

```
var list = images.ListBlobs(null, true, BlobListingDetails.All);
```

The output is the entire list of uploaded images in the container:

```
https://solexpstorage.blob.core.windows.net/images/en/bmp/logo.bmp
https://solexpstorage.blob.core.windows.net/images/en/jpg/logo.jpg
https://solexpstorage.blob.core.windows.net/images/sp/bmp/logo.bmp
https://solexpstorage.blob.core.windows.net/images/sp/jpg/logo.jpg
```

To filter only those with the prefix *en*, use this:

```
var list = images.ListBlobs("en", true, BlobListingDetails.All);
```

The output will be this:

```
https://solexpstorage.blob.core.windows.net/images/en/bmp/logo.bmp
https://solexpstorage.blob.core.windows.net/images/en/jpg/logo.jpg
```

Configuring custom domains

By default, the URL for accessing the Blob service in a storage account is *https://<your account name>.blob.core.windows.net*. You can map your own domain or subdomain to the Blob service for your storage account so that users can reach it using the custom domain or subdomain.

Scaling Blob storage

Blobs are partitioned by container name and blob name, which means each blob can have its own partition. Blobs, therefore, can be distributed across many servers to scale access even though they are logically grouped within a container.

Working with Azure File storage

Azure File storage provides a way for applications to share storage accessible via SMB 2.1 protocol. It is particularly useful for VMs and cloud services as a mounted share, and applications can use the File Storage API to access File storage.

Thought experiment
Partitioning strategy for localization

In this thought experiment, apply what you've learned about this objective. You can find answers to these questions in the "Answers" section at the end of this chapter.

You are localizing a mobile application for multiple languages. Some of your efforts revolve around having separate images for the regions you are targeting.

1. How will you structure the files in Blob storage so that you can retrieve them easily?

2. What can you do to make access to these images quick for users around the world?

Objective summary

- A blob container has several options for access permissions. When set to Private, all access requires credentials. When set to Public Container, no credentials are required to access the container and its blobs. When set to Public Blob, only blobs can be accessed without credentials if the full URL is known.

- To access secure containers and blobs, you can use the storage account key or a shared access signatures.

- AzCopy is a useful utility for activities such as uploading blobs, transferring blobs from one container or storage account to another, and performing these and other activities related to blob management in scripted batch operations.

- Block blobs allow you to upload, store, and download large blobs in blocks up to 4 MB each. The size of the blob can be up to 200 GB.

- You can use a blob naming convention akin to folder paths to create a logical hierarchy for blobs, which is useful for query operations.

Objective review

Answer the following questions to test your knowledge of the information in this objective. You can find the answers to these questions and explanations of why each answer choice is correct or incorrect in the "Answers" section at the end of this chapter.

1. Which of the following is *not* true about metadata? (Choose all that apply.)

   A. Both containers and blobs have writable system properties.

   B. Blob user-defined metadata is accessed as a key value pair.

   C. System metadata can influence how the blog is stored and accessed in Azure Storage.

   D. Only blobs have metadata; containers do not.

2. Which of the following are valid differences between page blobs and block blobs? (Choose all that apply.)

   A. Page blobs are much faster for all operations.

   B. Block blobs allow files to be uploaded and assembled later. Blocks can be resubmitted individually.

   C. Page blobs are good for all sorts of files, like video and images.

   D. Block blobs have a max size of 200 GB. Page blobs can be 1 terabyte.

3. What are good recommendations for securing files in Blob storage? (Choose all that apply.)

   A. Always use SSL.

   B. Keep your primary and secondary keys hidden and don't give them out.

C. In your application, store them someplace that isn't embedded in client-side code that users can see.

D. Make the container publicly available.

Objective 4.2: Implement Azure Storage tables

Azure Storage is a non-relational (NoSQL) entity storage service on Microsoft Azure. When you create a storage account, it includes the Table service alongside the Blob and Queue services. Table services can be accessed through a URL format. It looks like this:

http://<storage account name>.table.core.windows.net/<table name>.

There are many forms of NoSQL databases:

- Key-value stores that organize data with a unique key per record and often allow for jagged entries where each row might not have a complete set of values.
- Document databases that are similar to key-value stores with semi-structured, easy-to-query documents. Usually, information is stored in JavaScript Object Notation (JSON) format.
- Columnar stores that are used to organize large amounts of distributed information.
- Graph databases that do not use columns and rows; instead, they use a graph model for storage and query, usually for large amounts of highly distributed data.

Table storage is a key-value store that uses a partition key to help with scale out distribution of data and a row key for unique access to a particular entry. Together, these keys are used to uniquely identify a record in the account.

> **This objective covers how to:**
> - Implement CRUD with and without transactions
> - Query using OData
> - Design, manage, and scale table partitions

Using basic CRUD operations

In this section, you learn how to access table storage programmatically.

Creating a table

1. Create a C# console application.

2. In your app.config file, add an entry under the Configuration element, replacing the account name and key with your own storage account details:

```
<configuration>
  <appSettings>
    <add key="StorageConnectionString" value="DefaultEndpointsProtocol=https;Accou
ntName=<your account name>;AccountKey=<your account key>" />
  </appSettings>
</configuration>
```

3. Use NuGet to obtain the Microsoft.WindowsAzure.Storage.dll. An easy way to do this is by using the following command in the NuGet console:

```
Install-package windowsazure.storage -version 3.0.3
```

4. Add the following using statements to the top of your Program.cs file:

```
using Microsoft.WindowsAzure.Storage;
using Microsoft.WindowsAzure.Storage.Auth;
using Microsoft.WindowsAzure.Storage.Table;
using Microsoft.WindowsAzure;
using System.Configuration
```

5. Add a reference to System.Configuration.

6. Type the following command to retrieve your connection string in the Main function of Program.cs:

```
var storageAccount = CloudStorageAccount.Parse(
var storageAccount =CloudStorageAccount.Parse( ConfigurationManager.AppSettings["S
torageConnectionString"]);
```

7. Use the following command to create a table if one doesn't already exist:

```
CloudTableClient tableClient = storageAccount.CreateCloudTableClient();
CloudTable table = tableClient.GetTableReference("customers");
table.CreateIfNotExists();
```

Inserting records

To add entries to a table, you create objects based on the TableEntity base class and serialize them into the table using the Storage Client Library. The following properties are provided for you in this base class:

- **Partition Key** Used to partition data across storage infrastructure
- **Row Key** Unique identifier in a partition
- **Timestamp** Time of last update maintained by Azure Storage
- **ETag** Used internally to provide optimistic concurrency

The combination of partition key and row key must be unique within the table. This combination is used for load balancing and scaling, as well as for querying and sorting entities.

Follow these steps to add code that inserts records:

1. Add a class to your project, and then add the following code to it:

```
using Microsoft.WindowsAzure.Storage.Table;
public class OrderEntity : TableEntity
{
 public OrderEntity(string customerName, String orderDate)
 {
  this.PartitionKey = customerName;
  this.RowKey = orderDate;
 }
 public OrderEntity() { }
 public string OrderNumber { get; set; }
 public DateTime RequiredDate { get; set; }
 public DateTime ShippedDate { get; set; }
 public string Status { get; set; }
}
```

2. Add the following code to the console program to insert a record:

```
CloudStorageAccount storageAccount = CloudStorageAccount.Parse(
CloudConfigurationManager.GetSetting("StorageConnectionString"));
CloudTableClient tableClient = storageAccount.CreateCloudTableClient();
CloudTable table = tableClient.GetTableReference("orders");
OrderEntity newOrder = new OrderEntity("Archer", "20141216");
newOrder.OrderNumber = "101";
newOrder.ShippedDate = Convert.ToDateTime("20141218");
newOrder.RequiredDate = Convert.ToDateTime("20141222");
newOrder.Status = "shipped";
TableOperation insertOperation = TableOperation.Insert(newOrder);
table.Execute(insertOperation);
```

Inserting multiple records in a transaction

You can group inserts and other operations into a single batch transaction. All operations in the batch must take place on the same partition. You can have up to 100 entities in a batch. The total batch payload size cannot be greater than 4 MB.

The following code illustrates how to insert several records as part of a single transaction:

```
CloudStorageAccount storageAccount = CloudStorageAccount.Parse(
CloudConfigurationManager.GetSetting("StorageConnectionString"));
CloudTableClient tableClient = storageAccount.CreateCloudTableClient();
CloudTable table = tableClient.GetTableReference("orders");
TableBatchOperation batchOperation = new TableBatchOperation();

OrderEntity newOrder1 = new OrderEntity("Lana", "20141217");
newOrder1.OrderNumber = "102";
newOrder1.ShippedDate = Convert.ToDateTime("1/1/1900");
newOrder1.RequiredDate = Convert.ToDateTime("1/1/1900");
newOrder1.Status = "pending";
OrderEntity newOrder2 = new OrderEntity("Lana", "20141218");
newOrder2.OrderNumber = "103";
newOrder2.ShippedDate = Convert.ToDateTime("1/1/1900");
```

```
newOrder2.RequiredDate = Convert.ToDateTime("12/25/2014");
newOrder2.Status = "open";
OrderEntity newOrder3 = new OrderEntity("Lana", "20141219");
newOrder3.OrderNumber = "103";
newOrder3.ShippedDate = Convert.ToDateTime("12/17/2014");
newOrder3.RequiredDate = Convert.ToDateTime("12/17/2014");
newOrder3.Status = "shipped";

batchOperation.Insert(newOrder1);
batchOperation.Insert(newOrder2);
batchOperation.Insert(newOrder3);
table.ExecuteBatch(batchOperation);
```

> **MORE INFO**   **ENTITY GROUP TRANSACTIONS**
>
> You can batch transactions that belong to the same table and partition group for insert,
> update, merge, delete, and related actions programmatically or by using the Storage
> API. For more information, see the reference at *http://msdn.microsoft.com/en-us/library/
> dd894038.aspx*.

Getting records in a partition

You can select all of the entities in a partition or a range of entities by partition and row key.
Wherever possible, you should try to query with the partition key and row key. Querying
entities by other properties does not work well because it launches a scan of the entire table.

Within a table, entities are ordered within the partition key. Within a partition, entities are
ordered by the row key. RowKey is a string property, so sorting is handled as a string sort. If
you are using a date value for your RowKey property use the following order: year, month,
day. For instance, use 20140108 for January 8, 2014.

The following code requests all records within a partition using the PartitionKey property
to query:

```
CloudStorageAccount storageAccount = CloudStorageAccount.Parse(
CloudConfigurationManager.GetSetting("StorageConnectionString"));
CloudTableClient tableClient = storageAccount.CreateCloudTableClient();
CloudTable table = tableClient.GetTableReference("orders");
TableQuery<OrderEntity> query = new TableQuery<OrderEntity>().Where(
TableQuery.GenerateFilterCondition("PartitionKey", QueryComparisons.Equal, "Lana"));

foreach (OrderEntity entity in table.ExecuteQuery(query))
{
 Console.WriteLine("{0}, {1}\t{2}\t{3}", entity.PartitionKey, entity.RowKey,
 entity.Status, entity.RequiredDate);
}
```

Updating records

One technique you can use to update a record is to use InsertOrReplace(). This creates the record if one does not already exist or updates an existing record. Here's an example:

```
CloudStorageAccount storageAccount = CloudStorageAccount.
Parse(CloudConfigurationManager.GetSetting("StorageConnectionString"));
CloudTableClient tableClient = storageAccount.CreateCloudTableClient();
CloudTable table = tableClient.GetTableReference("orders1");
TableOperation retrieveOperation = TableOperation.Retrieve<OrderEntity>("Lana",
"20141217");
TableResult retrievedResult = table.Execute(retrieveOperation);
OrderEntity updateEntity = (OrderEntity)retrievedResult.Result;
if (updateEntity != null)
{
  updateEntity.Status = "shipped";
  updateEntity.ShippedDate = Convert.ToDateTime("12/20/2014");
  TableOperation insertOrReplaceOperation = TableOperation.
InsertOrReplace(updateEntity);
  table.Execute(insertOrReplaceOperation);
}
```

Deleting a record

To delete a record, first retrieve the record as shown in earlier examples, and then delete it with code, such as this:

```
TableOperation deleteOperation = TableOperation.Delete(deleteEntity);
table.Execute(deleteOperation);
Console.WriteLine("Entity deleted.");
```

Querying using ODATA

The Storage API for tables supports OData, which exposes a simple query interface for interacting with table data. Table storage does not support anonymous access, so you must supply credentials using the account key or a Shared Access Signature (SAS) (discussed in "Manage Access") before you can perform requests using OData.

To query what tables you have created, provide credentials, and issue a GET request as follows:

```
https://myaccount.table.core.windows.net/Tables
```

To query the entities in a specific table, provide credentials, and issue a GET request formatted as follows:

```
https://<your account name>.table.core.windows.net/<your table
name>(PartitionKey='<partition-key>',RowKey='<row-key>')?$select=<comma separated
property names>
```

> **NOTE QUERY LIMITATIONS**
>
> The result is limited to 1,000 entities per request, and the query will run for a maximum of five seconds.

> **MORE INFO ODATA**
>
> For more information on OData, see the reference at *http://msdn.microsoft.com/en-us/library/azure/dn535600.aspx*.

Designing, managing, and scaling table partitions

The Azure Table service can scale to handle massive amounts of structured data and billions of records. To handle that amount, tables are partitioned. The partition key is the unit of scale for storage tables. The table service will spread your table to multiple servers and key all rows with the same partition key co-located. Thus, the partition key is an important grouping, not only for querying but also for scalability.

There are three types of partition keys to choose from:

- **Single value**   There is one partition key for the entire table. This favors a small number of entities. It also makes batch transactions easier since batch transactions need to share a partition key to run without error. It does not scale well for large tables since all rows will be on the same partition server.

- **Multiple values**   This might place each partition on its own partition server. If the partition size is smaller, it's easier for Azure to load balance the partitions. Partitions might get slower as the number of entities increases. This might make further partitioning necessary at some point.

- **Unique values**   This is many small partitions. This is highly scalable, but batch transactions are not possible.

For query performance, you should use the partition key and row key together when possible. This leads to an exact row match. The next best thing is to have an exact partition match with a row range. It is best to avoid scanning the entire table.

Objective summary

- Table storage is a non-relational database implementation (NoSQL) following the key-value database pattern.

- Table entries each have a partition key and row key. The partition key is used to logically group rows that are related; the row key is a unique entry for the row.

- The Table service uses the partition key for distributing collections of rows across physical partitions in Azure to automatically scale out the database as needed.

- A Table storage query returns up to 1,000 records per request, and will time out after five seconds.

- Querying Table storage with both the partition and row key results in fast queries. A table scan is required for queries that do not use these keys.

Objective review

Answer the following questions to test your knowledge of the information in this objective. You can find the answers to these questions and explanations of why each answer choice is correct or incorrect in the "Answers" section at the end of this chapter.

1. Which of the following is not a method for replicating a Table storage account?

   A. Transactional replication

   B. Zone redundant storage

   C. Read access geo-redundant storage

   D. Geo-redundant storage

2. How should you choose a good partition key for a Table storage implementation? (Choose all that apply.)

   A. They should always be unique, like a primary key in a SQL table.

   B. You should always use the same partition key for all records.

   C. Think about how you're likely to update the data using batch transactions.

   D. Find an even way to split them so that you have relatively even partition sizes.

3. Which of the following statements are correct for submitting operations in a batch? (Choose all that apply.)

   A. All operations have to be in the same partition.

   B. Total batch size can't be greater than 4 MB.

   C. Max operation count is 100.

   D. Minimum operation count is three.

Objective 4.3: Implement Azure storage queues

The Azure Storage Queue service provides a mechanism for reliable inter-application messaging to support asynchronous distributed application workflows. This section covers a few fundamental features of the Queue service for adding messages to a queue, processing those messages individually or in a batch, and scaling the service.

> **MORE INFO** **QUEUE SERVICE**
>
> For a general overview of working with the Queue service, see the reference at *http://azure.microsoft.com/en-us/documentation/articles/storage-dotnet-how-to-use-queues/*.

This objective covers how to:
- Add and process messages
- Retrieve a batch of messages
- Scale queues

Adding messages to a queue

You can access your storage queues and add messages to a queue using many storage browsing tools; however, it is more likely you will add messages programmatically as part of your application workflow.

The following code demonstrates how to add messages to a queue:

```
string connection = "DefaultEndpointsProtocol=https;AccountName=<ACCOUNTNAME>;AccountKey
=<ACCOUNTKEY>";
CloudStorageAccount account;
if (!CloudStorageAccount.TryParse(connection, out account))
{
 throw new Exception("Unable to parse storage account connection string.");
}
CloudQueueClient queueClient = account.CreateCloudQueueClient();
CloudQueue queue = queueClient.GetQueueReference("workerqueue");
queue.AddMessage(new CloudQueueMessage("Queued message 1"));
queue.AddMessage(new CloudQueueMessage("Queued message 2"));
queue.AddMessage(new CloudQueueMessage("Queued message 3"));
```

NOTE **MESSAGE IDENTIFIERS**

The Queue service assigns a message identifier to each message when it is added to the queue. This is opaque to the client, but it is used by the Storage Client Library to identify a message uniquely when retrieving, processing, and deleting messages.

MORE INFO **LARGE MESSAGES**

There is a limit of 64 KB per message stored in a queue. It is considered best practice to keep the message small and to store any required data for processing in a durable store, such as SQL Azure, storage tables, or storage blobs. This also increases system reliability since each queued message can expire after seven days if not processed. For more information, see the reference at *http://msdn.microsoft.com/en-us/library/azure/hh690942.aspx*.

Processing messages

Messages are typically published by a separate application in the system from the application that listens to the queue and processes messages. As shown in the previous section, you can create a CloudQueue reference and then proceed to call GetMessage() to de-queue the next available message from the queue as follows:

```
CloudQueueMessage message = queue.GetMessage(new TimeSpan(0, 5, 0));
if (message != null)
{
 string theMessage = message.AsString;
 // your processing code goes here
}
```

NOTE **INVISIBILITY SETTING**

By default, when you de-queue a message, it is invisible to the queue for 30 seconds. In the event message processing exceeds this timeframe, supply an alternate setting for this value when creating or updating the message. You can set the timeout to a value between one second and seven days. Visibility can also exceed the message expiry time.

Retrieving a batch of messages

A queue listener can be implemented as single-threaded (processing one message at a time) or multi-threaded (processing messages in a batch on separate threads). You can retrieve up to 32 messages from a queue using the GetMessages() method to process multiple messages in parallel. As discussed in the previous sections, create a CloudQueue reference, and then proceed to call GetMessages(). Specify the number of items to de-queue up to 32 (this number can exceed the number of items in the queue) as follows:

```
IEnumerable<CloudQueueMessage> batch = queue.GetMessages(10, new TimeSpan(0, 5, 0));
foreach (CloudQueueMessage batchMessage in batch)
{
 Console.WriteLine(batchMessage.AsString);
}
```

> **NOTE PARALLEL PROCESSING OVERHEAD**
>
> Consider the overhead of message processing before deciding the appropriate number of messages to process in parallel. If significant memory, disk space, or other network resources are used during processing, throttling parallel processing to an acceptable number will be necessary to avoid performance degradation on the compute instance.

Scaling queues

When working with Azure Storage queues, you need to consider a few scalability issues, including the messaging throughput of the queue itself and the design topology for processing messages and scaling out as needed.

Each individual queue has a target of approximately 2,000 messages per second (assuming a message is within 1 KB). You can partition your application to use multiple queues to increase this throughput value.

As for processing messages, it is more cost effective and efficient to pull multiple messages from the queue for processing in parallel on a single compute node; however, this depends on the type of processing and resources required. Scaling out compute nodes to increase processing throughput is usually also required.

As discussed in Chapter 2, "Create and manage virtual machines," and Chapter 3, "Design and implement cloud services," you can configure VMs or cloud services to auto-scale by queue. You can specify the average number of messages to be processed per instance, and the auto-scale algorithm will queue to run scale actions to increase or decrease available instances accordingly.

MORE INFO   **BACK OFF POLLING**

To control storage costs, you should implement a back off polling algorithm for queue message processing. This and other scale considerations are discussed in the reference at *http://msdn.microsoft.com/en-us/library/azure/hh697709.aspx*.

Thought experiment
Asynchronous design patterns

In this thought experiment, apply what you've learned about this objective. You can find answers to these questions in the "Answers" section at the end of this chapter.

Your application must, on user request, generate PDF reports that include both data stored in SQL Azure and images stored in storage blobs. Producing these reports requires significant memory per report and local disk storage prior to saving reports in Blob storage. There are 50,000 users that could potentially request these reports daily; however, the number of requests per day varies widely.

1. How would you design the system to handle asynchronous processing of these PDF reports?

2. Which type of compute instance would you choose?

3. How many reports would you process on a single compute instance?

4. How would you approach scaling the number of compute instances according to the number of requests?

Objective summary

- Applications can add messages to a queue programmatically using the .NET Storage Client Library or equivalent for other languages, or you can directly call the Storage API.

- Messages are stored in a storage queue for up to seven days based on the expiry setting for the message. Message expiry can be modified while the message is in the queue.

- An application can retrieve messages from a queue in batch to increase throughput and process messages in parallel.

- Each queue has a target of approximately 2,000 messages per second. You can increase this throughput by partitioning messages across multiple queues.

Objective review

Answer the following questions to test your knowledge of the information in this objective. You can find the answers to these questions and explanations of why each answer choice is correct or incorrect in the "Answers" section at the end of this chapter.

1. Which of the following statements are true about queuing messages? (Choose all that apply.)

   A. Storage queue messages have no size restrictions. The reason for using smaller messages sizes is to increase throughput to the queue.

   B. Storage queue messages are limited to 64 KB.

   C. Storage queue messages are durable.

   D. The client application should save the message identifier returned after adding a message to a queue for later use.

2. Which of the following are valid options for processing queue messages? (Choose all that apply.)

   A. A single compute instance can process only one message at a time.

   B. A single compute instance can process up to 32 messages at a time.

   C. A single compute instance can retrieve up to 32 messages at a time.

   D. Messages can be read one at a time or in batches of up to 32 messages at a time.

   E. Messages are deleted as soon as they are read.

3. Which of the following are valid options for scaling queues? (Choose all that apply.)

   A. Distributing messages across multiple queues

   B. Automatically scaling websites based on queue metrics

   C. Automatically scaling VMs based on queue metrics

   D. Automatically scaling cloud services based on queue metrics

Objective 4.4: Manage access

All storage accounts can be protected by a secure HTTPS connection and by using storage account keys to access all resources. In this section, you'll learn how to manage storage account keys, how to generate shared access keys with more granular control over which resources are accessible and for how long, how to manage policies for issued keys, and how to allow browser access to storage resources.

> **MORE INFO** **MANAGING ACCESS TO STORAGE SERVICES**
>
> For an overview of some of the topics discussed in this section, see *http://msdn.microsoft. com/en-us/library/azure/ee393343.aspx*.

Generating shared access signatures

By default, storage resources are protected at the service level. Only authenticated callers can access tables and queues. Blob containers and blobs can optionally be exposed for anonymous access, but you would typically allow anonymous access only to individual blobs. To authenticate to any storage service, a primary or secondary key is used, but this grants the caller access to all actions on the storage account.

An SAS is used to delegate access to specific storage account resources without enabling access to the entire account. An SAS token lets you control the lifetime by setting the start and expiration time of the signature, the resources you are granting access to, and the permissions being granted.

The following is a list of operations supported by SAS:

- Reading or writing blobs, blob properties, and blob metadata
- Leasing or creating a snapshot of a blob
- Listing blobs in a container
- Deleting a blob
- Adding, updating, or deleting table entities
- Querying tables
- Processing queue messages (read and delete)
- Adding and updating queue messages
- Retrieving queue metadata

This section covers creating an SAS token to access storage services using the Storage Client Library.

MORE INFO   **CONTROLLING ANONYMOUS ACCESS**

To control anonymous access to containers and blobs, follow the instructions provided at *http://msdn.microsoft.com/en-us/library/azure/dd179354.aspx*.

MORE INFO   **CONSTRUCTING AN SAS URI**

SAS tokens are typically used to authorize access to the Storage Client Library when interacting with storage resources, but you can also use it directly with the storage resource
URI and use HTTP requests directly. For details regarding the format of an SAS URI, see
http://msdn.microsoft.com/en-us/library/azure/dn140255.aspx.

Creating an SAS token (Blobs)

The following code shows how to create an SAS token for a blob container:

```
string connection = "DefaultEndpointsProtocol=https;AccountName=<ACCOUNTNAME>;AccountKey
=<ACCOUNTKEY>";
CloudStorageAccount account;
if (!CloudStorageAccount.TryParse(connection, out account))
{
 throw new Exception("Unable to parse storage account connection string.");
}
CloudBlobClient blobClient = account.CreateCloudBlobClient();
SharedAccessBlobPolicy sasPolicy = new SharedAccessBlobPolicy();
sasPolicy.SharedAccessExpiryTime = DateTime.UtcNow.AddHours(1);
sasPolicy.SharedAccessStartTime = DateTime.UtcNow.Subtract(new TimeSpan(0, 5, 0));
sasPolicy.Permissions = SharedAccessBlobPermissions.Read | SharedAccessBlobPermissions.
Write | SharedAccessBlobPermissions.Delete | SharedAccessBlobPermissions.List;
CloudBlobContainer files = blobClient.GetContainerReference("files");
string sasContainerToken = files.GetSharedAccessSignature(sasPolicy);
```

The SAS token grants read, write, delete, and list permissions to the container (rwdl). It
looks like this:

```
?sv=2014-02-14&sr=c&sig=B6bi4xKkdgOXhWg3RWIDO5peekq%2FRjvnuo5o41hj1pA%3D&st=2014
-12-24T14%3A16%3A07Z&se=2014-12-24T15%3A21%3A07Z&sp=rwdl
```

You can use this token as follows to gain access to the blob container without a storage
account key:

```
StorageCredentials creds = new StorageCredentials(sasContainerToken);
CloudBlobClient sasClient = new CloudBlobClient("https://<ACCOUNTNAME>.blob.core.
windows.net/", creds);
CloudBlobContainer sasFiles = sasClient.GetContainerReference("files");
```

With this container reference, if you have write permissions, you can create a blob, for
example as follows:

```
ICloudBlob blob = sasFiles.GetBlockBlobReference("note.txt");
blob.Properties.ContentType = "text/plain";
string fileContents = "my text blob contents";
byte[] bytes = new byte[fileContents.Length * sizeof(char)];
System.Buffer.BlockCopy(fileContents.ToCharArray(), 0, bytes, 0, bytes.Length);
blob.UploadFromByteArray(bytes,0, bytes.Length);
```

Creating an SAS token (Queues)

Assuming the same account reference as created in the previous section, the following code shows how to create an SAS token for a queue:

```
CloudQueueClient queueClient = account.CreateCloudQueueClient();
CloudQueue queue = queueClient.GetQueueReference("workerqueue");
SharedAccessQueuePolicy sasPolicy = new SharedAccessQueuePolicy();
sasPolicy.SharedAccessExpiryTime = DateTime.UtcNow.AddHours(1);
sasPolicy.Permissions = SharedAccessQueuePermissions.Read |
SharedAccessQueuePermissions.Add | SharedAccessQueuePermissions.Update |
SharedAccessQueuePermissions.ProcessMessages;
sasPolicy.SharedAccessStartTime = DateTime.UtcNow.Subtract(new TimeSpan(0, 5, 0));
string sasToken = queue.GetSharedAccessSignature(sasPolicy);
```

The SAS token grants read, add, update, and process messages permissions to the container (raup). It looks like this:

```
?sv=2014-02-14&sig=wE5oAUYHcGJ8chwyZZd3Byp5jK1Po8uKu2t%2FYzQsIhY%3D&st=2014-12-2
4T14%3A23%3A22Z&se=2014-12-24T15%3A28%3A22Z&sp=raup
```

You can use this token as follows to gain access to the queue and add messages:

```
StorageCredentials creds = new StorageCredentials(sasToken);
CloudQueueClient sasClient = new CloudQueueClient("https://<ACCOUNTNAME>.queue.core.
windows.net/", creds);
CloudQueue sasQueue = sasClient.GetQueueReference("workerqueue");
sasQueue.AddMessage(new CloudQueueMessage("new message"));
```

> **IMPORTANT** SECURE USE OF SAS
>
> Always use a secure HTTPS connection to generate an SAS token to protect the exchange of the URI, which grants access to protected storage resources.

Creating an SAS token (Tables)

The following code shows how to create an SAS token for a table:

```
CloudTableClient tableClient = account.CreateCloudTableClient();
CloudTable table = tableClient.GetTableReference("$logs");
SharedAccessTablePolicy sasPolicy = new SharedAccessTablePolicy();
sasPolicy.SharedAccessExpiryTime = DateTime.UtcNow.AddHours(1);
sasPolicy.Permissions = SharedAccessTablePermissions.Query |
SharedAccessTablePermissions.Add | SharedAccessTablePermissions.Update |
SharedAccessTablePermissions.Delete;
sasPolicy.SharedAccessStartTime = DateTime.UtcNow.Subtract(new TimeSpan(0, 5, 0));
string sasToken = table.GetSharedAccessSignature(sasPolicy);
```

The SAS token grants query, add, update, and delete permissions to the container (raud). It looks like this:

```
?sv=2014-02-14&tn=%24logs&sig=dsnI7RBA1xYQVr%2FTlpDEZMO2H8YtSGwtyUUntVmxstA%3D&s
t=2014-12-24T14%3A48%3A09Z&se=2014-12-24T15%3A53%3A09Z&sp=raud
```

Renewing an SAS token

SAS tokens have a limited period of validity based on the start and expiration times requested. You should limit the duration of an SAS token to limit access to controlled periods of time. You can extend access to the same application or user by issuing new SAS tokens on request. This should be done with appropriate authentication and authorization in place.

Validating data

When you extend write access to storage resources with SAS, the contents of those resources can potentially be made corrupt or even be tampered with by a malicious party, particularly if the SAS was leaked. Be sure to validate system use of all resources exposed with SAS keys.

Creating stored access policies

Stored access policies provide greater control over how you grant access to storage resources using SAS tokens. With a stored access policy, you can do the following after releasing an SAS token for resource access:

- Change the start and end time for a signature's validity
- Control permissions for the signature
- Revoke access

The stored access policy can be used to control all issued SAS tokens that are based on the policy. For a step-by-step tutorial for creating and testing stored access policies for blobs, queues, and tables, see *http://azure.microsoft.com/en-us/documentation/articles/storage-dotnet-shared-access-signature-part-2*.

> **IMPORTANT RECOMMENDATION FOR SAS TOKENS**
>
> Use stored access policies wherever possible, or limit the lifetime of SAS tokens to avoid malicious use.

> **MORE INFO STORED ACCESS POLICY FORMAT**
>
> For more information on the HTTP request format for creating stored access policies, see *http://msdn.microsoft.com/en-us/library/azure/ee393341.aspx*.

Regenerating storage account keys

When you create a storage account, two 512-bit storage access keys are generated for authentication to the storage account. This makes it possible to regenerate keys without impacting application access to storage.

The process for managing keys typically follows this pattern:

1. When you create your storage account, the primary and secondary keys are generated for you. You typically use the primary key when you first deploy applications that access the storage account.

2. When it is time to regenerate keys, you first switch all application configurations to use the secondary key.

3. Next, you regenerate the primary key, and switch all application configurations to use this primary key.

4. Next, you regenerate the secondary key.

Regenerating storage account keys (existing portal)

To regenerate storage account keys using the management portal, complete the following steps:

1. Navigate to the Dashboard tab for your storage account in the management portal accessed via *https://manage.windowsazure.com*.

2. Select Manage Access Keys from the bottom of the page.

3. Click the regenerate button for the primary access key or for the secondary access key, depending on which key you intend to regenerate, according to the workflow above

4. Click the check mark on the confirmation dialog box to complete the regeneration task.

> **IMPORTANT   MANAGING KEY REGENERATION**
>
> It is imperative that you have a sound key management strategy. In particular, you must be certain that all applications are using the primary key at a given point in time to facilitate the regeneration process.

Regenerating storage account keys (Preview portal)

To regenerate storage account keys using the Preview portal, complete the following steps:

1. Navigate to the management portal accessed via *https://portal.azure.com*.

2. Click Browse on the command bar.

3. Select Storage from the Filter By list.

4. Select your storage account from the list on the Storage blade.

5. Click the Keys box.

6. On the Manage Keys blade, click Regenerate Primary or Regenerate Secondary on the command bar, depending on which key you want to regenerate.

7. In the confirmation dialog box, click Yes to confirm the key regeneration.

Configuring and using Cross-Origin Resource Sharing

Cross-Origin Resource Sharing (CORS) enables web applications running in the browser to call web APIs that are hosted by a different domain. Azure Storage blobs, tables, and queues all support CORS to allow for access to the Storage API from the browser. By default, CORS is disabled, but you can explicitly enable it for a specific storage service within your storage account.

> *MORE INFO* **ENABLING CORS**
>
> For additional information about enabling CORS for your storage accounts, see *http://msdn.microsoft.com/en-us/library/azure/dn535601.aspx.*

> ## Thought experiment
> ### Access control strategy
>
> In this thought experiment, apply what you've learned about this objective. You can find answers to these questions in the "Answers" section at the end of this chapter.
>
> Your web application generates large reports for your customers, and you are designing a strategy for granting access to those reports, which are stored in blobs. You want users to authenticate to download reports, but you want them to be able to share a link to the report with others in the company in a secure way that prevents unauthorized users from accessing content.
>
> 1. How would you approach granting access to these reports within the web application and sharing that with authenticated users?
>
> 2. How would you ensure that if the report is shared with others via link, the reports are not available long term without authentication?

Objective summary

- You can use SAS tokens to delegate access to storage account resources without sharing the account key.

- With SAS tokens, you can generate a link to a container, blob, table, table entity, or queue. You can control the permissions granted to the resource.

- Using Shared Access Policies, you can remotely control the lifetime of a SAS token grant to one or more resources. You can extend the lifetime of the policy or cause it to expire.

Objective review

Answer the following questions to test your knowledge of the information in this objective. You can find the answers to these questions and explanations of why each answer choice is correct or incorrect in the "Answers" section at the end of this chapter.

1. Which of the following are true regarding supported operations granted with an SAS token? (Choose all that apply.)

    A. You can grant read access to existing blobs.

    B. You can create new blob containers.

    C. You can add, update, and delete queue messages.

    D. You can add, update, and delete table entities.

    E. You can query table entities.

2. Which of the following statements are true of stored access policies? (Choose all that apply.)

    A. You can modify the start or expiration date for access.

    B. You can revoke access at any point in time.

    C. You can modify permissions to remove or add supported operations.

    D. You can add to the list of resources accessible by an SAS token.

3. Which of the following statements are true of CORS support for storage? (Choose all that apply.)

    A. It is recommended you enable CORS so that browsers can access blobs.

    B. To protect CORS access to blobs from the browser, you should generate SAS tokens to secure blob requests.

    C. CORS is supported only for Blob storage.

    D. CORS is disabled by default.

Objective 4.5: Monitor storage

Azure Storage has a built-in analytics feature called Azure Storage Analytics used for collecting metrics and logging storage request activity. You enable Storage Analytics Metrics to collect aggregate transaction and capacity data, and you enable Storage Analytics Logging to capture successful and failed request attempts to your storage account. This section covers how to enable monitoring and logging, control logging levels, set retention policies, and analyze the logs.

> *NOTE* **STORAGE ANALYTICS AVAILABILITY**
>
> At the time of this writing, Storage Analytics is not available for Azure Files.

> **This objective covers how to:**
> - Enable monitoring and logging
> - Set retention policies and logging levels
> - Analyze logs

Configuring storage metrics

Storage Analytics metrics provide insight into transactions and capacity for your storage accounts. You can think of them as the equivalent of Windows Performance Monitor counters. By default, storage metrics are not enabled, but you can enable them through the management portal, using Windows PowerShell, or by calling the management API directly.

When you configure storage metrics for a storage account, tables are generated to store the output of metrics collection. You determine the level of metrics collection for transactions and the retention level for each service—Blob, Table, and Queue.

Transaction metrics record request access to each service for the storage account. You specify the interval for metric collection (hourly or by minute). In addition, there are two levels of metrics collection:

- **Service level** These metrics include aggregate statistics for all requests, aggregated at the specified interval. Even if no requests are made to the service, an aggregate entry is created for the interval, indicating no requests for that period.
- **API level** These metrics record every request to each service only if a request is made within the hour interval.

> *NOTE* **METRICS COLLECTED**
>
> All requests are included in the metrics collected, including any requests made by Storage Analytics.

Capacity metrics are only recorded for the Blob service for the account. Metrics include total storage in bytes, the container count, and the object count (committed and uncommitted).

Table 4-1 summarizes the tables automatically created for the storage account when Storage Analytics metrics are enabled.

TABLE 4-1 Storage metrics tables

METRICS	TABLE NAMES
Hourly metrics	$MetricsHourPrimaryTransactionsBlob $MetricsHourPrimaryTransactionsTable $MetricsHourPrimaryTransactionsQueue
Minute metrics (cannot set through the management portal)	$MetricsMinutePrimaryTransactionsBlob $MetricsMinutePrimaryTransactionsTable $MetricsMinutePrimaryTransactionsQueue
Capacity (only for the Blob service)	$MetricsCapacityBlob

> **MORE INFO**   **STORAGE ANALYTICS METRICS TABLE SCHEMA**
>
> For additional details on the transaction and capacity metrics collected, see *http://msdn.microsoft.com/en-us/library/azure/hh343264.aspx*.

Retention can be configured for each service in the storage account. By default, Storage Analytics will not delete any metrics data. When the shared 20-terabyte limit is reached, new data cannot be written until space is freed. This limit is independent of the storage limit of the account. You can specify a retention period from 0 to 365 days. Metrics data is automatically deleted when the retention period is reached for the entry.

When metrics are disabled, existing metrics that have been collected are persisted up to their retention policy.

> **MORE INFO**   **STORAGE METRICS**
>
> For more information about enabling and working with storage metrics, see *http://msdn.microsoft.com/en-us/library/azure/dn782843.aspx*.

Configuring storage metrics and retention (existing portal)

To enable storage metrics and associated retention levels for Blob, Table, and Queue services in the existing management portal, follow these steps:

1. Navigate to the Configure tab for your storage account in the management portal accessed via *https://manage.windowsazure.com*.

2. If this storage account uses blobs, set the metrics level for blobs to Minimal. Set retention according to your retention policy.

3. If this storage account uses tables, set the metrics level for tables to Minimal. Set retention according to your retention policy.

4. If this storage account uses queues, set the metrics level for queues to Minimal. Set retention according to your retention policy.

5. Click Save to commit the settings.

> *NOTE* **CHOOSING A METRICS LEVEL**
>
> Minimal metrics yield enough information to provide a picture of the overall usage and health of the storage account services. Verbose metrics provide more insight at the API level, allowing for deeper analysis of activities and issues, which is helpful for troubleshooting.

Configuring storage metrics and retention (Preview portal)

To enable storage metrics and associated retention levels for Blob, Table, and Queue services in the Preview portal, follow these steps:

1. Navigate to the management portal accessed via *https://portal.azure.com*.

2. Click Browse on the command bar.

3. Select Storage from the Filter By drop-down list.

4. Select your storage account from the list on the Storage blade.

5. Scroll down to the Usage section, and click the Capacity Past Week check box.

6. On the Metric blade, click Diagnostics on the command bar.

7. Click the On button under Status. This shows the options for metrics and logging.

8. If this storage account uses blobs, select Blob Aggregate Metrics to enable service level metrics. Select Blob Per API Metrics for API level metrics.

9. If this storage account uses tables, select Table Aggregate Metrics to enable service level metrics. Select Table Per API Metrics for API level metrics.

10. If this storage account uses queues, select Queue Aggregate Metrics to enable service level metrics. Select Queue Per API Metrics for API level metrics.

11. Provide a value for retention according to your retention policy. Through the Preview portal, this will apply to all services. It will also apply to Storage Analytics Logging if that is enabled. Select one of the available retention settings from the drop-down list, or enter a number from 0 to 365.

Configuring storage metrics and retention using Windows PowerShell

To enable storage metrics and associated retention levels using Windows PowerShell, use the Set-AzureStorageMetricsProperty cmdlet.

To enable service level metrics collected by minute for blobs, tables, and queues with unlimited retention, run the following:

```
Set-AzureStorageServiceMetricsProperty -MetricsType Minute -ServiceType Blob -
MetricsLevel Service -RetentionDays 0
Set-AzureStorageServiceMetricsProperty -MetricsType Minute -ServiceType Table -
MetricsLevel Service -RetentionDays 0
Set-AzureStorageServiceMetricsProperty -MetricsType Minute -ServiceType Queue -
MetricsLevel Service -RetentionDays 0
```

To enable service and API level metrics collected hourly for blobs, tables, and queues with 90 days of retention, run the following:

```
Set-AzureStorageServiceMetricsProperty -MetricsType Hour -ServiceType Blob -MetricsLevel
ServiceAndApi -RetentionDays 90
Set-AzureStorageServiceMetricsProperty -MetricsType Hour -ServiceType Table -
MetricsLevel ServiceAndApi -RetentionDays 90
Set-AzureStorageServiceMetricsProperty -MetricsType Hour -ServiceType Queue -
MetricsLevel ServiceAndApi -RetentionDays 90
```

To disable the collection of metrics, run the following:

```
Set-AzureStorageServiceMetricsProperty-ServiceType Blob -MetricsLevel None
Set-AzureStorageServiceMetricsProperty-ServiceType Table -MetricsLevel None
Set-AzureStorageServiceMetricsProperty-ServiceType Queue -MetricsLevel None
```

Analyzing storage metrics

Storage Analytics metrics are collected in tables as discussed in the previous section. You can access the tables directly to analyze metrics, but you can also review metrics in both Azure management portals. This section discusses various ways to access metrics and review or analyze them.

> **MORE INFO** **STORAGE MONITORING, DIAGNOSING, AND TROUBLESHOOTING**
>
> For more details on how to work with storage metrics and logs, see *http://azure.microsoft. com/en-us/documentation/articles/storage-monitoring-diagnosing-troubleshooting*.

Monitoring metrics (existing portal)

To monitor metrics in the existing portal, complete the following steps:

1. Navigate to the Monitor tab for your storage account in the management portal accessed via *https://manage.windowsazure.com*.

2. Click Add Metric to choose metrics to monitor in the management portal.

3. In the Choose Metrics dialog box, select from the list of metrics for blobs, tables, or queues.

4. Click the check mark to commit the settings.

5. You may choose up to six metrics to show in the monitoring graph, as shown in Figure 4-8.

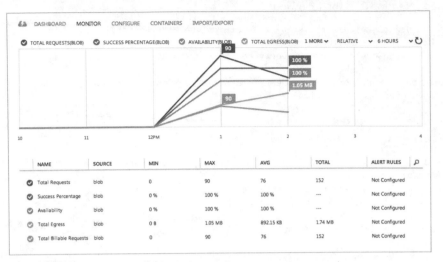

FIGURE 4-8 Monitoring metrics from the existing management portal

6. Select absolute or relative display of metrics from the appropriate drop-down list (RELATIVE is indicated in Figure 4-8).

7. Select the time range to display from the appropriate drop-down list (6 HOURS is indicated in Figure 4-8). Select 6 hours, 24 hours, or 7 days.

Monitoring metrics (Preview portal)

At the time of this writing, the Preview portal features for monitoring metrics is limited to some predefined metrics, including total requests, total egress, average latency, and availability (see Figure 4-9). Click each box to see a Metric blade that provides additional detail.

FIGURE 4-9 Monitoring overview from the Preview portal

To monitor the metrics available in the Preview portal, complete the following steps:

1. Navigate to the management portal accessed via *https://portal.azure.com*.

2. Click Browse on the command bar.

3. Select Storage from the Filter By drop-down list.

4. Select your storage account from the list on the Storage blade.

5. Scroll down to the Monitor section, and view the monitoring boxes summarizing statistics. You'll see TotalRequests, TotalEgress, AverageE2ELatency, and AvailabilityToday by default.

6. Click each metric box to view additional details for each metric. You'll see metrics for blobs, tables, and queues if all three metrics are being collected.

> **NOTE   CUSTOMIZING THE MONITORING BLADE**
>
> You can customize which boxes appear in the Monitoring area of the Preview portal, and you can adjust the size of each box to control how much detail is shown at a glance without drilling into the metrics blade.

Configuring Storage Analytics Logging

Storage Analytics Logging provides details about successful and failed requests to each storage service that has activity across the account's blobs, tables, and queues. By default, storage logging is not enabled, but you can enable it through the management portal, by using Windows PowerShell, or by calling the management API directly.

When you configure Storage Analytics Logging for a storage account, a blob container named $logs is automatically created to store the output of the logs. You choose which services you want to log for the storage account. You can log any or all of the Blob, Table, or Queue services. You can also choose which type of requests to log: read, write, or delete. Logs are created only for those services that have activity, so you will not be charged if you enable logging for a service that has no requests. The logs are stored as block blobs as requests are logged and are periodically committed so that they are available as blobs.

> **NOTE   DELETING THE LOG CONTAINER**
>
> After Storage Analytics has been enabled, the log container cannot be deleted; however, the contents of the log container can be deleted.

Retention can be configured for each service in the storage account. By default, Storage Analytics will not delete any logging data. When the shared 20-terabyte limit is reached, new data cannot be written until space is freed. This limit is independent of the storage limit of the account. You can specify a retention period from 0 to 365 days. Logging data is automatically deleted when the retention period is reached for the entry.

Configuring storage logging and retention (existing portal)

To enable storage logging and associated retention levels for Blob, Table, and Queue services in the existing portal, follow these steps:

1. Navigate to the Configure tab for your storage account in the management portal accessed via *https://manage.windowsazure.com*. Scroll to the logging section.

2. If this storage account uses blobs, select Read, Write, and Delete requests to log all activity. Set retention according to your retention policy.

3. If this storage account uses tables, select Read, Write, and Delete requests to log all activity. Set retention according to your retention policy.

4. If this storage account uses queues, check Read, Write, and Delete requests to log all activity. Set retention according to your retention policy.

5. Click Save to commit the settings.

Configuring storage logging and retention (Preview portal)

To enable storage logging and associated retention levels for Blob, Table, and Queue services in the Preview portal, follow these steps:

1. Navigate to the management portal accessed via *https://portal.azure.com*.

2. Click Browse on the command bar.

3. Select Storage from the Filter By drop-down list.

4. Select your storage account from the list on the Storage blade.

5. Scroll down to the Usage section, and select the Capacity Past Week check box.

6. On the Metric blade, click Diagnostics on the command bar.

7. Click the On button under Status. This shows the options for enabling monitoring features.

8. If this storage account uses blobs, select Blob Logs to log all activity.

9. If this storage account uses tables, select Table Logs to log all activity.

10. If this storage account uses queues, select Queue Logs to log all activity.

11. Provide a value for retention according to your retention policy. Through the Preview portal, this will apply to all services. It will also apply to Storage Analytics Metrics if that is enabled. Select one of the available retention settings from the drop-down list, or enter a number from 0 to 365.

> **NOTE CONTROLLING LOGGED ACTIVITIES**
>
> From the Preview portal, when you enable or disable logging for each service, you enable read, write, and delete logging. To log only specific activities, use Windows PowerShell cmdlets.

Configuring storage logging and retention using Windows PowerShell

To enable storage metrics and associated retention levels using Windows PowerShell, use the Set-AzureStorageServiceLoggingProperty cmdlet.

To enable logging for read, write, and delete actions with retention of 30 days, run the following:

```
Set-AzureStorageServiceLoggingProperty –ServiceType Blob –LoggingOperations
read,write,delete –RetentionDays 30
Set-AzureStorageServiceLoggingProperty –ServiceType Table –LoggingOperations
read,write,delete –RetentionDays 30
Set-AzureStorageServiceLoggingProperty –ServiceType Queue –LoggingOperations
read,write,delete –RetentionDays 30
```

To disable the collection of metrics, run the following:

```
Set-AzureStorageServiceLoggingProperty –ServiceType Blob –LoggingOperations none
Set-AzureStorageServiceLoggingProperty –ServiceType Table –LoggingOperations none
Set-AzureStorageServiceLoggingProperty –ServiceType Queue –LoggingOperations none
```

Enabling client-side logging

You can enable client-side logging using Microsoft Azure storage libraries to log activity from client applications to your storage accounts. For information on the .NET Storage Client Library, see *http://msdn.microsoft.com/en-us/library/azure/dn782839.aspx*. For information on the Storage SDK for Java, see *http://msdn.microsoft.com/en-us/library/azure/dn782844.aspx*.

Analyzing storage logs

Logs are stored as block blobs in delimited text format. When you access the container, you can download logs for review and analysis using any tool compatible with that format. Within the logs, you'll find entries for authenticated and anonymous requests, as listed in Table 4-3.

TABLE 4-3 Authenticated and anonymous logs

Request Type	Logged Requests
Authenticated requests	<ul><li>Successful requests</li><li>Failed requests such as timeouts, authorization, throttling issues, and other errors</li><li>Requests that use an SAS</li><li>Requests for analytics data</li></ul>
Anonymous requests	<ul><li>Successful requests</li><li>Server errors</li><li>Timeouts for client or server</li><li>Failed GET requests with error code 304 (Not Modified)</li></ul>

Logs include status messages and operation logs. Status message columns include those shown in Table 4-4. Some status messages are also reported with storage metrics data. There are many operation logs for the Blob, Table, and Queue services.

> **MORE INFO STATUS MESSAGES AND OPERATION LOGS**
>
> For a detailed list of specific logs and log format specifics, see *http://msdn.microsoft.com/en-us/library/azure/hh343260.aspx* and *http://msdn.microsoft.com/en-us/library/hh343259.aspx*.

TABLE 4-4 Information included in logged status messages

Column	Description
Status Message	Indicates a value for the type of status message, indicating type of success or failure
Description	Describes the status, including any HTTP verbs or status codes
Billable	Indicates whether the request was billable
Availability	Indicates whether the request is included in the availability calculation for storage metrics

Finding your logs

When storage logging is configured, log data is saved to blobs in the $logs container created for your storage account. You can't see this container by listing containers, but you can navigate directly to the container to access, view, or download the logs.

To view analytics logs produced for a storage account, do the following:

1. Using a storage browsing tool, navigate to the $logs container within the storage account you have enabled Storage Analytics Logging for using this convention: *https://<accountname>.blob.core.windows.net/$logs*.

2. View the list of log files with the convention *<servicetype>/YYYY/MM/DD/HHMM/<counter>.log*.

3. Select the log file you want to review, and download it using the storage browsing tool.

> **MORE INFO** **LOG METADATA**
>
> The blob name for each log file does not provide an indication of the time range for the logs. You can search this information in the blob metadata using storage browsing tools or Windows PowerShell.

Accessing logs with Windows PowerShell

Using Windows PowerShell, you can access logs with the Get-AzureStorageBlob cmdlet and then filter logs by filename and metadata. The following example illustrates how to filter a list of write logs for Blob storage entries on a particular date during the ninth hour:

```
Get-AzureStorageBlob -Container '$logs' |
where {
  $_.Name -match 'blob/2014/12/01/09' -and
  $_.ICloudBlob.Metadata.LogType -match 'write'
} |
foreach {
  "{0} {1} {2} {3}" -f $_.Name,
  $_.ICloudBlob.Metadata.StartTime,
  $_.ICloudBlob.Metadata.EndTime,
  $_.ICloudBlob.Metadata.LogType
}
```

Downloading logs

To review and analyze your logs, first download them to your local machine. You can do this with storage browsing tools, programmatically, or with AzCopy.

> **MORE INFO** **AZCOPY**
>
> AzCopy is part of the Azure SDK. You can download the latest version directly from *http://aka.ms/AzCopy*.

Viewing logs with Microsoft Excel

Storage logs are recorded in a delimited format so that you can use any compatible tool to view logs. To view logs data in Excel, follow these steps:

1. Open Excel, and on the Data menu, click From Text.

2. Find the log file and click Import.

3. During import, select Delimited format. Select Semicolon as the only delimiter, and Double-Quote (") as the text qualifier.

Analyzing logs

After you load your logs into a viewer like Excel, you can analyze and gather information such as the following:

- Number of requests from a specific IP range
- Which tables or containers are being accessed and the frequency of those requests
- Which user issued a request, in particular, any requests of concern
- Slow requests
- How many times a particular blob is being accessed with an SAS URL
- Details to assist in investigating network errors

> **MORE INFO** **LOG ANALYSIS**
>
> You can run the Azure HDInsight Log Analysis Toolkit (LAT) for a deeper analysis of your storage logs. For more information, see *https://hadoopsdk.codeplex.com/releases/view/117906*.

> ### Thought experiment
> #### Proactive and reactive diagnostics
>
> In this thought experiment, apply what you've learned about this objective. You can find answers to these questions in the "Answers" section at the end of this chapter.
>
> Your application is now live, and you are planning how you will monitor the overall health of your storage account resources.
>
> 1. What features would you use to give you a proactive, early warning of problems with storage services?
>
> 2. What features could you use to diagnose an issue retroactively so that you can perform root cause analysis and fix the problem?

Objective summary

- Storage Analytics metrics provide the equivalent of Windows Performance Monitor counters for storage services.
- You can determine which services to collect metrics for (Blob, Table, or Queue), whether to collect metrics for the service or API level, and whether to collect metrics by the minute or hour.
- Capacity metrics are only applicable to the Blob service.
- Storage Analytics Logging provides details about the success or failure of requests to storage services.
- Storage logs are stored in blob services for the account, in the $logs container for the service.
- You can specify up to 365 days for retention of storage metrics or logs, or you can set retention to 0 to retain metrics indefinitely. Metrics and logs are removed automatically from storage when the retention period expires.
- Storage metrics can be viewed in the management portal. Storage logs can be downloaded and viewed in a reporting tool such as Excel.

Objective review

Answer the following questions to test your knowledge of the information in this objective. You can find the answers to these questions and explanations of why each answer choice is correct or incorrect in the "Answers" section at the end of this chapter.

1. Which statements are true of Storage Analytics Metrics? (Choose all that apply.)

    A. Capacity metrics are recorded only for blobs.

    B. You can set hourly or by minute metrics through the management portal.

    C. By default, metrics are retained for one year.

    D. If you disable metrics, existing metrics are deleted from storage.

2. Which statements are true of Storage Analytics Logging? (Choose all that apply.)

    A. Logs are stored in the same storage account where they are enabled and are measured as part of your storage quota.

    B. Logs can have duplicate entries.

    C. Logs cannot be deleted.

    D. You can log all read, write, and delete requests to blobs, queues, and tables in a storage account.

3. Which of the following are captured by Storage Analytics Logging? (Choose all that apply.)

   A. Successful requests for authenticated calls only

   B. Failed requests for authenticated calls only

   C. Server errors

   D. Requests using SAS URIs

Objective 4.6: Implement SQL databases

In this section, you learn about Microsoft Azure SQL Database, a PaaS offering for relational data.

> **This objective covers how to:**
>
> - Choose the appropriate database tier and performance level
> - Configure and perform point in time recovery
> - Enable geo-replication
> - Import and export data and schema
> - Scale SQL databases

Choosing the appropriate database tier and performance level

Choosing a SQL Database tier used to be simply a matter of storage space. Recently, Microsoft added new tiers that also affect the performance of SQL Database. This tiered pricing is called Service Tiers. There are three service tiers to choose from, and while they still each have restrictions on storage space, they also have some differences that might affect your choice. The major difference is in a measurement called database throughput units (DTUs). A DTU is a blended measure of CPU, memory, disk reads, and disk writes. Because SQL Database is a shared resource with other Azure customers, sometimes performance is not stable or predictable. As you go up in performance tiers, you also get better predictability in performance.

- **Basic** Basic tier is meant for light workloads. There is only one performance level of the basic service tier. This level is good for small use, new projects, testing, development, or learning.

- **Standard** Standard tier is used for most production online transaction processing (OLTP) databases. The performance is more predictable than the basic tier. In addition, there are four performance levels under this tier, levels S0 to S3.

- **Premium** Premium tier continues to scale at the same level as the standard tier. In addition, performance is typically measured in seconds. For instance, the basic tier can handle 16,600 transactions per hour. The standard/S2 level can handle 2,570 transactions per minute. The top tier of premium can handle 735 transactions per second. That translates to 2,645,000 per hour in basic tier terminology.

MORE INFO   SQL DATABASE TIERS AND THROUGHPUT

For more information on SQL Database tiers, see *http://msdn.microsoft.com/en-us/library/azure/dn741336.aspx.*

There are many similarities between the various tiers. Each tier has a 99.9 percent uptime SLA, backup and restore capabilities, access to the same tooling, and the same database engine features. Fortunately, the levels are adjustable, and you can change your tier as your scaling requirements change.

The management portal can help you select the appropriate level. You can review the metrics on the Monitor tab to see the current load of your database and decide whether to scale up or down.

1. Click the SQL database you want to monitor.

2. Click the Monitor tab, as shown in Figure 4-10.

3. Add the following metrics:

   - CPU Percentage

   - Physical Data Reads Percentage

   - Log Write Percentage

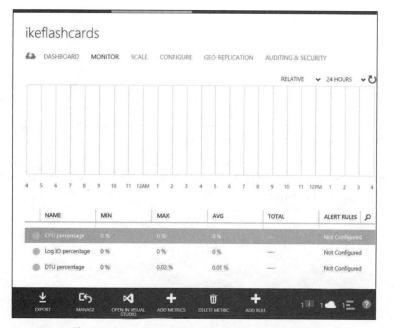

FIGURE 4-10 The Monitor tab

All three of these metrics are shown relative to the DTU of your database. If you reach 80 percent of your performance metrics, it's time to consider increasing your service tier or performance level. If you're consistently below 10 percent of the DTU, you might consider decreasing your service tier or performance level. Be aware of momentary spikes in usage when making your choice.

In addition, you can configure an email alert for when your metrics are 80 percent of your selected DTU by completing the following steps:

1. Click the metric.

2. Click Add Rule.

3. The first page of the Create Alert Rule dialog box is shown in Figure 4-11. Add a name and description, and then click the right arrow.

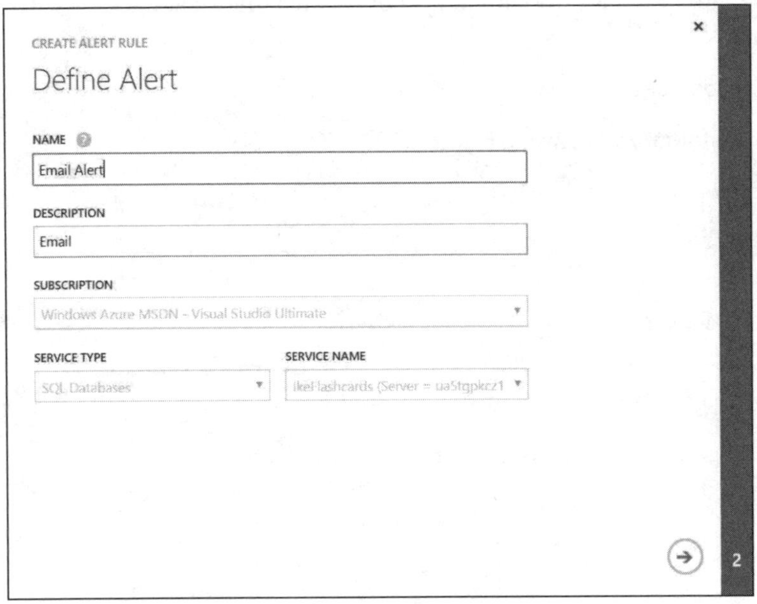

FIGURE 4-11 The first page of the Create Alert Rule dialog box

4. On the next page of the Create Alert Rule dialog box, shown in Figure 4-12, select the condition and the threshold value.

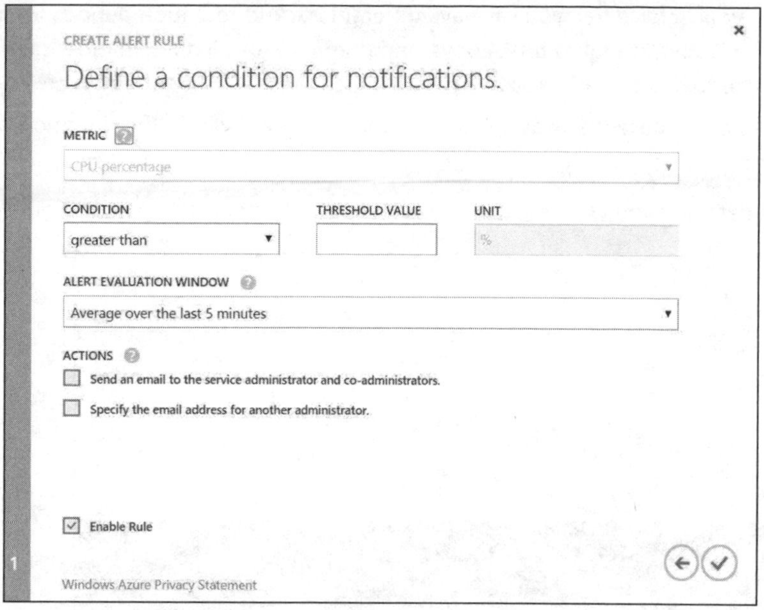

FIGURE 4-12 The second page of the Create Alert Rule dialog box

5. Select your alert evaluation window. An email will be generated if the event happens over a specific duration. You should indicate at least 10 minutes

6. Select the action. You can choose to send an email either to the service administrator(s) or to a specific email address.

Configuring and performing point in time recovery

Azure SQL Database does a full backup every week, a differential backup each day, and an incremental log backup every five minutes. The incremental log backup allows for a point in time restore, which means the database can be restored to any specific time of day. This means that if you accidentally delete a customer's table from your database, you will be able to recover it with minimal data loss if you know the timeframe to restore from that has the most recent copy.

The length of time it takes to do a restore varies. The further away you get from the last differential backup determines the longer the restore operation takes because there are more log backups to restore. When you restore a new database, the service tier stays the same, but the performance level changes to the minimum level of that tier.

Depending on your service tier, you will have different backup retention periods. Basic retains backups for 7 days, standard for 14 days, and premium for 35 days. In most cases, 14 days is enough time to determine that you have a problem and how to correct it.

You can restore a database that was deleted as long as you are within the retention period. Follow these steps to restore a database:

1. Select the database you want to restore, and then click Restore, as shown in Figure 4-13.

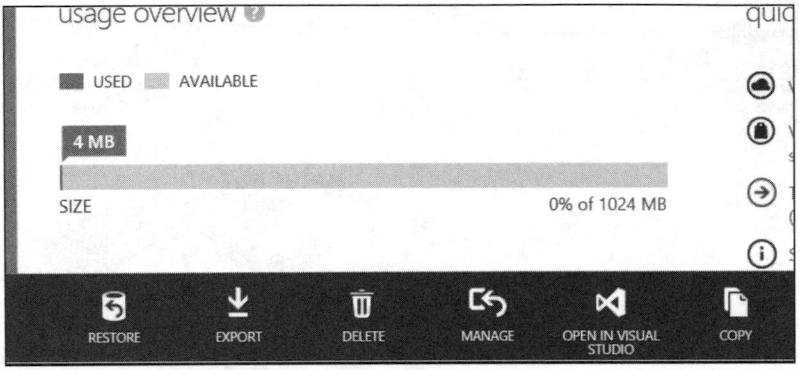

FIGURE 4-13 The Restore button

2. The Restore dialog box opens, as shown in Figure 4-14.

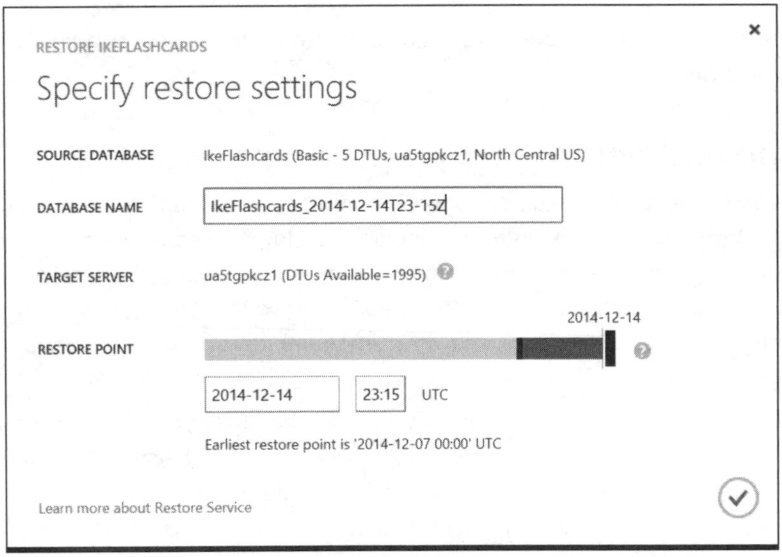

FIGURE 4-14 The Restore dialog box

3. Select a database name.

4. Select a restore point. You can use the slider bar or manually enter a date and time.

5. You can also restore a deleted database. Select the Deleted Databases tab, as shown in Figure 4-15.

FIGURE 4-15 The Deleted Databases tab for SQL databases in the management portal

6. Select the database you want to restore.

7. Click Restore as you did in step 1.

8. Specify a database name for the new database.

9. Click Submit.

Enabling geo-replication

Every Azure SQL Database subscription has built-in redundancy. Three copies of your data are stored across fault domains in the datacenter to protect against server and hardware failure. This is built in to the subscription price and is not configurable. You can configure two more fault-tolerant options: standard geo-replication and active geo-replication.

Standard geo-replication allows the user to fail over the database to a different region when a database is not available. It is available on the standard and premium service tiers. The main difference between active and standard geo-replication is that standard geo-replication does not allow clients to connect to the secondary server. It is offline until it's needed to take over for the primary. The target region for the offline secondary server is pre-determined. For instance, if your primary server is in North Central US, then your secondary server will be in South Central US. The source and target servers must belong to the same subscription.

Creating an offline secondary database (existing portal)

Follow these steps to configure an offline secondary database:

1. Click the Geo-Replication tab for the database, as shown in Figure 4-16, and click Add Secondary.

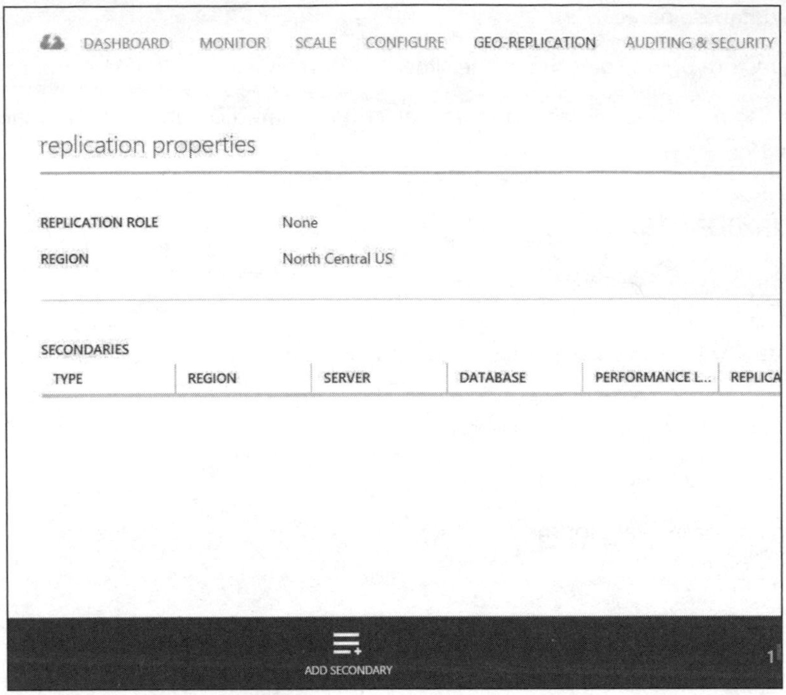

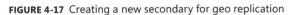

DASHBOARD   MONITOR   SCALE   CONFIGURE   GEO-REPLICATION   AUDITING & SECURITY

replication properties

| REPLICATION ROLE | None |
| REGION | North Central US |

SECONDARIES

TYPE	REGION	SERVER	DATABASE	PERFORMANCE L...	REPLICA

ADD SECONDARY

1

FIGURE 4-16 Replication properties

2. On the Specify Secondary Settings page, shown in Figure 4-17, select a server from the server list or click New SQL Database Server, and then click the right arrow.

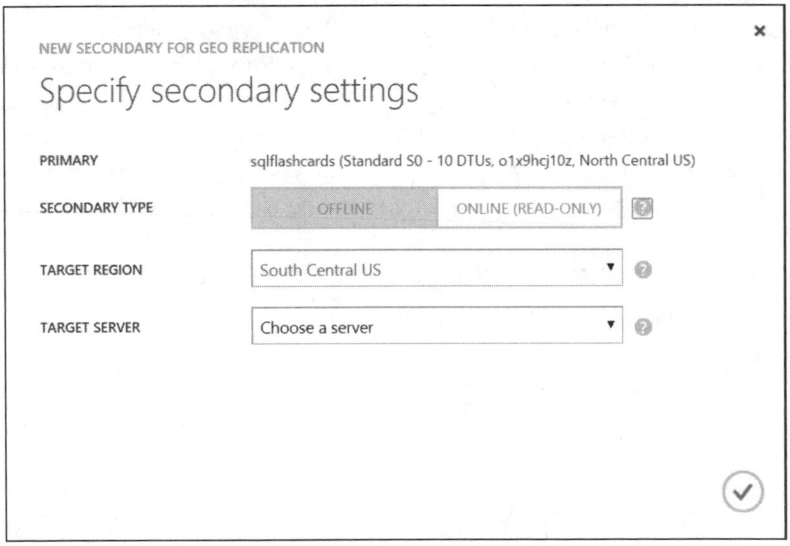

NEW SECONDARY FOR GEO REPLICATION

Specify secondary settings

PRIMARY	sqlflashcards (Standard S0 - 10 DTUs, o1x9hcj10z, North Central US)
SECONDARY TYPE	OFFLINE ONLINE (READ-ONLY)
TARGET REGION	South Central US ▾
TARGET SERVER	Choose a server ▾

FIGURE 4-17 Creating a new secondary for geo replication

3. If you select a new server, the SQL Database Server Settings page opens (see Figure 4-18). Enter a login name and password, and select the Allow Windows Azure Services To Access The Server check box.

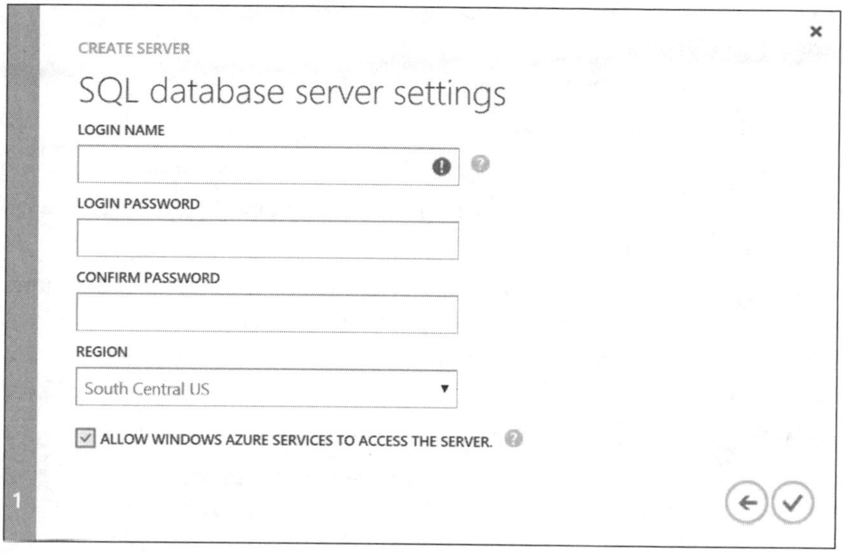

FIGURE 4-18 The SQL Database Server Settings page

4. Monitor the Geo-Replication page for the progress of building the new secondary. You can watch the Replication Status of the database switch from Pending to Active.

   If there is a datacenter failure, the same page shows the Replication Status of your database as Unavailable. You will also see the Failover Enabled property set to true for the database and be able to initiate a failover by clicking Failover on the command bar.

> *NOTE* **USES FOR CREATING AN OFFLINE SECONDARY**
>
> Another use for this feature has to do with the ability to terminate the continuous copy relationship between a primary and secondary database. You can terminate the relationship and then upgrade the primary database to a different schema to support a software upgrade. The secondary database gives you a rollback option.

Creating an offline secondary database (Preview portal)

To create an offline secondary database in the Preview portal, follow these steps:

1. Navigate to your SQL database in the management portal accessed via *https://portal.azure.com*.

2. Scroll to the Geo Replication section, and click the Configure Geo Replication box.

3. On the Geo Replication blade, select your target region.

4. On the Create Secondary blade, click Create.

Creating an online secondary database (existing portal)

There are some differences between standard geo-replication and active geo-replication. Active geo-replication is different in these ways:

- You can have four secondary copies of your database.
- It is available only at the premium service tier.
- The online secondary will be consistent with the primary eventually.
- Of the four secondary copies of the database, four can be active, or three can be active and one can be an offline secondary.
- The online secondary server is readable. This allows you to put reports or ETL processes on the secondary, freeing up the locking overhead on the primary. Since the secondary copies are located in different regions, you can put readable databases close to remote users.

Before you create an online secondary, the following requirements must be met:

- The secondary database must have the same name as the primary.
- They must be on separate servers.
- They both must be on the same subscription.
- The secondary server cannot be a lower performance tier than the primary.

The steps for configuring an active secondary is the same as creating an offline secondary, except you can select the target region, as shown in Figure 4-19.

NEW SECONDARY FOR GEO REPLICATION

Specify secondary settings

PRIMARY	sqlflashcards (Premium P1 - 100 DTUs, o1x9hcj10z, North Central US)
SECONDARY TYPE	OFFLINE ONLINE (READ-ONLY)
TARGET REGION	South Central US (Microsoft Recommended) ▾
TARGET SERVER	New SQL database server ▾

FIGURE 4-19 The New Secondary For Geo Replication dialog box for creating an active secondary

Creating an online secondary database (Preview portal)

If your SQL database is a Premium database, you will be able to create an online secondary. To create an online secondary in the Preview portal, follow these steps:

1. Navigate to your SQL database in the management portal accessed via *https://portal.azure.com*.

2. On the Create Secondary blade, change the Secondary Type to Readable.

3. Click Create to create the secondary.

Creating an online or offline secondary with Windows PowerShell

Creating an online or offline secondary can be done with Windows PowerShell using the Start-AzureSqlDatabaseCopy cmdlet.

To create an online secondary, use the following command:

```
Start-AzureSqlDatabaseCopy -ServerName "SecondarySrv" -DatabaseName "Flashcards"
-PartnerServer "NewServer" -ContinuousCopy
```

To create an offline secondary, use the following command:

```
Start-AzureSqlDatabaseCopy -ServerName "SecondarySrv" -DatabaseName "Flashcards"
-PartnerServer "NewServer" -ContinuousCopy -OfflineSecondary
```

Importing and exporting data and schema (existing portal)

Importing and exporting data and schema from a SQL database is essential for a number of situations, including creating a local development or test copy, moving a database to a local instance of SQL Server, or archiving data before you clean up a production database.

To export a database, follow these steps:

1. In the management portal, click the database you want to export.

2. On the task bar, click Export.

3. Enter values for the following:
   - FileName
   - Subscription
   - Blob Storage Account
   - Container
   - Login Name
   - Password

This will create a BACPAC file that can be used to create a database with either an on-premises SQL server, a SQL server in an Azure VM or in Azure SQL Database.

To import the BACPAC into Azure SQL Database, perform the following steps:

4. Click New, Data Services, SQL Database, Import.

5. Click the folder under the BACPAC URL to navigate to the BACPAC file stored in the storage account.

6. Click Open.

7. Enter the following information:
   - Subscription
   - Service Tier
   - Performance Level
   - Server

8. Click the Next arrow.

9. Enter the login details for the new server.

10. Click the check mark. Your new database appears online shortly.

The import process is faster if you use the standard service tier and at least the S2 performance level.

Importing and exporting data and schema (Preview portal)

The Preview portal does not currently support importing and exporting data and schema.

Thought experiment
Managing schema changes

In this thought experiment, apply what you've learned about this objective. You can find answers to these questions in the "Answers" section at the end of this chapter.

Your have 20 developers. They work on a central development copy of SQL Database hosted on Azure. They are constantly changing schema. Sometimes they overwrite each other's changes, which leads to frustration. These developers are not in the same city. Some are in Europe and some are in the United States.

1. What are some things you should consider to make schema changes easier for the developers?

2. What should you consider when creating a backup and restore strategy for this database?

3. What level of SQL Database is probably adequate for the developers? How would you determine that?

Objective summary

- The different editions of Azure SQL Database affect performance, SLAs, backup/restore policies, pricing, geo-replication options, and database size.
- The edition of Azure SQL Database determines the retention period for point in time restores. This should factor into your backup and restore policies.
- It is possible to create an online secondary when you configure Azure SQL Database geo-replication. It requires the Premium Edition.
- If you are migrating an existing database to the cloud, you can use the Azure management portal to move schema and data into your Azure SQL database.

Objective review

Answer the following questions to test your knowledge of the information in this objective. You can find the answers to these questions and explanations of why each answer choice is correct or incorrect in the "Answers" section at the end of this chapter.

1. Which of the following is *not* a requirement for creating an online secondary for SQL Database? (Choose all that apply.)

    A. The secondary database must have the same name as the primary.

    B. They must be on separate servers.

    C. They both must be on the different subscription.

    D. The secondary server cannot be a lower performance tier than the primary.

2. Which metrics should you add to monitoring that will help you select the appropriate level of SQL Database?

    A. CPU Processor Count

    B. CPU Percentage

    C. Physical Data Reads Percentage

    D. Log Writes Percentage

3. From what you know about SQL Database architecture, what should you include in your client application code?

    A. Connection resiliency, because you could failover to a replica.

    B. Transaction resiliency so you can resubmit a transaction in the event of a failover.

    C. Query auditing so you can baseline your current query times and know when to scale up the instance.

    D. A backup and restore operation for the database.

Answers

This section contains the solutions to the thought experiments and answers to the objective review questions in this chapter.

Objective 4.1: Thought experiment

1. You would consider structuring the blob hierarchy so that one of the portions of the path represented the language or region.

2. You would consider creating a CDN on a publicly available container to cache those files locally around the world.

Objective 4.1: Objective review

1. **Correct answers:** A and D

    A. **Correct:** Only blobs have writable system properties.

    B. **Incorrect:** Blob user-defined metadata is accessed as a key value pair.

    C. **Incorrect:** System metadata can influence how the blob is stored and accessed in Azure Storage.

    D. **Correct:** Containers also have system properties and user-defined metadata.

2. **Correct answers:** B and D

    A. **Incorrect:** Page files are not faster for streaming files, but are very good for random I/O files like VHDs.

    B. **Correct:** Block blobs allow files to be uploaded and assembled later. Blocks can be resubmitted individually.

    C. **Incorrect:** Page blobs are for hard disks, not files for streaming.

    D. **Correct:** Block blobs have a maximum size of 200 GB. Page blobs can be 1 terabyte.

3. **Correct answers:** A, B, and C

    A. **Correct:** SSL encrypts all data between client and server and prevents network sniffing.

    B. **Correct:** If the keys are hidden, they can't be compromised and used to gain access to Table storage.

    C. **Correct:** Client-side code can easily be seen in the browser. Keep sensitive information stored where few people can access it.

    D. **Incorrect:** Public containers are not secured.

Objective 4.2: Thought experiment

1. Machine ID seems like a logical candidate for PartitionKey.

2. Shot count time stamp, ordered descending.

3. There might be two tables, one for the machine metadata and one for the shots. You could also make an argument for consolidating both pieces of data into one table for speed in querying.

Objective 4.2: Objective review

1. **Correct answer:** A

   A. **Correct:** Transactional replication is used in Microsoft SQL Server. Table storage doesn't have anything like that.

   B. **Incorrect:** Zone redundant storage is valid.

   C. **Incorrect:** Read access geo-redundant storage is valid.

   D. **Incorrect:** Geo-redundant storage is valid.

2. **Correct answers:** C and D

   A. **Incorrect:** They should not necessarily be unique, although they can be for rare-use cases.

   B. **Incorrect:** You should only use the same partition key if you have a very small entity set.

   C. **Correct:** Batches can only have operations that exist in the same partition, with the same partition key.

   D. **Correct:** Even partition sizes will give your application predictable performance because one partition server won't be unevenly loaded with more entities than the others.

3. **Correct answers:** A, B, and C

   A. **Correct:** All operations have to be in the same partition.

   B. **Correct:** Total batch size can't be greater than 4 MB.

   C. **Correct:** Maximum operation count is 100.

   D. **Incorrect:** There is no minimum operation count for a batch.

Objective 4.3: Thought experiment

1. Typically, the application will store any relevant data and content to be used to produce reports in durable storage. When a report is requested, the request is written to a queue to trigger processing. The queue message must include enough information so that the compute instance listening to the queue can gather the information required for the specific user's report. In some cases, the message may point to a report request stored in a database record. In other cases, the queue message holds enough data to look up all the information required for the report. The work to generate a PDF should be performed on a compute instance that does not compete with mainline application resources, such as the core application web applications and services. This will allow the system to scale PDF generation separately from the main application as needed.

2. The most likely candidate for the compute instance for PDF generation is a cloud service worker role because it provides a built-in mechanism to deploy a Windows Service equivalent in a PaaS environment, but also provides some level of VM customization with startup tasks—possibly necessary for whatever PDF generation tool you may select. If no special software requirements are necessary for producing PDFs, you could also use a WebJob trigger to process queued messages. A VM can also be used, likely with a Windows Service deployed that processes the queue.

3. It will be important to take note of the average memory and disk space used while processing a single message to generate the PDF report. If you monitor the compute instance statistics and slowly begin to scale the number of concurrent messages processed on a single instance, you'll be able to see how much a single instance can handle for configuring auto-scale properties.

4. When you have an idea of the number of concurrent messages that can be processed on a single compute instance, you can identify the number of queued items that should trigger scaling the number of instances. For VMs and cloud services, you can automate this with auto-scale by metrics. For websites and WebJobs, you do not have the option to auto-scale by metric.

Objective 4.3: Objective review

1. **Correct answer:** B

   A. **Incorrect:** Storage queue messages have a size limit of 64 KB. It is true, however, that a smaller message size can increase throughput since the storage service can support more requests per second when those requests hold a smaller amount of data.

   B. **Correct:** Storage queues can only store up to 64 KB per message.

   C. **Incorrect:** Storage queue messages expire after seven days, unlike Service Bus Queue messages, which are persisted until explicitly read and removed.

   D. **Incorrect:** The message identifier should be considered opaque to the client, although it is returned from the AddMessage() method. When retrieving messages from the queue for processing, the message identifier is provided so that you can use it to subsequently delete the message.

2. **Correct answers:** C and D

   A. **Incorrect:** A single compute instance can process as many messages as its resources allow for. For example, if processing a message is memory intensive, the number of parallel messages that can be processed will depend on the amount of memory to be consumed for each message that is processed.

   B. **Incorrect:** A single compute instance can process as many messages as its resources allow for. For example, if processing a message is memory intensive, the number of parallel messages that can be processed will depend on the amount of memory to be consumed for each message that is processed.

   C. **Correct:** The queue client can request up to 32 messages in a single batch and then process them sequentially or in parallel. Each request from the queue client can request another 32 messages.

   D. **Correct:** The queue client can request a single message or request up to 32 messages in a batch for processing.

   E. **Incorrect:** Messages are not deleted when the message is read. Messages must be explicitly deleted.

3. **Correct answers:** A, C, and D

   A. **Correct:** By creating multiple queues for the application, broken down by logical heuristics that make sense to the application for distributing messages, you can increase scalability by reducing the pressure on a single queue for message processing and throughput.

   B. **Incorrect:** Websites do not support auto-scale by metric at this time.

   C. **Correct:** VMs can be scaled based on the number of items in a specified queue.

   D. **Correct:** Cloud services can be scaled based on the number of items in a specified queue.

Objective 4.4: Thought experiment

1. Users who authenticate to the application should be able to request the report, but since the reports are stored in blobs, it is convenient to be able to share the link directly to the blob. You could have the web application present a page that generates an SAS URI for a report on demand. The user could then copy that link and share in email with others even if they don't have access to the web application.

2. The duration that the link should be valid depends on the typical workflow for your customers who access these reports. For example, if it is acceptable to expect the user who authenticated to download the report right away, or to send the link to someone who will do so right away, limit the SAS token to 30 minutes so that if the email with the link is found at a later time by an unauthorized user, it will be expired. If the link should be shared with someone who may need more time to access the report, but you want to enforce that links can be revoked when some other action has taken place in the application, use a stored access policy with an initial duration that will be acceptable for this workflow. You can then allow users to extend the validity of the SAS token through the web application, or you can programmatically revoke access if you note suspicious activity on the report links through storage logs.

Objective 4.4: Objective review

1. **Correct answers:** A, C, D, and E

   A. **Correct:** You can generate an SAS token that grants read access to blobs. You can also grant access to modify a blob's contents.

   B. **Incorrect:** You cannot grant access to create new containers using SAS. This operation requires the storage access key.

   C. **Correct:** You can grant access to an existing queue and allow add, update, and delete operations using SAS tokens.

   D. **Correct:** You can grant access to an existing table and allow add, update, and delete operations on entities within that table.

   E. **Correct:** You can grant access to query the entities of an existing table using SAS tokens.

2. **Correct answers:** A, B, and C

   A. **Correct:** You can change both the start and expiration dates of an SAS token that is attached to a stored access policy.

   B. **Correct:** You can revoke all access by an SAS token that is attached to a stored access policy.

   C. **Correct:** You can revoke specific operations by an SAS token that is attached to a stored access policy. For example, you can remove support for delete operations that were originally granted.

D. Incorrect: You can use the same stored access policy for multiple resources (such as multiple blobs, for example) but this is done at the time of producing the SAS token and associating the stored access policy to the token. You cannot add resources at the policy level.

3. **Correct answers:** B and D

   A. Incorrect: CORS is not generally recommended but is a necessary evil for certain types of browser applications to allow for efficient access to storage resources. Try to avoid the use of CORS by using an alternate design if possible.

   B. Correct: If blobs are protected resources that require authentication, you should avoid using the storage account key to access them, in particular if this means sharing it with a browser. Instead, generate an SAS token that will be included in any links for requesting the resource and limit the duration the token is valid either with a short duration or a stored access policy you can revoke when the user session ends.

   C. Incorrect: CORS is now supported for all storage services, including blobs, queues, and tables.

   D. Correct: CORS is not enabled for a new storage account. You have to explicitly enable this feature.

Objective 4.5: Thought experiment

1. You should be looking at using monitoring (through the management portal) and configuring alerts based on latency and availability.

2. You should enable and review the Storage Analytics logs. You can look for usage patterns based on the type of activity seen or errors logged. You can also look for specific types of logs related to a specific event that occurred.

Objective 4.5: Objective review

1. **Correct answer:** A

   A. Correct: Capacity metrics include total storage in bytes, the container count, and the object count for blob storage only.

   B. Incorrect: You can only set minute metrics programmatically or by using Windows PowerShell cmdlets.

   C. Incorrect: By default, retention is not specified, therefore metrics are retained indefinitely. You should set the retention policy to match your compliance requirements and seek to archive if beyond one year.

   D. Incorrect: If you disable metrics, all metrics previously collected will be retained until the retention period expires.

2. **Correct answers:** B and D

    A. **Incorrect:** Logs are stored in a $logs container in Blob storage for your storage account, but the log capacity is not included in your storage account quota. A separate 20-terabyte allocation is made for storage logs.

    B. **Correct:** Logs can have duplicate entries within a one-hour period; however, you can identify a log entry uniquely with a RequestId and operation number.

    C. **Incorrect:** The log container cannot be deleted once in use, but the logs within that container can be deleted by authorized callers.

    D. **Correct:** You can log all or individual operations to all storage services.

3. **Correct answers:** C and D

    A. **Incorrect:** A log entry is created for all successful authenticated and anonymous requests.

    B. **Incorrect:** For authenticated calls, all known failed requests are logged, and for anonymous calls, only failed Get requests for error code 304 are logged.

    C. **Correct:** Server errors generate a log entry.

    D. **Correct:** All requests to storage resources using SAS tokens are logged.

Objective 4.6: Thought experiment

1. You might consider giving each developer his or her own copy of the database with SQL Database. Then create a central one for merging changes.

2. If developers write database objects and then don't access them again, you might need more than a 14-day backup retention policy. This might lead to a higher edition of SQL Database being used for reasons different than raw performance. You might also consider manually exporting the database if a developer says he or she will be doing something particularly risky.

3. If the developers don't need access to a database the same size as production, they might get away with the basic level of SQL Database. If they do need development databases that are just like production, then choose the level of SQL Database that corresponds with the right size. Developers don't usually put a high load on their servers, so you can ignore the hardware metrics when selecting the appropriate level.

Objective 4.6: Objective review

1. **Correct answer:** D

   A. **Incorrect:** The secondary database must have the same name as the primary.

   B. **Incorrect:** They must be on separate servers.

   C. **Incorrect:** They need to be on the same subscription

   D. **Correct:** The secondary server cannot be a lower performance tier than the primary.

2. **Correct answers:** B, C, and D

   A. **Incorrect:** CPU Processor Count is not a valid metric

   B. **Correct:** CPU Percentage is a valid metric.

   C. **Correct:** Physical Data Reads Percentage is a valid metric

   D. **Correct:** Log Writes Percentage is a valid metric.

3. **Correct answers:** A, B, and C

   A. **Correct:** Connection resiliency, because you could failover to a replica.

   B. **Correct:** Transaction resiliency so you can resubmit a transaction in the event of a failover.

   C. **Correct:** Query auditing so you can baseline your current query times and know when to scale up the instance.

   D. **Incorrect:** You can handle backup and restore operations from the Azure management portal. There's no reason to write custom code for this.

Manage application and network services

Beyond compute and storage features, Microsoft Azure also provides a number of infra-structure services for security, virtual networking, communication mechanisms to support many messaging patterns, and caching strategies. In this chapter you learn about those core services.

Objectives in this chapter

- Objective 5.1: Integrate an app with Azure Active Directory
- Objective 5.2: Configure a virtual network
- Objective 5.3: Modify network configuration
- Objective 5.4: Design and implement a communication strategy
- Objective 5.5: Monitor communication
- Objective 5.6: Implement caching

Objective 5.1: Integrate an app with Azure Active Directory

Azure Active Directory (Azure AD) provides a cloud-based identity management service for application authentication, Single Sign-On (SSO), and user management. Azure AD can be used for the following core scenarios:

- A standalone cloud directory service
- Corporate access to Software-as-a-Service (SaaS) applications with directory synchronization
- SSO between corporate and SaaS applications
- Application integration for SaaS applications using a number of protocols
- User management through a Graph API

In this section, you learn about the protocols used to set up your directory; how to integrate applications with Azure AD, including WS-Federation, SAML-P, and OAuth; and how to query the user directory with the Graph API.

MORE INFO **AZURE AD DOCUMENTATION**

You can find the Azure AD documentation at *http://azure.microsoft.com/en-us/documentation/services/active-directory/*.

This objective covers how to:

- Create a directory
- Manage users
- Integrate applications
- Query the directory using the Graph API

Creating a directory

MORE INFO **USING WINDOWS POWERSHELL TO MANAGE AZURE AD**

You might want to manage some aspects of Azure AD with Windows PowerShell. For example to initialize the deployment, you would create applications, permissions, users, and groups. For more information, see *http://msdn.microsoft.com/library/azure/jj151815.aspx*.

Creating a directory (existing portal)

To create a directory using the management portal, follow these steps:

1. Navigate to the management portal accessed via *https://manage.windowsazure.com*.
2. Click New on the command bar, and select New, App Services, Active Directory, Directory, Custom Create.
3. In the Add Directory dialog box that opens (see Figure 5-1), make sure Create New Directory is selected from the drop-down list, supply a name and domain name for the directory, and select your region.

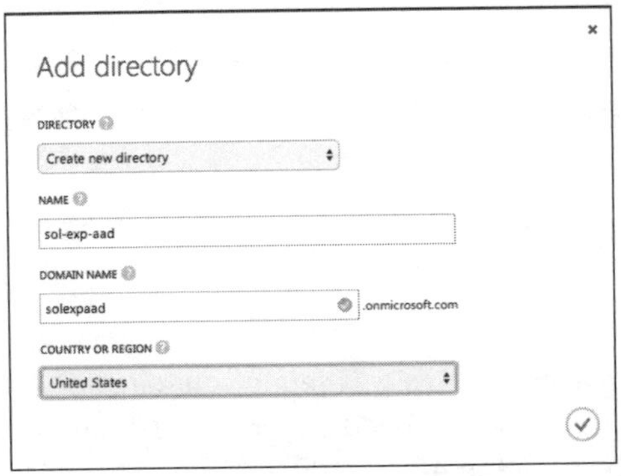

FIGURE 5-1 The Add Directory dialog box

4. Click the check mark to close the dialog box and to create the directory. This might take a few minutes.

Creating a directory (Preview portal)

At the time of this writing, the Preview portal does not support any Azure AD features.

Managing users

You can provision users in your Azure AD directory a number of ways:

- Create, edit, and delete users from the management portal
- Use the Graph API to manage users in your directory
- Sync users from an existing Windows Server Active Directory

> **NOTE   AZURE AD CONNECT**
>
> Azure Active Directory Connect (Azure AD Connect) is currently in preview and includes features that were previously released as DirSync and Azure AD Sync.

> **MORE INFO   DIRECTORY INTEGRATION**
>
> For additional information on directory integration, Azure AD Sync, and Azure AD Connect see *http://msdn.microsoft.com/en-us/library/azure/jj573653.aspx*.

Creating users (existing portal)

You can create new users from the existing portal by following these steps:

1. Navigate to the directory from the management portal accessed via *https://manage.windowsazure.com*.

2. Click the Users tab, and then click Add User on the command bar.

3. In the Add User dialog box, select New User In Your Organization, and provide a unique username prefix. The full username will become the prefix followed by @ and the fully qualified domain name. For example:

   ```
   user1@solexpaad.onmicrosoft.com
   ```

   Click the right arrow to move to the next page.

4. Provide a first, last, and display name for the new user. Leave User selected as the role. Click the right arrow.

5. Generate a temporary password for this user. The user will be asked to change the password on first login. You can optionally email this password to the user's email address.

6. Click the check mark to close the dialog box and to add the user to your directory.

Assigning administrative roles

You can choose from a number of pre-defined organizational roles for users you create in a directory. Most users are assigned the user role, which means they are not granted any additional administrative permissions for managing the directory. Outside of the user role, there are five administrator roles available:

- Global administrator
- Billing administrator
- Service administrator
- User administrator
- Password administrator

When you create a new user, you can choose from these roles. You can also use the management portal to modify the organizational role of an existing user.

Creating and assigning groups (existing portal)

You can create groups for a directory and assign users to those groups. This is useful for application authorization scenarios.

1. Navigate to the directory from the management portal accessed via *https://manage. windowsazure.com.*

2. Click the Groups tab, and click Add Group on the command bar.

3. In the Add Group dialog box, provide a name and description for the group. Click the check mark to create the group.

4. From the list of groups on the Groups tab (see Figure 5-2), click a group to select it.

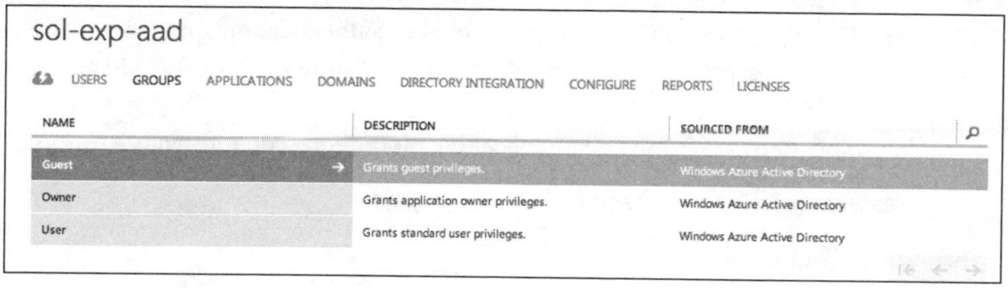

FIGURE 5-2 The Groups tab for a directory with a list of existing groups

5. Click Add Members on the command bar.

6. In the Add Members dialog box, click the Users tab, and select one of the users to assign to a group.

7. After assigning one or more users to the group, click the check mark to save the changes.

> **NOTE   GROUP HIERARCHY**
>
> You can assign a child group to a parent group to create a hierarchy of groups so that a parent group can include users that belong to multiple child groups.

> **MORE INFO   USER MANAGEMENT**
>
> For additional information about managing users from the management portal, see *http://msdn.microsoft.com/en-us/library/azure/hh967609.aspx*.

Integrating applications

There are several common scenarios for application integration with Azure AD, including the following:

- Users sign in to browser-based applications
- Browser-based applications call Web APIs from JavaScript
- Users sign in to mobile applications that call Web APIs
- Asynchronous server applications call Web APIs

For the first scenario, you can choose from a few protocols: WS-Federation, SAML-P, or OpenID Connect. OpenID Connect is the recommended path because it is the most modern protocol available. The other three scenarios can be implemented using OAuth 2.0 flows, though this is not a strict requirement.

The following steps are involved in application integration scenarios with Azure AD:

1. Create your Azure AD directory. This is your tenant.

2. Create your application.

3. Register the application with Azure AD with information about your application.

4. Write code in your application to satisfy one of the scenarios for user authentication or token requests to call APIs.

5. Receive protocol-specific responses to your application from Azure AD, including a valid token for proof of authentication or for authorization purposes.

In this section, you'll learn how to register an application in the management portal, learn how to find integration endpoints for each protocol, and receive an overview of the relationship between your applications and the protocol.

Registering an application (existing portal)

You can manually add an application using the existing portal by following these steps:

1. Navigate to the directory from the management portal accessed via *https://manage. windowsazure.com*.

2. Select the Applications tab, and click Add on the command bar.

3. In the Add Application dialog box, click Add An Application My Organization Is Developing.

4. In the Add Application dialog box, provide a friendly name for the application, and select Web Application and/or Web Api. Click the right arrow to continue to the next screen.

5. For Sign-On URL, provide the URL to your application.

6. For App ID URI, provide a unique URL that will identify your application. This does not have to be a live endpoint, but it must be in the form of a URL and be unique across all of your applications.

7. Click the check mark to add the application registration.

8. Navigate to the Configure tab to view these settings and customize additional settings such as the following:

   - Uploading a logo for login branding
   - Indicating if the application is single or multi-tenant
   - Managing keys for OAuth scenarios
   - Setting additional permissions

> **NOTE   REPLY URL AND APPLICATION ID**
>
> The sign-on URL is used as the reply URL for browser-based scenarios so that the response from user authentication can be sent to your application. You should provide the URL that will process this response for this value. You can optionally use the same value for your application ID URI since it is a well-formed URL and would likely be unique across your Azure AD tenant applications.

Viewing integration endpoints (existing portal)

Azure AD exposes endpoints for many protocols including:

- WS-Federation metadata and sign-on endpoints
- SAML-P sign-on and sign-out endpoints
- OAuth 2.0 token and authorization endpoints
- Azure AD Graph API endpoints

To view these endpoints, do the following.

1. Navigate to the directory from the management portal accessed via *https://manage.windowsazure.com*.

2. Select the Applications tab, and click View Endpoints on the command bar.

3. The dialog box (see Figure 5-3) lists protocol endpoints, such as the following:

```
https://login.windows.net/4a3779e5-8c00-478d-b2cd-7be06a8b236e/
    federationmetadata/2007-06/federationmetadata.xml
https://login.windows.net/4a3779e5-8c00-478d-b2cd-7be06a8b236e/wsfed
https://login.windows.net/4a3779e5-8c00-478d-b2cd-7be06a8b236e/saml2
https://login.windows.net/4a3779e5-8c00-478d-b2cd-7be06a8b236e/saml2
https://graph.windows.net/4a3779e5-8c00-478d-b2cd-7be06a8b236e
https://login.windows.net/4a3779e5-8c00-478d-b2cd-7be06a8b236e/oauth2/
    token?api-version=1.0
https://login.windows.net/4a3779e5-8c00-478d-b2cd-7be06a8b236e/oauth2/
    authorize?api-version=1.0
```

App Endpoints

If you are developing an app that integrates with Windows Azure AD, update your code to use these endpoints for single sign-on and directory access.

FEDERATION METADATA DOCUMENT

https://login.windows.net/4a3779e5-8c00-478d-b2cd-7be06a8b236e/

WS-FEDERATION SIGN-ON ENDPOINT

https://login.windows.net/4a3779e5-8c00-478d-b2cd-7be06a8b236e/

SAML-P SIGN-ON ENDPOINT

https://login.windows.net/4a3779e5-8c00-478d-b2cd-7be06a8b236e/

SAML-P SIGN-OUT ENDPOINT

https://login.windows.net/4a3779e5-8c00-478d-b2cd-7be06a8b236e/

WINDOWS AZURE AD GRAPH API ENDPOINT

https://graph.windows.net/4a3779e5-8c00-478d-b2cd-7be06a8b236e

OAUTH 2.0 TOKEN ENDPOINT

https://login.windows.net/4a3779e5-8c00-478d-b2cd-7be06a8b236e/

OAUTH 2.0 AUTHORIZATION ENDPOINT

https://login.windows.net/4a3779e5-8c00-478d-b2cd-7be06a8b236e/

FIGURE 5-3 A list of protocol endpoints for an Azure AD tenant

EXAM TIP

You can substitute the tenant identifier with the tenant name for protocol endpoint URLs. See, for example, *https://login.windows.net/solexpaad.onmicrosoft.com/wsfed*.

MORE INFO **AZURE AD PROTOCOLS**

For more information about each of these protocols, see *http://msdn.microsoft.com/en-us/library/azure/dn151124.aspx*.

Integrating with WS-Federation

WS-Federation is an identity protocol used for browser-based applications. For example, WS-Federation integration with Azure AD might follow steps like this:

1. Users navigate to your application.

2. Your application redirects anonymous users to authenticate at Azure AD, sending a WS-Federation protocol request that indicates the application URI for the realm parameter. The URI should match the App ID URI shown in the single sign-on settings (see Figure 5-4):

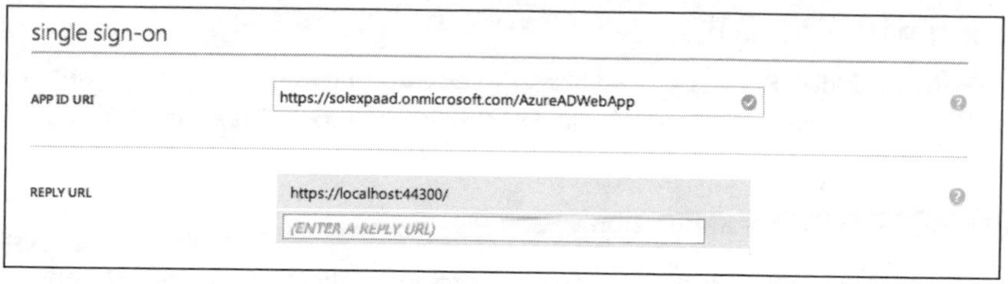

FIGURE 5-4 Single sign-on settings for an Azure AD tenant

3. The request is sent to your tenant WS-Federation endpoint, for example:

```
https://login.windows.net/solexpaad.onmicrosoft.com/wsfed
```

4. The user is presented with a login page, unless he or she already has a valid cookie for the Azure AD tenant.

5. When authenticated, a SAML token is returned in the HTTP POST to the application URL with a WS-Federation response. The URL to use is specified in the single sign-on settings as the Reply URL.

6. The application processes this response, verifies the token is signed by a trusted issuer (Azure AD), and confirms that the token is still valid.

7. The application can optionally use claims in the token to personalize the application experience for the logged in user.

8. The application can optionally query Azure AD for groups for authorization purposes.

> **NOTE FEDERATION METADATA**
>
> WS-Federation exposes two endpoints, one for metadata and one for sign-in and sign-out. The metadata endpoint exposes the standard federation metadata document that many identity tools know how to consume to discover the address of the sign-in and sign-out endpoint, the certificate required to validate signatures in a response, and other endpoints available at the service, such as SAML-P endpoints. If you use the metadata endpoint, your application should dynamically receive updates, such as new certificates used by the service. The sign-in and sign-out endpoint expects parameters indicating the purpose of the request.

> **MORE INFO WS-FEDERATION SAMPLE**
>
> For more information on integrating an ASP.NET MVC application using the OWIN framework to handle WS-Federation requests and responses, see *https://github.com/AzureADSamples/WebApp-WSFederation-DotNet*.

Integrating with SAML-P

SAML 2.0 Protocol (SAML-P) can be used like WS-Federation to support user authentication to browser-based applications. For example, SAML-P integration with Azure AD might follow steps like this:

1. Users navigate to your application.

2. Your application redirects anonymous users to authenticate at Azure AD, sending a SAML-P request that indicates the application URI for the ConsumerServiceURL element in the request.

3. The request is sent to your tenant SAML2 endpoint, for example:

    ```
    https://login.windows.net/solexpaad.onmicrosoft.com/saml2
    ```

4. The user is presented with a login page, unless he or she already has a valid cookie for the Azure AD tenant.

5. When authenticated, a SAML-P response is returned in the HTTP POST to the application URL. The URL to use is specified in the single sign-on settings as the Reply URL. This response contains a SAML2 token.

6. The application processes this response, verifies the token is signed by a trusted issuer (Azure AD), and confirms that the token is still valid.

7. The application can optionally use claims in the token to personalize the application experience for the logged in user.

8. The application can optionally query Azure AD for groups for authorization purposes.

> **NOTE SAML-P ENDPOINTS**
>
> SAML-P support in Azure AD includes a sign-on and sign-out endpoint, and they are both the same URL. The protocol describes how to format each request so that the endpoint knows which action is requested.

> **MORE INFO SAML PROTOCOL**
>
> SAML-P tools are not provided as part of the .NET Framework libraries; however, there are a few third-party libraries available for building applications based on this protocol. Typically, support for SAML-P becomes important when you are integrating other SaaS applications with your Azure AD because some applications do not support WS-Federation or OpenID Connect. For more information on SAML-P and Azure AD, see *http://msdn. microsoft.com/en-us/library/azure/dn195591.aspx.*

Integrating with OpenID Connect

OAuth 2.0 is an authorization protocol and is not used for classic browser-based authentication scenarios. OpenID Connect (OIDC) is an identity protocol that extends OAuth 2.0 to provide a mechanism for authenticating users. With OIDC, you can provide a modern approach to identity in your web applications that redirects the user to authenticate in a similar fashion to WS-Federation and SAML-P, as follows:

1. Users navigate to your application.

2. Your application redirects anonymous users to authenticate at Azure AD, sending an OpenID Connect authentication request that indicates the application URI for the client_id element in the request. The client_id can be found in your configuration properties for the directory (see Figure 5-5):

FIGURE 5-5 Client ID configuration for an Azure AD tenant

3. The request is sent to your tenant OAuth authorize endpoint, for example:

    ```
    https://login.windows.net/solexpaad.onmicrosoft.com/oauth2/authorize?api-
    version=1.0
    ```

4. The user is presented with a login page, unless he or she already has a valid cookie for the Azure AD tenant.

5. When authenticated, a response is returned in the HTTP POST to the application URL. The URL to use is specified in the single sign-on settings as the Reply URL, and this value should match the redirect_uri element in the request. The response contains a JSON Web Token (JWT).

6. The application processes this response, verifies the token is signed by a trusted issuer (Azure AD), and confirms that the token is still valid.

7. The application can optionally use claims in the token to personalize the application experience for the logged in user.

8. The application can optionally query Azure AD for groups for authorization purposes.

> **NOTE OAUTH ENDPOINTS**
>
> Azure AD exposes two OAuth endpoints: one for token requests and one for authorization requests typical of OAuth 2.0. Frameworks that build OpenID Connect and OAuth requests usually use a well-known OpenID metadata endpoint at the identity service to discover which endpoint to send requests to. This metadata endpoint looks something like *https://login.windows.net/solexpaad.onmicrosoft.com/.well-known/openid-configuration*.

Integrating with OAuth

OAuth 2.0 is typically useful in scenarios where user consent is required to access resources, but it can also be employed to request tokens for server side client applications. In both cases, your application must supply a client identifier and a key (secret) when requesting a token from the OAuth token endpoint.

To generate a key for your application, complete the following steps:

1. Navigate to the directory from the management portal accessed via *https://manage. windowsazure.com*.

2. Click the Applications tab, and select the application you want to grant access to request tokens via OAuth.

3. Scroll to the Keys section. Select a duration of one or two years for the key to be valid. Click Save on the command bar, and then the key appears.

4. Copy the key somewhere safe; it will not be presented again.

5. You can now use the client_id and key (secret) to perform OAuth token requests from your application.

The following section, "Querying directories with the Graph API," covers an example of an OAuth token request authorizing an application to use the Graph API.

Querying directories with the Graph API

Using the Graph API, you can interact with your Azure AD tenant to manage users, groups, and more. If the application is limited to read access only, query activity will be allowed. With read and write access, the application can perform additional management activities:

- Add, update, and delete users and groups

- Find users
- Request a user's group and role membership
- Manage group membership
- Create applications
- Query and create directory properties

In this section, you learn how to set up an application to query a directory programmatically using the Graph API.

> **MORE INFO** **QUERYING AZURE AD**
>
> For additional information about querying Azure AD with the Graph API, see *http://msdn. microsoft.com/en-us/library/azure/dn151791.aspx*. For an overview of the Azure AD Graph API, see *http://msdn.microsoft.com/en-us/library/azure/hh974476.aspx*.

Granting application access to the Graph API

Before you can interact with the Graph API programmatically, you must grant the calling application access.

1. After adding an application to your Azure AD tenant, navigate to the Configure tab for the application.

2. Scroll down to the Keys section.

3. Select one or two years for the duration, and then click Save on the command bar to produce the key. Figure 5-6 shows the Keys section with the newly generated key. Store the key somewhere safe—it will not be shown when you return to this page.

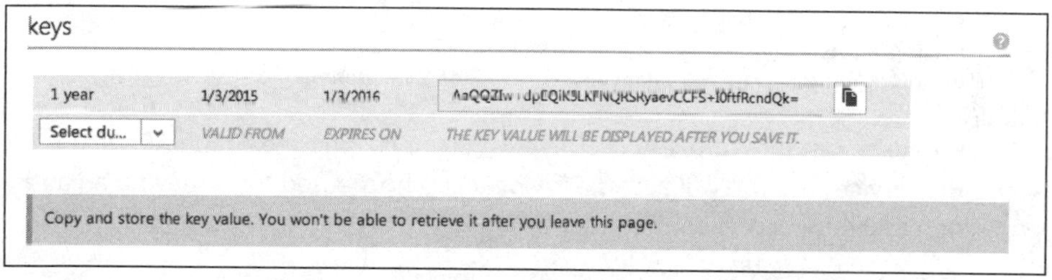

keys				
1 year	1/3/2015	1/3/2016	AaQQZIw dpEQiK5LKFNUKSKyaevCCFS+I0ftfRcndQk=	
Select du... ⌄	*VALID FROM*	*EXPIRES ON*	*THE KEY VALUE WILL BE DISPLAYED AFTER YOU SAVE IT.*	

Copy and store the key value. You won't be able to retrieve it after you leave this page.

FIGURE 5-6 The Keys section on the Configuration tab showing a newly generated key

4. Scroll down to the Permissions To Other Applications section.

5. Beside Windows Azure Active Directory, select Application Permissions, and from the drop-down list, select Read Directory Data or Read And Write Directory Data permissions (see Figure 5-7).

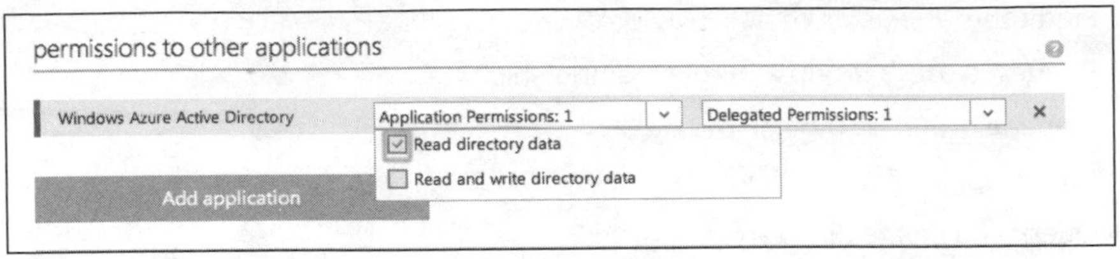

permissions to other applications

Windows Azure Active Directory | Application Permissions: 1 ▾ | Delegated Permissions: 1 ▾ | ✕
☑ Read directory data
☐ Read and write directory data

Add application

FIGURE 5-7 The permissions section on the Configuration tab for an Azure AD tenant

6. Click Save on the command bar to save these changes.

> **MORE INFO** **ACCESSING THE GRAPH API**
>
> For more information on granting access to the Graph API, see *http://msdn.microsoft.com/ en-us/library/azure/dn132599.aspx#BKMK_Graph.*

Accessing the Graph API tenant

Using the Active Directory Client Library, you can write code to securely reference the Graph API for your Azure AD tenant. Using the ActiveDirectoryClient reference, you can then access tenant details, users, groups, and other information about your Azure AD tenant.

1. Create a new console project, and add the following NuGet packages:

   Active Directory Authentication Library

   Microsoft Azure Active Directory Graph Client Library

2. Gather the following information about your Azure AD tenant, for example:

```
string graphUrl = "https://graph.windows.net";
string tenantId = "4a3779e5-008c-478d-cdb2-7be06a8b236e";
string loginUrl = "https://login.windows.net/solexpaad.onmicrosoft.com";
string clientId = "dafe0335-446b-9845-8653-6f920b0623dc";
string clientSecret = "Xha6cdPlVdABiz+StfSZZBwP4eWntuxokLtSPSaiOFg=";
```

3. Create an instance of the ActiveDirectoryClient passing the Graph API tenant URL as the service root you will access. Provide an async method for retrieving an authorization token for accessing the Graph API:

```
using Microsoft.Azure.ActiveDirectory.GraphClient;
string serviceRoot = graphUrl + "/" + tenantId;
ActiveDirectoryClient graphClient = new ActiveDirectoryClient(new
Uri(serviceRoot), async () => await GetTokenAsync());
```

4. In the async method, supply the login URL to your Azure AD tenant, the client identifier and key to be used for authorizing this application's access to the Graph API, and the Graph API URL as the resource you will access:

```
AuthenticationContext authContext = new AuthenticationContext(loginUrl, false);
ClientCredential creds = new ClientCredential(clientId, clientSecret);
Task<AuthenticationResult> result = authContext.AcquireTokenAsync(graphUrl,
creds);
```

5. When the application is authenticated, a token is returned validating the ActiveDirectoryClient instance so that you can proceed to interact with the Graph API reference:

```
string token = result.Result.AccessToken;
```

> **MORE INFO** **GRAPH API CODE SAMPLES**
>
> For an example showing how to connect to your Graph API and perform user management, see *https://github.com/AzureADSamples/ConsoleApp-GraphAPI-DotNet*.

Querying directories

When you have a Graph API reference using an ActiveDirectoryClient instance, you can use it to interact with your Azure AD tenant.

The following code illustrates how to retrieve a sorted collection of users:

```
List<IUser> users = activeDirectoryClient.Users.OrderBy(user =>
user.UserPrincipalName).Take(maxUsers).ExecuteAsync().Result.CurrentPage.ToList();
```

To search for a user by UPN, use the following:

```
string upn = "admin@solexpaad.onmicrosoft.com";
List<IUser> matchingUsers = activeDirectoryClient.Users
                .Where(user -> user.UserPrincipalName Equals(upn))
                .ExecuteAsync().Result.CurrentPage.ToList();
User foundUser = (User)matchingUsers.First();
```

To gather the groups for a user, paging through the collection of directory objects looking for groups, use the following:

```
IUserFetcher userFetcher = foundUser;
IPagedCollection<IDirectoryObject> result = userFetcher.MemberOf.ExecuteAsync().Result;
do
{
  List<IDirectoryObject> objects = result.CurrentPage.ToList();
  foreach (IDirectoryObject o in objects)
  {
    if (o is Group)
    {
      Group g = o as Group;
      Console.WriteLine(g.DisplayName, g.Description);
    }
  }
  result = result.GetNextPageAsync().Result;
} while (result != null && result.MorePagesAvailable);
```

Thought experiment
Authentication and authorization

In this thought experiment, apply what you've learned about this objective. You can find answers to these questions in the "Answers" section at the end of this chapter.

You are in the process of designing the authentication and authorization strategy for your web applications and APIs using Azure AD. Users will authenticate to Azure AD, and you will create groups for role-based authorization in your application.

1. Describe your choice of protocol for authentication and why you chose it.

2. Describe how you will approach setting up users and groups.

3. Describe how you will access groups for role-based authorization.

Objective summary

- You can manage Azure AD users from the management portal or programmatically with the Graph API.

- Azure AD users can optionally be added to one of the built-in administrator roles, including Global administrator, Billing administrator, Service administrator, User administrator, and Password administrator. These roles apply to directory administration.

- You can create groups and group hierarchies and assign users to groups. Applications can optionally use group information for authorization and access control.

- Azure AD supports WS-Federation, SAML-P, OAuth 2, and OpenID Connect protocols for application integration.

- You can use the Graph API to query directories; to find and manage users, groups and role assignment; and to create applications for integration with Azure AD.

Objective review

Answer the following questions to test your knowledge of the information in this objective. You can find the answers to these questions and explanations of why each answer choice is correct or incorrect in the "Answers" section at the end of this chapter.

1. Which of the following are true about Azure AD roles and groups? (Choose all that apply.)

   A. Azure AD roles can be used for role-based authorization in your applications.

   B. Both Azure AD roles and groups can be used for role-based authorization in your applications.

   C. Azure AD groups can be used to authorize access to Azure AD resources such as user management and password resets.

   D. Azure AD roles and groups can be queried using the Graph API.

2. Which of the following statements are true of application integration with Azure AD? (Choose all that apply.)

   A. You can use WS-Federation, SAML-P, or OAuth for user authentication in a browser application.

   B. A client application identifier and key are required for OpenID Connect and OAuth requests.

   C. OAuth application client keys can be issued for one or two years.

   D. The sign-on URL and application ID URI must be set to the same value for an Azure AD application.

3. Which of the following are valid uses for the Graph API? (Choose all that apply.)

   A. Adding users and assigning them to groups

   B. Finding a user in the directory

   C. Creating new roles for users

   D. Requesting the roles or groups a user belongs to

Objective 5.2: Configure a virtual network

When you deploy a VM to Microsoft Azure, it can be configured to allow Internet access. While this is typical of a public-facing web server, it might not be acceptable for all servers in your system topology, for example file servers and database servers. In addition, if you have a private network at your organization, you might want to access servers hosted by Azure as if they are part of your local network.

An Azure virtual network supports several scenarios, including:

- Creating a virtual network for a collection of servers, including Azure virtual machines, web roles, or websites in your system topology

- Joining on-premises machines and servers hosted in Azure to the same virtual network.

In this section, you learn how to deploy a VM or cloud service into a virtual network and how to configure a site-to-site virtual network.

> **This objective covers how to:**
> - Deploy a VM into a virtual network
> - Deploy a cloud service into a virtual network

Creating a virtual network

You typically create a virtual network prior to adding VMs to it. In this section, you learn how to create a virtual network and add VMs and cloud services to it.

> *MORE INFO*   **MOVING A VM TO AN EXISTING NETWORK**
>
> You can move a VM to a previously created virtual network, but it requires some down-time. Virtual networks are typically chosen when you create a VM. To change the virtual network of an existing VM, you can remove it from the first network and then create a new VM with the same VHD as part of the new network. There is no method to move the VM itself to a different network after it is created.
>
> When you remove an existing VM from a network, the VHD is still attached and registered as a disk in the management portal. When you create a new VM, you can select that disk under My Disks in the management portal to reuse it.

Creating a virtual network (existing portal)

To create a virtual network in the management portal, complete the following steps:

1. Navigate to the management portal accessed via *https://manage.windowsazure.com.*

2. Click New on the command bar, and select New, Network Services, Virtual Network, Custom Create.

3. In the dialog box that appears, provide a name and location for the network. When you deploy VMs on this virtual network, they will reside in this location.

4. Select a subscription, and click the arrow to continue.

5. Leave the defaults for DNS Servers and VPN Connectivity, and click the arrow to continue.

6. Leave the default IP address settings for your VPN unless you want to configure a specific IP address range. Often, organizations need to control the subnet IP range to

match existing VMs on-premises when moving to the cloud or to add additional VMs to an existing range that conjoins with on-premises VMs.

7. Optionally, add multiple subnets to allocate VMs in your network to different layers in your virtual network.

8. Click the check mark to create the virtual network.

EXAM TIP

Using shared DNS servers with a virtual network allows resources on the network to use a DNS server that you specify. You can use one that Azure provides, but if you need more control over DNS settings, or if you have needs outside normal, you can specify your own DNS servers. DNS servers are not round-robin load balanced. The first DNS server on the list will always be used unless it is unavailable, in which case then the next one will be used.

Creating a virtual network (Preview portal)

To create a virtual network in the Preview portal, complete the following steps:

9. Navigate to the management portal accessed via *https://portal.azure.com*.

10. Click New on the command bar.

11. Navigate to the Marketplace by clicking the Everything link located near the top-right blade that appears. Scroll down and select Virtual Network from the Networking section (see Figure 5-8).

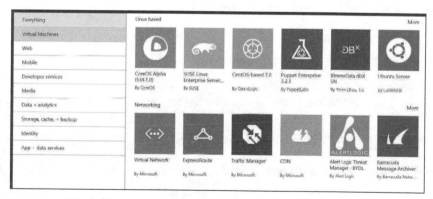

FIGURE 5-8 Networking options shown in the management portal

12. On the Virtual Network blade (see Figure 5-9), provide a name, location, and subscription. Click Create to create the new virtual network.

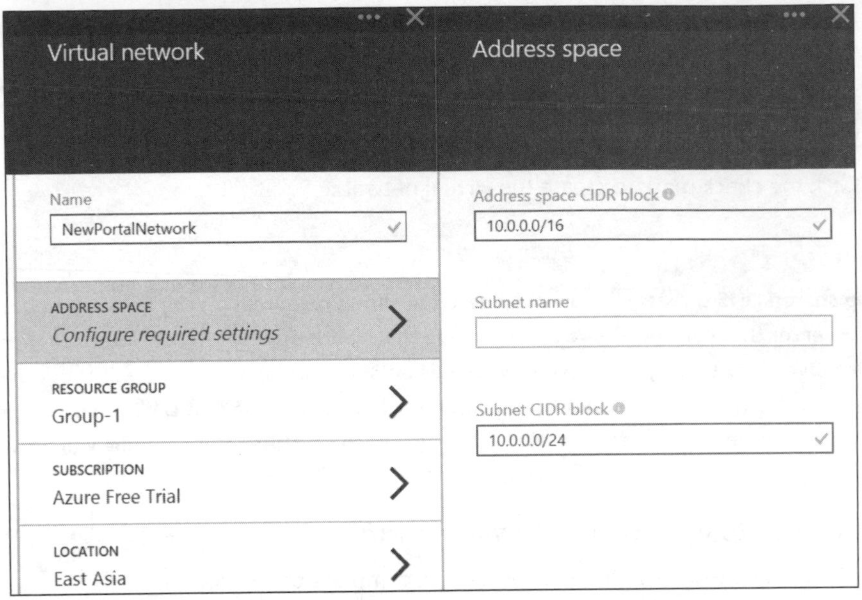

FIGURE 5-9 Creating a new virtual network

> **MORE INFO** **NETWORK CONFIGURATION FILES**
>
> You can export a network configuration file after creating a network within the management portal. You can also manually create a network configuration file. For more information, see *http://msdn.microsoft.com/en-us/library/azure/jj156097.aspx*.

Adding a VM to a virtual network

When you create a new VM, you can easily add it to an existing virtual network. Chapter 2, "Create and manage virtual machines," discusses different ways to create a new VM through the management portal or by using Windows PowerShell. This section describes how to create a new VM and specify the virtual network through the management portal.

Creating a new VM in a virtual network (existing portal)

To create a new VM and specify a virtual network for it to join, complete the following steps:

1. Navigate to the management portal accessed via *https://manage.windowsazure.com*.

2. Click New on the command bar, and select New, Compute, Virtual Machine, From Gallery.

3. Provide information for the new VM, as discussed in Chapter 2. In this case, set the region by choosing a virtual network from the list (see Figure 5-10).

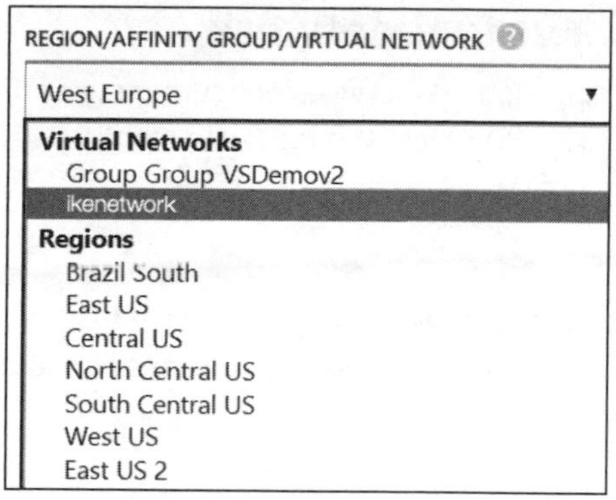

FIGURE 5-10 Selecting a virtual network for a new VM

Creating a new VM in a virtual network (Preview portal)

To create a new VM in a virtual network using the Preview portal, complete the following steps:

4. Navigate to the management portal accessed via *https://portal.azure.com*.

5. Click New on the command bar, navigate to the virtual machines, and select an image from the gallery.

6. Provide settings for the new VM as discussed in Chapter 2. To join a virtual network, select Optional Configuration, Network, Virtual Network, and then select the virtual network you previously created (see Figure 5-11).

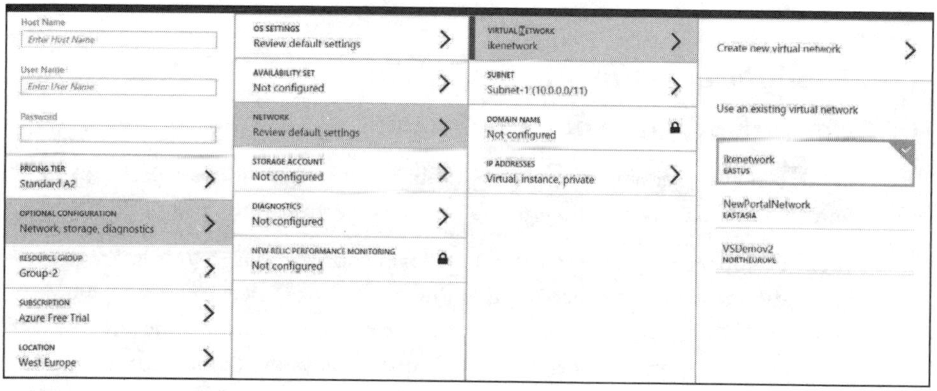

FIGURE 5-11 Selecting an existing virtual network for a new VM

7. Click OK on each blade and notice that the Location setting should reflect the virtual network location.

Deploying a cloud service to a virtual network

You deploy a cloud service to a virtual network through its service configuration, not through the management portal. To deploy a cloud service, complete the following steps:

1. Open your cloud service solution in Visual Studio and open the service configuration file (.cscfg).

2. Add a <NetworkConfiguration> section to the service configuration file that indicates the site name and the roles to include in the virtual network with a specific subnet, if applicable:

```
<NetworkConfiguration>
  <VirtualNetworkSite name="SampleNetwork" />
  <AddressAssignments>
    <InstanceAddress roleName="ContactManager.Web">
      <Subnets>
        <Subnet name="FrontEnd" />
      </Subnets>
    </InstanceAddress>
  </AddressAssignments>
</NetworkConfiguration>
```

3. Deploy the solution to reflect these changes.

> **MORE INFO**   **NETWORKCONFIGURATION SECTION**
>
> For a complete set of options for cloud services network configuration settings, see
> *http://msdn.microsoft.com/en-us/library/azure/jj156091.aspx.*

> ## Thought experiment
> ### Network deployment considerations
>
> In this thought experiment, apply what you've learned about this objective. You can find answers to these questions in the "Answers" section at the end of this chapter.
>
> Your developers are concerned about deploying applications to VMs in Azure for integration testing. The concern is that they have to use RDP to access each VM individually to deploy the application using *.cloudapp.net DNS names. They'd prefer to run a Windows PowerShell script that deploys the Continuous Integration server inside the network and interact with their servers like they would if it were on-premises. In addition, they're concerned that SQL VMs are publicly available on the Internet, rather than protected behind a DMZ.
>
> 4. What architecture using Virtual Networks would address their concerns about network connectivity and security?
>
> 5. What needs to be done inside your organization's network to implement this solution?

Objective summary

- A virtual network allows your services to communicate securely without granting public Internet access to VMs.
- Virtual networks can be used by virtual machines, cloud services, and websites.
- Virtual networks can be used to create a secure connection between your organization's network and your Azure applications.

Objective review

Answer the following questions to test your knowledge of the information in this objective. You can find the answers to these questions and explanations of why each answer choice is correct or incorrect in the "Answers" section at the end of this chapter.

1. What are some valid use cases for creating a virtual network? (Choose all that apply.)

   A. You want to spread VMs across Azure datacenters in several regions and use the same virtual network.

   B. You want to configure more endpoints on the VMs to allow more services.

   C. You want to access Azure as if it was locally connected to your on-premises network.

   D. You want a virtual network to be fault tolerant in case your other networks go down.

2. Which of the following are valid methods to deploy a cloud service to a virtual network? (Choose all that apply.)

   A. From the existing portal

   B. From the Preview portal

   C. Using the service configuration file

   D. None of the above

3. When should you create a VM on your virtual network? (Choose all that apply.)

   A. Create the VM first, then create the virtual network, and then migrate it.

   B. Create the virtual network at the same time you create the VM.

   C. Create the virtual network first, and then create the VM.

   D. The order you create them in doesn't matter.

Objective 5.3: Modify network configuration

After creating a virtual network, you are able to modify the network configuration. For example, you might want to take any of the following actions:

- Add DNS servers
- Create point-to-site connectivity
- Change virtual network address spaces
- Add and delete subnets
- Expand or shrink a subnet
- Add, remove, expand, or shrink any prefixes

You can take any of these actions through the management portal or by using Windows PowerShell cmdlets.

> **This objective covers how to:**
> - Modify a subnet
> - Import and export network configuration

EXAM TIP

You cannot modify or delete a subnet after services or VMs have been deployed to it. You can modify prefixes as long as the subnets containing existing VMs or services are not affected by the change.

Modifying a subnet (existing portal)

To modify a subnet using the management portal, complete the following steps:

1. Navigate to the management portal accessed via *https://manage.windowsazure.com*.
2. Click the Networks icon in the navigation pane.
3. From the list of networks, select the network you want to modify.
4. Navigate to the Configure tab for the network.
5. In the Virtual Network Address Spaces section (see Figure 5-12), modify subnet settings as desired, and click Save on the command bar to save those changes.

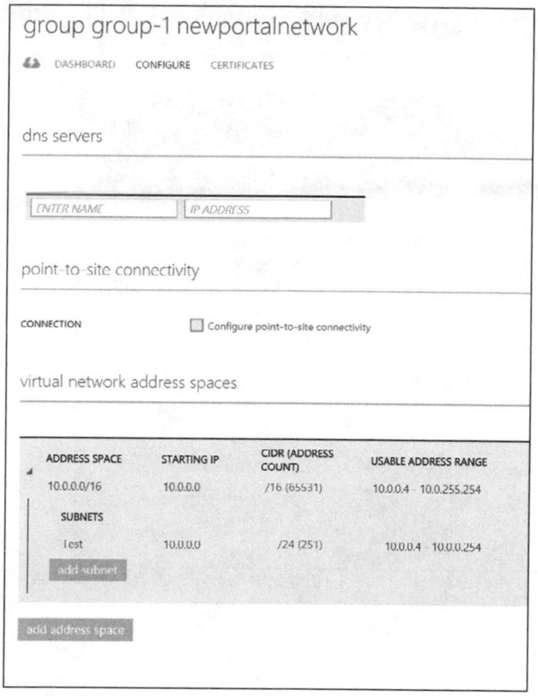

FIGURE 5-12 Editing subnet settings for a virtual network

Modifying a subnet (Preview portal)

To modify a subnet using the Preview portal, complete the following steps:

1. Navigate to the management portal accessed via *https://portal.azure.com*.

2. Click Browse on the navigation bar, navigate to Virtual Networks Machines, and select the virtual network from the list on the Virtual Networks blade.

3. On the Virtual Network blade, click the Subnets box (see Figure 5-13).

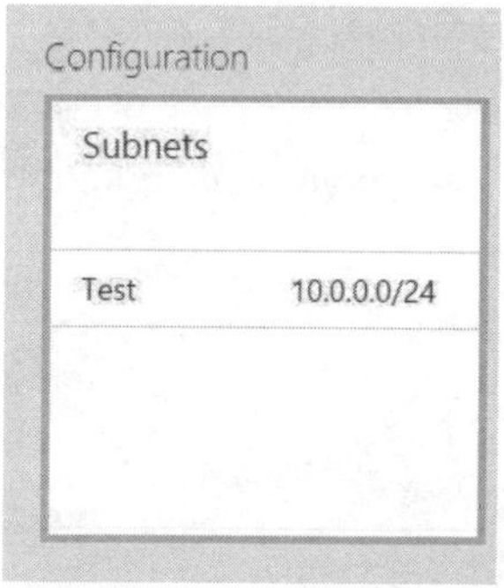

FIGURE 5-13 The Subnets box in the Configuration section of the Virtual Network blade

4. The Subnet Configuration blade appears on the right (see Figure 5-14). Make the desired changes, and click Save.

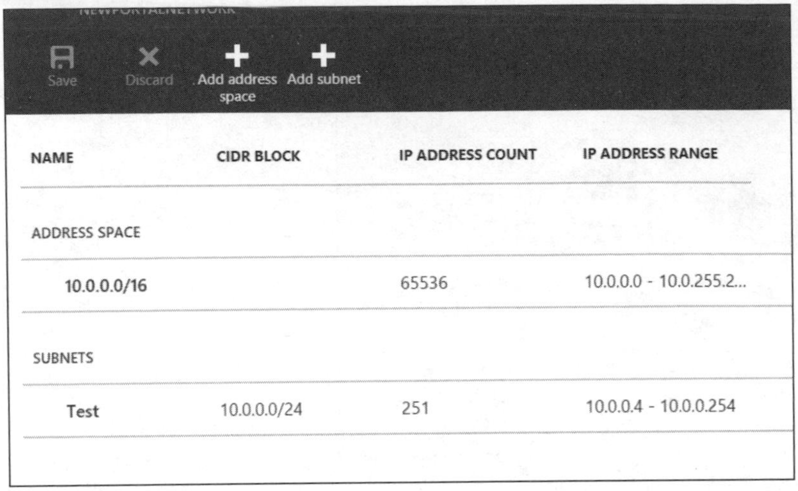
Save
Discard
Add address space
Add subnet
NAME
CIDR BLOCK
IP ADDRESS COUNT
IP ADDRESS RANGE
ADDRESS SPACE
10.0.0.0/16
65536
10.0.0.0 - 10.0.255.2...
SUBNETS
Test
10.0.0.0/24
251
10.0.0.4 - 10.0.0.254

FIGURE 5-14 The Subnet Configuration blade

Moving a VM or cloud service to a new subnet

If you find it necessary to reorganize your network topology and the servers running within each subnet, you can move existing VMs or cloud services from one subnet to another. In this section, you learn how to accomplish this.

Moving a VM to a new subnet using Windows PowerShell

You can move a VM from one subject to another using the Set-AzureSubnet Windows PowerShell cmdlet. After you modify the subnet, you can restart the VM with Update-AzureVM cmdlet as follows:

```
Get-AzureVM -ServiceName TestVMCloud -Name TestVM | Set-AzureSubnet -SubnetNames
Subnet-2 | Update-AzureVM
```

Moving a cloud service role to a new subnet

To move a cloud service role from one subnet to another, edit the service configuration file (.cscfg) to reflect the new configuration as follows:

```
<NetworkConfiguration>
    <VirtualNetworkSite name="VNETName" />
    <AddressAssignments>
       <InstanceAddress roleName="Role0">
            <Subnets><Subnet name="Subnet-2" /></Subnets>
       </InstanceAddress>
    </AddressAssignments>
</NetworkConfiguration>
```

Exporting network configuration

You can export your virtual network settings to a network configuration file. This creates an XML file that can be used to re-create your network. This can be useful in situations where you accidentally modify or delete your network or when you want to reproduce a similar environment with the same topology.

Exporting network configuration (existing portal)

To export the network configuration file for a specific virtual network, complete the following steps:

1. Navigate to the virtual network list in the management portal accessed via *https://manage.windowsazure.com*.

2. Select the network from the list, and click Export on the command bar. In the Export Network Configuration dialog box, click the check mark to generate the file and download it in your browser.

Exporting network configuration (Preview portal)

The Preview portal does not currently support exporting a virtual network configuration.

Importing network configuration

When you export a network configuration file, it includes the following settings:

- The IP addresses of DNS servers to use for name resolution
- The IP address space and IP subnet definitions
- The local (on-premises) network site name and IP address space.
- Your VPN gateway IP address
- The region that you want to associate with your virtual network

You can create a network configuration file manually, or you can export it from an existing virtual network configuration (see previous section) and use that to create a network topology.

Importing network configuration (existing portal)

To import an existing network configuration XML file, complete the following steps:

1. Navigate to the management portal accessed via *https://manage.windowsazure.com*.

2. Click New on the command bar, and select New, Virtual Network, Import Configuration.

3. In the dialog box that opens, browse to your network configuration file. Click the right arrow.

4. On the Building Your Network page, a list of potential changes to the virtual network configuration are presented. Browse through those changes and then click the check mark to accept the changes and produce the new virtual network.

Importing network configuration (Preview portal)

The Preview portal does not currently support exporting a virtual network configuration.

> **Thought experiment**
> **Smooth migration**
>
> In this thought experiment, apply what you've learned about this objective. You can find answers to these questions in the "Answers" section at the end of this chapter.
>
> You are migrating an existing infrastructure to Microsoft Azure. You currently have over 300 VMs that you locally host that you'll be moving one at a time. You'll be performing the migration slowly over 12 months. The new VMs in Azure still need access to the old VMs that haven't migrated yet.
>
> 1. How should you configure the Virtual Network?
>
> 2. If you run out of IP addresses, what are your options

Objective summary

- If you run out of IP addresses, you can either add IP addresses to an existing subnet, or you can add add subnets.
- You can move a VM to a new subnet with the management portal or Windows PowerShell.
- You can export your network configuration so you can re-create it during a recovery operation, or reproduce it in another environment.

Objective review

Answer the following questions to test your knowledge of the information in this objective. You can find the answers to these questions and explanations of why each answer choice is correct or incorrect in the "Answers" section at the end of this chapter.

1. You have run out of IP addresses on the only subnet of your virtual network. What can you do to correct this? (Choose all that apply.)

   A. Delete the existing subnet and re-create it with more IP addresses.

   B. Expand the existing subnet.

   C. Add a new subnet, and add new VMs to the new subnet.

   D. Add a new subnet, migrate all resources to the new subnet, and then delete the old subnet.

2. Why would you need to export your network configuration to an XML file? (Choose all that apply.)

   A. To back it up.

   B. To make update changes to it.

   C. To learn from it so you can make new networks manually.

   D. To use it as a template.

Objective 5.4: Design and implement a communication strategy

Microsoft Azure Service Bus is a hosted infrastructure service that provides multi-tenant services for communications between applications. It supports service publishing, communication, and distribution of events at scale. Core scenarios for Service Bus features include:

- **Relays** Expose secure endpoints for synchronous calls to service endpoints across a network boundary, for example to expose on-premises resources to a remote client

- **Queues** Implement brokered messaging patterns where the message sender can deliver a message even if the receiver is temporarily offline

- **Topics and subscriptions** Implement publish and subscribe patterns where messages can be received by more than one receiver (subscriber)

- **Event hubs** Implement scenarios where receivers choose events to register for, to support high-volume message processing at scale

- **Notification hubs** Push notifications to mobile devices

Relays are used for relayed, synchronous messaging. The remaining scenarios are a form of brokered, asynchronous messaging patterns. In this section, you learn how to implement and scale each Service Bus resource.

> **MORE INFO**   **SERVICE BUS RESOURCES AND SAMPLES**
>
> See these references for a collection of overviews, tutorials, and samples related to Service Bus:
>
> - *http://msdn.microsoft.com/en-us/library/azure/ee732537.aspx*
> - *http://msdn.microsoft.com/en-us/library/azure/dn194201.aspx*

> **This objective covers how to:**
>
> - Create Service Bus namespaces
> - Develop messaging solutions using Service Bus relays, queues, topics, event hubs, and notification hubs

NOTE **TIERS**

Choosing a tier and scaling Service Bus might also fall under this objective. You'll find more information about these topics later in this chapter under Objective 5.4.

Creating a Service Bus namespace

The Service Bus namespace is a container for Service Bus resources including queues, topics, relays, notification hubs, and event hubs. You can group these resources into a single namespace or separate them according to management and scale requirements. In this section, you learn how to create a new Service Bus namespace. Scalability considerations are discussed in a later section.

Creating a Service Bus namespace (existing portal)

To create a Service Bus namespace, complete the following steps:

1. Navigate to the management portal accessed via *https://manage.windowsazure.com*.
2. Click the Service Bus icon in the left navigation pane.
3. Click Create on the command bar.
4. In the Create A Namespace dialog box that appears, type a unique name for the namespace name, and select a region (see Figure 5-15).
5. If the namespace will be used only for queues, topics, and event hubs, select Messaging for type. If the namespace will include notification hubs, select Notification Hub for type.
6. Select Basic as the messaging tier. You select your tier according to expected usage. This is discussed in a later section.

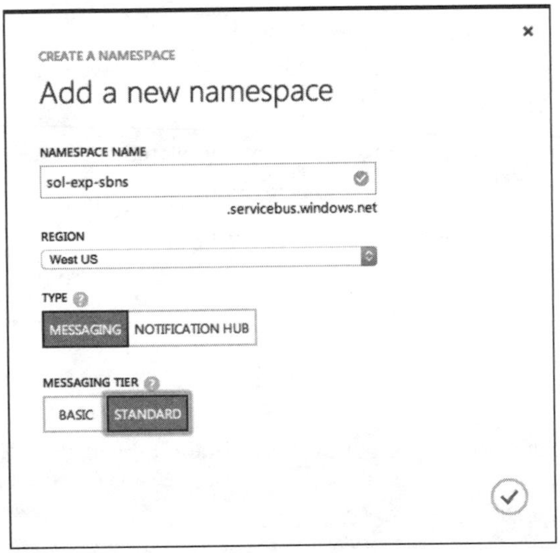

FIGURE 5-15 Creating a new Service Bus namespace

Creating a Service Bus namespace (Preview portal)

At the time of this writing, Service Bus management is not available from the Preview portal.

Creating a Service Bus namespace using Windows PowerShell

To create a new Service Bus namespace using Windows PowerShell cmdlets use the New-AzureSBNamespace command as follows:

```
New-AzureSBNamespace –Name sol-exp-svcbus –Location West US
```

By default when you create a namespace with Windows PowerShell it will use NamespaceType of Messaging. To create a namespace that can support Notification Hubs you must specify a parameter for NamespaceType as follows:

```
New-AzureSBNamespace –Name sol-exp-svcbus –Location West US –NamespaceType
NotificationHub
```

Selecting a protocol for messaging

By default, Service Bus supports several communication protocols. Table 5-1 lists the protocol options and required ports.

TABLE 5-1 Service Bus protocols and ports

Protocol	PORTS	Description
SBMP	9350-9354 (for relay) 9354 (for brokered messaging)	Service Bus Messaging Protocol (SBMP), is a proprietary SOAP-based protocol that typically relies on WCF under the covers to implement messaging with between applications through Service Bus. Relay services use this protocol by default when non-HTTP relay bindings are chosen. The brokered messaging client library uses this by default unless the Service Bus environment is set to use HTTP. See this reference for port settings per binding: *http://msdn.microsoft.com/en-us/library/azure/ee732535.aspx*

Protocol	PORTS	Description

HTTP	80, 443	HTTP protocol can be used for relay services when one of the HTTP relay bindings are selected and the Service Bus environment is set to use HTTP connectivity. The brokered messaging client library uses this if you do not specify AMQP protocol and set the Service Bus environment to HTTP as follows:
		
		`ServiceBusEnvironment.SystemConnectivity.Mode =`
		`ConnectivityMode.Http;`

AMQP	5671, 5672	Advanced Message Queuing Protocol (AMQP) is a modern, cross-platform asynchronous messaging standard. The brokered messaging client library uses this protocol if the connection string indicates TransportType of Amqp.

> **MORE INFO** **AMQP PROTOCOL**
>
> Advanced Message Queuing Protocol (AMQP) is the recommended protocol to use for brokered message exchange if firewall rules are not an issue. For additional information, see *http://msdn.microsoft.com/en-us/library/azure/jj841071.aspx*.

EXAM TIP

Connectivity issues are common for on-premises environments that disable ports other than 80 and 443. For this reason, it is still often necessary for portability to use HTTP protocol for brokered messaging.

Using Service Bus relays

The Service Bus Relay service is frequently used to expose on-premises resources to remote client applications located in the cloud or across network boundaries. It involves creating a Service Bus namespace for the Relay service, creating shared access policies to secure access to management, and follow these high level implementation steps:

1. Create a service contract defining the messages to be processed by the Relay service

2. Create a service implementation for that contract. This implementation includes the code to run when messages are received.

3. Host the service in any compatible WCF hosting environment, expose an endpoint using one of the available WCF relay bindings, and provide the appropriate credentials for the service listener.

4. Create a client reference to the relay using typical WCF client channel features, providing the appropriate relay binding and address to the service, with the appropriate credentials for the client sender.

5. Use the client reference to call methods on the service contract to invoke the service through the Service Bus relay.

The Relay service supports different transport protocols and Web services standards. The choice of protocol and standard is determined by the WCF relay binding selected for service endpoints. The list of bindings supporting these options are as follows:

- BasicHttpRelayBinding
- WS2007HttpRelayBinding
- WebHttpRelayBinding
- NetTcpRelayBinding
- NetOneWayRelayBinding
- NetEventRelayBinding

Clients must select from the available endpoints exposed by the service for compatible communication. HTTP services support two-way calls using SOAP protocol (optionally with extended WS* protocols) or classic HTTP protocol requests (also referred to as REST services). For TCP services, you can use synchronous two-way calls, one-way calls, or one-way event publishing to multiple services.

Managing relay credentials

Service Bus relay credentials are managed on the Configure tab for the namespace as follows:

1. Create a Service Bus namespace as described in the section "Create a Service Bus namespace." It can be either a Messaging or Notification Hub type.

2. To create a shared access policy for the namespace, select the namespace in the management portal, and navigate to the Configure tab. Scroll to Shared Access Policies (see Figure 5-16). It is not recommended to use the root shared access policy. Instead, create an entry for a receiver and sender policy that respectively can only listen or send. Click Save to produce the policy entries.

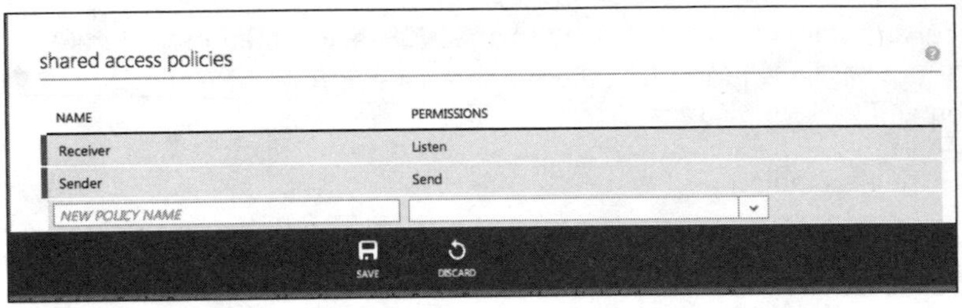

FIGURE 5-16 Creating shared access policies for a Service Bus namespace

3. In the Shared Access Key Generator section, after creating one or more policies, you can manage their keys (see Figure 5-17). Select Receiver from the Policy Name drop-down list and note the primary key for use with the relay service listener.

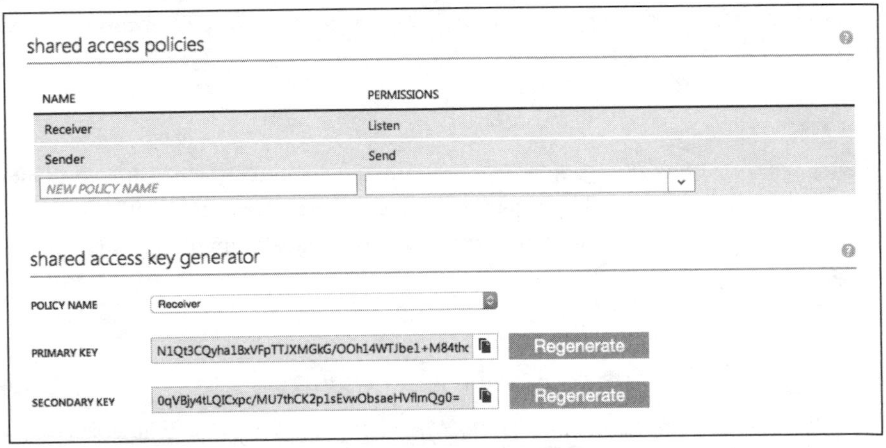

FIGURE 5-17 Managing keys for shared access policies

4. In the same section, also select Sender from the Policy Name drop-down list and note the primary key for use with the relay service client.

> **NOTE** **SENDER AND RECEIVER KEYS**
>
> It is considered best practice to create separate keys for the sender and receiver, and possibly multiple keys according to different groups of senders and receivers. This allows you to more granularly control which applications have send, receive, and management rights to Service Bus relays created in the namespace.

Creating a relay and listener endpoint

After you have created the namespace and noted the listener policy name and key, you can write code to create a relay service endpoint. Here is a simple example with steps:

1. Open Visual Studio 2013 and create a new console application.

2. Add the Microsoft Azure Service Bus NuGet package to the console application.

3. Create a WCF service definition to be used as a definition for the relay contract and an implementation for the relay listener service. Add a class file to the project with the following service contract and implementation. Include the using statement at the top of the file:

```
using System.ServiceModel;
[ServiceContract]
public interface IrelayService
{
  [OperationContract]
  string EchoMessage(string message);
}
public class RelayService:IrelayService
{
  public string EchoMessage(string message)
  {
    Console.WriteLine(message);
    return message;
  }
}
```

4. Host the WCF service in the console application by creating an instance of the WCF ServiceHost for the service. Add an endpoint using NetTcpRelayBinding, passing the name of the Service Bus namespace, policy name, and key. Include the using statements at the top of the file:

```
using System.ServiceModel;
using Microsoft.ServiceBus;
    class Program
    {
        static void Main(string[] args)
        {
            string serviceBusNamespace = "sol-exp-msg";
            string listenerPolicyName = "Receiver";
            string listenerPolicyKey = "r/k1r5kLuH1gYPnaj/
L1rt1Gi+SRTTzFJNNnci0ibhU=";
            string serviceRelativePath = "Relay";
            ServiceHost host = new ServiceHost(typeof(RelayService));

            host.AddServiceEndpoint(typeof(IrelayService), new
NetTcpRelayBinding(),
                ServiceBusEnvironment.CreateServiceUri("sb", serviceBusNamespace,
serviceRelativePath))
                .Behaviors.Add(new TransportClientEndpointBehavior
                {
```

```
                      TokenProvider = TokenProvider. CreateSharedAccessSignatureToke
        nProvider(listenerPolicyName, listenerPolicyKey)
                      });

             host.Open();

             Console.WriteLine("Service is running. Press ENTER to stop the
        service.");
             Console.ReadLine();

             host.Close();
           }
        }
```

5. Run the console, and the WCF service listener is now waiting for messages.

EXAM TIP

You can configure WCF relay endpoints programmatically or by using application configuration in the <system.servicemodel> section. The latter is more appropriate for dynamically configuring the host environment for production applications.

Sending messages through relay

After you have created the relay service, defined the endpoint and related protocols, and noted the sender policy name and key, you can create a client to send messages to the relay service. Here is a simple example with steps building on the previous sections:

1. In the existing Visual Studio solution created in the previous section, add another console application called RelayClient.

2. Add the Microsoft Azure Service Bus NuGet package to the client console application.

3. Add a new class to the project, copy the WCF service interface, and create a new interface to be used by the WCF client channel creation code. Include the using statement at the top of the file:

```
using System.ServiceModel;
[ServiceContract]
public interface IrelayService
{
  [OperationContract]
  string EchoMessage(string message);
}
public interface IrelayServiceChannel:IrelayService,IclientChannel {}
```

4. Add code in the main entry point to call the relay service. You will create a WCF client channel for the client channel interface, provide an instance of the NetTcpRelayBinding for the client endpoint, and provide an EndpointAddress for the namespace and

relative path to the service. You will also provide the sender policy name and key. Include the using statement at the top of the file:

```
using System.ServiceModel;
    class Program
    {
        static void Main(string[] args)
        {
            string serviceBusNamespace = "sol-exp-msg";
            string listenerPolicyName = "Sender";
            string listenerPolicyKey = "17AplxvMO4FLJsntP+nrlwctEkYMWwJ4VLxpts621
gk=";
            string serviceRelativePath = "Relay";

            var client = new ChannelFactory<IrelayServiceChannel>(
                new NetTcpRelayBinding(),
                new EndpointAddress(
                    ServiceBusEnvironment.CreateServiceUri("sb",
serviceBusNamespace, serviceRelativePath)));

            client.Endpoint.Behaviors.Add(
                new TransportClientEndpointBehavior { TokenProvider =
TokenProvider.CreateSharedAccessSignatureTokenProvider(listenerPolicyName,
listenerPolicyKey) });

            using (var channel = client.CreateChannel())
            {
                string message = channel.EchoMessage("hello from the relay!");
                Console.WriteLine(message);
            }
            Console.ReadLine();
        }
    }
```

5. To test sending messages to the service created in the previous section, first run the service listener console, and then the client console. You will see the message written to both consoles.

> **NOTE** **RELAY ALTERNATIVES**
>
> Practically speaking, most systems today employ an asynchronous architecture that involves queues, topics, or event hubs as a way to queue work for on-premises processing from a remote application.

Using Service Bus queues

Service Bus queues provide a brokered messaging service that supports physical and temporal decoupling of a message producer (sender) and message consumer (receiver). Queues are based on the brokered messaging infrastructure of Service Bus and provide a First In First Out (FIFO) buffer to the first receiver that removes the message. There is only one receiver per message.

Properties of the Service Bus queue influence its behavior, including the size and partitions for scale out, message handling for expiry and locking, and support for sessions. Table 5-2 shows the core properties of a Service Bus queue. Properties prefixed with an asterisk (*) indicate a property not shown in the management portal while creating the queue, but can be edited in the management portal after they are created.

TABLE 5-2 Queue properties

Property	Description
Max Size	The size of the queue in terms of capacity for messages. Can be from 1 GB to 5 GB.
Default message time to live	Time after which a message will expire and be removed from the queue. Defaults to 14 days.
Move expired messages to dead-letter sub-queue	If enabled, automatically moves expired messages to the dead letter queue.
Lock duration	Duration of time a message is inaccessible to other receivers when a receiver requests a peek lock on the message. Defaults to 30 seconds. Can be set to a value up to 5 minutes.
Enable duplicate detection	If enabled, the queue will retain a buffer and ignore messages with the same message identifier (provided by the sender). The window for this buffer is by default 10 seconds, and can be set to a value up to 7 days.
*Duplicate detection history	Window of time for measuring duplicate detection. Defaults to 10 seconds, and can be set to a value up to 7 days.
Enable sessions	If enabled, messages can be grouped into sequential batches to guarantee ordered delivery of a set of messages.
Enable partitioning	If enabled, messages will be distributed across multiple message brokers and can be grouped by partition key. Up to 100 partitioned queues are supported within a namespace.
*Maximum delivery count	The maximum number of times Service Bus will try to deliver the message before moving it to the dead-letter sub-queue. The maximum value is 2,000.
*Queue state	Allows for disabling publishing or consumption without removing the queue. Valid choices are Enabled, Disabled, Receive Disabled (send only mode) or Send Disabled (receive only mode).

In this section you learn how to create a queue, send messages to a queue, and retrieve messages from a queue.

Creating a queue

You can create a queue directly from the management portal or programmatically using the management API, using Windows PowerShell, or using code.

CREATING A QUEUE (EXISTING PORTAL)

To create a queue in the management portal, complete the following steps:

1. Navigate to the management portal accessed via *https://manage.windowsazure.com.*

2. Click New on the command bar, and select New, App Services, Service Bus, Queue, Custom Create.

3. On the first page of the Create A Queue dialog box (see Figure 5-18), select a region, and then select a namespace for the queue. Type a unique queue name for the namespace. Click the right arrow to continue to the next page.

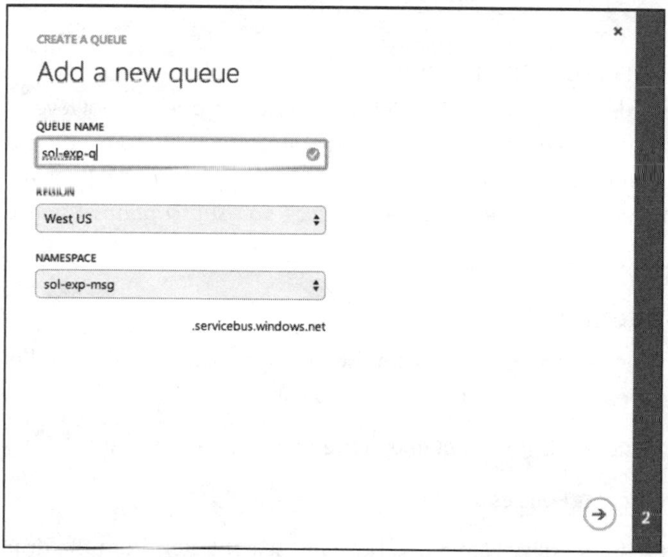

FIGURE 5-18 Adding a new queue to a Service Bus namespace

4. Accept the defaults on the Configure Queue page (see Figure 5-19), and click the check mark to create the queue.

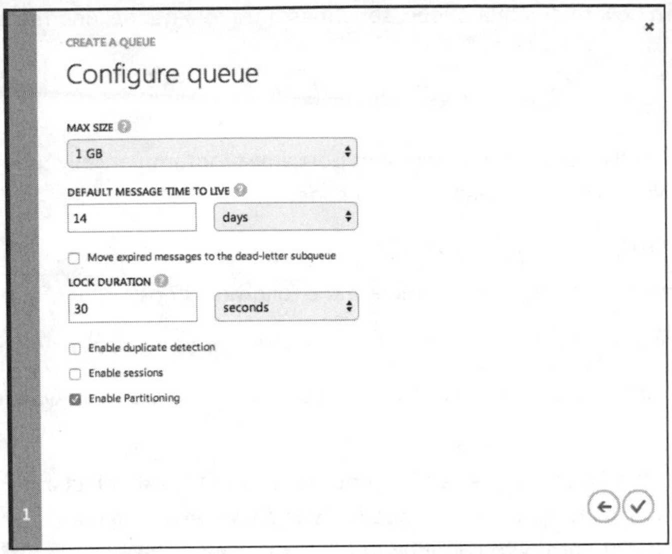

CREATE A QUEUE

Configure queue

MAX SIZE ⓘ

| 1 GB | ⇅ |

DEFAULT MESSAGE TIME TO LIVE ⓘ

| 14 | | days | ⇅ |

☐ Move expired messages to the dead-letter subqueue

LOCK DURATION ⓘ

| 30 | | seconds | ⇅ |

☐ Enable duplicate detection

☐ Enable sessions

☑ Enable Partitioning

1

← ✓

FIGURE 5-19 Additional setting available when creating a new queue

CREATING A QUEUE WITH WINDOWS POWERSHELL

There are no direct commands for creating and deleting Service Bus queues; however, you can construct a custom Windows PowerShell script that includes code to produce a queue programmatically. For more information, see *http://blogs.msdn.com/b/paolos/archive/2014/12/02/how-to-create-a-service-bus-queues-topics-and-subscriptions-using-a-powershell-script.aspx*.

Managing queue credentials

Service Bus queue credentials can be managed from the management portal. The following example illustrates how to create a sender and receiver policy:

1. Navigate to the Configure tab for the queue in the management portal.

2. Scroll to the Shared Access Policies section.

3. Enter **Receiver** in the New Policy Name text box, and select Listen from the drop-down list in the Permissions column.

4. Enter **Sender** in the New Policy Name text box, and select Send from the drop-down list in the Permissions column.

5. Click Save on the command bar.

6. In the Shared Access Key Generator section, select the Receiver and Sender policy individually and copy the primary key for each to use in their respective applications.

Finding queue connection strings

To communicate with a queue, you provide connection information including the queue URL and shared access credentials. The management portal provides a connection string for each shared access policy you have created. For example, the following are the connection strings for the Receiver and Sender policies created in the previous section:

```
Endpoint=sb://sol-exp-msg.servicebus.windows.
net/;SharedAccessKeyName=Receiver;SharedAccessKey=N1Qt3CQyha1BxVFpTTJXMGkG/
OOh14WTJbe1+M84tho=
Endpoint=sb://sol-exp-msg.servicebus.windows.net/;SharedAccessKeyName=Sender;
SharedAccessKey-f9rWrHfJlns7iMFbWQxxFi2KyssfpqCFIHJtOuLS178=
```

You can access this information as follows:

1. Navigate to the Dashboard tab for the queue in the management portal.

2. On the command bar, click Connection Information.

3. In the dialog box that appears showing the shared access policies and their associated connection strings, click the Copy To Clipboard icon to access the information.

Sending messages to a queue

After you have created the namespace and queue and you've noted the sender connection string, you can write code to create a queue client that sends message to that queue. Here is a simple example with steps:

1. Open Visual Studio 2013 and create a new console application called QueueSender.

2. Add the Microsoft Azure Service Bus NuGet package to the console application.

3. In the main entry point, add code to send messages to the queue. Get the connection string with a TransportType setting for AMQP, create an instance of the Messaging-Factory, and create a reference to the queue with QueueClient. You can then create a

BrokeredMessage (in this case, a string) and send that using the queue reference. The following listing shows the entire implementation, including required namespaces:

```
using Microsoft.ServiceBus;
using Microsoft.ServiceBus.Messaging;
using Microsoft.WindowsAzure;
class Program
{
    static void Main(string[] args)
    {
        string queueName = "sol-exp-q-nopart";
        string connection = "Endpoint=sb://sol-exp-msg.servicebus.windows.net/;Sha
redAccessKeyName=Sender;SharedAccessKey=17AplxvMO4FLJsntP+nrlwctEkYMWwJ4VLxpts62lg
k=;TransportType=Amqp";
        MessagingFactory factory = MessagingFactory.CreateFromConnectionString(co
nnection);
        QueueClient queue = factory.CreateQueueClient(queueName);
        string message = "queue message over amqp";
        BrokeredMessage bm = new BrokeredMessage(message);
        queue.Send(bm);
    }
}
```

EXAM TIP

The BrokeredMessage type can accept any serializable object or a stream to be included in the body of the message. You can also set additional custom properties on the message and provide settings relevant to partitions and sessions.

Receiving messages from a queue

There are two modes for processing queue messages:

- **ReceiveAndDelete** Messages are delivered once, regardless of whether the receiver fails to process the message.

- **PeekLock** Messages are locked after they are delivered to a receiver so that other receivers do not process them unless they are unlocked through timeout or if the receiver that locked the message abandons processing.

By default, PeekLock mode is used, and this is preferred unless the system can tolerate lost messages. The receiver should manage aborting the message if it can't be processed to allow another receiver to try to process the message more quickly.

After you have created the namespace and queue and you've noted the receiver connection string, you can write code to read messages from the queue using the client library. Here is a simple example with steps:

1. In the existing Visual Studio solution created in the previous section, add another console application called QueueListener.

2. Add the Microsoft Azure Service Bus NuGet package to the console application.

3. In the main entry point, add code to read messages from the queue. Get the connection string with a TransportType setting for AMQP, create an instance of the MessagingFactory, and create a reference to the queue with QueueClient. You can then create a BrokeredMessage (in this case, a string) and send that using the queue reference. The following listing shows the entire implementation, including required namespaces:

```
using Microsoft.ServiceBus.Messaging;
class Program
{
    static void Main(string[] args)
    {
        string queueName = "sol-exp-q-nopart";
        string connection = "Endpoint=sb://sol-exp-msg.servicebus.windows.net/;Sha
redAccessKeyName=Receiver;SharedAccessKey=r/k1r5kLuHlgYPnaj/L1rt1Gi+SRTTzFJNNnci0i
bhU=;TransportType=Amqp";

        MessagingFactory factory = MessagingFactory.CreateFromConnectionString(co
nnection);
        QueueClient queue = factory.CreateQueueClient(queueName);
        while (true)
        {
            BrokeredMessage message = queue.Receive();
            if (message != null)
            {
                try
                {
                    Console.WriteLine("MessageId {0}", message.MessageId);
                    Console.WriteLine("Delivery {0}", message.DeliveryCount);
                    Console.WriteLine("Size {0}", message.Size);
                    Console.WriteLine(message.GetBody<string>());
                     message.Complete();
                }
                catch (Exception ex)
                {
                    Console.WriteLine(ex.ToString());
                    message.Abandon();
                }
            }
        }
    }
}
```

> **NOTE DUPLICATE MESSAGES**
>
> Service Bus queues support at-least-once processing. This means that under certain circumstances, a message might be redelivered and processed twice. To avoid duplicate messages, you can use the MessageId of the message to verify that a message was not already processed by your system.

Using Service Bus topics and subscriptions

Service Bus queues support one-to-one delivery from a sender to a single receiver. Service Bus topics and subscriptions support one-to-many communication in support of traditional publish and subscribe patterns in brokered messaging. When messages are sent to a topic, a copy is made for each subscription, depending on filtering rules applied to the subscription. Messages are not received from the topic; they are received from the subscription. Receivers can listen to one or more subscriptions to retrieve messages.

Properties of the Service Bus topic influence its behavior, including the size and partitions for scale out and message handling for expiry. Table 5-3 and Table 5-4 respectively show the core properties of a Service Bus topic and subscription. Properties prefixed with an asterisk (*) indicate a property not shown in the management portal while creating the topic or subscription, but can be edited in the management portal after they are created.

TABLE 5-3 Topic properties

Property	Description
Max size	The size of the topic buffer in terms of capacity for messages. Can be from 1 GB to 5 GB.
Default message time to live	Time after which a message will expire and be removed from the topic buffer. Defaults to 14 days.
Enable duplicate detection	If enabled, the topic will retain a buffer and ignore messages with the same message identifier (provided by the sender). The window for this buffer is by default 10 seconds and can be set to a value up to 7 days.
*Duplicate detection history	Window of time for measuring duplicate detection. Defaults to 10 seconds and can be set to a value up to 7 days.
*Filter message before publishing	If enabled, the publisher will fail to publish a message that will not reach a subscriber.
*Topic state	Allows for disabling publishing without removing the topic. Valid choices are Enabled, Disabled, or Send Disabled (receive only mode).
Enable partitioning	If enabled, messages will be distributed across multiple message brokers and can be grouped by partition key. Up to 100 partitioned topics are supported within a namespace.

TABLE 5-4 Subscription properties

Property	Description
Default message time to live	Time after which a message will expire and be removed from the subscription buffer. Defaults to 14 days.
Move expired messages to dead-letter sub-queue	If enabled, automatically moves expired messages to the dead letter sub-queue.
Move messages that cause filter evaluation exceptions to the dead-letter sub-queue	If enabled, automatically moves messages that fail filter evaluation to the dead letter sub-queue.
Lock duration	Duration of time a message is inaccessible to other receivers when a receiver requests a peek lock on the message. Defaults to 30 seconds. Can be set to a value up to 5 minutes.
Enable sessions	If enabled, messages can be grouped into sequential batches to guarantee ordered delivery of a set of messages.
Enable batched operations	If enabled, server-side batch operations are supported.
Maximum delivery count	The maximum number of times Service Bus will try to deliver the message before moving it to the dead-letter sub-queue. The maximum value is 2,000.
*Topic subscription state	Allows for disabling consumption without removing the subscription. Valid choices are Enabled, Disabled, or Receive Disabled (send only mode).

Creating a topic and subscriptions

You can create a topic and subscriptions directly from the management portal or programmatically using the management API, using Windows PowerShell, or using code.

CREATING A TOPIC AND SUBSCRIPTIONS (EXISTING PORTAL)

To create a topic and subscriptions using the management portal, complete the following steps:

1. Navigate to the management portal accessed via *https://manage.windowsazure.com*.

2. Click New on the command bar, and select New, App Services, Service Bus, Topic.

3. On the first page of the Create A Topic dialog box, select a region and a namespace for the topic. Type a unique topic name for the namespace. Click the right arrow to continue to the next page.

4. Accept the defaults on the Configure Topic page (see Figure 5-20), and click the check mark to create the topic.

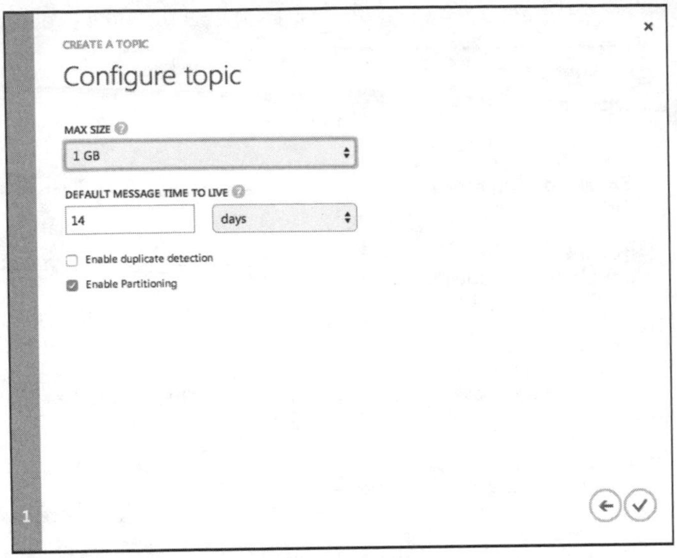

CREATE A TOPIC

Configure topic

MAX SIZE ⍰

| 1 GB | ⇕ |

DEFAULT MESSAGE TIME TO LIVE ⍰

| 14 | | days | ⇕ |

☐ Enable duplicate detection

☑ Enable Partitioning

FIGURE 5-20 Creating a new topic for a Service Bus namespace

5. To create subscriptions for the topic, select the topic in the management portal, and navigate to the Subscriptions tab.

6. Click Create on the command bar. In the Create A Subscription dialog box that appears, provide a unique subscription name. Click the right arrow to advance to the next page.

7. Accept the defaults on the Configure Topic page, and click the check mark to create the subscription.

CREATING A TOPIC AND SUBSCRIPTIONS WITH WINDOWS POWERSHELL

There are no direct commands for creating and deleting Service Bus topics and subscriptions; however, you can construct a custom Windows PowerShell script that includes code to produce topics and subscriptions programmatically. For more information, see *http://blogs. msdn.com/b/paolos/archive/2014/12/02/how-to-create-a-service-bus-queues-topics-and-subscriptions-using-a-powershell-script.aspx*.

Managing topic credentials

Service Bus topic credentials can be managed from the management portal. The following example illustrates creating a sender and receiver policy:

1. Navigate to the Configure tab for the topic in the management portal.

2. Scroll to the Shared Access Policies section.

3. Enter **Receiver** in the New Policy Name text box, and select Listen from the drop-down list in the Permissions column.

4. Enter **Sender** in the New Policy Name text box, and select Send from the drop-down list in the Permissions column.

5. Click Save on the command bar.

> **NOTE** **SHARED ACCESS POLICIES FOR TOPICS**
>
> By default, there are no shared access policies created for a new topic. You will usually create at least one policy per subscriber to isolate access keys and one for send permissions to separate key access between clients and services.

Finding topic connection strings

Connection strings for topics are similar to the queues discussed earlier. To access your topic connection strings, complete the following steps:

1. Navigate to the Dashboard tab for the topic in the management portal.

2. On the command bar, click Connection Information.

3. In the dialog box that appears showing the shared access policies and their associated connection strings, click the Copy To Clipboard icon to access the information.

Sending messages to a topic

With topics and subscriptions, you send messages to a topic and retrieve them from a subscription. After you have created the namespace, the topic, and one or more subscriptions, and you've noted the sender connection string, you can write code to create a topic client that sends messages to that topic. Here is a simple example with steps:

1. Open Visual Studio 2013 and create a new console application called TopicSender.

2. Add the Microsoft Azure Service Bus NuGet package to the console application.

3. In the main entry point, add code to send messages to the topic. Create an instance of the MessagingFactory, and create a reference to the topic with TopicClient. You can then create a BrokeredMessage and send that using the topic reference. Here is the heart of the main method:

```
string topicName = "sol-exp-t";
string connection = "Endpoint=sb://sol-exp-msg.servicebus.windows.net/;SharedAcces
sKeyName=Sender;SharedAccessKey=17AplxvMO4FLJsntP+nrlwctEkYMWwJ4VLxpts621gk=";
MessagingFactory factory = MessagingFactory.CreateFromConnectionString(connecti
on);
TopicClient topic = factory.CreateTopicClient(topicName);
topic.Send(new BrokeredMessage("topic message"));
```

Receiving messages from a subscription

Processing messages from a subscription is similar to processing messages from a queue. You can use ReceiveAndDelete or PeekLock mode. The latter is the preferred mode and the default.

After you have created the namespace, topic, and subscriptions, and you've noted the subscription connection string, you can write code to read messages from the subscription using the client library. Here is a simple example with steps:

1. In the existing Visual Studio solution created in the previous section, add another console application called TopicListener.

2. Add the Microsoft Azure Service Bus NuGet package to the console application.

3. In the main entry point, add code to read messages from a subscription. Get the connection string for the subscription, create an instance of the MessagingFactory, and create a reference to the subscription with SubscriptionClient. You can then call Receive() to get the next BrokeredMessage from the subscription for processing. Here is the heart of the receive code:

```
string topicName = "sol-exp-t";
string subA = "SubscriptionA";
string connection = "Endpoint=sb://sol-exp-msg.servicebus.windows.net/
;SharedAccessKeyName=SubscriptionA;SharedAccessKey=r/k1r5kLuHlgYPnaj/
L1rt1Gi+SRTTzFJNNnci0ibhU=";
MessagingFactory factory = MessagingFactory.CreateFromConnectionString(connecti
on);
SubscriptionClient clientA = factory.CreateSubscriptionClient(topicName, subA);
while (true)
{
    BrokeredMessage message = clientA.Receive();
    if (message != null)
    {
        try
        {
            Console.WriteLine("MessageId {0}", message.MessageId);
            Console.WriteLine("Delivery {0}", message.DeliveryCount);
            Console.WriteLine("Size {0}", message.Size);
            Console.WriteLine(message.GetBody<string>());
            message.Complete();
        }
        catch (Exception ex)
        {
            Console.WriteLine(ex.ToString());
            message.Abandon();
        }
    }
}
```

EXAM TIP

If you enable batch processing for the subscription, you can receive a batch of messages in a single call using ReceiveBatch() or ReceiveBatchAsync(). This will pull messages in the subscription up to the number you specify, or fewer if applicable. Note that you must be aware of the potential lock timeout while processing the batch.

MORE INFO   **BATCHING AND PREFETCH**

You can batch messages from a queue or topic client to avoid multiple calls to send messages to Service Bus, including them in a single call. You can also batch receive messages
from a queue or subscription to process messages in batch. For more information on batch
processing and prefetch, an alternative to batch, see *http://msdn.microsoft.com/library/
azure/hh528527.aspx.*

Filtering messages

One of the powerful features of topics and subscriptions is the ability to filter messages based
on certain criteria, such as the value of specific message properties. Based on criteria, you can
determine which subscription should receive a copy of each message. In addition, you can
configure the topic to validate that every message has a valid destination subscription as part
of publishing.

By default, subscriptions are created with a "match all" criteria, meaning all topic messages
are copied to the subscription. You cannot create a subscription with filter criteria through the
management portal, but you can create it programmatically using the NamespaceManager object and its CreateSubscription() method. The following code illustrates creating an instance
of the NamespaceManager for a topic and creating a subscription with a filter based on a
custom message property:

```
string topicName = "sol-exp-t";
string connection = "Endpoint=sb://sol-exp-msg.servicebus.windows.net/;SharedAccessKeyNa
me=Admin;SharedAccessKey=17AplxvMO4FLJsntP+nrlwctEkYMWwJ4VLxpts62lgk=";
var ns = NamespaceManager.CreateFromConnectionString(connectionString);
SqlFilter filter = new SqlFilter("Priority == 1");
ns.CreateSubscription(topicName, "PrioritySubscription", filter);
```

To send messages to the topic, targeting the priority subscription, set the Priority property
to 1 on each message:

```
BrokeredMessage message = new BrokeredMessage("priority message");
message.Properties["Priority"] = 1;
```

Using event hubs

Service Bus event hubs support very high-volume message streaming as is typical of enterprise application logging solutions or Internet of Things (IoT) scenarios. With event hubs, your
application can support the following:

- Ingesting message data at scale

- Consuming message data in parallel by multiple consumers

- Re-processing messages by restarting at any point in the message stream

Messages to the event hub are FIFO and durable for up to seven days. Consumers can
reconnect to the hub and choose where to begin processing, allowing for the re-processing

scenario or for reconnecting after failure. Event hubs differ from queues and topics in that there are no enterprise messaging features. Instead there is very high throughput and volume. For example, there isn't a Time-to-Live (TTL) feature for messages, no dead-letter sub-queue, no transactions or acknowledgements. The focus is low latency, highly reliable, message streaming with order preservation and replay.

Table 5-5 shows the core properties of an event hub. Properties prefixed with an asterisk (*) indicate a property not shown in the management portal while creating the queue, but they can be edited in the management portal after they are created.

> **MORE INFO   EVENT HUBS OVERVIEW**
>
> For more details on the event hubs architecture, see *http://msdn.microsoft.com/en-us/library/azure/dn836025.aspx*.

> **EXAM TIP**
>
> Event hubs can by default handle 1-MB ingress per second, 2-MB egress per second per partition. This can be increased to 1-GB ingress per second and 2-GB egress per second through a support ticket.

TABLE 5-5 Event hub properties

Property	Description
Partition count	Determines the number of partitions across which messages are distributed. Defaults to 8. Can be set to a value between 8 and 32 and cannot be modified after it is created.
Message retention	Determines the number of days a message will be retained before it is removed from the event hub. Can be between 1 and 7 days.
*Event hub state	Allows for disabling the hub without removing it. Valid choices are Enabled or Disabled.

Creating an event hub

You can create an event hub directly from the management portal, programmatically using the management API, using Windows PowerShell, or using code.

CREATING AN EVENT HUB (EXISTING PORTAL)

To create and event hub using the management portal, complete the following steps:

1. Navigate to the management portal accessed via *https://manage.windowsazure.com*.

2. Click New on the command bar, and select New, App Services, Service Bus, Event Hub.

3. Select a region and a namespace for the event hub. Type a unique event hub name. Click the right arrow to move to the next page.

4. Enter **8** for the partition count (can be from 8 to 32) and **7** for the message retention (can be from 1 to 7 days). Click the check mark to create the event hub (see Figure 5-21).

EXAM TIP

You can create between 8 and 32 partitions, but with a support ticket you can increase that number up to 1,024.

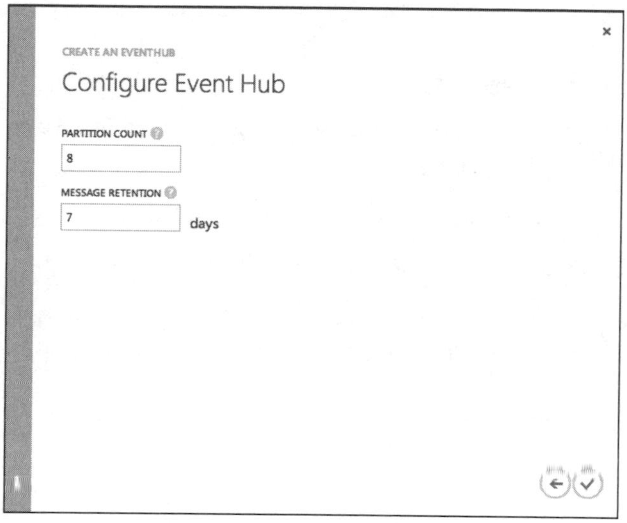

CREATE AN EVENTHUB

Configure Event Hub

PARTITION COUNT

8

MESSAGE RETENTION

7   days

FIGURE 5-21 Configuring settings for a new Event Hub

CREATING AN EVENT HUB WITH WINDOWS POWERSHELL

There are no direct commands for creating and deleting event hubs; however, you can construct a custom Windows PowerShell script that includes code to produce event hubs programmatically. For more information, see *http://blogs.msdn.com/b/paolos/archive/2014/12/01/how-to-create-a-service-bus-namespace-and-an-event-hub-using-a-powershell-script.aspx*.

Managing event hub credentials

Service Bus event hub credentials can be managed from the management portal. The following example illustrates creating a sender and receiver policy:

1. Navigate to the Configure tab for the event hub in the management portal.

2. Scroll to the Shared Access Policies section.

3. Enter **Receiver** in the New Policy Name text box, and select Listen from the drop-down list in the Permissions column.

4. Enter **Sender** in the New Policy Name text box, and select Send from the drop-down list in the Permissions column.

5. Click Save on the command bar.

EXAM TIP

By default, there are no shared access policies created for a new event hub. You will usually create at least one policy for each receiver and one for send permissions to separate key access between clients and services.

Finding event hub connection strings

Connection strings for event hubs are similar to the queues discussed earlier. To access your connection strings, complete the following steps:

1. Navigate to the Dashboard tab for the event hub in the management portal.

2. On the command bar, click Connection Information.

3. In the dialog box that appears showing the shared access policies and their associated connection strings, click the Copy To Clipboard icon to access the information.

Sending messages to an event hub

With event hubs, you send streamed messages as EventData instances to the event hub, and Service Bus leverages the allocated partitions to distribute those messages. Messages are stored for up to seven days and can be retrieved multiple times by consumers.

After you have created the namespace and event hub and you've noted the sender connection string, you can write code to create an event hub client that sends messages. Here is a simple example with steps:

1. Open Visual Studio 2013 and create a new console application called EventHubSender.

2. Add the Microsoft Azure Service Bus NuGet package to the console application.

3. In the main entry point, add code to send messages to the event hub. Create an instance of the MessagingFactory and a reference to the EventHubClient. You can then create an EventData instance and send. Here is the heart of the main method:

```
string ehName = "sol-exp-eh";
string connection = "Endpoint=sb://sol-exp-msg.servicebus.windows.net/;SharedAcce
ssKeyName=Sender;SharedAccessKey=17AplxvMO4FLJsntP+nrlwctEkYMWwJ4VLxpts62lgk=;Tra
nsportType=Amqp";
MessagingFactory factory = MessagingFactory.CreateFromConnectionString(connecti
on);
EventHubClient client = factory.CreateEventHubClient(ehName);
string message = "event hub message";
EventData data = new EventData(Encoding.UTF8.GetBytes(message));
client.Send(data);
```

Receiving messages from a consumer group

When you create the event hub, you allocate a number of partitions to distribute message ingestion. This helps you to scale the event hub ingress alongside settings for throughput (to be discussed in the next section). To consume messages, consumers connect to a partition. In this example, a default consumer is created to consume events.

After you have created the namespace, topic, and subscriptions, and you've noted the subscription connection string, you can write code to read messages from the consumer group using the client library. Here is a simple example with steps:

1. In the existing Visual Studio solution created in the previous section, add another console application called EventHubListener.

2. Add the Microsoft Azure Service Bus NuGet package to the console application.

3. In the main entry point, add code to read data from the event hub using the default consumer group. You can then call Receive() to get the next BrokeredMessage from the subscription for processing. Here is the heart of the receive code:

```
string ehName = "sol-exp-eh";
string connection = "Endpoint=sb://sol-exp-msg.servicebus.windows.net/;SharedAcces
sKeyName=Receiver;SharedAccessKey=r/k1r5kLuHlgYPnaj/L1rt1Gi+SRTTzFJNNnci0ibhU=;Tr
ansportType=Amqp";
MessagingFactory factory = MessagingFactory.CreateFromConnectionString(connecti
on);
EventHubClient ehub = factory.CreateEventHubClient(ehName);
EventHubConsumerGroup group = ehub.GetDefaultConsumerGroup();
EventHubReceiver receiver = group.CreateReceiver("1");
while (true)
{
    EventData data = receiver.Receive();
    if (data != null)
    {
```

```
        try
        {
            string message = Encoding.UTF8.GetString(data.GetBytes());
            Console.WriteLine("EnqueuedTimeUtc: {0}", data.EnqueuedTimeUtc);
            Console.WriteLine("PartitionKey: {0}", data.PartitionKey);
            Console.WriteLine("SequenceNumber: {0}", data.SequenceNumber);
            Console.WriteLine(message);
        }
        catch (Exception ex)
        {
            Console.WriteLine(ex.ToString());
            }
        }
    }
```

MORE INFO **EVENTPROCESSORHOST**

To simplify scaling event hub consumers for .NET developers, there is a NuGet package that supplies a hosting feature for event hubs called EventProcessorHost. For more information, see *https://www.nuget.org/packages/Microsoft.Azure.ServiceBus. EventProcessorHost/.*

NOTE **CONSUMER GROUPS**

A default consumer group is created for each new event hub, but you can optionally create multiple consumer groups (receivers) to consume events in parallel.

Using notification hubs

Notification hubs provide a service for push notifications to mobile devices, at scale. If you are implementing applications that are a source of events to mobile applications, notification hubs simplify the effort to send platform-compatible notifications to all the applications and devices in your ecosystem.

In this section, you learn how to create a notification hub and implement solutions for various application platforms.

Creating a notification hub

You can create a notification hub directly from the management portal, programmatically using the management API, using Windows PowerShell, or using code.

CREATING A NOTIFICATION HUB (EXISTING PORTAL)

To create a notification hub using the management portal, complete the following steps:

1. Navigate to the management portal accessed via *https://manage.windowszaure.com.*

2. Click New on the command bar, and select New, App Services, Service Bus, Notification Hub, Quick Create.

3. Select a region and a namespace for the notification hub. Type a unique notification hub name. Click the check mark to create the notification hub.

CREATING A NOTIFICATION HUB WITH WINDOWS POWERSHELL

There are no direct commands for creating and deleting Service Bus notification hubs; however, you can construct a custom Windows PowerShell script that includes code to produce notification hubs programmatically following a similar pattern as discussed in previous sections for queues, topics, and event hubs.

Implementing solutions with notification hubs

A solution that involves notification hubs typically has the following moving parts:

- A mobile application deployed to a device and able to receive push notifications
- A back-end application or other event source that will publish notifications to the mobile application
- A platform notification service, compatible wi th the application platform
- A notification hub to receive messages from the publisher and handle pushing those events in a platform-specific format to the mobile device

The implementation requirements vary based on the target platform for the mobile application. For a set of tutorials with steps for each platform supported, including the steps for setting up the mobile application, the back-end application, and the notification hub, see *http://azure.microsoft.com/en-us/documentation/articles/notification-hubs-windows-store-dotnet-get-started.*

> **MORE INFO** NOTIFICATION HUB GUIDES
>
> The following references provide additional background and programming guidance for notification hubs and mobile services:
>
> - Notification hubs overview and tutorials: *http://msdn.microsoft.com/en-us/library/azure/jj891130.aspx*
> - Notification hubs documentation: *http://azure.microsoft.com/en-us/documentation/services/notification-hubs/*
> - Mobile services documentation: *http://azure.microsoft.com/en-us/documentation/services/mobile-services/*

Objective summary

- A Service Bus namespace is a container for relay and message broker communication through relays, queues, topics and subscriptions, event hubs, and notification hubs.

- Relay enables access to on-premises resources without exposing on-premises services to the public Internet. By default, all relay messages are sent through Service Bus (relay mode), but connections might be promoted to a direct connection (hybrid mode).

- Queues and topics are message brokering features of Service Bus that provide a buffer for messages, partitioning options for scalability, and a dead letter feature for messages that can't be processed.

- Queues support one-to-one message delivery while topics support one-to-many delivery.

- Event hubs support high-volume message streaming and can ingest message data at scale. Messages are stored in a buffer and can be processed multiple times.

- Service Bus features can require authentication using a key. You can create multiple keys to isolate the key used for management and usage patterns, such as send and receive.

Objective review

Answer the following questions to test your knowledge of the information in this objective. You can find the answers to these questions and explanations of why each answer choice is correct or incorrect in the "Answers" section at the end of this chapter.

1. Which of the following statements are true of Service Bus relays? (Choose all that apply.)

   A. WCF is required for implementing server-side listeners to a relay.

   B. Relays can help avoid communication issues by using port 80 or 443.

   C. Relays have a limited number of client and listener connections.

   D. Relays do not support any inbound communications.

2. Which of the following statements are true of queues and topics? (Choose all that apply.)

   A. Service Bus queues can provide an alternative strategy to relays for communicating with on-premises resources.

   B. Both queues and topics can be used in publish and subscribe messaging implementations.

   C. To disable processing for Service Bus queues, topics, or event hubs, you must remove the entity from the subscription.

   D. Both queues and topics rely on partitions to increase throughput.

3. Which of the following statements about event hubs are true? (Choose all that apply.)

   A. Event hubs do not support TTL for messages. Messages are deleted as soon as they are consumed.

   B. Event hubs provide a dead-letter queue for messages that cannot be processed.

   C. Event hubs support processing messages multiple times until they expire.

   D. Event hubs, like queues and topics, support sending and receiving messages in batches.

Objective 5.5: Scale and monitor communication

In this section, you learn how to choose a Service Bus pricing tier, scale Service Bus features, and monitor communication.

> **This objective covers how to:**
>
> - Choose a pricing tier
> - Scale Service Bus
> - Monitor Service Bus relays, queues, topics, event hubs, and notification hubs

Choosing a pricing tier

The Service Bus has two types of tiers: a messaging tier for brokered messaging entities and a notification hubs tier. When you create a Service Bus namespace, you choose a messaging tier for all entities that will belong to that namespace. The tier you choose controls which entities you have access to as follows:

- **Basic tier**   Queues and event hubs (up to 100 connections)
- **Standard tier**   Queues, event hubs, topics, and relays (up to 1000 connections)

Standard tier also supports advance brokered messaging features such as transactions, de-duplication, sessions, and forwarding, so if you need these features for your solution, select the standard tier.

> **MORE INFO   SERVICE BUS TIERS**
>
> For information on Service Bus tier pricing, see *http://azure.microsoft.com/en-us/pricing/details/service-bus/*.

Specifically related to event hubs, the basic tier only supports a single consumer group, so if you want to support parallelized processing across partitions, choose standard messaging tier. In addition, standard tier provides additional storage up to seven days for event hubs.

> **MORE INFO   EVENT HUB TIERS**
>
> For information on event hub tier pricing, see *http://azure.microsoft.com/en-us/pricing/details/event-hubs/*.

Notification hubs have a separate tier selection strategy outside of the namespace tier. When you create a namespace that supports notification hubs, you choose a messaging tier for brokered messaging entities, if applicable, and select a notification hub tier appropriate to your expected push notification strategy. All tiers support unlimited devices, but there are some differences between the tiers:

- **Free tier**   Up to 1 million messages per month; no support for auto-scale nor a number of other enterprise features
- **Basic tier**   10 million messages per month plus unlimited overage for a fee; support for auto-scale; no support for other enterprise features
- **Standard tier**   The same as basic tier with all enterprise features

> **MORE INFO   NOTIFICATION HUB TIERS**
>
> For information on notification hub tier pricing, see *http://azure.microsoft.com/en-us/pricing/details/notification-hubs/*.

Scaling Service Bus features

Service Bus entities scale based on a variety of properties, including

- Namespaces
- Partitions
- Message size
- Throughput units
- Entity instances

Not all of these properties impact every Service Bus entity in the same manner.

A Service Bus namespace is a container for one or more entities, such as relays, queues, topics, event hubs, and notification hubs. In most cases, the namespace itself is not a unit of scale, with some exceptions specifically related to pricing (referenced earlier), event hub throughput (to be discussed), and the following:

- For relays, there is a limit to the number of endpoints, connections overall, and listeners.
- The number of topics and queues are limited, and separately a smaller number of partitioned topics and queues are supported.

Since pricing is not directly related to namespace allocation between relays, queues, topics, and event hubs, you can avoid reaching some of these limits by isolating entities that could be impacted into separate namespaces. For example, consider isolating individual relays that might grow their connection requirements, or consider isolating partitioned queues and topics.

> **MORE INFO** **SERVICE BUS QUOTAS**
>
> For the latest information related to namespace and other quotas for individual Service Bus entities, see *http://msdn.microsoft.com/en-us/library/azure/ee732538.aspx*.

Beyond namespace selection, each entity has slightly different requirements for scale as is discussed in this section.

Scaling relays

This section discusses how to scale relays for potential namespace limitations.

NAMESPACE

As mentioned previously, relay endpoints have a limited number of overall connections and listeners that can be supported per namespace. When you are considering the design for a relay service, you should consider the number of concurrent connections that might be required for communicating with the endpoint.

If the scale of the solution has the potential to exceed the quota per namespace, the following approach can help to mitigate the limitation:

- Design the solution to support publishing an instance of each relay service into multiple namespaces. This will allow for growth so that additional listeners can be added by adding namespaces with a new relay service instance.

- Design the solution so that clients sending messages to the relay service can distribute calls across a selection of service instances. This implies building a service registry.

EXAM TIP

Relay services can be replaced with queues or topics to provide greater throughput, scalability, and design flexibility.

Scaling queues and topics

This section discusses how to scale queues and topics for potential namespace or storage limitations and discusses the use of batching and partitions to help with scaling.

NAMESPACE

Queues and topics are similar in their scale triggers. Neither is particularly bound by the namespace it belongs to except in the total number of queues or topics supported and the limited number of partitioned queues and topics. Ideally, you will have a pattern for your solution in terms of namespace allocations by Service Bus entities.

STORAGE

When you create a new queue or topic, you must choose the maximum expected storage from 1 GB to 5 GB, and this cannot be resized. This impacts the amount of concurrent storage supported as messages flow through Service Bus.

BATCHING

To increase throughput for a queue or topic, you can have senders batch messages to Service Bus and listeners batch receive or pre-fetch from Service Bus. This increases overall throughput across all connected senders and listeners and can help reduce the number of messages taking up storage.

> **MORE INFO   BATCHING AND PRE-FETCHING**
>
> For more information on batch send, batch receive, or pre-fetch, see *http://msdn.microsoft.com/en-us/library/azure/hh528527.aspx*.

PARTITIONS

Adding partitions increases the number of message brokers available for incoming messages, as well as the number available for consuming messages. For high throughput queues and topics, you should enable partitioning when you create the queue or topic.

MORE INFO **PARTITIONED ENTITIES**

For more information on partitions, see *http://msdn.microsoft.com/en-us/library/azure/dn520246.aspx.*

Scaling event hubs

This section discusses how to scale event hubs for potential namespace limitations and discusses how to set throughput units or use partitions to help with scaling.

NAMESPACE

Each namespace can have multiple event hubs, but those event hubs share the throughput units allocated to the namespace. This means that multiple event hubs can share a single throughput unit to conserve cost, but conversely, if a single event hub has the potential of scaling beyond the available throughput units for a namespace, you might consider creating a separate namespace for it.

EXAM TIP

You can request additional throughput units for a namespace by calling Microsoft support.

THROUGHPUT UNITS

The primary unit of scale for event hubs is throughput units. This value is controlled at the namespace level and thus applies to all event hubs in the namespace. By default, you get a single throughput unit which provides ingress up to 1 MB per second, or 1,000 events per second, and egress up to 2 MB per second. You pre-purchase units and can by default configure up to 20 units.

PARTITIONS

A single event hub partition can scale to a single throughput unit; therefore, the number of partitions across event hubs in the namespace should be equal to or greater than the number of throughput units selected.

Scaling notification hubs

You can scale push notifications through notification hubs to millions of devices if you choose basic or standard tier. With basic or standard tier, you can push an unlimited number of notifications, but the fees per notification will vary between these two tiers.

Monitoring Service Bus features

In this section you learn how to monitor queues, topics, event hubs, and notification hubs.

Monitoring queues

To monitor a Service Bus queue from the existing portal, complete the following steps:

1. Navigate to the Dashboard tab for the queue, where metrics are presented in a graph (see Figure 5-22).

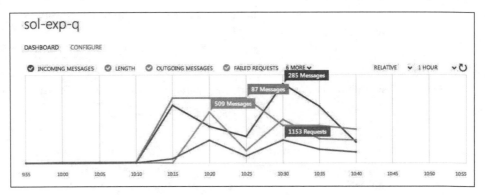

FIGURE 5-22 The metrics graph shown on the Dashboard tab for a queue

2. You can show relative or absolute values by selecting from the drop-down list above the graph (click the down arrow beside the word Relative shown in Figure 5-22).

3. You can choose the number of hours or days to include based on a predefined list shown in the drop-down list above the graph (click the down arrow beside 1 Hour shown in Figure 5-22).

It is useful to compare the number of incoming and outgoing messages to note any behavior that indicates burst activities for messages received or reduced ability to process requests as they are received. In addition, you can monitor queue length to note increases indicating requests not yet processed.

Monitoring topics

To monitor a Service Bus topic from the existing portal, complete the following steps:

1. Navigate to the Monitor tab for the topic, where metrics are presented in a graph (see Figure 5-23).

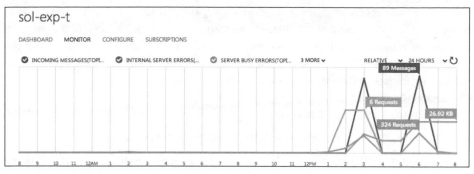

FIGURE 5-23 The metrics graph presented on the Monitor tab for a topic

2. Click Add Metrics on the command bar to choose from a list of metrics, including topic or specific subscription metrics. After selecting additional metrics to monitor, you will be able to filter which metrics to show in the graph.

As describedw in the previous section for queues, you can show relative or absolute values in the graph, and you can choose the number of hours or days to include based on a pre-defined list.

As with queues, it is useful to compare the number of incoming and outgoing messages to note any behavior that indicates burst activities for messages received or reduced ability to process requests as they are received across all subscriptions in aggregate. In addition, monitor the length of each subscription to look for problems with throughput to those endpoints.

Monitoring event hubs

To monitor a Service Bus event hub from the existing portal, navigate to the Dashboard tab for the event hub, where metrics are presented in a graph.

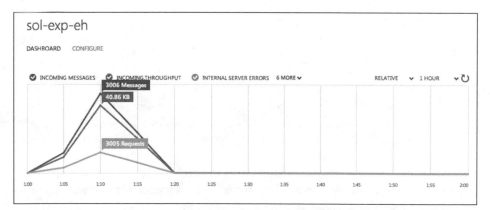

FIGURE 5-24 The metrics graph presented on the Dashboard tab for an event hub

As described in the previous section for queues, you can show relative or absolute values in the graph, and you can choose the number of hours or days to include based on a predefined list.

It is useful to compare the number of incoming and outgoing messages to note any behavior that indicates burst activities for messages received or reduced ability to process requests as they are received. You can also monitor incoming and outgoing throughput to measure throughput usage of this event hub for ingress and egress. Again, you are typically looking for bursts or decreases in usage indicating a need to adjust scale.

Monitoring notification hubs

To monitor a Service Bus notification hub from the existing portal:

1. Navigate to the Monitor tab for the notification hub, where metrics are presented in a graph.

2. You can show relative or absolute values, and you can choose the number of hours or days to include based on a predefined list.

3. Click Add Metrics on the command bar to choose from a list of metrics, including platform-specific metrics across each respective notification service and additional metrics for notification hub messaging (see Figure 5-25).

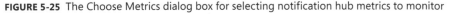

CHOOSE METRICS

Select Metrics to Monitor

GENERAL   WNS   APNS   GCM   MPNS

NAME	UNIT
☑ Incoming Messages	Messages
☐ Installation Management Operations	Count
☐ Patch Installation Operations	Count
☐ Payload Errors	Errors
☐ Pending Scheduled Notifications	Messages
☐ Registration Create Operations	Count
☐ Registration Delete Operations	Count
☑ Registration Operations	Count
☐ Registration Read Operations	Count
☐ Registration Update Operations	Count
☐ Scheduled Push Notifications Sent	Messages
☑ Successful Notifications	Count

FIGURE 5-25 The Choose Metrics dialog box for selecting notification hub metrics to monitor

It is useful to monitor registration operations to note when there are bursts or decreases in those requests. In addition, monitoring errors for each platform notification service might help you identify specific issues related to that platform.

Objective summary

- Service Bus pricing tiers fall into a few categories: a Service Bus messaging tier, an event hub tier, and a notification hub tier.
- Relay services are primarily scaled by adding namespaces and listeners for processing messages.
- Queues and topics are primarily scaled by choosing a larger storage size, adding partitions, and batching messages on both send and receive.
- Notification hubs are scaled by adjusting the tier to allow for increased message volume.
- You can monitor queues, topics, event hubs, and notification hubs in the existing management portal.

Objective review

Answer the following questions to test your knowledge of the information in this objective. You can find the answers to these questions and explanations of why each answer choice is correct or incorrect in the "Answers" section at the end of this chapter.

1. Which of the following are valid statements about choosing a pricing tier for Service Bus? (Choose all that apply.)

   A. Relays are supported in basic or standard messaging tier.

   B. Event hubs are only supported in standard messaging tier.

   C. Standard messaging tier is limited to 1,000 connections.

   D. Notification hub tiers all support unlimited messaging, but the price varies.

   E. Free messaging tier only supports queues and topics.

2. Which of the following statements about scaling Service Bus are true? (Choose all that apply.)

   A. Allocating relays to individual namespaces improves scalability per relay.

   B. Increasing queue and topic partitions improves capacity to process messages at the server.

   C. Event hubs scale with paid throughput units.

   D. Notification hubs scale to more devices by adding namespaces.

3. Which of the following statements about monitoring Service Bus entities in the management portal are true? (Choose all that apply.)

   A. You can monitor incoming and outgoing messages for queues, topics, and event hubs.

   B. You can monitor ingress and egress for topics and event hubs.

   C. Monitoring queue and topic length can indicate issues with throughput.

   D. Monitoring notification hubs by device can help isolate issues local to a device.

Objective 5.6: Implement caching

Microsoft Azure offers several options for distributed, in-memory, and scalable caching solutions over time. At present, the following options are available:

- Azure Redis Cache
- Azure Managed Cache Service
- In-Role Cache

The first two options offer an SLA of 99.9 percent (with the right configuration of Redis Cache) and the latter does not since you are effectively self-hosting a caching service. Both Managed Cache Service and In-Role Cache are primarily offered for backward compatibility for existing customers using those features. Azure Redis Cache is considered the modern and preferred approach for green field distributed cache implementations.

> **This objective covers how to:**
> - Implement Redis Cache
> - Implement Azure Managed Cache Service

Implementing Redis Cache

Azure Redis Cache is based on the open source project Redis Cache, allowing you to leverage the vast resources in this open source community while leaving the reliability, security, and hosting to Azure. Redis offers many features beyond a traditional key-value pair cache, including manipulating existing entries with atomic operations such as the following capabilities:

- Appending to a string
- Incrementing or decrementing a value
- Adding to a list
- Computing results or intersections and unions
- Working with sorted sets

In this section you learn how to create a cache, connect clients to a cache, and add or retrieve objects.

> **EXAM TIP**
>
> The large Redis Cache size is 53 GB.

> **MORE INFO** REDIS DOCUMENTATION
>
> For Redis Cache features, tutorials, and other documentation, see *http://redis.io/documentation*.

Creating a cache (existing portal)

This feature is currently not available in the existing management portal.

Creating a cache (Preview portal)

To create a cache in the Preview portal, complete the following steps:

1. Navigate to the management portal accessed via *https://portal.azure.com*.
2. Click New on the command bar, and then click Everything.
3. Select Storage, Cache + Backup, and click the Redis Cache box on the Storage, Cache + Backup blade.
4. On the Redis Cache blade, click Create.
5. For DNS name, supply a unique subdomain name for the cache. Select a pricing tier, subscription, and location near the cache clients in your topology (see Figure 5-26). You can choose a resource group or allow a new resource group to be generated (the default behavior).

FIGURE 5-26 Creating a new Redis cache in the Preview portal

6. Click Create to create the new Redis Cache instance.

> **NOTE PRICING TIERS FOR REDIS CACHE**
>
> You can select options from each pricing tier. Basic tier has several options that supports single node topology. Standard tier supports two-node master/subordinate topology with 99.9 percent SLA.

Configuring the cache

To configure the cache, complete the following steps:

1. To view your cache in the management portal after it is created, click Browse in the left navigation panel, and select Redis Caches under Filter By.

2. From the list presented on the Redis Caches blade, select your cache to open the blade for your cache.

3. To view your cache properties, select the Properties box on the cache blade. The Properties blade shows the host name address to your cache and indicates if SSL is required and what port is used (see Figure 5-27). By default, the cache requires SSL and assigns a port.

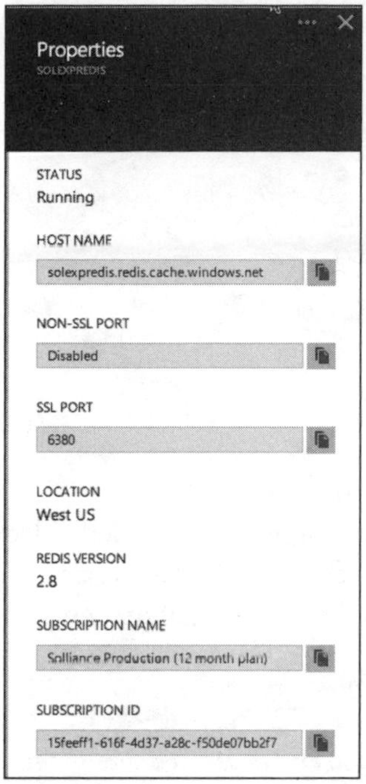

FIGURE 5-27 Editing Redis cache properties on the Properties blade

4. To access your management keys, select the Keys box on the cache blade (see Figure 5-28).

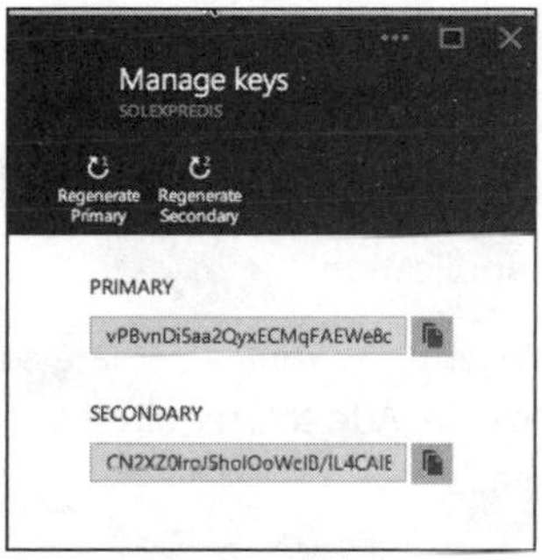

FIGURE 5-28 Managing keys for a Redis cache

5. To configure access ports, scroll to the Configuration section of the cache blade and click the Access Ports box (see Figure 5-29).

FIGURE 5-29 Setting access ports for a Redis cache

6. To configure how the cache behaves when maximum memory is exceeded, select the Maxmemory Policy box on the cache blade. You can choose the desired behavior of Redis Cache when clients add keys to the cache and the cache is out of memory.

> ***MORE INFO***   **REDIS CACHE CONFIGURATION**
>
> For information about the default Redis Cache configuration and how to configure features such as Maxmemory policy, see *http://msdn.microsoft.com/en-us/library/azure/dn793612. aspx*.

Adding and retrieving values

To add and retrieve values, complete the following steps:

1. Open Visual Studio 2013, and create a new console application called RedisCacheClient.

2. Add the StackExchange.Redis NuGet package to the application.

3. To connect to your cache, use the ConnectionMultiplexer type. You can create a single instance of this type and reuse it for each call to the cache. Add the required using statement and the following code to connect to the cache:

```
using StackExchange.Redis;
ConnectionMultiplexer connection = ConnectionMultiplexer.Connect("solexpredis.
redis.cache.windows.net,ssl=true,password=vPBvnDi5aa2QyxECMqFAEWe8d5Z2nXyLWhK+DAX
wE6Q=");
```

4. To add an entry to the cache, get a reference to the cache and call StringSet() to add simple integral types, such as string and integer:

```
IDatabase cache = connection.GetDatabase();
cache.StringSet("stringValue", "my string");
cache.StringSet("intValue", 42);
```

5. You can augment existing cache entries with functions such as StringAppend() and Increment(). For example, the following code appends to the previous string entry and increments the number value:

```
IDatabase cache = connection.GetDatabase();
cache.StringAppend("stringValue", "more added to my string");
cache.StringIncrement("intValue");
```

6. To retrieve entries from the cache, use StringGet() as follows:

```
IDatabase cache = connection.GetDatabase();
string entry = cache.StringGet("stringValue");
entry = cache.StringGet("intValue");
```

EXAM TIP

You can add any non-primitive type to the cache when it is serialized. Use any of your favorite serializers, such as JSON format, and then store the result as a string with StringSet(). When you retrieve it, use the same serializer to de-serialize the value after StringGet().

MORE INFO   ASP.NET SESSION STATE AND OUTPUT CACHE

You can use Redis Cache to back your ASP.NET session state for a fast, in-memory distributed session shared by multiple servers. For more information, see *http://msdn. microsoft.com/en-us/library/dn690522.aspx*. You can also use Redis Cache for output cache, as described at *http://msdn.microsoft.com/en-us/library/dn798898.aspx*.

Controlling expiration

You can control the expiration of any item you store in the cache by passing the parameter to StringSet(). When the string expires, it will be automatically removed from the cache. The following example sets the cache expiry to 30 minutes:

```
IDatabase cache = connection.GetDatabase();
cache.StringAppend("expiringString", "this string will expire in 30 mins", TimeSpan.
FromMinutes(30));
```

Implementing Azure Managed Cache Service

The Azure Managed Cache Service is similar to the role caching features discussed in Chapter 3; however, it is a service managed by Azure. This service provides a secure cache that you can leverage from your cloud applications in a region of your choice.

While this cache offering is still supported, it is no longer available through the Azure management portal and is being maintained primarily for existing customers who have investments that use it. New customers should look at Redis Cache for a hosted cache service on Azure.

EXAM TIP

Azure Managed Cache Service can only be created using Windows PowerShell cmdlets. You can then manage the cache settings from the management portal.

MORE INFO   CREATE AND CONFIGURE CACHE SERVICE

The following reference shows you how to create Azure Managed Cache Service using Windows PowerShell and then configure it from the management portal: *http://msdn. microsoft.com/en-us/library/azure/dn448831.aspx*.

Thought experiment
Migrating to Redis Cache

In this thought experiment, apply what you've learned about this objective. You can find answers to these questions in the "Answers" section at the end of this chapter.

You have an existing application the uses Azure Managed Cache Service for its distributed cache. You are working on some significant improvements to your caching implementation throughout your application. You've heard that Redis Cache is now the preferred strategy for applications.

1. How will you determine the best course of action for your business scenario in terms of retiring Azure Managed Cache Service and implementing Redis Cache?

2. What are the benefits of developing a strategy to move to Redis Cache?

Objective summary

- Microsoft Azure offers three caching solutions at present: Redis Cache, Azure Managed Cache Service, and In-Role Caching. Redis Cache is the preferred option.
- Redis Cache is an open source project implemented in Microsoft Azure for its Redis Cache service.
- With Redis Cache, you can perform traditional key-value pair cache management, but you can also perform atomic operations that append to existing values, increment or decrement values, and perform other operations on cached values.
- The Azure Managed Cache Service can only be created using Windows PowerShell commands.

Objective review

Answer the following questions to test your knowledge of the information in this objective. You can find the answers to these questions and explanations of why each answer choice is correct or incorrect in the "Answers" section at the end of this chapter.

1. Which of the following statements about working with Azure Redis Cache entries are true? (Choose all that apply.)

   A. You can use only JSON serializer to insert entries for complex types.

   B. You can append to an entry in a single operation.

   C. You can add to a list in a single operation.

   D. You can perform intersections and unions on cache entries in a single operation.

2. Which statement about Azure Redis Cache is true?

   A. Only HTTPS is supported.

   B. Both HTTP and HTTPS communication are supported.

   C. You can create custom access keys for sending and reading from the cache.

   D. You can create a Redis Cache instance using the existing portal and the Preview portal.

Answers

This section contains the solutions to the thought experiments and answers to the objective review questions in this chapter.

Objective 5.1: Thought experiment

1. Consider standardizing on the OAuth 2.0 protocol with OpenID Connect for user authentication. This is the standard that is most commonly selected for new applications unless there is a legacy application in the mix that requires WS-Federation or SAML-P.

2. Consider using the Graph API to provision users through your application, long term. For testing and development, you can manually create some users and groups.

3. You will request a user's groups post-authentication by sending a request to the Graph API.

Objective 5.1: Objective review

1. **Correct answer:** D

   A. **Incorrect:** Azure AD roles are assigned only to users who have access to administer the Azure AD instance. These roles are not used for application-specific authorization.

   B. **Incorrect:** You can optionally create Azure AD groups to use for application authorization of users in your directory; however, Azure AD roles are used to authorize access to Azure AD functionality.

   C. **Incorrect:** Azure AD groups are application specific. Azure AD roles are used to authorize administrative access to directory features.

   D. **Correct:** Azure AD roles and groups can both be queried using the Graph API. You will typically query groups for a logged in user to authorize access within your application.

2. **Correct answer:** C

   A. **Incorrect:** OAuth is an authorization protocol, not an authentication protocol. You can use WS-Federation, SAML-P, or OpenID Connect (an extension to OAuth) as browser-based authentication protocols.

   B. **Incorrect:** OpenID Connect requires that the application is trusted by identifying the application URI provided in the request for user authentication, but the client identifier is not used for this flow. The client identifier is required for OAuth requests, and, in cases where the user is not authenticating, the client key (secret) is also required.

C. **Correct:** Azure AD supports generating client keys for one or two years in the management portal.

D. **Incorrect:** The sign-on URL identifies the URL that Azure AD will redirect back to after authenticating the user. The application URI is an identifier and does not have to be a live endpoint, but it must be unique across all applications in the Azure AD tenant.

3. **Correct answers:** A, B, and D

A. **Correct:** You can create a user management interface using the Graph API and add, update, and delete users, as well as assign them to groups.

B. **Correct:** You can use the Graph API to (for example) create a directory query functionality in your applications for looking up users to find users by their UPN, and to gather other directory properties.

C. **Incorrect:** Roles are defined by Azure AD for administering specific directory features; groups are customizable for the application and are typically assigned to users for authorization.

D. **Correct:** You can use the Graph API to query both roles and groups for a user in the directory.

Objective 5.2: Thought experiment

1. You could configure a virtual network in Azure with a subnet that does not conflict with the existing on-premises network. To connect to the Azure virtual network, you can use a VPN device on-premises.

2. You should purchase a hardware VPN device, although you can use RRAS with Windows if necessary. You would need to decide what IP addresses to use. You might consider what should be done about shared security, like syncing Active Directory or joining the VMs to your domain.

Objective 5.2: Objective review

1. **Correct answers:** A and C

A. **Correct:** You can use virtual networks to make resources in separate regions behave as if they are on one network.

B. **Incorrect:** Resources on a virtual network don't go through endpoints for connectivity.

C. **Correct:** Virtual networks will make Azure VMs and cloud services available as if they were local to the on-premises users.

D. **Incorrect:** Virtual networks do not make your local network fault tolerant.

2. **Correct answer:** C

    A. **Incorrect:** You cannot deploy a cloud service from the existing portal.

    B. **Incorrect:** You cannot deploy a cloud service from the Preview portal.

    C. **Correct:** You can deploy a cloud service by supplying virtual network configuration details in the network configuration file.

    D. **Incorrect:** You can deploy a cloud service using the network configuration file.

3. **Correct answer:** C

    A. **Incorrect:** You would incur downtime by creating the VM first.

    B. **Incorrect:** You can't create both at the same time.

    C. **Correct:** Create the virtual network first and then create the VM. This makes configuration faster and easier, with no future downtime.

    D. **Incorrect:** Create the virtual network first, and then create the VM

Objective 5.3: Thought experiment

1. You should use a compatible subnet with your existing network so that when you create a site-to-site VPN they can co-exist. You should use a shared DNS server.

2. You can either increase the number of IP addresses in the subnet or you can add additional subnets.

Objective 5.3: Objective review

1. **Correct answers:** C and D

    A. **Incorrect:** You can't do this with existing services on it.

    B. **Incorrect:** You can't do this with existing services on it.

    C. **Correct:** You can always add a new subnet.

    D. **Correct:** This is how you would migrate and keep all your resources on one subnet.

2. **Correct answers:** A, B, C and D

    A. **Correct:** To back it up.

    B. **Correct:** To make update changes to it.

    C. **Correct:** To learn from it so you can make new networks by hand.

    D. **Correct:** To use it as a template

Objective 5.4: Thought experiment

1. Consider using Service Bus queues to offload processing of report generation from the main website to a separate compute tier that can be scaled as needed. Since this is not a publish-and-subscribe scenario, queues can satisfy this requirement. Actual processing can be performed by any compute tier, including a VM, cloud service worker role, or web job in an isolated VM.

2. Consider using event hubs for logging whereby all applications can provide custom properties to isolate the source of the message, while all messages can be somehow correlated in a FIFO manner for troubleshooting user sessions that span different websites and applications. The site is multi-tenant and could potentially expansively grow in number of users across each tenant, and event hubs have the potential scale to handle log volumes.

Objective 5.4: Objective review

1. **Correct answer:** B, C, and D

   A. **Incorrect:** Relays are optimized to work with WCF; however, it is possible to implement non-WCF endpoints to listen to relay services.

   B. **Correct:** Although well-known ports like 80 and 443 can also be restricted on a network, it is less likely than the other ports required to perform TCP communications using non-HTTP relay bindings. By requiring HTTP, you can ensure that only an HTTP binding is used for relay communications.

   C. **Correct:** The number of client and server listeners are restricted by the messaging tier chosen for the namespace. The limit is 100 for basic tier and 1,000 for standard tier.

   D. **Correct:** Relays use an outbound connection to establish communications with Service Bus. No inbound communication is supported.

2. **Correct answers:** A, B, and D

   A. **Correct:** Since both relays and queues rely on Service Bus for implementation, queues can be a substitute for relays in that they allow for the on-premises listener to request messages using a protocol that is suitable for the environment. In addition, it provides a temporal and physical decoupling of client and server, which can also improve scalability in the overall design.

   B. **Correct:** Theoretically, you can build a publish-and-subscribe solution using queues; however, the implementation requires quite a lot of custom coding, so that is not recommended. Topics and subscriptions are built for publish-and-subscribe solutions and provide out-of-the-box infrastructure for this purpose using coding similar to that of queues at the client and service. For publish and subscribe, choose topics.

   C. **Incorrect:** You can disable any Service Bus feature with the state property without removing the entity from the subscription. Each Service Bus entity provides a state property that can be disabled in the management portal or programmatically through management tools like Windows PowerShell. This allows you to disable processing while still maintaining the actual entity for later use.

   D. **Correct:** Partitions can be set when you create the queue or topic. This allocates additional message brokers for handling incoming messages to the entity, and this increases scale.

3. **Correct answers:** C and D

   A. **Incorrect:** It is true that event hubs do not support a TTL for messages; however, messages are not deleted as soon as they are consumed. Messages remain in the buffer until the designated global expiry for the buffer.

   B. **Incorrect:** Only queues and topics support a dead-letter sub-queue. Event hubs do not have this concept; instead, they retain messages up to the expiry for reprocessing.

   C. **Correct:** The buffer allows for different consumers to receive data from the buffer multiple times by requesting a particular part of the message stream.

   D. **Correct:** You can batch send and receive for all three entities: queues, topics and subscriptions, and event hubs.

Objective 5.5: Thought experiment

1. To understand how to scale the queue, you need to estimate how many customers are using the system and how many requests they will make on average throughout the month and during the peak request period. This leads you to an estimation of the number of concurrent requests and throughput required at a given time, which influences decisions about queue partitioning and the number of listeners required to effectively process and maintain throughput. You should also find out the average request size to calculate the best queue size for messages stored at any given moment.

   To understand how to scale the event hub, you need an estimation of the number of devices, the growth trajectory expected, and the amount of data/second (and its size) to be sent per device on average. This helps you estimate the required throughput units and, therefore, the expected growth of event hub consumers.

2. To implement event hubs, you must choose standard messaging tier. If you implement queues and they are stored in a separate namespace from the event hub, and the number of connections does not exceed 100, the queue can possibly start at basic messaging tier and later be upgraded to standard messaging tier. Since namespaces affect addressing, making a decision to separate event hubs and queues early on to isolates the two namespaces might be helpful to avoid refactoring the application at a later date.

3. Consider optimizing queue throughput by sending messages in batch and prefetching or receiving messages in batch at the server. This reduces connection usage and increases overall throughput on both client and server. Also, consider adding listeners across multiple servers as needed to process additional messages in parallel.

4. Consider optimizing event hub throughput by increasing throughput units as needed and parallelizing how you process data using multiple consumers and, as needed, multiple hosts to process additional data in parallel.

Objective 5.5: Objective review

1. **Correct answer:** C

   A. **Incorrect:** Relays are only supported in the standard messaging tier.

   B. **Incorrect:** Event hubs are supported in both basic and standard messaging tiers.

   C. **Correct:** For basic tier, 100 connections are supported and applied to queues and event hubs. For standard tier, 1,000 connections are supported and applied to queues, event hubs, topics, and relays.

   D. **Incorrect:** Notification hubs support unlimited devices across all tiers. For the free notification hub tier, messages are limited to 1 million per month. Basic and standard notification hub tiers support 10 million messages per month and unlimited additional messages for a per message fee.

   E. **Incorrect:** Free messaging tier does not exist. You must select from basic or standard tier. Basic tier supports queues and event hubs. Standard tier supports queues, topics, event hubs, and relays.

2. **Correct answers:** A and C

   A. **Correct:** Each namespace messaging tier has a limited number of connections to the Service Bus. If the number of sender and listener connections are approaching the limit of 1,000 for a namespace with basic tier, isolating resources to another tier will make it possible to allocate another 1,000 connections to resources in that namespace.

   B. **Incorrect:** Adding partitions increases throughput to Service Bus. Server listeners to queues and subscriptions are responsible for scaling out to process additional messages. This can be improved by prefetching or receiving messages in batch and by adding listeners to consume messages.

   C. **Correct:** Event hubs have a prepaid set of throughput units that can be shared across all partitions. The number of partitions should exceed the number of throughput units for optimal performance. Consumers are also responsible for scaling throughput to the server. Adding event hub consumers allows for parallel processing of additional message data.

   D. **Incorrect:** Notification hubs support unlimited devices for all tiers for a single namespace. Unlimited messages are also supported on a paid notification tier basis.

3. **Correct answer:** A, C, and D

   A. **Correct:** You can monitor the number of messages both incoming and outgoing for queues, topics, and event hubs. When there is disparity growing between these values, it can be an indicator of issues with exceptions or throughput.

   B. **Incorrect:** Topics do not have a concept of ingress or egress. You can monitor ingress and egress for event hubs, and this is helpful for managing usage expectations for throughput unit pre-purchase.

   C. **Correct:** When the queue or topic length increases in bursts, it can be an indicator of a problem or an indication that you should increase the number of listeners or optimize message processing using prefetch or batches.

   D. **Correct:** You can monitor errors and other types of counters by device, which can be helpful in isolating issues that are local to a particular device format or its notification service.

Objective 5.6: Thought experiment

1. Consider the amount of work and your timeline for delivering the business requirements you have defined for the upcoming release. It will be less painful to modify the work to use Redis Cache while you are actively implementing new features for your solution's use of cache, than to revisit this later.

2. Redis Cache has many features that Azure Managed Cache Service lacks, such as the ability to do atomic operations on individual cache entries while modifying them. These features might be useful to your application now or in future. Further, any improvements to caching features are likely to be focused on Redis Cache going forward.

Objective 5.6: Objective review

1. **Correct answers:** B, C, and D

   A. **Incorrect:** You can use any serializer of your choosing to produce serialized results to save to an entry.

   B. **Correct:** You can append to a string in a single atomic operation and also increment or decrement values.

   C. **Correct:** You can also add to a list using an atomic operation.

   D. **Correct:** You can use Redis Cache to perform intersections, unions, and sorting on cached entries.

2. **Correct answer:** B

   A. **Incorrect:** Both HTTP and HTTPS are supported; however, only HTTPS is enabled by default.

   B. **Correct:** Only HTTPS is supported by default, but you can enable HTTP support.

   C. **Incorrect:** You use a single primary access key (similar to Azure Storage) to access the cache account. There is a secondary access key typically used for key rolling exercises.

   D. **Incorrect:** Redis Cache instances can be created using the Preview portal, but not using the existing portal.

Index

A

Q

U

V

X

About the authors

ZOINER TEJADA is a founder and CEO of Solliance, a Microsoft Azure MVP, and a Google Developer Expert (GDE) for Analytics. Additionally, he has been awarded the Azure Elite and Azure Insider status by Microsoft. Zoiner is passionate about the business of software and tackling innovative areas in software development that range from cloud computing, modern websites, graphics programming, networking, NoSQL/NewSQL distributed databases, scientific computing, digital privacy, and that side of security that involves thinking like hacker.

Zoiner has over 15 years of consulting experience, providing strategic, architectural, and implementation guidance to an array of enterprises and start-ups, all leveraging cutting-edge technologies. He enjoys engaging the greater community by speaking at conferences and user group meetings and by extending his reach through his online courses and published books. Zoiner has earned MCSD certification and has a degree in computer science from Stanford University. You can reach Zoiner at *zoinertejada@solialiance.net*.

MICHELE LEROUX BUSTAMANTE is a founder and CIO of Solliance (solliance.net), the founder of Snapboard.com, a Microsoft Regional Director, and a Microsoft Azure MVP. Additionally, she has been awarded Azure Elite and Azure Insider status and the ASP.NET Insider designation. Michele is a thought leader recognized in many fields, including software architecture and design, identity and access management, cloud computing technologies, security and compliance, and DevOps. During the past 20 years, Michele has held senior executive positions at several corporations, has assembled software development teams and implemented processes for all aspects of the software development lifecycle, and has facilitated numerous successful large-scale enterprise application deployments.

Michele has also been active in the start-up community, bringing a keen understanding of the technical and business needs of a startup. At Solliance, she provides "Start-up Architect" services for activities such as guiding Minimum Viable Product design and delivery, providing necessary preparations to secure funding events, and offering overall advice and guidance to select start-ups.

Michele shares her experiences through presentations and keynote addresses all over the world and has been publishing regularly in technology journals over her entire career. Michele has written several books, including the best-selling book *Learning WCF* (O'Reilly Media, 2007). Find out more about Michele at *linkedin.com/in/michelebusta*.

IKE ELLIS is a data and cloud architect for Solliance. He loves data in all its forms and shapes, whether relational, NoSQL, MPP, JSON, or just sitting in a CSV. Ike consults on SQL Server performance tuning, SQL Server architecture, data warehouse design, and business intelligence projects. Ike is well-known in the industry and speaks at SQL PASS, TechEd, SQL in the City, and other conferences around the world. Ike has been a Microsoft SQL Server MVP for four consecutive years and is a member of Microsoft Azure Insiders. He has MCDBA, MCSE, MCSD, and MCT certifications. Find out more about Ike at *linkedin.com/in/ikeellis* and at *ikeellis.com*.

STILL HAVE QUESTIONS?

Michele Leroux Bustamante
Security
Azure
DevOps

Zoiner Tejada
Azure
Web
Analytics
Open Source

Brian Noyes
WPF
Windows Store
Prism
Web

Ike Ellis
Data
BI & DW
Perf Tuning

Lynn Lang
Big Data
BI
NoSQL & New

solliance

Our experts have you covered. We love to hear from you!
Connect with a Solliance expert today!

azurebook@solliance.net | http://azurebook.solliance.net

...and
30+
experts worldwide ac
many technologies

Free ebooks

From technical overviews to drilldowns on special topics, get free ebooks from Microsoft Press at:

www.microsoftvirtualacademy.com/ebooks

Download your free ebooks in PDF, EPUB, and/or Mobi for Kindle formats.

Look for other great resources at Microsoft Virtual Academy, where you can learn new skills and help advance your career with free Microsoft training delivered by experts.

Now that you've read the book...

Tell us what you think!

Was it useful?
Did it teach you what you wanted to learn?
Was there room for improvement?

Let us know at http://aka.ms/tellpress

Your feedback goes directly to the staff at Microsoft Press,
and we read every one of your responses. Thanks in advance!